Latin America's Radical Left

This book examines the emergence, development, and demise of a network of organizations of young leftist militants and intellectuals in South America. This new generation, formed primarily by people who in the late 1960s were still under the age of thirty, challenged traditional politics and embraced organized violence and transnational strategies as the only ways of achieving social change in their countries during the Cold War. This lasted for more than a decade, beginning in Uruguay as a result of the rise of authoritarianism in Brazil and Argentina, and expanding with Che Guevara's Bolivia campaign in 1966. These coordination efforts reached their highest point in Buenos Aires from 1973 to 1976, until the military coup d'état in Argentina eliminated the last refuge for these groups. Aldo Marchesi offers the first in-depth, regional and transnational study of the militant left in Latin America during the turbulent 1960s and 1970s.

Aldo Marchesi teaches history at the Universidad de la República (Montevideo, Uruguay). He is the Director of the Uruguayan Interdisciplinary Studies Center (CEIU), a specialized center on Uruguayan Recent History.

Books in the Series

(*continued after the index*)

Latin America's Radical Left

Rebellion and Cold War in the Global 1960s

ALDO MARCHESI

Universidad de la Republica (Uruguay)

Translated by LAURA PEREZ CARRARA

CAMBRIDGE
UNIVERSITY PRESS

University Printing House, Cambridge CB2 8BS, United Kingdom

One Liberty Plaza, 20th Floor, New York, NY 10006, USA

477 Williamstown Road, Port Melbourne, VIC 3207, Australia

314-321, 3rd Floor, Plot 3, Splendor Forum, Jasola District Centre, New Delhi - 110025, India

79 Anson Road, #06-04/06, Singapore 079906

Cambridge University Press is part of the University of Cambridge.

It furthers the University's mission by disseminating knowledge in the pursuit of education, learning and research at the highest international levels of excellence.

www.cambridge.org
Information on this title: www.cambridge.org/9781316630716
DOI : 10.1017/9781316822968

First published 2018
First paperback edition 2019

A catalogue record for this publication is available from the British Library

ISBN 978-1-107-17771-0 Hardback
ISBN 978-1-316-63071-6 Paperback

Contents

Figures

Acknowledgments

The acknowledgments for this book are inevitably tied to my decision to pursue my PhD studies in Latin American History in the United States, more specifically at New York University. That decision emerged gradually over a series of conversations with Eric Herschberg, Steve Stern, and Elizabeth Jelin (Shevi) at the start of the century, in the framework of the SSRC program on Collective Memory of Repression. The three of them helped me considerably in that process and opened up possibilities that were unimaginable from where I stood, in my small and remote country of Uruguay.

Shevi provided enormous support throughout that whole process, both intellectually and as a friend. Generously sharing her experience as a researcher, she showed me that there was a way to conduct research in which the ethical and political commitments of the researcher need not be at odds with doing quality research and that, quite the contrary, they would help me examine more incisively the recent, turbulent past of the Southern Cone, especially in those aspects toward which I felt a certain sympathy. Shevi also created a collective space that played a key role in my studies on these issues. There I met and worked with many colleagues, including Claudio Barrientos, Azun Candina, Emilio Crenzel, Álvaro de Giorgi, Ponciano del Pino, Claudia Feld, Silvina Jensen, Victoria Langland, Cecilia Lesgart, Federico Lorenz, Ludmila Catela da Silva, Samantha Quadrat, Diego Sempol, and many more, several of whom I am still in contact with and are now great friends. It was in those Southern Cone exchanges that I began forming the idea of carrying out a project that considered the region as a whole.

In the process of deciding on my PhD studies, the Uruguayan historians Gerardo Caetano, José Rilla, and Álvaro Rico were also of great assistance. Over a series of conversations with them I traced a line of work, which was what enabled me to apply for a PhD with a clear idea of what I wanted to do. Vania Markarian was also very supportive in this whole process. In addition to being a close friend, she was something of a "pioneer" who showed me that it was possible to study abroad and return to build an academic career in

Uruguay. Since then we have had a highly productive academic relationship, which I think has much to do with several of the concerns expressed in my dissertation. Jaime Yaffé, with whom I have worked at a number of events on the recent past, has also been a valuable friend throughout this process and someone with whom I could discuss ideas.

In 2004, I began my PhD studies at NYU thanks to a Fulbright/Laspau Scholarship and the McCracken funds assigned by the university. The experience was very enriching. Jeniffer Adair, Lina Britto, Joaquin Chavez, Michelle Chase, Joshua Frens String, Forrest Hylton, Yuko Miki, Ernesto Seman, Aaron Slater, and Mattew Vitz were great friends with whom I shared courses and exam preparations. In all those spaces we discussed the work we were doing and I am sure that some of the few merits of this book have much to do with those conversations.

The team of Latin Americanist scholars in the History Department provided essential support in the development of my dissertation project, as well as in the drafting of the final version. Sinclair Thomson showed ongoing interest and commitment with the project and its realization. The brilliant, intelligent, and insightful feedback he provided throughout the process helped enhance many aspects of my work. In his role as dissertation advisor, Greg Grandin helped me put my object of study into the broader context of the Latin American Cold War. His perspective pushed me to question certain common notions that I had interiorized and to identify what was relevant by taking a global approach to the conflict. Ada Ferrer was immensely helpful in the workshops and her insistence that I incorporate Cuba into the project was very useful. Although she joined the Department just as I was returning to the Southern Cone, Barbara Weinstein gave me valuable feedback during my defense and provided interesting input for examining the relationship of the middle classes with these organizations.

Peter Winn was also part of the examination committee when I defended my dissertation and I thank him in particular for his comments on the Chilean process, as well as his keen contribution regarding the more general conceptualization of the period.

From my experience as a student I would also like to highlight three courses from which my project's development profited greatly: Jeff Goodwin's course on social movements, Mary Nolan and Marilyn Young's course on the Cold War, and Pablo Piccato's course on Honor and Masculinity in Mediterranean societies.

In 2007, I began my journey back to the Southern Cone. Thanks to funding from New York University and an IDRF-SSRC grant, I was able to move back and forth from Chile to Argentina and back to Uruguay several times to gather the necessary information. Many colleagues helped me with my project in many different ways during these trips.

In Chile, historians Igor Goicovich, María Olga Ruiz, Claudio Pérez, and Alondra Peirano, Veronica Valdivia, Rolando Álvarez, Claudio Barrientos, Julio Pintos, and Hillary Heiffner all lent enormous support to my efforts. Last, but not least, I would like to thank my two great friends, the historians Alberto Harambour and Consuelo Figueroa, whom I met in New York and who were excellent hosts during my stays in Santiago.

In Argentina, Vera Carnovale and Maria Cristina Tortti were instrumental as guides for my work. But also, several conversations with Ludmila Da Silva Catela, Emilio Crenzel, and Marina Franco helped me in my research.

In Uruguay, my work was somewhat easier because I knew the people and the places I needed to focus on. Nonetheless, I have to thank Clara Aldrighi and David Cámpora, who were instrumental in my gaining access to militants as well as insight into perspectives that had not been included in my research.

During the writing stage I also had the chance to travel and present sections of the work in progress. Such opportunities are always good for gauging the impact of the work one is doing. In this sense, I would like to thank Eric Zolov, Tanya Harmer, Julio Pinto, Eugenia Pallieraki, Maud Chirio, and Andrew Kirkendall for the feedback they provided in different events held in the United States, Spain, Chile, and France. Also, Herbert Klein read the final draft thoroughly, providing valuable comments and suggesting additions that I believe have strengthened the manuscript. Klein also helped me in exploring the Hoover Archive collections, which contain material very relevant to my research.

While I was writing in Montevideo, I discussed my project with several friends with whom I met on various occasions to share the concerns that moved me to delve into these subjects. Although many of them are not engaged strictly in academic work, our talks contributed enormously to my research. In recognition of this I want to mention two groups I discussed my project with several times. First, *de la raíz* (Rodrigo Arim, Gabriel Burdín, Andres Dean, Anibal Corti, Damian Osta, Andres Prieto, Gustavo Rak, Adolfo Wassem, Isabel Wschebor), a political discussion group that began gathering at the start of the century to talk about left-wing politics. The other is a group of close friends with whom I got together regularly at a bar in the city. They insisted that their "key contribution" had to be included in the credits of my work. So here are my thanks to the great Eduardo Clouzet, Daniel Martirena, and Fernando Devicenzi, who sadly will not be here to see this work published.

And last, as is typical in acknowledgments, comes family. If, as I believe, creating something is a process of intersubjective construction, then it follows that those who have been closest to me have without a doubt played a major role in this process.

My stepsiblings Rafael and Analía have been an important presence in my life during this past decade and we have shared this experience in different ways. They have been there for me in difficult times and we have also enjoyed good moments together.

My parents, Carlos Marchesi and María Amelia Gordillo occupy a very important place in this history. This work studies their time. That time inevitably marked their youth and, through them, it marked me too, leaving a critical imprint that in many ways has always been with me and is still with me today.

Finally, Antonieta and Luca both played a leading role in this project. With her I traveled to the United States and with him we returned. They both saw me glued to my computer and sacrificed their time with me as a family so I could finish this book. Antonieta was a major pillar in all this. Besides having my back in the day-to-day during the times in which the dissertation absorbed me completely, talking to her always helped me gain a different perspective and understand how much of what I was writing made sense beyond the academic world. For all that, I am deeply grateful to her. Luca grew along with the dissertation. At times it was hard and painful having to travel and to concentrate on my writing, as I felt that was robbing me of the time to be with him and to accompany his growth. This was a learning experience for us both. The dissertation may have been a way of teaching me that, in these individualistic times in which we are living, in addition to family there are other things we need to care about and commit to. But that family, at least family as I see it, must also be part of those commitments.

Abbreviations

AC	Ação católica (Catholic Action) Brazil.
AP	Ação Popular (Popular Action) Brazil.
CNT	Convención nacional de trabajadores (Workers National Convention) Uruguay.
CIA	Central Intelligence Agency, United States.
CGT	Confederación general del trabajo (Labor General Confederation) Argentina.
CUT	Central unitaria de trabajadores (Workers United Center) Chile.
DINA	Dirección de inteligencia nacional (National Intelligence Directorate) Chile.
EGP	Ejército guerrillero del pueblo (People´s Guerrilla Army) Argentina.
ELN	Ejército de Liberación Nacional (National Liberation Army) Bolivia.
FA	Frente Amplio (Broad Front) Uruguay.
FAL	Fuerzas Armadas de Liberación (Liberation Armed Forces) Argentina.
FARN	Fuerzas Armadas de la revolución nacional (National Revolution of Armed Forces) Argentina.
FAP	Fuerzas Armadas Peronistas (Peronist Armed Forces) Argentina.
FAR	Fuerzas Armadas Revolucionarias (Revolutionary Armed Forces) Argentina.
FIDEL	Frente Izquierda de Liberación (Leftist Liberation Front) Uruguay.
FRA	Frente Revolucionario Antimperialista (Antimperialist Revolutionary Front) Bolivia.
FRIP	Frente Revolucionario Indoamericano Popular (Popular Indoamerican Revolutionary Front) Argentina.

GAP	Grupos de amigos personales (Group of Personal friends of Salvador Allende) Chile.
JCR	Junta de coordinación revolucionaria (Revolutionary Coordination Board) .
MAPU	Movimiento de acción popular unitaria (Popular Unitary Action Movement) Chile.
MIR	Movimiento de izquierda revolucionaria (Left Revolutionary Movement) Chile.
MLNT	Movimiento de liberación nacional Tupamaros (Tupamaros´s National Liberation Movement) Uruguay.
OAS	Organization of American States.
OLAS	Organización Latinoamericana de Solidaridad (Latin American Solidarity Organization) Cuba.
OSPAAL	Organización de solidaridad de los pueblos de Asia, África y América Latina (Organization of Solidarity with the People of Asia, Africa and Latin America) Cuba.
PCC	Partido Comunista Cubano (Cuban Communist Party) Cuba.
PO	Palabra obrera (Worker Word)Argentina.
POLOP	Politica operaia (Worker Policy) Brazil.
PRT-ERP	Partido Revolucionario de los trabajadores-Ejército revolucionario del pueblo (Workers Revolutionary Party-People Revolutionary Army) Argentina.
PRT	Partido Revolucionario de los trabajadores-Bolivia (Workers Revolutionart Party) Bolivia.
PSV	Partido Socialista de Vanguardia (Socialist Party of Vangard) Argentina.
VPR	Vanguarda Popular Revolucionária (Popular Revolutionary Vangard) Chile.
SIDE	Secretaría de Inteligencia del Estado (State Secretariat of Intelligence) Argentina.
UP	Unidad popular (Popular Unity) Chile.
UTAA	Unión de Trabajadores del Azúcar de Artigas (Artigas´s Sugar Workers Union) Uruguay.

Introduction: Actions, Ideas, and Emotions in the Construction of a Transnational Radicalism in the Southern Cone

In the late 1960s, the Uruguayan Enrique Lucas joined the urban guerilla organization Movimiento de Liberación Nacional Tupamaros (Tupamaros National Liberation Movement, or MLN-T). In 1972, after several months in prison, Lucas went into exile in Allende's Chile, making use of a constitutional provision that enabled prisoners to leave the country. In Chile he participated in mobilizations organized by the Movimiento de Izquierda Revolucionaria (Revolutionary Left Movement, or MIR). After the coup he fled to Argentina. Following a short stay in Cuba, Lucas participated as an MLN-T member in the activities conducted in Buenos Aires by the Junta de Coordinación Revolucionaria (Revolutionary Coordination Board, or JCR), a coordinating body formed by members of his organization, Chile's MIR, Bolivia's Ejército de Liberación Nacional Boliviano (Bolivian National Liberation Army, or ELN), and Argentina's Ejército Revolucionario del Pueblo (People's Revolutionary Army, or ERP). However, amid-a strong internal crisis in the MLN-T, Lucas decided to leave his organization and join Bolivian ELN militants who were planning an insurrectional campaign to demand the return of General Juan José Torres, who during his year as president of Bolivia (1970–1971) had built a left-wing government in alliance with peasant and mining sectors. In 1974 he crossed the border. There he met Graciela Rutilo Artes, an Argentine activist with whom he had a daughter. On April 2, 1976 Graciela was kidnapped, along with their daughter Carla and they were taken illegally to a clandestine detention center in Argentina. Five months later, Lucas was killed, along with a group of Bolivian guerrillas, in a clash with members of Bolivia's repressive forces in Cochabamba. Graciela was disappeared and is still missing today, and Carla was illegally appropriated by an Argentine military officer with whom she lived into her teenage years.[1]

Enrique Lucas' story is just one example among thousands that reveal the epic, violent, and dramatic dimensions that political struggles in Latin America's Southern Cone took on during the late 1960s and early 1970s. Lucas belonged to a generation of political activists that emerged in a context marked by increasing social protests, the rise of authoritarian regimes

(Brazil, 1964; Bolivia, 1966; Argentina, 1966; Bolivia, 1971; Uruguay, 1972–3; Chile, 1973; Argentina, 1976), and growing expectations fueled by the social alternatives opened up by the Cuban Revolution. This new political generation – composed primarily of young people, who in the late 1960s had not yet reached their thirties – challenged the traditional ways of doing politics and proposed new forms of social, political, and cultural mobilization. The activists of this "New Left" criticized the legalism and reformism of the communist and socialist parties – the parties of the traditional Left. They also proposed new, more radical methods, which they considered more effective for ensuring the social changes that, in their view, popular sectors demanded. Armed organizations gradually became the leading players in this wave of "New Left" movements that spread across the region and which are the subject of study of this investigation.[2]

This book examines the emergence, development, and demise of a network of organizations of young leftist militants in the Southern Cone, who in the late 1960s and early 1970s advocated organized political violence and transnational strategies as the only ways of achieving social change in their countries. The research conducted for this study traces the path taken by Argentine, Chilean, Uruguayan, and, to a lesser extent, Brazilian and Bolivian activists to develop a regional network of armed organizations. The exchanges among these organizations spanned more than ten years.

The origins of the organizations that participated in this network date back to the mid-1960s. In Argentina, the Partido Revolucionario de los Trabajadores (Revolutionary Workers' Party, or PRT), which would later become the ERP, was formed through the merging of the Trotskyist group Palabra Obrera (Workers' Word, or PO), which had participated in the intense urban labor struggles of the early 1960s, and the Frente Revolucionario Indoamericano Popular (Popular Indo-American Revolutionary Front, or FRIP), a Latin Americanist and Indigenist organization influenced by the ideas of Peruvian APRA leader Víctor Haya de la Torre, with influence in northern Argentina. Both organizations came together in their efforts to raise political awareness among sugar workers in the north, and in 1965 they came to an agreement that established the PRT. One of the leaders of the FRIP, Roberto Mario Santucho, prevailed as head of the new organization over Nahuel Moreno, the traditional leader of Argentine Trotskyism.[3] The Chilean MIR was formed that same year as the result of the coming together of various activists who were critical of the traditional (communist and socialist) Left and its commitment to electoral politics in Chile. These activists, who belonged to Trotskyist and anarchist sectors but were also from groups that had broken away from the communist and socialist parties, were for the most part trade unionists and students who saw social protest as the path to Chile's revolution. Although initially traditional Trotskyist sectors had a significant presence, they were eventually replaced by a new generation of activists, as occurred in Argentina.[4] The Uruguayan Tupamaros were a small group created in January 1966 by various activists who for the most part had broken away from the Socialist Party, but also from the Communist Party and anarchist and minor left-wing groups. From 1962 to 1965, several of these activists had met in an informal group, which they called "the Coordinator," with the aim of supporting the protests of sugarcane workers in northern Uruguay who were occupying land and demanding agrarian reform. This movement was headed by a young law student, Raul Sendic, a member of the Socialist Party who had gone up north to work with rural laborers and would later be the leader of the Tupamaros.[5]

Although initially small and with little awareness of each other, these and other groups gradually started to come together in meetings across the region. They began in Uruguay as a result of rising authoritarianism in neighboring Brazil and Argentina. Che Guevara's Bolivia campaign in 1966 furthered these interactions, which were formalized in Chile under the Unidad Popular (Popular Unity, or UP) government, where a number of groups started to consider the possibility of creating a new regional organization. This idea eventually took form in the Junta de Coordinación Revolucionaria, formed by Bolivia's ELN, Chile's MIR, Argentina's ERP, and Uruguay's MLN-T.

These coordination efforts reached their highest point in Buenos Aires in the period spanning from 1973 to 1976. With the coup d'état in Argentina in 1976, these organizations lost their last remaining "refuge" in the region. Following the harsh blows suffered as a result of the repressive actions of their governments, they tried to regroup during the transition to democracy in the 1980s and adapt to that new political context.

To understand the evolution that led these armed organizations to attempt a broad continental strategy, I will look at the convergence of these national movements through the critical events that defined this generation. I will do this through a multiple-scale approach, considering transnational, regional, and local developments, and will seek to gain insight into the numerous political and cultural processes on which this generation gradually built its political projects. In this way, I aim to contribute to three fields of study connected with the recent history of Latin America: the global 60s; the evolution of the Latin American Left; and the rise of authoritarianism in the Southern Cone.

South America and the Global 60s

An extensive literature has discussed the implications that the global 60s had for the Left in different parts of the world. Most approaches agree that the 1960s opened up fresh possibilities for the emergence of a novel global political movement called the New Left that challenged the political assumptions of the traditional Left. However, the main features of this new political movement have been a matter of debate around the world. While for Jeremi Suri, the global unrest was linked to an elusive "international language of dissent" furthered by a new generation of young people (the post-World War II baby-boomer generation) socialized in universities, for Immanuel Wallerstein and others, 1968 marked the beginning of a revolutionary cycle comparable to that of 1848. But, in contrast to that earlier cycle's critique of the old regime of the nineteenth century, this mobilization focused on questioning the global hegemony of the United States and emerged in reaction to the traditional Left's failure to stop that process.[6] Although in the long term, New Left activists ultimately failed to achieve their aims, according to Wallerstein their efforts were justified by their belief that their actions would be more effective.

Both approaches reveal a tension in the literature of the 1960s. While some emphasize the relative vagueness of the supposedly global counterculture, others insist on the political dimension and revolutionary nature of the movements of the 1960s. Although these two dimensions should not necessarily be seen as antithetical, this antagonism has shaped much of the debate on the 1960s, as is illustrated by Kristin Ross' study on the memory of the French May, *May '68 and its Afterlives*.[7]

Most of the approaches on Latin America, however, have put forward a much less antagonistic view of the relationship between the New Left and the traditional Left. Jeffrey Gould and Eric Zolov – in regional approaches – and Vania Markarian, Victoria Langland, and María Cristina Tortti – in studies that look at specific cases – have all suggested that, while conflicts did exist, there was also some convergence between this "movement of movements" (intellectual trends, aesthetic sensibilities, popular culture expressions, and new behaviors, social movements, political organizations, armed political groups) that the New Left embodied, on the one hand, and the traditional Left, on the other.[8]

Initially, these groups emerged as a reaction against the traditional Left. Their main criticism had to do with the traditional Left's inability to come up with strategies for mobilizing the masses in a way that would create enabling conditions for the revolution. This generation was also very critical of Soviet socialism and stressed the Latin American nature of the revolution as opposed to traditional leftist views that were Eurocentric in their approach to politics. Lastly, these groups sought to organize lower-class sectors from rural areas and urban slums, which had been relatively ignored by the traditional Left. Besides these political differences, there was a distinction that arose from the strong generational imprint that these movements had. From the way they dressed, their cultural products, and their lifestyles, it was evident they sought to be part of the "language of dissent" described by Suri, but this gesture had deep political implications that went far beyond Suri's superficial view.[9]

While they disagreed over strategy, the old and new Left nonetheless had many points in common in terms of their ultimate aims, and there were certain aspects of a highly hierarchical internal political culture that marked significant continuities between the two.

In this sense, this study seeks to put into a broader context the emergence of armed groups and to contribute to an understanding of how their members were part of that "movement of movements," as they engaged in a wide range of innovative experiences in social and cultural spheres in each of their respective countries, where the old and new Left had specific configurations, which differed from those in Europe and the United States.

In addition to this historiographical discussion, I would like to put into question the geography of the 1960s. As with the nineteenth-century revolutions, 1968 is conceptualized to a large extent with a focus on Western Europe and the United States. The vast majority of studies acknowledge the role of the Third World and its struggles in the unrest that stirred the First World. However, these aspects are limited to a mere context and are not included as part of the same network of circulation of ideas and actors.[10] But events in Europe and the United States were also influenced by what was happening in Latin America. One of the most popular icons in central countries during the year 1968 was the image of Che Guevara. Beyond the romantic nostalgia evoked by Guevara's life, the impact of his image illustrates the weight that Latin America's recent history had in the ideas and political strategies that fueled the global 60s. In this sense, it is necessary to reconstruct the place that the Southern Cone had in the global 60s, as the emergence of these actors cannot be explained from the centrality of what happened in Europe and the United States. On the contrary, several major local events that played a role in shaping this political generation also impacted the global 60s. From Che Guevara's Bolivia campaign, with the networks it spawned in the Southern Cone and the emergence of the Tupamaros with their urban guerrilla proposal that was better suited for more urbanized societies, to the debates on the transition to socialism under the Unidad Popular government, all of these developments affected the more radical sectors of the New Left in Europe and the United States.

In sum, the 1960s were global but studies of this period, for the most part, seem to downplay the active role played by the countries of the periphery in the generation of ideas and repertoires of contention in the countries of the center. Studying this experience can thus provide greater insight into the global nature of the 1960s, enable a reflection on the role of processes that have been largely overlooked by the bibliography on the subject, and, lastly, propose new approaches to the tension between the New Left and the traditional Left under which these issues have been examined.

Political Violence and the Left in Latin America

One of the most salient characteristics of this political generation was its defense of revolutionary political violence as a legitimate and necessary form of collective action for countering the advancing hegemony of the United States that thwarted any attempt to bring social change through peaceful and legal means. This option does not only have to do with the global unrest of the 1960s. To a large extent the radicalization that emerges among young people and lower-class sectors in the mid-1960s is one more layer in a process that had been building up through several experiences during Latin America's Cold War.

In his influential study The Last Colonial Massacre, Greg Grandin draws on the revolution/counter-revolution dynamics in twentieth-century Latin America to describe the emergence of the New Left as the last response to a series of failed attempts to bring about social change that were effectively contained by state terrorism practices, as epitomized by the coup against Jacobo Árbenz in Guatemala staged by local elites with U.S. support in the context of the Latin American Cold War.[11]

As of the end of the democratic Spring of the late 1940s, the United States began to view any left-leaning political expressions and labor organization efforts in Latin America with increasingly hostile eyes.[12] The overthrow of Árbenz in Guatemala with major involvement from the CIA marked a watershed moment in the role played by the United States in the region, which continued with the Bay of Pigs in 1961, and was firmly consolidated with the 1964 coup d'état in Brazil. For South America, the Brazilian dictatorship ushered in a new form of authoritarian political regime based on a new role played by the armed forces, trained in the national security doctrine, which was to be replicated in the coming years in most of the countries of the Southern Cone. It also gradually shattered the reformist expectations that the Alliance for Progress had generated at the start of the decade.

Many intellectuals and activists who eventually embraced armed struggle in the late 1960s were forming their opinion on the role of the United States in the decade spanning from the coup in Guatemala to the coup in Brazil. Guevara's phrase "Cuba will not be Guatemala" is representative of this generation of activists who witnessed the growing interventionism of the United States that sought to stifle various alternatives of social reform, and who came to view armed struggle as the only possible response to that interventionism. Cuba must be considered against this backdrop. Revolution raised expectations among groups of activists who were already becoming radicalized in reaction to U.S. intervention in Latin America and the economic crises of the industrialist projects that had begun before Cuba in the context of the Cold War. Revolution offered replicable models that in South America were viewed with favorable eyes, but also from a critical distance, as will be shown in this book. Although several authors, such as Hal Brands in his recent study, have stressed Cuba's centrality, the individual paths taken by the activists studied here show that Cuba was not the starting point. Rather it was one moment in a process of radicalization whose origins could be traced back, as Grandin posits, to the mid-1950s.[13]

Beside their connection with the Latin American Cold War, the explanations for left-wing violence have also prompted heated debates both in academia and in national public spheres. During the dictatorships, these groups were stigmatized, accused of being foreign agents, and used to justify the authoritarian backlash that the military regimes claimed was necessary to defend national security. In the context of the democratic transitions, the violence of these groups was mostly interpreted as the result of an ideological fanaticism that fought against another fanaticized minority formed by the military. This narrative portrayed civil society as a hostage in a polarization between actors that were removed from society and ideologically alienated from it. Different variations of this kind of narrative have been used in experiences as diverse as those of Argentina, Chile, Peru, and Guatemala.[14]

It was also in the context of the transitions to democracy that the subject began to be of interest to academics, essayists, and journalists. While the body of works focusing on the subject is so extensive as to make a thorough review difficult, the most relevant moments and approaches for explaining the ways in which armed struggle was perceived as of the 1980s must be highlighted.[15] In a climate of positive expectations regarding the return to democracy, a significant number of studies emphasized the anti-liberal nature of these groups. In the debates of the time, these practices were condemned by the general public and some sectors of the human rights movements even avoided the subject as they were reluctant to bring up the most controversial aspects of the political violence in which some left-wing groups had engaged.[16] Most academics were influenced by the model of democratic breakdown proposed by Juan Linz, and focused on the ways in which the emergence of such groups contributed to the process of political polarization that eroded the region's democratic regimes. In Linz's model, based on their ideology, these organizations were characterized as actors disloyal to democracy, whose actions spurred a process of political polarization that tended to undermine democratic procedures, creating a political environment in which sectors at the center of the political spectrum – who were thought to be key for the preservation of stable democratic regimes – failed in their leadership role.[17]

In addition, several academic works insisted on the ideological influence of the Cuban Revolution and the ways in which the intellectual mood of the 1960s set the tone for a radicalization that was largely portrayed as alienated from the political process and which fueled the increasing polarization. For instance, in his book on the breakdown of democracy in Chile, Arturo Valenzuela argued that radical left-wing groups furthered a "self-fulfilling prophecy" as they not only denounced the inevitability of an authoritarian reaction with their maximalist discourses and practices, they also ultimately weakened center forces that would have been the only ones capable of overcoming the polarization faced by Chilean democracy.[18] Similar arguments were put forward by Luis Eduardo González for Uruguay and Liliana de Riz for Argentina.[19] In all of these cases the crises of democracy that preceded the coups were explained as being rooted in multiple causes, but when it came to armed leftist groups the descriptions focused on the major role that ideology had played in pushing them away from a democratic culture in which their views would have led the fate of these societies down a better path.

Starting in the 1990s, new studies, based on oral history and written sources, centered their attention more specifically on the armed actors themselves, offering an interpretation more focused on the internal life of these organizations than on their role in the crises of democracy. An early example of these is Richard Gillespie's book Soldiers of Perón: Argentina's Montoneros, published in Spanish in 1987, which emphasized the intersection of middle-class Catholic nationalism with Marxism to explain the emergence of this organization and its subsequent militarist deviation.[20] Other historians followed his example, attributing a significant role to the ideological aspects and cultural identity dimension of these new organizations in explaining their emergence, as well as the moments of increasing political isolation that had resulted in relatively irrational actions. This line of work was particularly prolific in the case of Argentina. In analyzing the military development of these organizations, authors such as Pilar Calveiro, Hugo Vezzetti, and Vera Carnovale highlighted the part played by ideology and internal culture.[21]

Along with these works, an abundant literature of testimony emerged, largely in the last two decades, which seeks to recover the experience of the militants who were active during this period. This literature, based mainly on testimonial accounts and produced by academics who are also activists, contributed to expand the chorus of voices engaged in the discussion of the issue of political violence. These approaches called attention to the weaknesses of the democracies of the 1950s and 1960s that the political and intellectual works seem to disregard.[22]

All of these studies on ideology and culture were useful because they reconstructed the language and ideas of armed groups in the pre-coup period. Most, however, failed to provide elements to historically approach the ways in which such groups developed their proposals. Despite the diversity of views that they represented, they all shared a methodological principle that entailed ignoring the possibility of a link between ideological and cultural processes and political and economic transformations, which had been the focus of the academic studies conducted in the 1970s. This resulted in ideas being understood as coherently organized bodies, disconnected from the contradictory historical processes in which they emerged and from the structural changes that were affecting these societies. This type of approach made it difficult to comprehend the sinuous and conflicting paths taken by the left-wing and center-left activists and parties studied in this book, many of whom had supported reformist projects in the mid-1950s and had gone on to adopt radical postures in the late 1960s, while backing electoral initiatives even as they took up arms, and that, as of the 1980s and in the context of re-democratization, resumed their political activities through non-violent means.

In this sense, the 1980s marked a starting point for a way of thinking about political violence in academia that still influences us today and which consisted in conceiving ideology and culture as an autonomous sphere without major links to other social, economic, and political processes on which these ideas and identities were built.

By contrast, the first authors – for the most part sociologists, who in the late 1960s and in the 1970s had sought to explain this phenomenon of political violence, had always pointed to structural frameworks derived from the process of modernization or the crisis of the Latin American industrialist model. Texts such as Political Order in Changing Societies by Samuel Huntington and Why Men Rebel by Ted Gurr provided significant theoretical inspiration for sociologists of modernization who explained the anomic behavior of this political generation as the result of the divorce between the middle classes' expectations of upward social mobility and the limited material possibilities of underdeveloped societies.[23] Or, in the framework of the Latin American dependency theory in its various forms, they all explained the radicalization of sectors of the middle classes as resulting from the crisis of the model of import substitution industrialization and the increasing demands that the state could not satisfy.[24] Even in Guillermo O'Donnell's first works, the radicalization of certain sectors of the Left is presented as the result of the "stirring of the lower classes" as these countries transitioned from the populist or welfare models of the 1950s to the authoritarian bureaucratic states that would ultimately be consolidated in the 1970s.[25] These studies, marked by structural sociological approaches that established diverse connections between political regimes and economic processes, provided important contextual insights for understanding the radicalization of the Left, but they failed to address the concrete paths taken by that radicalization.

In short, left-wing radicalization in the region was described, either as an inevitable structural consequence, or as the result of ideological convictions that for some spurred dictatorial authoritarianism. In this dichotomic view, those who have insisted on the more structural phenomena have tended to assign a central importance to local causalities, while those who emphasized ideological or cultural aspects have focused on the influence that the global context had on local processes.

I seek to combine the structural approaches of the 1970s, with the most recent political and cultural approaches, toward understanding the unique ways in which the ideas of the global 60s were read and reinterpreted in this part of the globe, and to provide insight into how this regional movement was shaped by the dialog between the inside and the outside. More precisely, the aim is to recreate the ways in which this political generation gradually built its political categories, based on the socioeconomic conditions and the political opportunities that the conflict with the state created or precluded. In this sense, the ideological or cultural definitions adopted by these groups must not be viewed as fixed aspects that were determined once and for all, but as symbolic resources that these movements took up, reinterpreted, and adapted depending on the historical circumstances.

In my research, the methodological tools for analyzing such dynamics from a historical perspective are inspired essentially on the reading of the works produced in the field of sociology of social movements. These are relevant to the case studied here, because they offer categories for examining the conflict dynamics that occur between social movements and the state in contemporary societies.[26] In this sense, categories such as "political process," "structure of political opportunities," and "protest repertoire" developed by social movement studies are useful for organizing an analysis of the relationship between the state and the methods of struggle implemented by these organizations. Moreover, recent studies conducted under this paradigm, which have contributed to an understanding of the complex dynamics between state repression and social protest in Europe and the United States in the 1960s and 1970s, and the development of armed leftist organizations, may also have implications for this research.[27] Also, the more recent contributions that have stressed the ethical and emotional dimensions of the development of social movements, offer valuable insight for examining the historical processes of construction of these groups' identities, where subjectivity coexists with specific rationalities.[28] Thus, while this is an eminently historical study, I will take certain categories used by social movement researchers and apply them to the examination of the origin, development, and resignification of the violent practices and representations adopted by these organizations.

I also seek to examine the political violence of the Latin American Left, and more specifically of the Southern Cone Left, through a transnational approach that transcends the national-foreigner dichotomy in which this subject has been primarily discussed. Generally speaking, the international dimension was used as an argument to invalidate an opponent's positions. The Right denounced the antinational nature of left-wing movements, whether they acted legally and illegally, due to their affinity with communist countries, and attributed their growth to the alleged influence of the Soviet Union and Cuba. The Left, for its part, explained the growth of civil and dictatorial authoritarianism as the result of the influence of U.S. imperialism on national political processes. While this is not the place to assess the effect that each of these international actors had on national processes, what I am interested in highlighting here is the negativity that characterized the analysis of the connections between domestic and non-national actors.[29] This has certainly impacted the ways in which issues connected with political violence have been addressed in national historiographies. Although transnational exchanges were evident for any analyst in the region – and in the cases studied here most activists of the period proclaimed explicitly that their revolutionary project was continental – as evidenced by the literature reviewed above, these political processes have thus far been explained, for the most part, in national terms, or through comparative approaches that ultimately reinforced national differences without addressing the ways in which these regional dialogs were constructed.[30]

Some works have proposed research lines that have reflected on the circulation of Latin American actors in the context of the Cold War.[31] The studies of Southern Cone militaries conducted by Ariel C. Armony and John Dinges are good examples of how the national security doctrine led to a circulation of ideas, practices, and resources in the region that was a departure from the traditional practices of the national armies.[32] Other works have highlighted the role of Cuba in the circulation of cultural and political actors from the region.[33] The recent study by Tanya Harmer, *Allende's Chile, and the Inter-American Cold War*, offers the most interesting and innovative approach with respect to the methodology and contents of my research.[34] In studying Allende's foreign policy, Harmer provides a "multidimensional, comprehensive, and decentralized perspective" involving various actors connected with the states of Brazil, Chile, Cuba, the United States, and the Soviet Union, along with Chilean left-wing political parties, Brazilian extreme right groups, and a range of regional actors. All of these groups participated in the unique scenario of the global Cold War that was the Inter-American system. For Harmer, thinking in terms of a system entails focusing on a closer examination of multilateral relations as opposed to bilateral ones. In this way, it is clear that several different aspects of U.S. bilateral relations with Mexico, Peru, and, in particular, Brazil were strongly influenced by the policies implemented by Washington for Allende's Chile. Moreover, in her approach to the Inter-American system she not only looks at states, but also at political actors and networks that imprinted certain dynamics to the process. In this sense, Harmer's contribution is significant because of the perspective for understanding the unique political dynamics of the region and for considering non-state actors in that system.[35]

My aim is to reconstruct the specific ways in which ideas, political and social movements, and networks connected with crucial historical events originating in the Inter-American system shaped the transnational development of a political culture with strong revolutionary undertones, which influenced these militants in their choice of violent options. The historical reconstruction of these processes provides an understanding of how the tension between the limitations of the Cold War and the ideas of social change proposed by various political and social actors set the tone of the debate on the need for political violence in the 1960s and 1970s.

The lasting significance of these movements has to do with the fact that they were instrumental in forging a common path for a range of left-wing organizations that, starting in the 1960s, had been gradually distancing themselves from the international experiences of socialism, communism, and Trotskyism, and which, as a result of their decision to take up arms and their close relationship with the Cuban Revolution, had been contributing to create a Left delimited by a historically-determined space: Latin America. The impact of that political culture marked a significant stage in the construction of a Left that identified with the continent's history, leaving universalist aspirations behind, and which today seems to be playing a key role in Latin American politics.[36] The meetings and experiences shared during the 1960s and 1970s by these Southern Cone militants and the ways in which they tried to adapt in the 1980s are important elements toward explaining the present situation of contemporary Latin American Left. Although the policies of the recent progressive governments differ from the maximalist agendas of the 1960s, there are many aspects that originated in that period and were recast during the transitions of the 1980s, when several survivors began to combine some of their political intentions of the 1960s with liberal democratic values associated with the human rights organizations and other social movements.

The Southern Cone and the Emergence of Modern Authoritarianism

In contrast to other regions, such as the Caribbean, Central America, or the Andean region, the Southern Cone had not been a significant space of joint collective action for the leftist organizations of the region. However, the political dynamics of the 1960s and early 1970s brought these militants together. This was a major development. It was true that the region had a common history, including their colonial past, successive waves of reforms that transformed the oligarchic regimes of the first half of the twentieth century without the need for a revolution – in contrast to Mexico – and high levels of social development in the context of Latin America in the 1960s.[37] But, while there had been attempts at integration agreements since the beginning of the twentieth century, the region lacked a strong tradition of shared identity.[38] Moreover, until the 1960s, the region's political processes did not merit it being classified as a discrete area of South America.

A search on WorldCat reveals that in the 1970s the term "Southern Cone" was used mainly as a category of analysis in connection with the dictatorial experience. Prior to that, we find it used only in an early testimonial novel published in the 1960s by Uruguayan writer Hiber Conteris, under the title Cono Sur (Southern Cone). The novel tells the story of a Bolivian refugee's experience in Uruguay at the beginning of the decade and anticipates what would happen in the coming years.[39] The idea of the Southern Cone as a distinct region gained increasing currency as scholars began to reflect on the cycle of authoritarian regimes that was inaugurated by Brazil with its 1964 coup d'état, continued by Argentina in 1966, furthered by Uruguay and Chile with their 1973 coups, and fully consolidated by Argentina with a new coup in 1976, and which spread military dictatorships across the territory of the Southern Cone with the firm support of conservative civilian sectors. This authoritarianism was not of the traditional sort found in scarcely urbanized societies, nor was it a populist authoritarianism: it rested, among other things, on the neutralization of social movements through repression. Neither was it an authoritarianism based on a cult of personality, as regimes were backed by the military, or a police dictatorship that sought to restore order, as its aim was to radically transform the lives of these countries. It was precisely the unprecedented nature of this new form of authoritarianism that led scholars to reflect on this phenomenon from a regional perspective.[40]

It is in this context that armed groups started acting regionally. The military, which already had a common ideological component that drew on the national security doctrine, and which in the 1960s had suggested forms of joint action under the Organization of American States (OAS), also began to act on a regional scale, deploying a repressive plan called Operation Condor, which involved illegally crossing national borders to control, kidnap, and murder political opponents in neighboring countries.

In this sense, the establishment of the JCR is the result of an awareness of the regionalization of political processes that begins to emerge in the 1960s and would later be adopted by a number of very diverse actors – the military, trade unions, political parties of the center, and human rights organizations – which, in the coming decades, would develop forms of coordination.

Building on prior contributions to the subject, as reviewed above, I have set out to map the origins and the development of a transnational political culture that emerged from dialogs and meetings among militants of the region's New Left from the mid-1960s to the 1976 coup in Argentina. This political culture would later be linked to the outcome of local political experiments, movements of exiles across the region, and the growing regionalization of authoritarianism.

While initially considered part of the "New Left," these groups – which in the mid-1960s were still unable to articulate a political alternative – gradually converged in a regional dialog that led them to strengthen their proposals and boost their political influence in each country. As activists were forced to leave their countries in the face of escalating repression and the establishment of authoritarian regimes, they came together in exile, and their joint regional experience spurred the circulation of ideas and individuals, thus contributing to fully develop a body of common ideas among militants from different countries.

In these movements across borders the groups constructed a shared conception of Latin Americanism and a criticism of the viability of liberal democracy in the context of underdevelopment and the Cold War. They also advocated a form of political violence that was linked to a particular morality where politics were understood in terms of good and evil, social change was reduced to an aspect of revolutionary will, and political commitment was associated with individual sacrifice.

For the purposes of this investigation I will use the term political culture to refer to a diversity of aspects ranging from ideology, morals, sentiments, class, subjectivities, and art, and which, at the same time, cannot be reduced to just one of these individualized categories. This notion of political culture is drawn from cultural history contributions. These works have helped understand how political activism is constructed historically from different political cultures. In a study of the French Revolution, Lynn Hunt – one of the first to develop this approach – defines the notion of political culture as follows: "The values, expectations, and implicit rules that expressed and shaped collective intentions and actions."[41] This research seeks to follow the ways in which each of these aspects was incorporated and reinterpreted in the construction of a particular political culture that included and furthered the development of a group of armed organizations in the Southern Cone.

Four aspects have been selected to trace how different elements came together to form a transnational political culture: actions, ideas, and interpretations of the regional political process, experiences that built a common political subjectivity, and transnational identity. This will first involve looking at the ways in which these groups with diverse ideological origins converged through a common repertoire of radical practices in a series of shared political ideas and interpretations of the events that were unfolding in the region. By drawing on concepts such as structure of feelings, or emotions, we will then look at how various events that occurred in the region had repercussions on the constitution of this political generation. Lastly, the book will examine the processes of regional exile to determine how these Southern Cone militants gradually came together, forging ties among groups from different countries that helped construct the idea of a transnational community.

These approaches offer possibilities but they also, admittedly, present certain limitations. On the one hand, they clearly enable us to think of these national processes in broader contexts. But as with any delimitation of scale, it entails emphasizing certain aspects and disregarding others. In this case, the experience of these militants traveling across the region largely concerns middle-ranking members and leaders of these organizations more than the rank-and-file of these groups. These militants were, for the most part, middle-class in origin and, to a lesser extent, urban working-class. It was middle-class militants who had the material and intellectual resources to move with relative ease in neighboring countries. In these movements across national borders we find few rank-and-file militants from rural areas or urban peripheries involved in the period's unprecedented social mobilization experiences. In this sense, the project places greater emphasis on the political involvement of middle sectors as opposed to other, lower-class actors, whose mobilization can be traced better at the local level.[42]

In terms of the sources used, the scale of the subject of study has imposed a research strategy that is relatively eclectic, adapting heuristic criteria to the degree of development of each country's archives. Generally speaking, the project was based primarily on written sources and to a lesser extent on oral sources. Three types of written sources were used for this study: (1) internal and public documentation of the organizations researched and news and cultural magazines close to the organizations; (2) state documents; and (3) written testimonial accounts from members of the organizations.[43] Each of these types of sources presents specific methodological problems that require a critical analysis of the conditions in which they were produced and the target audience of each source. Testimonial accounts have an added difficulty in that special attention must also be paid to the post-dictatorial context in which such accounts were given, as they generally tended to highlight aspects connected with political repression by the state and to minimize aspects related to the organization's own violent and illegal practices.

Many of these are unpublished sources, not previously used, which constitute a significant contribution to the study of the emergence and development of left-wing political violence in the region. Adopting a transnational approach also offered the possibility of rereading several sources that have been used to study national cases, but which are interpreted differently when compared with similar sources from neighboring countries. Although initially the aim was to rely heavily on oral history, a number of factors connected with the situation of the potential interviewees and the scale of the project led to a minimization of the role of oral accounts in the research. This study also draws on previous interviews conducted by colleagues in the region.[44]

Writing about the movements of militants across national borders is not a simple task. Recounting their history presents a number of difficulties that are both methodological and narrative. There is a real risk of producing a regional narrative that minimizes the importance of national scenarios. Also, the simultaneity of multiple meeting processes can result in a narrative that in its attempt to cover every process is rendered historically incomprehensible. For these reasons, the narrative will be delimitated by focusing on transnational meetings in certain national spaces at key moments of this regional history. Each of these transnational meetings will be studied to identify the ways in which emotions, ideas, and transnational loyalty ties contributed to create a transnational political culture. Each chapter deals with a different period, in which militants from various countries met in a particular city: Montevideo in the mid-1960s, Santiago from 1970 to 1973, and Buenos Aires from 1973 to 1976. Each experience furthered the expansion of a network of militants and the development of a common political culture.

Notes

1 For information on this case, see: Matilde Artés, Crónica de una desaparición. La lucha de una abuela de Plaza de Mayo (Madrid: Espasa, 1997), as well as John Dinges, The Condor Years: How Pinochet and his Allies Brought Terrorism to Three Continents (New York: The New Press 2004), and Madres y Familiares de Detenidos Desaparecidos (Uruguay), A todos ellos: informe de Madres y Familiares de Uruguayos Detenidos Desaparecidos (Montevideo: Madres y Familiares de Uruguayos Detenidos Desaparecidos, 2004), and Osvaldo "Chato" Peredo, Volvimos a las montañas (Santa Cruz, Bolivia: Osvaldo Peredo Leigue Edición, 2003).

2 For a more general analysis of the debates of the New Left in Latin America, see Jorge G. Castañeda, Utopia Unarmed: The Latin American Left after the Cold War (New York: Knopf 1993), and the recent compilation by Verónica Oikón Solano, Eduardo Rey Tristán, and Martín López Ávalos (eds.), El estudio de las luchas revolucionarias en América Latina (1959–1996): Estado de la cuestión (Colegio de Michoacan, Universidad de Santiago de Compostela: Santiago de Compostela, 2014). For Argentina's case, see: Oscar Terán, Nuestros años sesentas: la formación de la nueva izquierda intelectual en la Argentina, 1956–1966 (Buenos Aires, Argentina: Puntosur Editores, 1991), as well as María Cristina Tortti, El "viejo" partido socialista y los orígenes de la "nueva" izquierda: 1955–1965 (Buenos Aires: Prometeo Libros, 2009), and Pilar Calveiro, Política y/o violencia: una aproximación a la guerrilla de los años 70 (Buenos Aires: Norma, 2005), Richard Gillespie, Soldiers of Perón, Argentina's Montoneros

(Oxford, New York: Clarendon Press; Oxford University Press, 1982), María José Moyano, Argentina's Lost Patrol: Armed Struggle, 1969–1979 (New Haven: Yale University Press, 1995), Pablo A. Pozzi, Por las sendas argentinas: el PRT-ERP, la guerrilla marxista (Buenos Aires: Eudeba, 2001), and Vera Carnovale, Los combatientes: historia del PRT-ERP (Buenos Aires: Siglo Veintiuno Editores, 2011). For Chile's case, see: Daniel Avendaño and Mauricio Palma, El rebelde de la burguesía: la historia de Miguel Enríquez (Santiago, Chile: Ediciones CESOC, 2001), and García Naranjo, Historias derrotadas: opción y obstinación de la guerrilla chilena (1965–1988), as well as Pedro Naranjo et al., Miguel Enríquez y el proyecto revolucionario en Chile, Carlos Sandoval, M.I.R. (una historia) (Santiago: Sociedad Editorial Trabajadores, 1990) and Movimiento de Izquierda Revolucionaria. Coyunturas y vivencias (1973–1980) (Concepción, Chile: Escaparate Ediciones, 2011), Eugenia Palieraki, ¡La revolución ya viene!: el MIR chileno en los años sesenta (Santiago: LOM Ediciones, 2014); Julio Pinto Vallejo "¿Y la historia les dio la razón? El MIR en dictadura, 1973–1981," in Verónica Valdivia, Rolando Álvarez, and Julio Pinto, Su revolución contra nuestra revolución. Izquierdas y derechas en el Chile de Pinochet (1973–1981) (Santiago: LOM, 2006); and Igor Goicovic, Movimiento de Izquierda Revolucionaria (Concepción, Chile: Equipo Editorial, 2012). With respect to Uruguay, see: Clara Aldrighi, La izquierda armada: ideología, ética e identidad en el MLN-Tupamaros (Montevideo: Ediciones Trilce, 2001); Hebert Gatto, El cielo por asalto: el Movimiento de Liberación Nacional (Tupamaros) y la izquierda uruguaya (1963–1972) (Montevideo: Taurus, 2004); Alfonso Lessa, La revolución imposible: los tupamaros y el fracaso de la vía armada en el Uruguay del siglo XX (Montevideo: Editorial Fin de Siglo, 2002); and Eduardo Rey Tristan, A la vuelta de la esquina, la izquierda revolucionaria uruguaya, 1955–1973 (Montevideo: Editorial Fin de Siglo, 2006).

3 See: Pozzi, Por las sendas argentinas; Carnovale, Los combatientes: historia del PRT-ERP, and Maria Seoane, Todo o nada. La historia secreta y pública de Mario Roberto Santucho, el jefe guerrillero de los años setenta (Buenos Aires: Ed. Sudamericana, 2003).

4 See: Daniel Avendaño and Mauricio Palma, El rebelde de la burguesía: la historia de Miguel Enríquez (Santiago, Chile: Ediciones CESOC, 2001), Eugenia Palieraki, ¡La revolución ya viene!: el MIR chileno en los años sesenta (Santiago: LOM Ediciones, 2014).

5 See: Aldrighi, La izquierda armada; Gatto, El cielo por asalto; and Samuel Blixen, Sendic (Montevideo: Ediciones Trilce, 2000).

6 Jeremi Suri, Power and Protest: Global Revolution and the Rise of Détente (Cambridge: Harvard University Press, 2003), and Immanuel Wallerstein et al., Anti-Systemic Movements (London, New York: Verso 1989), Chapter V. To see different ways in which this subject has been treated, see Kristin Ross, May '68 and its Afterlives (Chicago, London: Chicago Press, 2002) for France, Jeremy Varon, Bringing the War Home: The Weather Underground, the Red Army Faction, and Revolutionary Violence in the Sixties and Seventies (Berkeley: University of California Press, 2004), and Martin Klimke, The Other Alliance: Student Protest in West Germany and the United States in the Global 60s (Princeton, N.J.: Princeton University Press, 2010) for the United States and Germany.

7 See Ross, May '68 and its Afterlives.

8 Jeffrey Gould, "Solidarity under Siege: The Latin American Left, 1968," The American Historical Review (2009) 114 (2): 348–75, also Eric Zolov, "Expanding our Conceptual Horizons: The Shift from an Old to a New Left in Latin America," A Contracorriente, Vol. 5, no. 2, Winter 2008, 47–73, and Vania Markarian, El 68 uruguayo: el movimiento estudiantil entre molotovs y música beat (Bernal: Universidad Nacional de Quilmes, 2012), Victoria Langland, Speaking of Flowers. Student Movements and the

Making and Remembering of 1968 in Military Brazil (Durham and London: Duke University Press, 2013), Maria Cristina Tortti, "Post Scriptum: La construcción de un campo temático," in Alfredo Pucciarelli (ed.), La primacia de la política. Lanusse, Perón y la Nueva Izquierda en tiempos del GAN (Buenos Aires: EUDEBA, 1999).

9 For two different approaches on the subject, see the works by Vania Markarian, El 68 uruguayo, and Patrick Barr-Melej, "Hippismo a la chilena: Juventud y heterodoxia cultural en un contexto transnacional (1970–1973)," in Fernando Purcell, Alfredo Riquelme (eds.), Ampliando miradas. Chile y su historia e un tiempo global (Santiago: RIL editores-Instituto de Historia PUC, 2009). While Markarian finds that young Uruguayan communist activists and Tupamaro militants followed certain cultural trends of the global youth counterculture, such as psychedelia, protest songs, and artistic experimentation, Barr-Melej emphasizes the differences that existed between the Chilean hippie movement and the Left. Although the differences between these two authors may be attributed to the specific characteristics of each process, they also express two different ways of approaching the subject. In my opinion, what Barr-Melej describes identifies the problems and resistances posed by a non-critical translation of certain categories, but that does not necessarily preclude the interpretation that a large part of the youth cultural expressions of the time were associated with those meanings operating at the global level.

10 One of the few exceptions is Quinn Slobodian, Foreign Front: Third World Politics in Sixties West Germany (Duke University Press, 2012). Other works also note this influence. See: Varon, Bringing the War Hom; Klimke, The Other Alliance; Ross, May '68 and its Afterlives.

11 Greg Grandin, The Last Colonial Massacre: Latin America in the Cold War (Chicago: University of Chicago Press, 2004).

12 Leslie Bethell and Ian Roxborough, Latin America between the Second World War and the Cold War, 1944–1948 (New York and Cambridge: Cambridge University Press, 1992).

13 See Hal Brands, Latin America's Cold War (Cambridge, Massachusetts: Harvard University Press, 2010). Grandin's study, The Last Colonial Massacre, offers an alternative view.

14 Greg Grandin, "The Instruction of Great Catastrophe: Truth Commissions, National History, and State Formation in Argentina, Chile, and Guatemala," The American Historical Review, Vol. 110, no. 1 (February 2005), and Aldo Marchesi, "El pasado como parábola política: Democracia y derechos en los informes Nunca Más del Cono Sur," Stockholm Review of Latin American Studies, no. 9, Issue no. 7, December 2011, and Emilio Crenzel, La historia política del Nunca Más: la memoria de las desapariciones en la Argentina (Buenos Aires, Argentina: Siglo Veintiuno Editores, 2008).

15 For Argentina, see Luis Alberto Romero, "La violencia en la historia argentina reciente: un estado de la cuestión," in Anne Pérotin-Dumon (ed.), Historizar el pasado vivo en América Latina (2007), http://www.historizarelpasadovivo.cl/, and Eudald Cortina and Gabriel Rot, "Tendencias e interpretaciones sobre la lucha armada en Argentina. De la teoría de los dos demonios a la actualidad," in Verónica Oikón Solano et al., El estudio de las luchas revolucionarias en América Latina (1959–1996); for Brasil see: Vitor Amorim de Angelo, "Izquierda armada en Brasil. Un balance de la historia y de la producción académica reciente," in Oikon et al., El estudio de las luchas revolucionarias, and Marcelo Ridenti, "Esquerdas revolucionarias armadas nos anos 1960–1970," in Jorge Ferreira and Daniel Aarao Reis, Revolução e democracia: 1964. ... (Civilização Brasileira: Rio de Janeiro, 2007); for Chile see: Peter Winn, "El pasado está presente. Historia y memoria en el Chile contemporáneo," in Pérotin-Dumon, (ed.), Historizar el pasado vivo en América Latina; and Igor Goicovic, "Temas y debates en la historia

de la violencia política en Chile," Contenciosa, year II, no. 3, second semester 2014; for Uruguay see: Aldo Marchesi, Jaime Yaffé, "La violencia bajo la lupa. Una revisión de la literatura sobre violencia y política en los sesenta," Revista Uruguaya de Ciencia Política 19 (2010); Eduardo Rey Tristan and Jaime Yaffé, "Izquierda y revolución en el Uruguay (1959–1973)," in Oikon et al., El estudio de las luchas revolucionarias.

16 See Emilio Crenzel, La historia política del Nunca Más.

17 See Juan Linz, The Breakdown of Democratic Regimes (Baltimore, London: Johns Hopkins University Press, 1978).

18 Arturo Valenzuela's study, The Breakdown of Democratic Regimes: Chile (Baltimore: Johns Hopkins University Press, 1978) published in Chile in 1988. This literature is more diverse than the political science bibliography produced under Linz' influence.

19 Luis Eduardo González, Estructuras políticas y democracia en Uruguay (Montevideo: FCU – Fundación de Cultura Universitaria, 1993), and Liliana de Riz, La política en suspenso, 1966–1976 (Buenos Aires: Paidós, 2000).

20 Richard Gillespie, Soldados de Perón: los Montoneros (Buenos Aires: Grijalbo, 1987).

21 Hugo Vezzetti. Pasado y presente: guerra, dictadura y sociedad en la Argentina (Buenos Aires: Siglo XXI, 2002), and Pilar Calveiro, Política y/o violencia: una aproximación a la guerrilla de los años 70 (Buenos Aires: Norma, 2005); Carnovale, Los combatientes.

22 A recent example is Pablo A. Pozzi and Claudio Pérez (eds.), Historia oral e historia política: izquierda y lucha armada en América Latina, 1960–1990 (Santiago: LOM Ediciones: Universidad Academia de Humanismo Cristiano, 2012). For other examples, see: Clara Aldrighi, Memorias de la insurgencia, Historias de vida y militancia en el MLN Tupamaros (1965–1975) (Montevideo: Ediciones de la Banda Oriental, 2009); Daniel de Santis, La historia del PRT-ERP: por sus protagonistas (Buenos Aires: Editora Guevarista, 2010); Pozzi, "Por las sendas argentinas," and Carlos Sandoval Ambiado, M.I.R. (una historia) (Santiago, Chile: Sociedad Editorial Trabajadores, 1990). Also, Eduardo Anguita and Martín Caparrós, La voluntad. Una historia de la militancia revolucionaria en la Argentina (5 vols.) (Buenos Aires: Grupo Editorial Norma, 1997, 2001).

23 Ted Robert Gurr, Why Men Rebel (Princeton, N.J.: Princeton University Press, 1970), and Samuel P. Huntington, Political Order in Changing Societies (New Haven: Yale University Press, 1968). For some works influenced by this framework see: Robert Moss, Urban Guerrilla Warfare (London: International Institute for Strategic Studies, 1971) and Peter Waldmann, "Anomia social y violencia," in Alain Rouquié (comp.), Argentina, hoy (Mexico: Siglo XXI Editores, 1981).

24 By way of example see: Theotônio dos Santos, Socialismo o Fascismo, el nuevo carácter de la dependencia y el dilema latinoamericano (Argentina: Ed. Periferia, 1972), as well as Manuel Garretón and Tomás Moulian, "Procesos y bloques políticos en la crisis chilena, 1970–1973," Revista Mexicana de Sociología 41, no. 1, Análisis de Coyuntura (January–March 1979), and Juan Carlos Portantiero, "Clases dominantes y crisis política en la Argentina actual," in Pasado y Presente, no. 1, new series (April–June 1973).

25 For some developments of O'Donnell's argument and its influence, see Guillermo O'Donnell, Contrapuntos: ensayos escogidos sobre autoritarismo y democratización (Buenos Aires: Paidós, 1997), and David Collier et al. (ed.), The New Authoritarianism in Latin America (Princeton, N.J.: Princeton University Press, 1979).

26 One of the pioneer studies of this approach is Doug McAdam, Political Process and the Development of Black Insurgency, 1930–1970 (Chicago: University of Chicago Press, 1982). For an updated version of this approach, see Doug McAdam, Sidney G. Tarrow, and Charles Tilly, Dynamics of Contention (Cambridge; New York: Cambridge University Press, 2001).

27 See Donatella della Porta, Social Movements, Political Violence, and the State: A Comparative Analysis of Italy and Germany (Cambridge; New York: Cambridge University Press, 1995), and Christian Davenport, Hank Johnston, and Carol Mueller, Repression and Mobilization (Minneapolis: University of Minnesota Press, 2005).

28 See Jeff Goodwin, James M. Jasper, and Francesca Polletta (ed.) Passionate Politics. Emotions and Social Movements (Chicago: University of Chicago Press, 2001). For Wood's critique of the approaches that focus on the theory of rational choice for understanding collective action, see Elizabeth Jean Wood, Insurgent Collective Action and Civil War in El Salvador (New York: Cambridge University Press, 2003), chapter 8.

29 The foreignness of the Left has been most strongly emphasized by the military, who point to these groups' connections with international organizations and their affinities with the Russian, Chinese, and Cuban revolutions. This was a constant element in military discourse starting in the 1970s and can be seen clearly in the attempts made by dictatorships and armed forces to systematize an official history. By way of example, see: Poder Ejecutivo Nacional, El terrorismo en la Argentina: evolución de la delincuencia terrorista en la Argentina (Buenos Aires: Poder Ejecutivo Nacional, 1979), as well as Junta de Comandantes en Jefe, Las Fuerzas Armadas al pueblo oriental. La subversión, vol. 1 (Montevideo: Junta de Comandantes en Jefe, 1978), and Manuel Contreras Sepúlveda, La verdad histórica: el ejército guerrillero: primer período de la guerra subversiva, abril de 1967 al 10 de setiembre de 1973 (Chile: Ediciones Encina Ltda., 2000). There are multiple, more or less sophisticated, versions of the Left's interpretation of imperialism. A representative example are the documents against imperialism drafted in the OLAS conference by the Latin American Left as a whole: OLAS, El imperialismo: deformador de nuestra tradición histórica (Havana, 1967).

30 See Timothy P. Wickham-Crowley, Guerrillas and Revolution in Latin America: A Comparative Study of Insurgents and Regimes since 1956 (Princeton, N.J.: Princeton University Press, 1991), and Eduardo Rey Tristán, "Las luchas revolucionarias en América Latina en perspectiva regional," in Oikon et al., El estudio de las luchas revolucionarias.

31 See G. M. Joseph and Daniela Spenser. In from the Cold: Latin America's New Encounter with the Cold War (Durham: Duke University Press, 2008).

32 Ariel C. Armony, Argentina, the United States, and the Anti-Communist Crusade in Central America, 1977–1984 (Athens: Ohio University Center for International Studies, 1997); and Dinges, The Condor Years.

33 Claudia Gilman, Entre la pluma y el fusil: debates y dilemas del escritor revolucionario en América Latina (Buenos Aires: Siglo Veintiuno Editores Argentina, 2003), as well as Piero Gleijeses, Conflicting Missions, Havana, Washington, and Africa, 1959–1976 (Berkeley: The University of North Carolina Press, 2002).

34 Tanya Harmer, Allende's Chile and the Inter-American Cold War (Chapel Hill: University of North Carolina Press, 2011).

35 In recent decades, a series of studies of social movements have paid special attention to the transnational activities of non-state actors. In 1998, a study by Margaret Keck and Kathryn Sikkink inaugurated an interesting line of work on transnational advocacy networks connected with human rights, gender, and environmental issues. Despite their thematic differences, these works have important points in common with my investigation. The ways in which non-state actors transformed themselves when they began establishing international contacts coincide in certain aspects with what happened with the groups studied here. Margaret E. Keck and Kathryn Sikkink, Activists Beyond Borders (Ithaca, NY: Cornell University Press, 1998).

36 From different perspectives some authors have followed the trajectory of this Latin American Left. See among others: Jorge G. Castañeda, Utopia Unarmed: The Latin

American Left after the Cold War (New York: Knopf 1993), as well as Claudia Gilman, Entre la pluma y el fusil; and Emir Sader, El nuevo topo: los caminos de la izquierda latinoamericana (Buenos Aires: Siglo XXI, 2009).

37 On the levels of development in the late 1950s, see John J. Johnson, Political Change in Latin America: The Emergence of the Middle Sectors (Stanford, California: Stanford University Press, 1958). On the waves of political reforms, see: for Chile, Paul W. Drake, Socialism and Populism in Chile, 1932–52 (Urbana: University of Illinois Press, 1978); for Argentina, David Rock, El radicalismo argentino, 1890–1930 (Buenos Aires: Amorrortu, 1977), and Juan Caros Torre et al. (comp.), Los años peronistas, 1943–1955 (Buenos Aires: Editorial Sudamericana, 2002); for Uruguay, Milton Vanger, El creador y su época (Montevideo: Ediciones de la Banda Oriental, 1992), and German D'Elía, El Uruguay neobatllista (1946–1958) (Montevideo: Ediciones de la Banda Oriental, 1982). On the suspicions of military expansionism of the Peronist movement, see Juan Oddone, Vecinos en discordia: Argentina, Uruguay y la política hemisférica de los Estados Unidos: selección de documentos, 1945–1955 (Montevideo: Universidad de la República, Facultad de Humanidades y Ciencias de la Educación, Departamento de Historia Americana, 2003).

38 Mario Rapoport and Amado Luiz Cervo (comp.), El Cono Sur. Una historia común (Buenos Aires: FCE, 2001).

39 Hiber Conteris, Cono Sur (Montevideo: Ediciones de Marcha, 1963).

40 For initial reflections in this sense, see David Collier et al., The New Authoritarianism in Latin America.

41 See Lynn Hunt, Politics, Culture and Class in the French Revolution (Berkeley: University of California Press, 1984), 185. For an overview of the notion of political culture, see Javier de Diego Romero, "El concepto de 'cultura política' en ciencia política y sus implicaciones para la historia," Ayer 61 (2006): 233–66.

42 For studies that examine the relationship of these groups with lower-class sectors at the local level, see: Marian E. Schlotterbeck, Everyday Revolutions: Grassroots Movements, the Revolutionary Left (MIR), and the Making of Socialism in Concepción, Chile, 1964–1973 (PhD, Dissertation, Yale University, 2013), and Claudio Barrientos, Emblems and Narratives of the Past: the Cultural Construction of Memories and Violence in Peasant Communities of Southern Chile, 1970–2000 (PhD diss., University of Wisconsin-Madison, 2003).

43 For my research of internal documents of the various organizations, I consulted the following archives: Archivo de la Lucha Armada "David Cámpora," in Archivo del Centro de Estudios Interdisciplinarios Uruguayos, Montevideo, Uruguay; Archivo del Centro de Documentación e Investigación de la Cultura de Izquierda (CEDINCI) en Argentina, Buenos Aires, Argentina; and the online collections El topo blindado and Archivo Chile, as well as private collections. For my research of state documents, I consulted the following archives: AMRREE (Chile), Archivo General Histórico, Ministerio de Relaciones Exteriores, Santiago, Chile; AHDMRREE Archivo Histórico Diplomático, Ministerio de Relaciones Exteriores, Montevideo, Uruguay; DIPBA Archivo de la Dirección de Inteligencia de la Provincia de Buenos Aires, La Plata, Argentina; and Dirección Nacional de Inteligencia, Ministerio del Interior, Montevideo, Uruguay. And, lastly, various collections of the National Archive, NARA, College Park, Maryland, United States. In addition to these collections and archives, I visited national libraries in the three countries of the region to consult press and testimonial and journalistic literature from the period. Lastly, some personal collections donated to the Hoover Archives in Stanford University provided interesting information on specific events.

44 In Argentina's case, I based my research on oral history banks developed by Memoria Abierta and the Gino Germani Institute: AOMA, Archivo Oral Memoria Abierta, Buenos Aires, Argentina, and AHOIGG Archivo de Historia Oral del Instituto de Investigaciones Gino Germani, Buenos Aires, Argentina. In Uruguay's case, the accounts gathered by historian Clara Aldrighi, as well as by other historians, were very useful. Clara Aldrighi, Memorias de insurgencia (Montevideo: Ediciones de la Banda Oriental, 2009).

I

Revolution without the Sierra Maestra: The Tupamaros and the Development of a Repertoire of Dissent for Urbanized Countries. Montevideo, 1962–1968

In July 1967, as Ernesto "Che" Guevara tried, without much success, to create a rural *foco* in Bolivia, the first conference of the Organization for Latin American Solidarity (OLAS) was being held in Havana.[1] This meeting was presented as the application in Latin America of the definitions arising from the Tri-Continental Conference. Members of various Latin American left-wing organizations gathered for the first time ever to collectively answer the question of how to establish effective solidarity ties with countries that, like Cuba, had defeated imperialism, or countries that, like Venezuela, Colombia, Brazil, Bolivia, Guatemala, and Peru, had launched "a final battle" against it. Two approaches were taken to address this question. Some embraced the Cuban position that held that the development of a continental strategy of armed struggle was the only effective way of promoting solidarity. The communist parties closest to the Soviet Union, on the other hand, defended a more moderate view that included the possibility of armed struggle but only as one of many means of political activism, alongside participation in elections and labor mobilization. At the end of the conference, the Cuban position prevailed, generating a profound impact on the continent's leftist movements.

Cuba's initial report, however, had noted some exceptions to the feasibility of armed struggle in Latin America, arguing that "to speak today of armed struggle in Chile or in Uruguay is as absurd as denying that possibility in Venezuela, Colombia, Brazil, Guatemala, or Peru."[2] This report upset some left-wing sectors in the Southern Cone, which had hoped the OLAS would help blow revolutionary winds their way. At one of the receptions held after the conference's sessions, two journalists connected with the new Southern Cone Left – Augusto Olivares, of Chile's *Punto Final*, and Carlos María Gutiérrez, of Uruguay's *Marcha* – were able to speak with Fidel Castro and discuss this. They brought up the question of the impossibility of armed struggle, and declared that as Uruguayans and Chileans they felt "somewhat slighted by such a categorical statement," to which Fidel Castro said, "well, that [report] wasn't written by me; don't get worked up about it." And he added, "there is no denying that there are mass movements in Chile and Uruguay. But geographical conditions are also necessary. Chile has them." When asked about conditions in Chile, Castro's reply was straightforward: "*Chico*, that depends on you. Look, if I were in Chile, I'd be taking up arms. But I think you're still dwelling on that election business over there." His view of Uruguay was different. "Your country lacks the geographical conditions necessary for armed struggle," he told Gutiérrez. "It has no mountains, no jungles. A guerrilla organization has no chance of developing there." Consulted about the possibility of other formulas, such as urban armed insurrection, he said:

Well, in theory, it is possible.... Uruguay has a combative and politicized population. I think that, from that perspective, you do have certain conditions. But an armed insurrection in your country today would be quenched in less than two days. The country is wedged between two giants; they'd crush you immediately. No, in Uruguay, it's not possible.

Q: So, we should accept the OLAS Cuban thesis?

Well – Castro smiled – , if you want to create a guerrilla movement you don't have to look far: you have a chance right there in Bolivia. Listen, guerrilla forces throughout Latin America are one and the same: they have the same goal everywhere. When conditions aren't ripe in one country – he said turning to the Chileans – you have to support the struggle in the countries where they are.[3]

At the end of the conference this exception was removed from the final document. However, the above conversation reflects some of the problems and contradictions that the relationship with the Cuban Revolution posed for a number of Southern Cone groups in the mid-1960s. While these groups acknowledged the leadership of the Cuban Revolution and supported the continental revolution line it proposed, the characteristics of the Southern Cone countries did not seem to fit into the rural *foco* strategy defined as the model to imitate after the Revolution. As one of Guevara's assistants graphically put it: "we were absolutely convinced that we had discovered a foolproof method for freeing the people."[4] However, as Southern Cone militants would find out through their own experiences, the method was not as foolproof as was claimed and it was not adaptable to the geographical, political, and social conditions of the countries of Latin America's Southern Cone. The differences between Cuba and the Southern Cone countries were too obvious to ignore. Uruguay and Chile had democracies that were relatively stable in the context of Latin America, and Argentina, while marked by political instability, was still very far from the authoritarianism of the Batista regime and other Caribbean dictatorships. Although in terms of urbanization and social development, Cuba had been moving in a direction similar to that of the Southern countries, these were still more urbanized and their middle classes had attained a greater development.[5] Chilean, Argentine, and Uruguayan militants became aware of the enormous differences between their geographies, populations, and socioeconomic structures and Cuba's.

Sidney Tarrow argues that there are moments in history in which a new repertoire of contention emerges to question established traditions in a specific community.[6] Something like that happened with the Cuban Revolution. Through a demonstration effect, Cuba generated a new regional scenario that called for renewed protest methods. However, the specific forms that this renovation took in the Southern Cone did not enable an automatic replication of the Cuban experience. This led the self-proclaimed New Left groups to renew their repertoires of contention, adapting certain ideas of the Cuban Revolution to the radical political discourses and practices that were being attempted since the 1950s in their respective countries.

Interpreting the Sierra Maestra from the Southern Cone

As Guillermo O'Donnell – one of the shrewdest analysts of the new authoritarianism – has noted, the crises that affected the Southern Cone countries in the 1960s and led to the coups shared certain common aspects. In every country, the periods prior to the crises were marked by a surge of social unrest involving popular sectors. This surge was linked to strong redistributive conflicts generated within each national state by the drop or instability in international prices of raw materials that threatened the continuity of the inward-looking, state-centered development models implemented since the 1940s, which had achieved significant levels of economic growth, industrial development, and prosperity for certain urban popular sectors.[7] As states faced fiscal and monetary constraints, they tended to address them through inflationary processes. Due to its important role in the economy and in monetary policies, the state became a major redistributive agent and was disputed by a host of economic and social actors.

All of this led to a rise in social mobilization and the radicalization of protests in the late 1950s, heralding a period of intense turmoil, even before the impact of the Cuban Revolution had reached the south. In the months of March and April 1957, a series of protests broke out across Chile. What began with students demonstrating against rising urban transportation fares in the city of Valparaíso quickly turned into anti-government unrest that spread to the country's leading cities. Following the death of a student, the movement reached a greater level of radicalization and confrontation with police forces. On 2 April, mass protests shook the city of Santiago. The government tried to repress protesters but the great scope of the popular demonstration forced the police to withdraw from downtown

Santiago. The following day, the government declared a state of war and called in the army. After twelve days of repression, the situation went back to normal in the country's leading cities. However, these events had caused a rift in a society that was not used to such levels of popular and state violence. According to official reports, more than twenty people were killed and hundreds were injured. The events of April 1957 anticipated several of the dilemmas, challenges, and debates that society in general and the Left in particular would face in the coming decades. In the words of historian Pedro Milos, the uprising revealed a crisis that was not only economic, but political and moral as well.[8]

A year later, in 1958, Uruguayan high school and university students, accompanied by sectors of the working class, staged an intense mobilization demanding the legislative approval of the Organic Law of the University of the Republic, which granted political autonomy to the university and established a university government formed by faculty, alumni, and students.[9] The active presence of students in the streets, who in some cases engaged in clashes with the police, marked the emergence of a new, effective player firmly determined to participate in politics. This mobilization revealed the potential of an alliance between students and trade unions, which in addition to supporting student demands, were clamoring for an improvement in their living conditions, deteriorated by the impact of inflation on their wages.

The student movement, however, was not limited to the specific demands of these mobilizations but were part of a struggle framed in a more general denunciation of Uruguay's "imbalanced and unjust social and economic structure," aggravated "by political and administrative corruption and the absence of government plans, resulting in lucrative improvisations for the authorities, and which basically complete the picture of our current bleak state of affairs."[10]

The dimensions of the crisis were also expressed in the country's elections. Politically, the opposition was able to capitalize on the widespread discontent.[11] In 1958, after almost 100 years of prevailing at the polls, the Colorado Party lost the elections to the National Party. This also marked the end of the already exhausted neo-Batllista reformist project. The student protests and the Colorado Party's defeat were the prelude to a new political and social dynamic that would shape the 1960s, characterized by stagnation, economic crisis, and the failure of past traditional leaders to restore the social welfare and prosperity of the 1950s. It was in this context that essays and other works in Uruguay began to discuss the moral and political crisis of an elite that seemed unable to adapt to the new circumstances.[12]

In 1959, labor protests also peaked in Argentina. After winning a democratic election in 1958 with a nationalist and development-centered agenda supported by socialists, communists, and most sectors of the banned Peronist movement, Arturo Frondizi signed an agreement with the International Monetary Fund that was seen as a betrayal by a large part of the generation of activists and intellectuals who had backed him.[13] Frondizi also agreed to a stabilization plan aimed at reducing the fiscal deficit, cutting public expenditure, and encouraging foreign investment in different areas of the economy, including some sectors of the state.

In this context, in January 1959 the government privatized the Lisandro de la Torre meatpacking plant, a measure that sparked an unprecedented mobilization, with six thousand workers occupying the plant. The government deployed tanks and 1,500 policemen, who cleared out the workers after intense clashes. In the following days, a significant number of workers participated in a general strike. Three major nationwide conflicts occurred that year, involving banking, textile, and metal workers, respectively. This labor mobilization revealed the increasing strength of the more radical sectors within the Peronist movement, as well as the coming together of leftist sectors (socialists, Trotskyists, and communists) and the labor movement, which was primarily Peronist. The state responded with an escalation of repression, which culminated with the Plan Conmoción Interna del Estado (State Internal Unrest Plan, or CONINTES) that enabled the involvement of the armed forces in the repression of trade union conflicts.[14] Some 2,000 political activists and unionists were jailed under this plan.[15]

All of these events evidence the emergence of a large number of significant social movements with disruptive capacity, which reacted to the social impacts of the crisis of the import-substitution models in each country. In every case, these movements had a significant degree of autonomy from political leaderships and had diverse effects on the ways in which the Lefts – and in Argentina's case, the Peronist movement – interacted with labor and student activists in the 1960s. Another phenomenon evidenced by these events – although with different dimensions in each country – was the growing levels of street violence and the state's strong repressive reaction. This situation represented a prelude to the social conflicts that would characterize the next decade. Each of these events will be linked to successive fractures within the parties of the Left, with unionists and youth members rejecting these parties' election-based strategies and breaking away in search of alternatives connected with social mobilizations.

For example, in Chile, starting in the late 1950s, Clotario Blest, a leader of the Central Única de Trabajadores (United Workers' Federation, or CUT), played a key role in bringing together these activists who had become disenchanted with the traditional Left. This current of discontent culminated in 1965 with the forming of the MIR, which grouped unionists, youth sectors, dissatisfied members of the Socialist and Communist Parties and Trotskyist and anarchist groups. Similar processes occurred in Argentina and Uruguay, as will be shown later in this chapter. These Southern

Cone militants, discontented with their national political experiences and the experiences of their Lefts saw the Cuban experience as an example, but they also had to distinguish those aspects that could be incorporated to the experience of the south and those that were foreign to it.[16]

The Cuban Revolution had sparked interest in the Southern Cone even before the rebels' victory in the Sierra Maestra. The experiences of journalists Carlos María Gutiérrez, of Uruguay, and Jorge Ricardo Masetti, of Argentina, are representative of these first exchanges.[17] In February 1958, while working for *La Mañana* – one of the newspapers of Uruguay's Colorado Party – , Carlos María Gutiérrez traveled to Havana. From there he was able to reach the Sierra Maestra where he spent a few weeks with the rebels. During that time he became close to Ernesto Guevara and obtained the first interview in Spanish with Fidel Castro.[18] Upon his return, Gutiérrez contacted Guevara's family in Argentina and became involved in the cause of the revolution. This commitment was expressed through his active role in *Marcha* – where in the 1960s he represented a new generation of journalists who had a more radical approach than that of the publication's editor, Carlos Quijano – , his political relationship with sectors of Uruguay's New Left, and his participation in the Cuban news agency *Prensa Latina* in the late 1960s.

Jorge Ricardo Masetti was an Argentine reporter who first became politically active as a conservative Catholic nationalist, but later abandoned his activism to concentrate on his work as a journalist. He took a critical stance toward U.S. imperialism and, although he had originally opposed the Peronist movement, after Juan Domingo Perón was ousted in 1955 he was drawn to the more radical sectors of Peronist resistance. He too visited the Sierra Maestra in 1958.[19] In February 1958, Masetti obtained financing from *Radio El Mundo* to travel to Havana with the aim of conducting a radio interview with the rebels, and in particular with Guevara, who was the focus of great interest in Argentina. Masetti stayed in Cuba for two months. After a brief trip to Venezuela he returned to Argentina, where in October of that year he published his book *Los que luchan y los que lloran* (*Those Who Fight and Those Who Cry*).[20] The book was Masetti's first-person account of his experience in Cuba, from his arrival to Havana, his contacts with the opposition in the cities, his journey to the Sierra Maestra, and his interviews with Che Guevara and Fidel, which were broadcast by *Radio Rebelde* from the mountains. In the last chapter, Masetti describes his departure and says he was left with a strange feeling, as if he were "deserting" and returning to the world of those "who cry." The experience left an indelible mark on the journalist and determined his political choices from then on. In 1959, Masetti became the first director of *Prensa Latina*, the news agency of the Revolution, and in 1962 he would head the first guerrilla movement in Argentina.

The relationships these two journalists had with the Cuban Revolution and the process leading up to it illustrate the interest these events sparked in certain Southern Cone press media and the effect they had in political sectors beyond the traditional Left. Their experiences are paradigmatic of a new generation of journalists who, starting in the early 1960s, adopted increasingly radical positions with respect to Latin America's political process, which in several cases entailed a full commitment to the cause of the revolution. These positions will be expressed in the development of a number of news and cultural publications that will have a strong impact on the debates of the New Left.[21] Also, Chilean, Uruguayan, and Argentine politicians and activists from the Left, but also from sectors in the center of the political spectrum, connected with reformist and popular national movements of the 1950s, would visit Cuba repeatedly after the victory of the Revolution.[22]

In addition to these accounts by travelers, the first canonic texts of the Revolution reached the Southern Cone at this time. The experience of the rebel army became an example to study, and thus books describing its tactics and strategy began circulating rapidly across the region. Ernesto Guevara's works provided the main body of ideas that systematically set forth the lessons of the Cuban rebel army. His book *Guerrilla Warfare* – first published in 1960 in Cuba by the Ministry of the Revolutionary Armed Forces (MINFAR), and reprinted many times in several languages as of 1961 – and the 1963 essay *Guerrilla Warfare: A Method* are representative of the main points of the theory developed by Guevara during this period.[23]

Guerrilla Warfare is a political-military strategy handbook that draws on the Cuban experience to build a theory of the role of guerrilla warfare in Latin America's political struggles, a characterization of the figure of the guerrilla combatant, and, lastly, a series of practical steps to maintain the guerrilla front. The "lessons" that according to Guevara could be derived from the Cuban experience were categorical and they influenced many of the guerrilla projects that would later be attempted:

(1) Popular forces can win a war against the army;
(2) It is not necessary to wait until all conditions for making revolution exist; the insurrection can create them;
(3) In underdeveloped America, the countryside is the basic area for armed fighting.[24]

Despite the general nature of the lessons in this work, Guevara cautioned that:

where a government has come into power by some form of popular vote, fraudulent or not, and maintains at least an appearance of constitutional legality, guerrilla outbreak cannot be promoted, since the possibilities of peaceful struggle have not yet been exhausted.[25]

By the time he wrote his essay *Guerrilla Warfare: A Method*, in 1963, Guevara's opinion of democratic regimes had changed from what he had voiced in Montevideo in 1961. He now argued that democratic regimes led by oligarchies would inevitably turn into repressive regimes as the masses advanced, and that when that time came guerrilla forces had to be prepared. Near the end of the essay he set forth three conclusions that reaffirmed the principles set out in his book: (a) rural guerrilla warfare is the best way to form a rebel army; (b) peasants will constitute a leading force of the revolution; and (c) the strategy should be continental, with coordination among the different guerrilla groups of Latin America. In contrast to the book, the language of the essay is closer to the language used by the Left, with multiple references to Marx, Engels, and Lenin.[26]

Simultaneously to the publication of these political and strategic works, other books that depicted the experience of the rebels in the Sierra Maestra circulated in the Southern Cone. In addition to Masetti's book and several interviews and reports, a popular book that was widely read as a "history" of the revolution was Guevara's *Pasajes de la guerra revolucionaria* (*Reminiscences of the Revolutionary War*), where with a fresh narrative and in a colloquial tone he gives an account of the development of the rebel army from 1956 to 1958.[27]

The relationship between the strategic texts and these journalistic and testimonial writings is evident. The theory was demonstrated with history. However, this history was limited to the experience of the Sierra Maestra and it ignored the analysis of urban movements that had been instrumental in overthrowing Batista. The centrality of the Sierra Maestra rebels was politically significant in the internal conflicts that arose as of 1959 within the revolutionary group, and contributed to legitimize Fidel Castro's leadership. Paradoxically, the outcome of what was an internal conflict also had repercussions in the continent. This somewhat biased account of the Cuban experience was adopted as the general rule for all revolutionary processes in Latin America.[28]

This literature was read avidly by the members of these small nascent groups of the Southern Cone. However, these militants were unable to find concrete forms to apply such methods. There are, nonetheless, accounts by militants who would later participate in Chile's MIR or in the MLN-Tupamaros describing rural military training and the beginning of activities modeled after the actions of the Cuban rebel army. These attempts failed due to the great differences between these territories and Cuba: either because of the absence of a peasantry similar to that described by the accounts of the Cuban Revolution, or the lack, in some cases, of geographical features similar to the island's, or the practical realization that there were other, primarily urban sectors who showed greater willingness to "combat" the governments in power than the rural populations where the campaigns were being attempted.[29] In Argentina, the process was somewhat different. This difference may be due to a mere historical accident: the nationality of one of the main leaders of the Cuban Revolution. The fact that Guevara was an Argentine national was highly significant in this case.

These readings were in line with Cuba's policy for some areas of Latin America. While Cuba had been used since 1959 by Nicaraguan and Guatemalan groups of exiles as a place to conspire against their respective governments, in 1962 it began actively hosting such groups as a matter of state policy. This policy was promoted by Guevara, who created a secret agency for that purpose within the Interior Ministry. Initially known as the "Americas Department," it combined intelligence work and solidarity actions in support of revolutionary struggles across Latin America and the Caribbean. The goal of the agency was to train human resources and provide material resources for Latin American guerrilla groups.[30] The idea was to "export the revolution" by sharing the Cuban experience, which was thought to be a proven infallible method. Piero Gleijeses notes that the revolution prioritized training over direct incursions into other countries, as such actions would have further compromised its situation in Latin America.[31]

At first, Cuba supported revolutionary movements that shared certain elements with its experience. The common denominator of this first wave of guerrilla groups – which would conclude with Guevara's Bolivia experience in 1967 – was that they all chose the rural guerrilla option.[32] In 1962, in response to Cuba's exclusion from the OAS, Fidel Castro issued the *Second Declaration of Havana* where he clearly stated that the Cuban Revolution had become an example and an inevitable path for the peoples of Latin America.[33] This radicalization of Cuba's foreign policy had a profound impact among members of the Southern Cone Lefts. The campaigns organized in solidarity with the Cuban Revolution prompted discussions on how to interpret it. For some it was a unique case that had to be defended against U.S. aggression and which could be imitated in some of its reform programs, while for others it was an example to be followed not only in its reforms but also in its method of coming into power.

Among the former were those who sought to win votes by tapping into the sympathy that voters could have for the Revolution, so they explicitly supported Cuba in their election campaigns.[34] The other position was held by those who believed that the impact of the Cuban Revolution should lead the Lefts to rethink their political strategies. That was how journalist Carlos María Gutiérrez put it in his article "Electoralismo y Revolución" (Electioneering and Revolution), published in *Marcha* in the prelude to the 1962 elections. There he wrote that the Cuban experience had opened up the possibility of bringing about a "revolutionary change, which in our case does not entail taking up arms (as some fools pretend to understand it), but completely abandoning past structures and methods."[35] The Revolution put the issue of the methods of political struggle on the agenda.

As Gutiérrez noted, the Revolution seemed to offer an inspiration for alternative paths – still very hazy – for the construction of a new leftist way of doing politics. Irrespective of the electoral victories or defeats experienced by left-wing parties, the Left suffered a process of partial fragmentation of traditional forces and the emergence of new organizations that questioned the electoral strategies of the former while still unclear about alternative strategies to replace them.

Cuba's policy with respect to the Southern Cone, however, did not appear to fit this line of radicalization. Guevara's participation in the Inter-American Economic and Social Council meeting held in Punta del Este, Uruguay, in August 1961 revealed that the Cuban Revolution had a particular view of the region. After the Punta del Este meeting, Guevara participated in the "Popular Conference against Imperialism," organized in Montevideo as a counter-conference. Also present at that event were Chilean socialist senator Salvador Allende and Argentine journalist Gregorio Selser. On August 17, Guevara spoke at the University of the Republic in the framework of this conference. After discussing several of the issues he had addressed in Punta del Este, Guevara referred specifically to Uruguay's case, as in his view, "Uruguay is the only country [in Latin America] that allows the free expression of ideas." And he argued that that freedom had to be defended:

You have something that must be protected, which is precisely the possibility of voicing your ideas; the possibility of using democratic means to advance as far as one can go; the possibility, in sum, of gradually creating the conditions that we all hope to attain some day in America, so that we can all be brothers and sisters, so that there will be no exploitation of man by man, so we may put an end to exploitation (APPLAUSE), which will not be achieved the same way everywhere – without spilling blood, without events unfolding as they did in Cuba, because once the first shot is fired you never know when the last will come. Because the last day of the Revolution did not bring the last shot; we had to continue shooting. We were shot at, we had to be tough, we had to punish some people with death; again we were attacked, we have been attacked again, and we will be attacked again and again.[36]

A shooting occurred outside as participants were leaving the conference, resulting in the death of Arbelio Ramírez, a university professor who had been in the audience. Guevara assumed that he had been the intended target. While the direct perpetrator was never identified, it was believed that the attack had been ordered by extreme right groups who by 1961 had gained notoriety, condoned by some members of the government.[37] For some members of the Left, Arbelio Ramírez's death was the "first shot" Guevara had spoken of. *Marcha* reported this death with an explicit headline: "This Is How Fascism Started."[38] Ironically, Guevara's presence undermined precisely what he was trying to defend.

Across the river, in Argentina, Guevara's presence also had a great impact. The Argentine government was interested in meeting with Guevara to offer to mediate between Cuba and the United States. Moreover, during the conference, Argentina's delegate had shared the Cuban delegation's position on certain issues connected with national development. This led President Arturo Frondizi to secretly invite Guevara to Argentina. On August 19, a private aircraft took Guevara from Montevideo to the outskirts of Buenos Aires to meet with Frondizi in the presidential estate of Olivos, where they spoke for an hour. When Frondizi conveyed his wish that Cuba would continue in the inter-American system through a coexistence agreement with the United States, Guevara appeared skeptical as he believed a conflict with the northern power was inevitable.[39]

The news of Guevara's visit immediately sparked reactions from conservative sectors and the armed forces. The night of the meeting a bomb went off in front of the home of an uncle of Guevara's. The following day a group of navy officers demanded that Frondizi resign. In the weeks that followed a number of meetings between Frondizi and the military evidenced the discontent in the armed forces and added another element of military pressure, which ultimately led to Frondizi's overthrow in August 1962.

Guevara then traveled to Brasilia, where he received the National Order of the Southern Cross from President Janio Quadros. By awarding him this honorary decoration Quadros meant to explicitly declare his "independence" in international policy and, similarly to Frondizi, try to keep Cuba within the inter-American system. The award added to the discontent of the military and conservative sectors, which responded by threatening with a coup. The threat was averted by Quadros's resignation and the appointment by congress of João Goulart as his successor.[40]

The reactions in Uruguay, Argentina, and Brazil contradicted the moderate and conciliatory position that Guevara tried to develop during this tour. Shortly after Guevara finished speaking in an event in Montevideo, arguing that Uruguay had to preserve its democratic freedoms, a participant was killed as he left the venue. While Guevara met with Frondizi and Quadros to try to keep Cuba in the inter-American system and strike an agreement with the United States, his presence in Argentina and Brazil is opposed by the militaries of both countries, inflaming them and further deteriorating their relations with the democratic governments. The strong reactions sparked in conservative sectors appeared to strengthen the more radical positions of the groups of the New Left that highlighted the limitations of electoral politics and perhaps the positions of the Cubans themselves with respect to the region.

However, to examine the relationship of the Cuban Revolution with the Southern Cone and the importance of Ernesto Guevara as a representative of the Revolution we need to factor in another key aspect: the fact that he was originally from Argentina. Following the triumph of the Revolution, Guevara showed a personal interest in the possibility of developing a revolutionary rural *foco* in Argentina.[41] He began contacting sectors of the incipient New Left and the Peronist resistance. Moreover, Guevara had become immensely popular in Argentina. Although his involvement in Argentina's political life had been limited, his role in the Cuban Revolution earned him great admiration among the public and particularly among the sectors of the budding New Left. For example, in October 1960 a group of socialist and some communist activists took part in a major press project called *Che*.[42]

The year 1959 had also been an important year for Argentina. The Arturo Frondizi administration (1958–62) had garnered significant support in certain sectors of the Left and the Peronist movement as a result of Frondizi's promises to lift the ban on Peronism and of his nationalist and developmentalist economic program.[43] This attraction lasted little more than a year. The foreign investment policies, the austerity measures of a monetary stabilization plan, and the establishment of private universities sparked discontent among trade unions, university students, and leftist groups that had placed their trust in the new president. This growing social unrest was met with authoritarian measures. Strikes were outlawed, the Communist Party was banned, and the military was called in to repress labor protests. In 1960, as noted above, the government implemented the CONINTES plan, which resulted in 2,000 arrests and 500 convictions for special offences.[44]

Peronist and leftist activists who had participated in labor mobilizations in 1959 and some Peronist resistance militants who had been involved in minor armed actions in 1959 found refuge in Cuba, where they began planning future actions for Argentina. In 1962 there were approximately 400 Argentine militants living in Cuba. A significant number of these militants performed revolutionary support tasks in different areas of the state (public works, education, health, etc.), and others were simply visiting Cuba to learn more about the Revolution. There was also a minority group of socialist, Trotskyist, and Peronist militants who had traveled to Cuba in 1961 with the aim of planning a revolutionary incursion in Argentina that would be launched from Cuba. This group was linked to the Peronist John William Cooke – Perón's political representative in Argentina, during his exile, from 1955 to 1959 – who had forged a close personal and political relationship with Guevara.[45]

Manuel Gaggero, a member of the Peronist Youth, is one of the few surviving participants of a 1961 military training attempt aimed at launching a revolutionary strategy in Argentina. He recounts that experience in *El encuentro con el Che, aquellos años*.[46] Upon Guevara's initiative, Cooke's wife, Alicia Eguren, had settled in Montevideo and from there she arranged for a number of Argentine militants to travel to Cuba. These militants belonged to a sector of the Socialist Party headed by Elías Seman, a faction of Palabra Obrera led by Ángel Bengochea – who had broken away from Nahuel Moreno's Trotskyist group – , a group of Peronist militants who had been involved in an armed action in 1959, and other Peronist militants from various extractions. The idea was to prepare a revolutionary hub in Cuba, whose members would later return to Argentina.

In the Argentine camp, Guevara proposed that an armed *foco* be created in the mountains of northern Argentina (in the provinces of Salta or Tucumán), in line with his well-known strategy. He also urged the Argentine militants to form a unified command for all the revolutionaries, a move that entailed abandoning their old party identities.

Bengochea was a major labor leader with a Trotskyist background, connected with several trade unions from the meatpacking industry area of Berisso, and he had established close ties with the most radical sectors of the Peronist movement during the conflicts under Frondizi. In Cuba he proposed an alternative structure to Guevara's, suggesting that the leading setting for an armed insurrection should be the city. In military terms Bengochea backed his thesis with various examples of urban partisan resistance taken from Second World War Europe.[47]

In addition to this debate, the different groups disagreed strongly on how they should prepare for the revolution. While some accepted the military training Cuba offered, others called for a more political discussion about the nature of the revolution in Argentina. The existing conflicts that divided the Left – particularly the differences between socialists and Trotskyists – were aggravated by the differences of opinion on the role of the Peronist movement in this process. According to Gaggero, the disagreements were so acute that in late 1961 the Cubans decided to suspend the project and leave the militants who had participated in this experience free to pursue other actions.[48]

Despite this failure, Guevara did not abandon his ideas. In 1962, the recently-created Cuban-Argentine Institute held a barbecue for the Argentines who lived in Cuba. Guevara was invited to participate as speaker. He was initially reluctant because he was aware of the resistance that his position had generated in the Argentine Communist Party and also in certain Cuban sectors. But he finally agreed to take on the challenge and in his speech he focused on two aspects. On the one hand, he made an analogy between the continental nature of the nineteenth century wars for independence and the continental strategy that the Cuban

Revolution needed in order to ensure its survival. Aware of the conflicts of the previous year, Guevara did not at this time stress the rural nature of the revolution but he did highlight the need for military action: "The goal of revolutionary liberation requires taking up arms, however few there may be, and using those arms to seize more arms and build the small army into a large people's army."[49] Lastly, Guevara called on the militants to abandon certain political identities (communism, socialism, Peronism) that stood in the way of the development of a revolutionary movement in Argentina, and to join together in the struggle against imperialism. This speech garnered little support from Argentine communists in Cuba, who reported it to other Cuban authorities. According to Amalio Rey, who participated in that gathering, the other activists, while sharing Guevara's emphasis on armed insurrection, disagreed with the development of a rural *foco*, as they were more in favor of urban fighting.[50]

After the failure of the 1961 training camp, Guevara prepared a new group of Argentines in Cuba, this time under his strict supervision, with the clear aim of starting a rural guerrilla movement in northern Argentina. Guevara's close friend Alberto Granado, with whom he traveled across Latin America in the 1950s in a trip immortalized in *Motorcycle Diaries. Notes on a Latin American Journey*, was put in charge of recruiting militants for this project.[51] The commanding officer was Jorge Ricardo Masetti, who had returned to Cuba after the Revolution and had been appointed director of the news agency *Prensa Latina*. The journalist took on the responsibility of this new venture and appointed himself "second-in-command," thus implying that the first commander would come later.

After their training in Cuba and Algeria, the guerrilla group known as Ejército Guerrillero del Pueblo (People's Guerrilla Army, or EGP) traveled to Bolivia where they received the support of the Federation of Communist Youths. In mid-1963 they set up camp in a forest and mountainous area of the province of Salta, in northern Argentina. From there they made contact with a group of university students from Córdoba – for the most part former communists – who published the magazine *Cuadernos de Pasado y Presente*, edited by José Aricó. Aricó was a communist activist who had been involved in a number of publishing ventures undertaken by the Communist Party but was expelled from the party when he launched this new magazine.[52] Activists from other communist youth factions and from the University of Buenos Aires gradually joined the guerrilla group in Salta, reaching some twenty militants in all.

The region chosen to develop the guerrilla camps was sparsely populated, so that contact with the people who lived in the area was very limited. In March 1964, border patrolmen found the first camp and within a month the entire organization had been dismantled. The main leader,

Masetti, was taken by the military and disappeared, two militants – one of them Cuban – were killed, and most of the others were jailed.[53]

Another armed initiative which is thought to have been connected with the EGP project was aborted before it was even launched. In July 1964, four militants from a newly-formed armed organization headed by Bengochea – the Fuerzas Armadas de la Revolución Nacional (Armed Forces of the National Revolution) – died in an accidental explosion as they were preparing bombs in a Buenos Aires apartment. In the apartment was most of the arsenal that had been gathered for an armed operation planned for Tucumán, where Bengochea believed it was possible to resolve the rural-urban tension through political work with a significant number of rural workers connected with the sugar industry. The group had ties to the EGP. The explosion put an end to the first cycle of guerrilla organizations in Argentina.[54]

The EGP experience exposed the limitations of automatically replicating Guevara's strategy in contexts that differed from the Cuban reality. Cuba, however, continued to promote that strategy throughout Latin America. The new advocate of the strategy was Regis Debray, a French philosophy student who was to become the leading intellectual of the Revolution in the late 1960s. In January 1965, in his article "Castroism: The Long March in Latin America," published in the Sartrean magazine *Les Temps Moderns*, Debray described his recent experiences in Latin America. The publication of this article had a major impact on his life. Guevara read the article in Algeria and translated it for Fidel Castro. Castro decided to invite "this *Fidelista* who is a stranger to the regiment, who expertly describes the blind alleys of urban guerrilla warfare and the advantages of rural guerrilla warfare."[55] He sent Debray a telegram that would change his life dramatically, thrusting him into Latin American politics. After agreeing to Castro's invitation, Debray immediately traveled to Havana, where he would play a leading role over the next decades.[56]

Debray had enrolled in the École normale supérieure in 1960 where he studied philosophy, and after visiting Cuba for a semester in 1961 he traveled across Latin America from 1963 to 1964. He studied under Louis Althusser, the renowned Marxist philosopher who was strongly influenced by French structuralism and studied, among other things, ideological state apparatuses.

In 1965, Debray became an Agrégé de philosophie in France and returned to Latin America to take on new responsibilities. In his words: "The Paris Academy thought I was a philosophy professor at the University of Havana and, meanwhile, I was roughing it in the Pinar del Río province, in an 'action' service course."[57]

His essay was disseminated by the Cuban government. The first Spanish language edition of *Castroism* appeared in *Cuadernos de Pasado y Presente*, the Argentine magazine published by the group of Córdoba students and intellectuals led by José Aricó who had split from the Communist Party and were linked to Masetti's guerrilla venture.[58] It was through that connection that they obtained money from Cuba for the publication of issues seven to eight of the magazine, which had been delayed for financial reasons. The decision to publish the article spurred debates within the *Pasado y Presente* team. While some approved the publication, others opposed it but were ultimately persuaded by the prospect of receiving Cuban funds.[59] This disagreement prompted the inclusion of a note from the editor acknowledging the debatable nature of the article.[60] The article was then published in *Cuadernos de Marcha* and fragments appeared in *Punto Final*.[61]

In that essay, Debray argued that the Cuban experience represented an innovation with respect to the forms of political struggle conceived thus far by popular sectors in Latin America: the "revolutionary putschism" that acted without the masses; and the "action purely of the masses," which let itself be led by them. According to Debray, the solution to that dilemma was to be found in Lenin and his party of "professional revolutionaries." The Latin American version of that organization were the Sierra Maestra rebels and the principles set out by Guevara in *Guerrilla Warfare*. The idea was that in the underdeveloped Latin America guerrilla warfare had to begin in the countryside and spread to the city. This meant that peasants had a key role to play in the development of a military *foco*, while in the cities universities would provide the leading "reservation army" for that rural *foco*.[62] In sum, although more elaborately and acknowledging the diversity and historical complexity of the different regions of Latin America, Debray repeated and reasserted Guevara's principles that maintained that the rural *foco* was the engine of the revolution.

Of all of Debray's works, the one that had the greatest impact in Latin America and the rest of the world was his second essay, *Revolution in the Revolution?*, published in January 1967 in the first number of the *Cuadernos* series of the Casa de las Américas publishing house.[63] This essay did not present major innovations with respect to *Castroism*, but it was more ambitious as it was presented as a work of theoretical systematization of the Cuban experience based on various unpublished documents of the revolution.[64] Despite its academic rhetoric, in comparison to *Castroism* the essay was more markedly aligned with the positions of the Cuban Revolution than with other Latin American left-wing currents. His criticism of certain military strategies such as armed self-defense or certain forms of armed propaganda implied a criticism of other left-wing political actors (Trotskyists, Maoists, communists) that vied with Cuba for influence in Latin America's Lefts. In his words:

Trotskyism and reformism join hands in condemning guerrilla warfare, in hampering or sabotaging it. It is no mere accident that these two movements have taken the Cuban Revolution as a target for their attacks in Latin America as well as in the rest of the world.[65]

The rest of the essay repeats in more explicit terms some of the arguments put forward in *Castroism* regarding the central importance of rural guerrillas, the subordination of the political leadership to guerrilla command, the different stages in rural guerrilla development, the risks of destroying such accumulation of forces with insurrectional strategies or premature forms of armed propaganda, and the constitution of a political vanguard from a rural *foco*.

The Southern Cone countries are hardly mentioned in the text. Uruguay is mentioned explicitly as a counterexample of a country "where conditions for armed struggle do not exist at present" although "there is a strong and militant mass movement."[66] Chile is also mentioned in passing as a case in which there are no revolutionary conditions. Argentina is scarcely mentioned. Brazil is the only country of the region where armed struggle is identified as being "on the agenda."[67]

Revolution in the Revolution? was widely distributed by the Cuban government. The publication of this essay must be understood in the more general context of the Cuban Revolution's foreign policy. Debray knew of Guevara's preparatory work in Bolivia and other South American countries and that the OLAS marked the beginning of a huge effort to coordinate revolutionary actions in the region, thus boosting the plans in Bolivia.[68] The same year it was published, the book became something of a global bestseller. It was translated into eight languages and published by prestigious publishing houses in the United States and Europe. In Latin America it saw several editions. In Chile it came out as part of the *Documentos* series of the *Punto Final* magazine, and in Montevideo it was released by several publishing houses.[69]

Debray's growing popularity was also due to the fact that simultaneously with the dissemination of his writings in 1967 he was arrested for his involvement in Guevara's Bolivia operation.[70] The intellectual gained international renown due to the multiple solidarity campaigns that were organized in his defense and called for his release (by De Gaulle and Graham Greene, among others). Debray gained such popularity that in May 1968 a *New York Times* article hailed the 27-year-old as one of the "Seven Heroes of the New Left," along with Noam Chomsky, Albert Camus, Frantz Fanon, Paul Goodman, Herbert Marcuse, and Ernesto Guevara.[71]

In just three years, Debray had built a vertiginous career as a public intellectual. He had gone from philosophy professor in France to a model intellectual, who in the eyes of some combined political action with theoretical thinking, embodied the synthesis of European thought and the political practice of Latin America, one of the world's most effervescent regions, and was laying the foundations of a revolutionary strategy that had supposedly proved effective.[72] This fast ascent, however, seemed to have much more to do with his role as an organic intellectual of the Revolution than with the soundness of his theoretical arguments. As a Uruguayan intellectual of the time said, "He's no consecrated Sartre coming to consecrate Cuba, but rather a Frenchman who has been consecrated by Cuba's consecration."[73]

Despite its initial impact, Debray's book also prompted significant criticism. The fact that political theorizing on the Cuban Revolution had shifted from Guevara to Debray made it possible for many sectors of the Left to take greater critical distance. The almost sacred halo of respect that surrounded Guevara could not be transferred to Debray. As Debray said somewhat reproachfully seven years after the essay's publication: "We were nothing more than ideological scapegoats, and *Revolution in the Revolution?* would never have caused such an uproar if it had not allowed the Latin American representatives of a certain orthodoxy to spew out their long-repressed resentfulness, having lacked the courage to aim it at whom it was really intended for: the leadership of the revolution."[74] Within the Left, criticizing Debray was a way of criticizing the Cuban Revolution without the cost such criticism involved, given the prestige that the Revolution had gained by the late 1960s.

Three months after the publication of his essay, his former professor Louis Althusser wrote him a letter where in cordial terms he expressed doubts about Debray's arguments in *Revolution in the Revolution?* He noted that the text was effective as a negative demonstration of the methods Debray criticized. However, in his view, the essay's main fault was that it failed to demonstrate in positive terms that the guerrilla warfare strategy implemented in Cuba was the most suitable method for all of Latin America. Althusser criticized Debray's exaggerated contrasting of the countryside and the city where he is "almost tempted – if my memory doesn't fail me – to draw class lines between mountain and city," proposing a rather ahistorical and almost geographically deterministic conceptualization of the relationship between the countryside and the city.

Also many Latin American communist parties, as well as Trotskyist and Maoist parties, mostly European, found an opportunity to criticize the foreign policy of the Cuban Revolution through a harsh and insulting criticism of Debray's thesis.[75] In the new Southern Cone Left, not many dared discuss the essay publicly, but various internal documents criticize its arguments.[76] In some way, the distance between Guevara and Debray together with the failure of the EGP rural guerrilla campaign enabled a more open discussion of the concrete forms that armed struggle could take in the Southern Cone. As a result of regional exiles, Montevideo became a privileged scenario for this discussion.

Montevideo: "A Favorable Place for Conspiracy," 1962–1968

Montevideo was one of the sites where such discussions were particularly vigorous and led to concrete results through a new political experience that emerged in 1966. Uruguay's long-standing tradition of receiving asylum seekers, along with its respect for individual liberties – which will continue relatively unaffected until 1968 – turned this country into a hub of Brazilian, Argentine, and Paraguayan dissidents. Uruguay had had a stable democratic system of government since 1946 that respected individual guarantees, and a political ruling class formed mostly by the Colorado Party and the National Party, which, while adopting the Cold War rhetoric, had not banned left-wing parties, in contrast to what had happened in most Latin American countries, where communist parties had been outlawed as the Cold War advanced. This made it an almost unique example in the region, and the prevailing conditions turned the capital of Uruguay into a sanctuary and a space for conspiracy for various militants from the region who viewed the city as a haven of freedom in an increasingly authoritarian regional context. Flavio Tavares, a Brazilian exile linked to Governor Leonel Brizola, saw it as an "ideal place for conspiring," and described it as having:

absolute freedom, parties of every tendency and all of them legalized (even Trotskyists and anarchists, who are stigmatized in the rest of the world, have headquarters, flags, newspapers, and the such there). And, above all, many books and magazines depicting the utopia of revolution. All of that in plain sight, like those hundreds of Brazilian exiles, who filled the cafés of 18 de Julio Avenue or San José Street or Pocitos, and dreamed of returning.[77]

A CIA agent described Montevideo as having an "extremely permissible political atmosphere," which, among other things, allowed the Cuban Embassy to become intensely involved in local politics and work with exiles from the region.[78]

That climate of active political socializing in bars and cafés of downtown Montevideo, along with the dissemination of literature through numerous bookshops, publishing houses, and publications, as well as the weekly *Marcha* and the daily *Época*, whose columns featured a variety of foreign intellectuals banned from writing in their own countries, all contributed to build a community of political exchanges that fostered reflection on the processes in the region. A growing number of Argentines and Brazilians flocked to Montevideo and began organizing the resistance against the political regimes of their respective countries. While the resistance to the Adolfo Stroessner dictatorship in Paraguay was organized primarily from Argentina – given the anti-Peronism of post-1955 governments and the fact that Stroessner was a former ally of Perón – there was also a large community of Paraguayan exiles in Montevideo.[79]

Argentines of various political backgrounds had long used Montevideo as a meeting place for opponents of the government of the moment. As of 1955, after Perón was ousted, Montevideo was increasingly frequented by members of the Peronist resistance, and the city became a meeting ground for Peronists from different provinces, who planned actions against the ruling governments and established international contacts. A number of leftist militants not necessarily connected with the Peronist movement also turned to Montevideo, as once Argentina broke off diplomatic relations with Cuba their contacts with the Cubans had shifted to Montevideo.

After the March 1964 coup in Brazil, Montevideo also received a large number of exiles from that country. These included a group of anti-coup military officers, as well as politicians connected with Rio Grande governor Leonel Brizola, and members of Ação Popular (Popular Action), a leftist Christian group that had broken away from Ação Católica (Catholic Action).

Despite how promising Uruguay looked to exiles, the country was not in one of its best moments. In the mid-1950s Uruguay had achieved a level of social development that was significant in the context of Latin America. That period of high optimism, illustrated by the popular saying "There's no place like Uruguay," was characterized by economic growth, the development of the welfare state, advanced labor and social laws, and a stable democracy. According to the 1963 census, Uruguay presented features that were quite different from the more stereotypical conceptions of Latin America. The country's population was predominantly urban, with 80.7 percent of Uruguayans living in cities, it had an illiteracy rate of 8.7 percent, primary school enrolment stood at 91.6 percent, and the rate of unemployment was 6.3 percent.[80] As for wages, from 1946 to 1950 the country had seen an annual real wage growth of 7.9 percent, which made it possible for it to begin the 1950s with welfare levels comparable to some developed countries.[81] However, that progress proved fragile in the post-war period, as terms of trade deteriorated and the economy faced changes. In the mid-1950s, Uruguay entered a phase of stagnation, which was followed by a structural economic crisis that lasted two decades. The increasing failure of political parties to provide solutions for the country's economic problems was interpreted as a political legitimacy crisis of the traditional parties, which for some essayists proved that society was suffering a moral crisis, marked by years of state paternalism and political patronage.[82]

The leading feature of the exhaustion of the Batllista model was the economic aspect. During the first half of the twentieth century, a sector of the Colorado Party led by José Batlle y Ordoñez furthered an economic social, political, and moral reform project that shaped modern day Uruguay. Among other things, this method was characterized by progressive social laws, a strong separation of Church and state, the promotion of advanced women's rights legislation, and an economic program based on statization and the fostering of industrialization. By the mid-1950s, this model, which had brought about Uruguay's various comparative achievements, began to reveal its limits. This decline would prompt many readings in which the "crisis" took on multiple dimensions: political, moral, and social.[83]

In 1960, the writer Mario Benedetti, a Uruguayan intellectual who in the coming years would explicitly support armed struggle, wrote an essay entitled "El país de la cola de paja" (roughly, "The Country with its Tail between its Legs"), which reflected the mood of certain sectors that were critical of this decline.[84] For Benedetti, Uruguay was "a country of office clerks."[85] From this characterization, closely connected with a middle-class sensibility, Benedetti embarked on a moral critique of this figure of the clerk, a metonymic representation of the average Uruguayan. The book attracted criticism from both the Right and the Left: from the former because a significant part of the moral crisis was associated with the decline and corruption of the political class, and from the latter because of the emphasis it placed on morality and its negligence of economic matters. Notwithstanding, the book became a bestseller in Uruguay. Its straightforward, depoliticized tone ensured its appeal to the general public, which recognized itself in the sense of moral crisis expressed in the book. The essay was reprinted eight times and by 1973 it had sold 50,000 copies.[86]

As of the fourth edition, Benedetti included a postscript written in 1963 in response to certain criticisms received by the book; it attempted to deal with more recent events related to the Left's poor performance in the 1962 elections. In that postscript, the author's heightened political engagement is evident, along with an interest in using politics – and more specifically a revolution – as a vehicle to resolve the "moral crisis." It also raised questions about the feasibility of revolution in Uruguay and provided some answers, albeit somewhat ambiguous. Benedetti concluded that the pacifist and legalist route was unfeasible and went on to claim that the idea of revolution "in this country and at this moment in time" was also unfeasible, given that the average Uruguayan was "clearly moderate, indifferent to politics, opposed to violence, lacking in commitment, and superstitious of the word freedom."[87]

Further on, he suggested that a possibility for the Left lay "in developing new elements of propaganda, in creating a new propagandistic language." Citing the case of the kidnapping of Havana Grand Prix winner Juan-Manuel Fangio in pre-revolutionary Cuba and the paintings on loan from the Louvre that were stolen by young revolutionaries in Caracas, he proposed an approach based on

... non-conventional, creative propaganda ... a type of propaganda that to some extent follows a common schema, witty and surprising, one that keeps the public on its toes, caught up in a constant state of expectation. . . . In this respect, I believe humor has a central role to play. I am convinced that certain *Peloduro* caricatures were more effective, accurate, and more memorable than many of the speeches given at the political rallies of the Left.[88]

This emphasis on morality, together with the call to renew the political language and practices of the Left would become central aspects in the formation of the MLN-T in the years to come. Benedetti's assessment is a clear precedent of what the Tupamaros would call their *Política con Armas* (Politics with Arms) strategy and which was later described by several analysts as a unique form of armed struggle where the symbolic and the performative took on a significant preponderance. Conceptual artist Luis Camnitzer, for example, has noted in a recent study that the actions of the Tupamaros provided a major contribution to the development of Latin American vanguard art in the second half of the twentieth century, and other authors have focused on the symbolic dimensions of Tupamaro actions, as discussed at the end of this chapter.[89]

Beyond the subjective and theoretical aspects of the decline of the Batllista welfare model, the stagnation and crisis had very specific effects. Successive governments of the Colorado and National Parties were unable to curb inflation, which soared to at an annual rate of sixty percent in the second half of the 1960s.[90] This had a strong impact on the distribution of wealth, and among the working classes it led to rising labor protests as workers demanded wage increases that would compensate for the loss in purchasing power. Yet the Left failed to capitalize on this discontent. Throughout the 1960s it continued to perform poorly at the polls, never obtaining more than seven percent of the votes, and the National and Colorado Parties seemed unbeatable.[91] In 1958, the National Party won the elections after almost a century in the opposition, and in 1967 the Colorado Party returned to power.[92] Although the dominance of the traditional parties persisted, the presence of the Left grew stronger among trade unions and students, as the public mood worsened.

One response to the crisis was the politicization of the labor movement. In an article in the January 1963 issue of *Marcha*, union leader Héctor Rodríguez wrote that the crisis put the workers' movement at a crossroads: workers could make economic demands without becoming involved in politics, or they could address the crisis and its causes. The latter would require proposing their own solutions and "mobiliz[ing] the forces required to put them into action."[93]

The state's response to the growing social mobilization against the crisis was to step up repression and police control. Although most studies have emphasized the increase in state repression starting in 1967, a series of recent studies have shown how a significant proportion of the authoritarian practices consolidated by the state as of 1968, under the government of Pacheco Areco had already been part of the repertoire of repressive state practices, having been developed at the beginning of the decade.[94] Between 1960 and 1963, certain sectors of the National Party government, together with the Colorado opposition, embarked on an anticommunist campaign, specifically focused on the threat posed by the Cuban Revolution. The campaign unsuccessfully attempted to ban the Communist Party, regulate union activity, and break off relations with the Soviet Union and Cuba. Between 1962 and 1963, a number of extreme Right groups carried out attacks against political and social activists, exiles, and Jews. In 1963 and 1965, the government decreed prompt security measures, and individual rights were suspended to suppress strikes by public sector unions. These measures enabled the imprisonment of hundreds of union activists and, in some cases, the use of systematic torture, which was a first in Uruguay.[95]

The March 1964 military coup in Brazil added a regional component to the authoritarian escalation fueled by Uruguay's conservative sectors.[96] There were multiple reports in the press denouncing that the Brazilian military dictatorship was meddling in Uruguay's affairs and pressuring the government regarding the treatment and control of Brazilian exiles in Uruguay.[97] Also, two conspiracies were reported in the period between 1964 and 1965, which were backed by civilian and military groups that were concerned with the Uruguayan government's failure to take action against "communist activities" and hoped to stage a coup. These groups looked to Brazil as a model for their actions, as a U.S. State Department report explained.[98]

In September 1965, pressure began to mount in Argentina. In a meeting with Brazilian general Costa e Silva, the influential Argentine general Juan Carlos Onganía – who had given a speech that same year at the West Point Military Academy proposing that national borders be replaced by ideological borders – suggested that the two countries enter into a military pact to stop subversion in Latin America. The two generals saw Uruguay as the main threat, given the strong presence of exiles in that country and its political instability.[99] Nine months later a coup d'état in Argentina installed a new military dictatorship headed by Onganía. As of 1966, Uruguay was surrounded by military dictatorships.

It was in this context of rising state repression and authoritarianism, lack of electoral options for the Left, and increasing social protests that a group of activists from different political backgrounds (anarchists, socialists, former communists, and independent activists) who were dissatisfied with the traditional Left began to meet in what would later be known as the "Coordinator." This group was initially formed to support the actions of the sugarcane workers' movement in northern Uruguay: the Unión de

Trabajadores del Azúcar de Artigas (Union of Sugarcane Cutters of Artigas, or UTAA).

These protests staged by a rural union from the country's far north to denounce harsh working conditions acted as a social spur. They revealed an "unknown Uruguay" that had little to do with the exceptional conditions that supposedly set it apart in the context of Latin America. The marches exposed the lack of labor rights and the abuses committed by the police against rural labor leaders, which included torture. These mobilizations were also unprecedented because they involved radical methods of struggle, such as land occupations, under the union's demand of "land for those who work it." The movement's main slogan, "For the Right to Land and with Sendic," evidenced a specific leadership that expressed the connection between these rural sectors and a militant Left that was seeking alternative forms of struggle outside electoral politics.

Raúl Sendic was a former law student from a family of small landholders from the country's interior who had begun his political life as a socialist youth leader and would go on to become the head of the Tupamaros. He had dropped out of university in the mid-1950s to work with a network of socialist activists who were organizing rural workers in northern Uruguay. Sendic and these activists were the link between the UTAA and the Coordinator. The sugarcane workers' movement received special attention from various intellectuals linked to the awareness of a New Left. Writers including Eduardo Galeano, Mario Benedetti, Alfredo Errandonea, Julio Castro, Carlos María Gutiérrez, Mauricio Rosencoff, and María Esther Gilio published reports on the sugarcane workers, in which they attempted to show how their experience revealed a Uruguay that was less than exceptional and much closer to the tragedies of Latin America.[100] In July 1963, the Coordinator broke into a firing club and stole a number of firearms to use in a land occupation that the UTAA was planning. For several members of the Coordinator this was the "baptism of fire" that laid the foundations of what would later be the MLN-T. Raúl Sendic, who was thirty-eight at the time, joined this action; from then on he went underground and became the leading reference point for the sectors of the New Left that were seeking alternatives to democratic legality.[101]

This group, which existed from 1963 to 1965, was the seed of the MLN-Tupamaros movement.[102] Almost no written documents have survived from that period and there are conflicting accounts regarding what the initial aims of these coordination efforts were. These accounts range from those that claim the Coordinator was created to provide an instrument of self-defense for the labor movement and the legal Left against mounting state repression and the attacks from extreme Right gangs, to others that suggest that from the start there was an explicit intention of forming a revolutionary organization that would emulate the Cuban experience.[103]

Figure 1.a. Demonstration of Sugar workers in support of Raul Sendic. Aurelio Gonzalez Archive, Montevideo Center of Photography, Montevideo, Uruguay.

The only surviving texts from that period that can be attributed to the Coordinator are the articles of the first issue of the magazine *Barricada*, published in September 1964. The editorial "Ser y Hacer" (Being and Doing) summarized in one page the identity of this group. It was a call to prioritize "doing" over the paralyzing ideological debates of the Left. In what was a heterodox approach for the Left, moral imperative and commitment were the leading inspirations for "doing." In the years that followed, the Tupamaros condensed this appeal to action in the maxim "Actions Unite Us, Words Separate Us."[104]

The article entitled "La marcha de los cañeros y la reordenación de la izquierda uruguaya" (The March of the Sugarcane Cutters and the Transformation of Uruguay's Left) set forth some ideas that provide a clearer understanding of the political construction that the Coordinator was attempting.[105]

The article begins by analyzing the effects that the marches to Montevideo staged by the UTAA had on the Left. For *Barricada*, the sugarcane cutters' actions had been a "critical test for the Left," as they brought up a number of questions:

Should priority be given to the distressing and urgent problems of one sector, which cannot be solved without tackling the very roots of the system? Or should we address general problems, which, while not as pressing, affect all popular sectors?.... What is more important right now? DEFENDING our existing "democratic freedoms" or "legality?" Or launching a full-scale ATTACK on the system whenever the opportunity presents itself?

According to the author, these questions ultimately led to the more general question of whether conditions were ripe for a social revolution in Uruguay. He identified two different answers to this question. One was given by what the author called the Arismendi-Quijano line, which represented the traditional Left, and the other came from critical sectors committed to the mobilization of the sugarcane cutters.[106] In his opinion, the Arismendi-Quijano line opposed the radicalization of union actions. Radicalization was considered dangerous because it would trigger an authoritarian backlash that could not be resisted, as Uruguay lacked the conditions that were present in other countries where the revolution had succeeded. These two leaders called for steady and daily political work aimed at furthering the organization of the people, but that strategy had not seemed to work in the last decades:

Naturally, we all agree that what is most important is the slow and arduous work of organization. What we may need to discuss is what we are organizing for and what methods we should use.

We cannot be made to forget – through partial pictures and propaganda – that neither the rate of unionization nor the level of political organization has experienced a noticeable change over the last 20 years, and that should be telling us that the organization is not working out right.

The author then goes on to compare the Cuban experience to the situation in Uruguay. While most critics of the more radical positions tried to mark the differences between Uruguay and Cuba, the author criticized the stereotyped views that had been constructed around the Cuban Revolution, and, going against the grain, looked for similarities between Cuba and the Southern Cone in the 1950s:

Cuba was not in the group of extremely impoverished countries of Latin America. On the contrary, with a second exportable product like sugar, it has always enjoyed a relative economic prosperity comparable to that of other countries with the same advantage in their trade balance: Argentina, Uruguay, and Chile.

That was the starting point, as in Cuba, "the vast majority of the people did not fight in the revolution, at least not in the beginning, but was not willing either to be killed in the name of the ruling system." With respect to the initial question regarding the conditions for a revolution, the author did not seem to come to any final conclusion, but it was clear that in his opinion the "traditional Left" was not doing anything to further a revolution. The problem of the traditional Left was not in its diagnosis of the situation but in the will to change it.

In this context, the Left had to address the demands of "explosive minorities," of the "weakest links of capitalism," like the sugarcane workers who exposed the most obvious injustices they suffered without forgetting the demands of others:

The Left cannot ask the tens of thousands of unemployed workers to starve to death as quietly as possible, simply because that Left is not organized enough to defend them. Neither can it ask another generation of rural laborers, women and children to postpone their legitimate rebellion because the Left is not yet mature enough to stand by them. And what about Cuba? Can it wait while we organize ourselves and finally decide to carry out our historical mission? What will be left for us to do if we stand by while Cuba is strangled? Start again in America?

The author concluded that, after the protests of the sugarcane cutters, there were two paths open for the Left: try to capitalize on the denunciations of the sugarcane cutters for electoral growth; or radicalize, by joining its struggle with that of the sugarcane cutters. The latter is the path "taken by those who have assumed the duty of every revolutionary, which is making the revolution."

Although the text contained a harsh criticism of the sectors of the so-called traditional Left and convincingly explained how the strategy of those parties failed to offer ways to bring about change in the medium term, its political proposals were rather limited. They were reduced to a vague call to radicalization, an appeal to fuse with the movements of the most marginalized sectors of society, and to the acknowledgment that conditions in Uruguay were not yet ripe for revolution. The text evidences a firm intention of defying legality, but the way in which such defiance would take place was not yet clear.

A large part of this group went on to create the MLN-Tupamaros in January 1966. It was a small organization of no more than 50 people who defended the idea of launching a revolutionary strategy in Uruguay but were still unclear about "how" they would do it. Their first document was not published until 1967. In it they defined themselves as an urban guerrilla group and an alternative to the *foco* strategy proposed by the Cuban Revolution. The ways in which from 1964 to 1967 this small group developed a political and military strategy are explained to a large extent by some of the issues indicated earlier in this chapter regarding Uruguay's geopolitical position in the region.

This small group of militants had multiple contacts with militants from other countries, who in a way helped design the strategy of the Tupamaros. Many of the region's militants, who passed through Montevideo for different reasons, met with members of the Coordinator. The networks of political parties that these militants belonged to, along with the new political ties that were being forged in the activities to support the sugarcane cutters' movement and the solidarity campaigns with Cuba, helped build relationships between the militants coming to Montevideo and the members of the Coordinator. The networks of journalists also played an important role in these exchanges. The newspaper *Época* had an active role in coordination activities involving exiles in Montevideo. It had been founded in 1962 as an independent, non-communist left-wing paper and adopted increasingly radical positions as the political process unfolded, reporting on the sugarcane cutters' mobilization, sympathizing with the first actions of the Coordinator, and, later, promoting the "Época Agreement" to support the definitions of the OLAS Conference in Havana. By reporting on the Coordinator's development and supporting its conspiratorial activities, *Época* became – as the newspaper's administrator and future member of the MLN-T Andrés Cultelli put it – the "foreign affairs ministry" of the sectors close to the Coordinator.[107]

Although the actions of the EGP in northern Argentina were organized in Bolivia, contacts were also made in Montevideo. Various materials were distributed through this city, where contacts were also made with the Cubans, first through the Embassy and later, when diplomatic relations were severed in September 1964, through the staff that remained in the country and a significant network of contacts. The painter Ciro Bustos – a friend of Guevara's who participated in the EGP experience and later in Ñancahauzú, Bolivia – tells how, as one of the few survivors of the EGP in Argentina, he decided to flee to Montevideo, where he reconnected with the Cubans. In that trip, he met at the Sorocabana – one of the city's leading cafés – with the director of *Época* and with *Marcha* journalist Eduardo Galeano, who put him in contact with Raúl Sendic in Montevideo. News of the EGP's defeat had reached the Uruguayan press and Coordinator activists wanted to know what had happened. According to Bustos, he and Sendic talked for hours, discussing the reasons for the EGP's failure. Sendic told him he belonged to a group that was interested in launching an armed struggle effort but that they were still not sure what characteristics it would have in Uruguay. The result of that meeting was a collaboration agreement. Bustos gave Sendic some weapons his group had in Montevideo that could not be taken across the border to Argentina, and offered to give him a course in security. The meeting apparently coincided, as will be shown below, with the moment in which Coordinator members began to abandon the idea that rural guerrilla warfare was feasible in Uruguay.[108]

As noted above, since Perón's ouster in 1955, Montevideo had also been a sanctuary for many Peronist resistance activists and a place where they could retreat to.[109] John William Cooke – who had been appointed by Perón as the person initially in charge of politically organizing the resistance – used Montevideo as his base for operations when he had to flee Argentina.[110] It was in Montevideo that he married Alicia Eguren, in

1957, and there they set up a base of operations along with a small group of militants who fled Argentina at different moments, mainly to escape the repression unleashed by the CONINTES Plan mentioned above. Argentine exiles engaged in political discussions and made contacts in Montevideo, and it was from there that Cooke's correspondence with Havana was processed and sent. It was also from Montevideo that Alicia Eguren arranged the trips of Argentines from various Peronist and left-wing organizations who went to train in Cuba from 1961 to 1962.

Another activist linked to the Peronist movement who came to Montevideo around this time was Abraham Guillén.[111] This nearly fifty-year-old Spanish anarchist, who was a member of Spain's Confederación Nacional del Trabajo – Federación Anarquista Ibérica, (National Confederation of Labor – Iberian Anarchist Federation, or CNT-FAI) – and had fought under Cipriano Mera's command during the Spanish Civil War, had settled in Argentina as a refugee in the 1940s. There, he became close to Cooke and the more radical Peronist sectors. After the 1955 coup he advised Cooke on the Peronist resistance's military strategy and in particular on the strategy of the Uturuncos, a group of Peronist militants who in 1959 organized a short-lived insurgency attempt in the Tucumán hills. In 1960, Guillén was arrested and spent a few months in jail. Upon his release he traveled to Cuba, where, according to his own account, he spent a year training guerrilla groups. He then settled in Uruguay, where he found work as a journalist in the Colorado Party newspaper *Acción*.

In 1963, some twenty-five militant members of Tacuara, an extreme Right nationalist group from Argentina, decided to break away and join Peronist left-wing organizations, reformulating their nationalism in a popular and anti-imperialistic perspective. In August 1963, several of these militants robbed the Policlínico Bancario, coming away with 100,000 dollars. Some of them made their way to Montevideo and joined the Peronist resistance. In 1964, Joe Baxter, one of the group's leaders, traveled to Vietnam, where he made contact with officers of the Chinese Communist Party who invited the group and another Peronist resistance organization to receive military training in China. After the course, unable to go back to Argentina, the militants returned to Montevideo and joined the Uruguayan Coordinator, offering to form a leadership training school for Argentine and Uruguayan militants. Joe Baxter, Nell Taxi, and Pata Cataldo taught courses on theoretical aspects, urban fighting, and explosives.[112] Nell Tacci would later be arrested in 1967 for his involvement with the Tupamaros, Joe Baxter would flee to Havana, returning to Argentina in 1970 and leaving the Peronist movement to join the PRT-ERP, and Cataldo would return to Argentina in 1967.[113]

As of March 1964, Uruguay received a new wave of refugees, this time from Brazil. After the military coup in that country, Uruguay became one of the main organization centers for the resistance against the Brazilian dictatorship. Rio Grande do Sul Governor Leonel Brizola led various resistance activities from Uruguay. There were several insurgency attempts, mostly organized by military officers. The two attempts in Rio Grande do Sul were unsuccessful.[114] Although Brizola focused on the possibility of generating military uprisings in southern Brazil, the repeated failures led him to adopt other strategies, including supporting an initiative by a group of sergeants who had requested his backing to develop a rural *foco*.

The establishment of a rural *foco* in the Caparaó mountains in southeastern Brazil, between the states of Espírito Santo and Minas Gerais, was thus planned from Montevideo, Cuba, and Brazil. Cuba provided money through Uruguay and offered military training in the island. In October 1966, the group started a rural *foco* in Caparaó with fourteen activists, five of whom had been trained in Cuba. According to Denisse Rollemberg, the launching of this *foco* was coordinated by Cuba, as it was planned to coincide with Guevara's Bolivia campaign. After five months the *foco*'s militants were found in appalling conditions. While they had not encountered "enemy forces," the guerrillas had to face extremely harsh conditions, were poorly fed, isolated, injured, and some psychologically affected, so that they were no match for the police and the army when some 3,000 men were deployed in a large operation to suppress the *foco*.[115]

These plans were backed by support activities in Montevideo, which entailed contacts with Uruguayan militants and other exiles. Jorge Rulli remembers how after the coup some Peronist militants had been entrusted by Perón to express their solidarity to Goulart, who had initially sought refuge in Montevideo.[116] Uruguay's left-wing parties and media also expressed their support. Uruguayan communists, who were critical of the Brazilian Communist Party's failure to take up arms against the coup, offered their help directly to Brizola.[117] Sendic personally took weapons to Brazil, and forged a close political relationship with Brizola in Montevideo.[118] Moreover, *Época* provided a space for Brazilian refugees to denounce the dictatorship's attempts to pressure the Uruguayan government, as well as cases of direct intervention by Brazilian military or police officers targeting exiles in Uruguay, and gave a detailed coverage of any events these exiles wanted to make known.[119] The Peronists who were in Montevideo also had a very close relationship with Brizola. The correspondence between Pablo Vicente (a representative of Perón in Montevideo) and the Argentine leader reveal very frequent political conversations and coordination between Perón and Brizola.[120]

Through all of these exchanges, the Uruguayans of the Coordinator had firsthand knowledge of what was happening in the region. They not only witnessed the process of advancing authoritarianism, which was seen as a road that the Uruguayan ruling classes would take sooner or later, but also came into contact with the different radical experiences that had been attempted in the region. They saw the limitations of those who tried to mechanically replicate the Cuban process, as had happened to the EGP in Argentina or the Caparaó guerrillas in Brazil. They also held discussions with and took ideas from those who were attempting other ways, such as members of the Peronist resistance. All of these aspects are key for understanding how the Tupamaros came to build a body of urban guerrilla warfare ideas, which they would later present as an alternative to the Cuban model in the region.

One of the major debates within this small group had to do with the problem of defining the strategy that would be implemented. A flat, grassland country with no mountains or jungles and a sparsely populated countryside, Uruguay did not have ideal conditions for rural guerrilla warfare. Nonetheless, from 1964 to 1965, Sendic and a group of rural workers had been surveying bush areas, lagoons, and swamps in northern Uruguay that could be used as hideouts in a rural guerrilla warfare strategy. At the same time, other members of the Coordinator had begun studying different alternatives. In 1965, Jorge Torres, a young former communist, penned a document arguing that in Uruguay the revolution had to be fought from the cities. Rubén Navillat and the bank employee Eleuterio Fernández Huidobro had also contributed to the document.[121]

In 1966, Debray was in Montevideo and met with Torres, Navillat, and the Argentine militant Baxter. They had a heated discussion. While Debray said that in Uruguay a revolution was impossible given its geography, the Uruguayan militants and Baxter maintained the feasibility of urban guerrilla warfare, backing their claim with little-known experiences, like that of the FLN in Algeria, the Jewish resistance to British rule in Palestine, and some cases of partisan resistance during World War II. These began to be studied more closely by some members of the Coordinator and by some Argentine militants who were in Montevideo.[122] These experiences put into question the *foco* theory advocated by the Debray. Navillat recalls that at one point in the conversation he and Baxter had with Debray he was so frustrated with Frenchman's "smugness" in denying the possibility of an armed insurrection in Uruguay that he said to him, "Che is a fool, but he has balls. He's going to get himself killed."[123]

That same year, Abraham Guillén published his book *Estrategia de la guerrilla urbana* (*Strategy of the Urban Guerrilla*) in Uruguay. It was the twelfth book he published. Argentine activists had been avidly reading his works, which dealt primarily with Argentine economy and the oligarchy's economic and political ties with imperialism, since the 1950s.[124] In the 1960s, drawing on his own experience in the Spanish Civil War and in line with the debates underway in the Left, Guillén shifted his analysis to focus on political violence and military theory. In 1965, he published his *Teoria de la Violencia* (*Theory of Violence*) in Argentina, where he developed a political and philosophical justification of revolutionary violence in contemporary society. A year later, in 1966, he published *Estrategia de la guerrilla urbana*, questioning the applicability of rural *foquismo* in Latin America, in particular in highly urbanized countries such as the Southern Cone nations. The text had many points in common with Torres' 1965 document. The two met in 1965 and Torres accused Guillén of plagiarizing his work.[125] Both texts argued that demographic and economic conditions should determine the specific rules that would guide revolutionary strategy. In cases like Argentina and Uruguay, where 30 and 50 percent of the population, respectively, lived in the capital cities, the ideal place to build the basis of a guerrilla movement was the city. Unlike Guevara, they found that developing an urban guerrilla movement presented certain advantages over rural guerrilla warfare, as urban guerrillas – who work during the day and fight at night – are familiarized with their battleground and can fall back on their networks of relationships to ensure their survival.

In contrast to Torres, who illustrated his case for urban guerrilla warfare with the Algerian, Zionist, and Second World War experiences, Guillén looked to the Spanish Civil War resistance in the cities, and in particular, the Battle of Madrid, for past experiences that could be useful in developing an urban guerrilla strategy. Both arguments also had points in common with ideas that Bengochea had put forward in his discussion with Guevara in 1962.[126]

This discussion was settled in 1967. The Uruguayans in the MLN-T would be the first to apply these political and military ideas to a concrete organization. In their Document No. 1, adopted in June 1967, the Tupamaros included a section entitled *Urban Warfare*, where they explained that their strategy was drawn from the tactics that had allowed them to survive during their first years of existence.[127] The shift had occurred in the year 1966, when the police became aware of the organization and they were forced to turn to the city and the periphery of Montevideo for infrastructure and hiding places, abandoning Sendic's original plans.

The reasons for the shift toward urban guerrilla warfare are connected with two developments. First, the exchange of experiences and debates among different Argentine, Brazilian, and Uruguayan militants is likely to have contributed to a thorough assessment of the difficulties faced by past rural *foco* attempts in the region. Second, when the government became aware of the existence of the MLN-T as a result of a shooting in December 1966 and launched a vigorous campaign to hunt down its members, the organization was able to survive thanks to the many networks that they had established in Montevideo with political and labor activists. The experience they gained led to their option of the city as the ideal battleground. For that reason, the document argued that in Uruguay's case armed struggle could not be tied to "classical strategic ideas." It then listed the advantages of urban combat as opposed to rural combat: cities offer good communication and liaison conditions; the urban control capacities of the police and the army are relatively idle; there is no need for supply networks in the city; guerrillas can work during the day and fight at night; and guerrillas are in an environment they know. The document also recognized that there were certain aspects of this strategy that were still not fully worked out. One such aspect was the issue of transforming an urban guerrilla organization into a regular army. But it noted that "the continental scope of the process had to be considered and that that transformation could only be attempted in the final stage."

Toward the end of 1968, the Tupamaros emerged as an example of urban guerrilla warfare that challenged previous models. In July 1968, the Chilean magazine *Punto Final* featured a long piece on the Tupamaros and reproduced the document *30 preguntas a un tupamaro* (*Thirty Questions for a Tupamaro*), one of the movement's first public documents.[128] This article would later be reprinted in the Argentine magazine *Cristianismo y Revolución*.[129] Just a few days earlier the MLN-T had carried out its first kidnapping of a government official, a man close to the president who called for taking a hardline stance against the labor movement.[130] The action impacted Uruguay, as it proved the operational capacity of an organization that until then had kept a very low profile. After that first kidnapping, the organization conducted relatively successful actions that earned it a certain prestige in the region.

The *30 preguntas* document reaffirmed some of the ideas set forth in Document No. 1 regarding the possibilities the city offered for a revolution. Some of the answers seemed to respond to the objections made by Fidel Castro a year earlier in his address at the OLAS Conference. With respect to his geographical objections, it said:

Our territory has no unassailable places where we can set up a lasting guerrilla *foco*, although there are some places in our countryside that are hard to access. To compensate we have a big city with more than 300 square kilometers of buildings, which allows for the development of an urban struggle. This means that we cannot copy the strategy of countries whose geographic conditions allow them to establish a stable guerrilla *foco* in the hills, mountain ranges, or jungles. Instead we have to devise a home-grown strategy that is suitable for a reality that differs from that of most countries in America.

The questions about Uruguay's geopolitical conditions that had been discussed with Fidel Castro on that occasion were also addressed:

Q: Can the possibility of foreign intervention be a reason for postponing all forms of armed struggle in Uruguay?

A: If that were the case, then Cuba could not have had a revolution 90 miles from the United States, and there would be no guerrillas in Bolivia, a country that borders with Brazil and Argentina.... And in any case, our strategy falls within the continental strategy of "creating many Vietnams," and interventionist forces would have to wage many battles in numerous, scattered fronts.[131]

Another element that set the Tupamaros apart was the symbolic dimension of their practice. Historian Francisco Panizza has suggested that "despite their emphasis on armed actions, the Tupamaros actually developed one of the most elaborate strategies of symbolic politics in the history of Uruguay."[132] Actions that were initially conceived as thefts or kidnappings, with specific objectives that had to do with benefiting the organization in terms of infrastructure, took on other political connotations that entailed a political denunciation and represented an effort to build an alternative power by way of "armed propaganda." An example of this is the Financiera Monty heist, in which the Tupamaros stole six million pesos along with the financial house's accounting records, which they used to expose a number of irregularities and a list of politicians and businessmen connected with the finance company. Or the robbery of the San Rafael Hotel casino, where the Tupamaros made sure that the workers received their pay from the money they took. Or the Pando city raid, which was staged as a fake funerary procession traveling from Montevideo, with some fifty combatants in disguise who were to seize the police and fire stations, the telephone company offices, and some of the city's banks. Most operations had a measure of creativity and inventiveness, which mirrored the fictional actions portrayed by television series of the time, thus making them more popular, and initially heightening the concerns of the authorities. These early achievements led them to declare in 1969 that they were "invincible."[133]

Thanks to the relative success of its actions, the MLN-T was able to project itself as a heterodox alternative to the orthodoxy of the Cuban Revolution. The experience and the ideas of the MLN-T began circulating throughout the region. These ideas appealed to a number of organizations in the region that were looking for alternatives to Guevara's *foquismo*. A book entitled *Tupamaros: Fracaso del Che?* (*Tupamaros: Che's Failure?*), published by Argentine journalists in 1969, suggested that the actions by this group were ushering in a new stage in the development of Latin American guerrilla movements. For many analysts, the cycle of rural guerrilla movements had ended with Guevara's death in Bolivia. However, the Tupamaros were proposing an alternative to rural guerrilla warfare that revived the expectations of those who believed in revolutionary violence.[134]

The Tupamaro experience was replicated in Argentina by the Fuerzas Armadas Peronistas (Peronist Armed Forces) – the first armed organization formed in the second wave of armed organizations in Argentina, during the Onganía dictatorship – by way of a group of Argentine militants who had participated in Tupamaro actions. That replication in turn affected other armed organizations that gradually emerged within and outside the Peronist movement.[135] Members of the Fuerzas Armadas Revolucionarias (Revolutionary Armed Forces, or FAR) – another organization initially formed by communist militants to support Guevara's Bolivia campaign and which later joined Peronist forces – said in an interview that the Tupamaros' contribution had been to redefine the guerrilla *foco*.[136]

The Fuerzas Argentinas de Liberación (Argentine Liberation Forces) were also influenced by the Tupamaros. This organization, formed by militants from different left-wing groups (primarily Trotskyist and communist), existed for over a decade in an embryonic stage of development, and in the early 1970s it began staging significant public actions.[137] In 1970, it criticized the Argentine Left's tendency to theorize, and as an alternative proposed action as a unifying criterion. It illustrated that idea with the experience "of the Tupamaros, who are for us the most advanced and closest example of urban guerrilla warfare."[138]

The PRT-ERP – the only non-Peronist armed organization that was still active in the 1970s – appears to have been less inspired by the Tupamaros, although it also shared a somewhat heterodox approach to rural *foquismo*. While there are not many references to the Tupamaros in the documents of the PRT-ERP, some of the younger militants who joined the organization in the years 1969 and 1970 remember its impact. Daniel de Santis recalls one of his first PRT meetings in 1969:

The militants I met with were talking about the *Tupamarization*, an idea I agreed with immediately, as the brilliant operative line of the Tupamaros had won many of us over to the Guevarista strategy.[139]

During that period, ties were also established between the Tupamaros and members of the incipient guerrilla groups that emerged in Brazil after 1966. In 1969, Carlos Marighella published his *Minimanual do Guerrilheiro Urbano* (*Mini Handbook for the Urban Guerrilla*), which had obvious points in common with the ideas that had been discussed in Uruguay. Guillén says his text was translated into Portuguese and a mimeograph version of it was distributed in Brazil.[140] In a research study, historian Marlon Asseff points to the existence of intelligence reports by the Centro de Informaçoes do Exterior (Brazil's Foreign Information Center) mentioning both Carlos Marighella and Carlos Lamarca crossing the border during that period.[141]

According to Andrés Pascal Allende's and Max Marambio's memoirs, Chile's MIR also paid close attention to certain MLN-T actions. In 1967, a new generation emerged within the MIR that embraced armed struggle. In 1969, that strategy began to bear fruits. Although a large part of the rank-and-file militants focused on promoting "direct actions" in mass fronts, such as land occupations in the countryside and the city, a smaller group, with ties to the commanding members, concentrated on building a military force through bank robberies and other thefts. The "bank expropriations" were carried out according to the armed propaganda criteria developed by the Tupamaros.[142]

Conclusion

In sum, in the mid-1960s a number of activists from Argentina, Brazil, Chile, and Uruguay were developing new repertoires of contention in the region, inspired by the Cuban Revolution. While publicly supporting and acknowledging the revolution, they proposed alternatives to the rural *foquismo* formulas advocated by Cuba. These new repertoires were built in a subtle play of similarities and differences, not always explicit, with the discourse of the Cuban Revolution.

These groups agreed in particular with one of Guevara's ideas: all of these organizations incorporated the idea that an armed organization could elevate the conscience of the people through different violent combat actions. Politics meant taking up arms and war was the continuation of politics by other means. The differences had to do with the rural *foco* scheme that drew on the Cuban experience. For these groups, peasants were a social force that needed to be taken into account, but it was not the only one. Moreover, the cities were for them the center of political conflicts that would enable the development of the revolutionary army. The exchanges that took place in Montevideo among Argentine, Brazilian, and Uruguayan militants, along with refugees from the Spanish Civil War, show the wealth of experiences that were incorporated into these debates.

In late 1967 these new repertoires of contention, developed over the previous three years, began to be adopted and applied by organizations, which were not new but only now started having an increasing influence in their respective countries. The fact that the MLN-T was the first group to put these ideas into practice has to do with Uruguay's geopolitical conditions. To a certain extent, the MLN-T is the result of all these shared transnational experiences involving militants and ideas from various countries, which circulated in Uruguay during this period. This geopolitical situation explains why the initial actions of the Tupamaros had such a rapid impact throughout the region.

In 1972, in a prologue to the *Actas Tupamaras*, Regis Debray – who had opposed urban guerrilla warfare – advocated in favor of the Tupamaros, describing them as "[t]he only armed revolutionary movement in Latin America that – at least until now – has been able to, or has known how to, attack on all fronts."[143] Debray's remarks show how the Tupamaro experience – and later the experiences of other groups that were formed in the Southern Cone and engaged in forms of armed struggle that differed from the Cuban rural *foco* strategy – generated expectations among analysts of the Latin American Left, attracted support, and spurred new repertoires of contention that achieved significant levels of visibility and public support in the region.

This repertoire of dissent was a first aspect of the transnational revolutionary political culture that will gradually be forged among militants of the Southern Cone. These groups first converged on practical aspects regarding the conception of "armed struggle." The similarities between certain repertoires of armed protest that looked to the Cuban Revolution as a reference but at the same time distanced themselves from it was what initially led these emerging groups to recognize themselves in one another. In this sense, their shared political culture had to do more with definitions of collective action than with ideological issues, which until then had guided the internationalist experiences of the traditional Left. Ideological definitions or the more general political conceptions were always subordinated to agreements regarding collective action. As will be seen in the next chapter, the foreign policy of the Cuban Revolution will help these Southern Cone militants to conceptualize their political actions as part of an effective Latin American revolution.

Notes

1 See OLAS, *Primera conferencia de la Organización Latinoamericana de Solidaridad* (Montevideo: Nativa Libros, 1967).

2 Carlos Jorquera, "Lucha armada y lucha guerrillera," *Punto Final*, no. 35, 2nd fortnight of August 1967.

3 Carlos María Gutiérrez, "Conversación con Fidel: la guerrilla en toda América es una sola," *Marcha* (Montevideo), no. 1366, August 18, 1967, 23.

4 Quoted from Piero Gleijeses, *Conflicting Missions, Havana, Washington, and Africa, 1959–1976*, (Berkeley: The University of North Carolina Press, 2002), 22.

5 See John Johnson, *Political Change in Latin America*, (Stanford: Stanford University Press, 1958).

6 Sidney Tarrow, *Power in Movement. Social Movements and Contentious Politics.* 2nd ed. (New York: Cambridge Press, 1999), 91–105.

7 Guillermo O'Donnell makes this connection between social unrest and redistributive conflicts in "Las fuerzas armadas y el estado autoritario del Cono Sur de América Latina," in *Contrapuntos: ensayos escogidos sobre autoritarismo y democratización* (Buenos Aires: Paidós, 1997). In Chile's case this presents some particular characteristics. Although inflation during this period was significant and affected political processes, according to some authors, popular sectors in the 1960s fared well economically as they increased their participation in the GDP. See Allan Angell, *Chile de Alessandri a Pinochet: en busca de la utopía* (Santiago: Andrés Bello, 1993), 24. In any case, this does not put into question the idea that inflation fueled the sensation of political instability. Chile's difference with respect to Argentina and Uruguay is that in these two cases the decade seems to have regressed in terms of distribution. On Argentina, see Oscar Altimir, "Estimaciones de la

distribución del ingreso en la Argentina," *Desarrollo Económico* 25, no. 100. On Uruguay, see Instituto de Economía, *El proceso económico del Uruguay* (Montevideo: Universidad de la República, 1969).

8 For an analysis of this episode and its subsequent impact, see Pedro Milos, *Historia y memoria: 2 de abril de 1957* (Santiago: LOM: Ediciones, 2007).

9 Blanca París de Oddone, *La Universidad de la República. Desde la Crisis a la Intervención 1958–1973* (Montevideo: Universidad de la República, 2010), 17–26.

10 Vania Markarian et al., *1958 el gobierno autonómico* (Montevideo: Universidad de la República, 2008), 120.

11 Rosa Alonso and Carlos Demasi, *Uruguay, 1958–1968: crisis y estancamiento* (Montevideo: Ediciones de la Banda Oriental, 1986).

12 For an interpretation of the crisis, see Aldo Marchesi and Jaime Yaffé, "La violencia bajo la lupa: una revisión de la literatura sobre violencia y política en los sesenta," *Revista Uruguaya de Ciencia Política* 19, no. 1.

13 Viñas, "Una generacion traicionada." *Marcha*, 01/31/1959. See Tortti, *El "viejo" partido socialista y los orígenes de la "nueva" izquierda*, chapters 2 and 3; and Silvia Sigal, *Intelectuales y poder en Argentina en la década del sesenta* (Argentina: Siglo XXI, 2002), chapter 5. Oscar Terán, *Nuestros años sesentas. La formación de la nueva izquierda intelectual argentina, 1956–1966* (Buenos Aires: Ediciones El Cielo por Asalto, 1991).

14 Daniel James, *Resistance and Integration, Peronism and the Argentine Working Class 1946–1976* (Cambridge: Cambridge University Press, 1988), 101–159.

15 See Cesar Seveso, "Escuelas de militancia: La experiencia de los presos políticos en Argentina, 1955–1972," *A contracorriente* 6, no. 3, Spring 2009, 137–165.

16 A large part of these debates were conducted through publications that played a major role. For Chile, see *Punto Final*; for Uruguay, see *Marcha* and *Época*. *Marcha* would also prove to be a major vehicle for the dissemination of debates in Argentina whenever the government in that country censured left-wing media outlets. *Marcha* was distributed weekly in Santiago and Buenos Aires. During the Onganía dictatorship (1966–73), the weekly publication *Marcha*, the daily *Época*, and the fortnightly magazine *Punto Final* were banned in Argentina on several occasions. In Argentina, some of the ostensibly cultural magazines connected with former Communist Party members, such as *Pasado y Presente*, or *Che*, a magazine linked to the Socialist Party, or progressive Catholic publications, such as *Cristianismo y Revolución*, which came out during Onganía's government, also played a significant role. The Cuban news agency Prensa Latina also acted as a vehicle for this exchange of articles and journalists.

17 For a brief account of these exchanges, see Jon Lee Anderson, *Che Guevara: A revolutionary life* (New York: Grove Press, 1997), 307–12.

18 See Carlos María Gutiérrez, "Con Fidel, en la Sierra Maestra, La Mañana, 14–18/3/1958," in *En la Sierra Maestra y otros reportajes* (Montevideo: Ediciones Tauro, 1967).

19 For a study on Masetti's trajectory, see Gabriel Rot, *Los orígenes perdidos de la guerrilla en la Argentina: la historia de Jorge Ricardo Masetti y el Ejército Guerrillero del Pueblo* (Buenos Aires: Ediciones El Cielo por Asalto, 2000).

20 Jorge Ricardo Masetti, *Los que luchan y los que lloran* (Buenos Aires: Editorial Jorge Álvarez, 1969).

21 These journalists included Carlos María Gutierrez, Carlos Núñez, Eduardo H. Galeano, Julio Huasi, Rodolfo Walsh, Manuel Cabieses, Hernán Vidal, Andrés Cultelli, and Guillermo Chifflet. In Argentina, two such publications were the magazine *Che*, founded by breakaways from the Communist and Socialist Parties, and the cultural magazine *Pasado y Presente*, whose staff consisted primarily of former Communist Party members. In Chile, the magazine *Punto Final* would quickly become aligned with the MIR, and in Uruguay, a new generation led by Carlos María Gutierrez in the weekly *Marcha* and the daily paper *Época*.

22 During this period, a large number of books were written by political leaders of left-wing and center parties, as well as by intellectuals who traveled to Cuba and conveyed their experiences upon their return. Some of these included: Salvador Allende, *Cuba: un camino* (Santiago: Prensa Latinoamericana, 1960); Mario Benedetti, *Cuaderno cubano* (Montevideo: Ed. Arca, 1967); Guillermo Bernhard and Alberto Etchepare, *Reportaje a Cuba* (Montevideo: Ediciones América Nueva, 1961); Alejando Chelén, *La Revolución Cubana y sus proyecciones en América Latina* (Santiago: Ed. Prensa Latinoamericana, 1960); Ariel Collazo, *Regreso de Cuba; La crisis en el Uruguay; Reforma constitucional revolucionaria* (Montevideo, 1961); Silvio Frondizi, *La Revolución cubana: su significación histórica* (Montevideo: Editorial Ciencias Políticas, 1960); Ezequiel Martínez Estrada, *En Cuba y al servicio de la revolución. Mi experiencia cubana* (Montevideo: Siglo Ilustrado, 1965); Carlos Martínez Moreno, *El paredón* (Barcelona: Seix Barral, 1962); Elías Seman, *Cuba Miliciana* (Buenos Aires: Ediciones Ubicación, 1961).

23 For an in-depth analysis of Guevara's texts from this period, see Matt D. Childs, "An Historical Critique of the Emergence and Evolution of Ernesto Che Guevara's Foco Theory," *Journal of Latin American Studies* 27, no. 3 (October 1995): 593–624. Guevara's biographies, *Che* by Anderson and *Compañero: The Life and Death of Che Guevara* by Jorge Castañeda (New York: Knopf, 1997), also devote some pages to these issues. See also Paul Dosal, *Comandante Che. Guerrilla Soldier, Commander, and Strategist, 1956–1967* (Pennsylvania: Pennsylvania State University Press, 2003).

24 Ernesto Guevara, *La guerra de guerrillas* (Lima: Fondo de Cultura Popular, 1973), 15.

25 Ibid., 16.

26 The essay was written in the context of the ideological radicalization that began in the year 1961 as a result of the revolution's new ideological definitions and the missile crisis.

27 Ernesto Guevara, *Pasajes de la guerra revolucionaria* (Cuba: Unión, 1963).

28 On how historiographical works on the revolution focused on the Sierra Maestra, neglecting urban mobilizations, and the political implications of such bibliography, see the introduction in Julia Sweig, *Inside the Cuban Revolution: Fidel Castro and the Cuban Underground* (Cambridge, Mass.: Harvard University Press, 2002).

29 On Chile, see interview with Andrés Pascal Allende conducted by the author (9/8/2008). On Uruguay, see some of the activities carried out by some of the groups and militants that would form the MLN-T, in Samuel Blixen, *Sendic* (Montevideo: Ediciones Trilce, 2000), and Fernández Huidobro, *Historia de los Tupamaros*, vol. 1 and 2.

30 For information on the Americas Department, see Manuel Piñeiro, *Che Guevara y la revolución latinoamericana* (Colombia: Ocean Sur, 2006); Anderson, *Che*, 533, 759; Castañeda, *Utopia Unarmed*, 50–89.

31 In Piero Gleijeses, *Conflicting Missions, Havana, Washington, and Africa, 1959–1976*, 21–23.

32 For studies on this wave of guerrilla groups, see Richard Gott, *Guerrilla Movements in Latin America* (Calcutta, London, New York: Seagull Books, 1970); Timothy P. Wickham-Crowley, *Guerrillas and Revolution in Latin America. A Comparative Study of Insurgents and Regimes since 1956* (New Jersey: Princeton, 1992), Part II.

33 While this assertion was derived from a principle-based policy set out in Guevara's writings about the continental revolution, several authors have also pointed out its pragmatic aspects. At the height of its isolation in the inter-American system, Cuba used this policy as a means of pressure to reach some form of agreement that would enable it to coexist within that system. Ibid., 21–23; Jorge I. Dominguez, *To Make a World Safe for Revolution. Cuba's Foreign Policy* (Cambridge: Harvard University Press, 1989), chapter 5; Anderson, *Che Guevara*, 418–21.

34 Thus a markedly pro-Cuban discourse helped socialist candidate Alfredo Palacios secure a seat in the Buenos Aires province senate, having obtained a relative majority (21.63%

of the votes) in the city of Buenos Aires, and Uruguay's Communist Party improved its constituency base in the 1962 elections by creating a coalition under the name Frente Izquierda de Liberación (Leftist Liberation Front), which formed the acronym FIDEL. For Argentina, see Tortti, *El "viejo" partido socialista y los orígenes de la "nueva" izquierda*, 266–79; for Uruguay, see Gerardo Leibner, *Camaradas y compañeros. Una historia política y social de los comunistas del Uruguay* (Montevideo: Trilce, 2011), 433.

35 Carlos Maria Gutierrez, "Electoralismo y revolución," *Marcha*, 8/30/1962, 19.

36 Ernesto Guevara, "Discurso en la Universidad de la República," August 17, 1961, www.archivochile.com, 10.

37 See Mauricio Bruno, *La caza del fantasma. Benito Nardone y el anticomunismo en Uruguay (1960–1962)* (Montevideo: Universidad de la República, FHCE, 2007).

38 *Marcha* "Asi empezó el fascismo," August 24, 1961, cover.

39 See Hugo Gambini, *El Che Guevara* (Argentina: Stockcero, 2002), 237–8.

40 Ruth Leacock, *Requiem for Revolution* (Ohio: Kent University Press, 1990) 35.

41 See Anderson, *Che*, and Fernando Martínez Heredia (comp.), *Che, el argentino* (Buenos Aires: Ediciones De Mano en Mano, 1997).

42 Tortti, *El viejo Partido Socialista y los orígenes de la "nueva izquierda*," 174–5.

43 See Daniel Campione, "Hacia la convergencia cívico-militar. Partido Comunista y 'Frente Democrático,' 1955–1976," *II Jornadas de Historia de las Izquierdas*, Buenos Aires, December 11, 12, and 13, 2002, CEDINCI. Cecilia Blanco, "El socialismo argentino de la euforia a la crisis de identidad, 1955–1958. Un análisis de la ideología política del PS desde el periódico La Vanguardia," *II Jornadas de Historia de las Izquierdas*. Buenos Aires, December 11, 12, and 13, 2002, CEDINCI. Trotskyists were not very hopeful about Frondizi, but Palabra Obrera decided to accept Perón's call to vote for Frondizi. Within the national Left, Frondizi had the support of renowned intellectuals such as David Viñas and Arturo Jauretche, who identified with his anti-imperialist stance. Silvia Sigal, *Intelectuales y poder en la década del sesenta* (Buenos Aires, Argentina: Punto Sur Editores, 1991), and Oscar Terán, *Nuestros años sesentas: la formación de la nueva izquierda intelectual argentina, 1956–1966* (Buenos Aires: Ed. El Cielo por Asalto, 1993).

44 James, *Resistance and Integration*, 146.

45 For an idea of the different activities and positions of the Argentine militants who were in Cuba in 1961, see the account by one of the members of the board of the Argentine-Cuban Friendship Institute: Amalio Juan Rey, *Sobre el mensaje del Che Guevara a los argentinos el 25 de mayo de 1962* (Córdoba: Narvaja Editor, 1999).

46 Manuel Justo Gaggero, "El encuentro con el Che: aquellos años," in Martínez Heredia, *Che, el argentino*.

47 See Sergio Nicanoff and Alex Castellano, *Las primeras experiencias guerrilleras en la Argentina: la historia del "Vasco" Bengochea y las Fuerzas Armadas de la Revolución Nacional* (Buenos Aires: Centro Cultural de la Cooperación Floreal Gorini, 2006). A conference delivered by Bengochea in Montevideo can be found in *Guerra de Guerrillas*, a brief book published in Montevideo. While the book does not indicate the year of the conference, considering that Bengochea died in 1964, it is likely that much of the issues addressed in that conference were part of the discussions he maintained with Guevara in 1962. The book suggests that guerrilla operations could be based either in the city, the countryside, or border areas, and analyzed the advantages of each, without giving a prescriptive solution. Angel Bengochea and J.J. López Silveira, *Guerra de guerrillas* (Montevideo: Editorial Uruguay, 1970), 67–73.

48 See Gaggero, "El encuentro con el Che: aquellos años."

49 Ernesto Guevara, "Mensaje a los argentinos," in Claudia Korol, *El Che y los argentinos* (Buenos Aires: Ediciones Dialéctica, 1988), 267.

50 Amalio Rey, one of the organizers, gives an account of a long conversation he had with Guevara when he went to invite him to the barbecue. Guevara took out a map and started discussing a plan to launch rural guerrilla actions in the mountains of Córdoba. When Rey disagreed with this idea, Guevara ignored him. See Rey, *Sobre el mensaje del Che a los argentinos el 25 de mayo de 1962*, 61–80.

51 See Ernesto Guevara, *Diarios de motocicleta* (Buenos Aires: Planeta, 2005).

52 The magazine and books published by this group would, however, play a major role in the renovation of Marxism in Latin America during the 1960s and 1970s. See Burgos, *Los gramscianos argentinos*.

53 For an overview of the EGP experience, see Rot, *Los orígenes perdidos de la guerrilla en la Argentina*, and the account by Ciro Bustos, *El Che quiere verte: la historia jamás contada del Che en Bolivia* (Buenos Aires: Javier Vergara Editor, 2007), first part.

54 See Nicanoff and Castellano, *Las primeras experiencias guerrilleras en la Argentina: la historia del "Vasco" Bengochea y las Fuerzas Armadas de la Revolución Nacional*.

55 Regis Debray, *Alabados sean nuestros señores. Una educación política* (Barcelona: Editorial Sudamericana, 1999), 50.

56 "I answered Fidel's telegram and shortly after he sent me to prepare Che's arrival to Bolivia. It was as an old friend of Guevara that Salvador Allende received me when I came out of prison in 1971. I met Mitterrand when I delivered a message to him from Allende near Pau, in 1972. And it was in my alleged capacity as Third World expert that the president elect introduced me at the Elyseum, in 1981. Everything is linked, connected through a minimum gesture." Debray, *Alabados*, 49–50.

57 Debray, *Alabados*, 67.

58 Regis Debray, "El castrismo: la gran marcha de América Latina," *Pasado y Presente*, year 2, no. 7–8 (October 1964–March 1965).

59 See the account by Héctor Schmucler in Burgos, *Los gramscianos argentinos*, 91.

60 See "Nota de la redacción," *Pasado y Presente*, year 2, no. 7–8 (October 1964–March 1965), 122.

61 Regis Debray, "¿Qué es el Castrismo?," *Punto Final*, no. 11 (1st fortnight of October 1966), 19. Regis Debray, "El castrismo: la larga marcha de América Latina," *Cuadernos de Marcha*. no. 3. (1967).

62 Debray, "El castrismo: la gran marcha de América Latina."

63 Regis Debray, "¿Revolución en la revolución?," *Cuadernos de la Revista Casa de las Américas* 1 (Havana: Casa, 1967).

64 Regis Debray, "¿Revolución en la revolución?," *Punto Final, Documentos*, no. 25 (1–15 March, 1967), 12.

65 Ibid., 33–4. These disagreements are illustrated, for example, in the debate between Adolfo Gilly and Fidel Castro in late 1965 and 1966. In the closing speech at the Tricontinental Conference, in reference to an article by Gilly published in *Marcha* on October 22, 1965, where Gilly claimed Guevara had to leave Cuba due to differences with Castro over the Sino-Soviet conflict and to Guevara's interest in furthering the revolution in Latin America, Castro speaks harshly against the Trotskyist influence in Latin America and points to the negative consequences that Yon Sosa's November 3 movement had in Guatemala. See Adolfo Gilly, "La renuncia del Che," *Marcha*, October 22, 1965; Fidel Castro, "Discurso pronunciado en el acto clausura de la Primera Conferencia de Solidaridad de los Pueblos de Asia, África y América Latina (Tricontinental), en el Teatro Chaplin, La Habana, el 15 de enero de 1966," http://www.cuba.cu/gobierno/discursos/; Adolfo Gilly, "Respuesta a Fidel Castro," *Marcha*, February 18, 1966.

66 Debray, *Revolución*, 108.

67 Ibid., 107.

68 Régis Debray, *La crítica de las armas* (Mexico: Siglo XXI, 1975), 217.

69 Régis Debray, "¿Revolución en la revolución?," *Punto Final, Documentos*, no. 25 (2nd fortnight of March 1967), no. 26 (1st fortnight of April 1967), no. 27 (2nd fortnight of April 1967); Regis Debray, "América Latina algunos problemas de estrategia revolucionaria," *Punto Final, Documentos*, no. 29 (2nd fortnight of May 1967); Régis Debray, "El castrismo: la gran marcha de América Latina," *Punto Final, Documentos*, no. 30 (1st fortnight of June 1967).

70 See: *Elisabeth Burgos-Debray Papers*. Hoover Institution Archives. Box:13–14

71 Lionel Abel, "Seven Heroes of the New Left," *New York Times*, May 5, 1968.

72 See: Carlos Núñez, "Por Debray, por la revolución, por nosotros," *Punto Final*, 2nd fortnight of June, 1967, no. 31, 18

73 Alberto Methol Ferre, *Regis Debray y la ideología de la revolución en América Latina*, Cuadernos Latinoamericanos (Montevideo: Instituto de Estudios Americanos, 1968), 8.

74 Debray, Ibid., 210.

75 See "Reseña sucinta de la polémica suscitada por ¿Revolución en la Revolución?," in Ibid., 212.

76 See, for example, the PRT document by Sergio Domecq, Carlos Ramírez, and Juan Candela (pseudonyms), *El único camino para la toma del poder y el socialismo* (Ediciones Combate, 1969), Archivo CEDINCI, and Movimiento de Liberación Nacional Tupamaros, *Documento no. 1*, 1967, Archivo de la lucha armada, David Campora, CEIU.

77 Flavio Tavares, *Memórias do esquecimento* (Sao Paulo: Globo, 1999), 175.

78 Philip Agee, *La CIA por dentro, diario de un espía* (Buenos Aires: Editorial Sudamericana, 1987), 265. According to Agee, the Montevideo station was the only CIA station in the hemisphere where anti-Cuba operations were the top priority, taking precedence over operations against the Soviet embassy.

79 Victor R. Duré and Agripino Silva, "Frente Unido de Liberación Nacional (1959–1965), guerra de guerrillas como guerra del pueblo," and Roberto Céspedes and Roberto Paredes, "La resistencia armada al stronismo: panorama general," in *Revista Nova Polis* 8 (August 2004).

80 CLAEH, *Indicadores básicos, Cultura, sociedad y política* (Montevideo: CLAEH, 1991).

81 See Instituto de Economía, *El Uruguay del siglo XX, La economía* (Montevideo: Banda Oriental, 2003), 29, and Germán Rama, *La democracia en Uruguay* (Buenos Aires: Cuadernos del. Rial, Grupo Editor Latinoamericano, 1987), 75.

82 For an overview of the various uses of the concept of crisis, see Aldo Marchesi and Jaime Yaffé, "La violencia bajo la lupa. Una revisión de la literatura sobre violencia y política en los sesenta," *Revista Uruguaya de Ciencia Política* 19 (2010).

83 See Aldo Marchesi and Jaime Yaffé, "La violencia bajo la lupa."

84 Mario Benedetti, *El país de la cola de paja* (Montevideo: ARCA, 1966). For a description of Benedetti's political commitment, see Hortensia Campanella, *Mario Benedetti, un mito discretísimo* (Montevideo: Planeta, 2009); and José Gabriel Lagos, "Una 'zona intermedia' entre el Benedetti moral y el Benedetti político" (unpublished).

85 Benedetti, *El País*, p. 58.

86 See Lagos, "Una 'zona intermedia'."

87 Benedetti, *El País de la cola de paja*, p. 143.

88 Ibid., pp. 153–4. Cited by Lagos in "Una 'zona intermedia'."

89 See Luis Camnitzer, *Didáctica de la liberación. Arte conceptualista latinoamericano* (Montevideo: HUM, 2008); Francisco Panizza, "Los codigos y simbolos de la épica tupamara," *Cuadernos del CLAEH*, no. 36, Montevideo, 1985; and Fernando Andacht, *Signos reales del Uruguay imaginario* (Montevideo: Trilce, 1992). See page 86–7.

90 Instituto de Economía, *El proceso económico del Uruguay* (Montevideo: Universidad de la República, 1969), pp. 257–71.

91 In 1962, the Unión Popular (UP), a coalition led by the Socialist Party (PS), obtained 2.3 percent of the vote, with the Frente Izquierda de Liberación (FIDEL), led by the Communist Party, obtaining 3.5 percent. Added together, the Left's share remained less than 6 percent of the total. In 1966, FIDEL obtained 5.7 percent, while the Socialist Party coalition disbanded. The PS obtained 0.9 percent and the Unión Popular 0.2 percent.

92 In 1962, the National Party won the elections with 46.5 percent of the vote, while the Colorado Party obtained 44.5 percent. In 1966, the Colorado Party won the elections with 49.3 percent of the vote, with the National Party obtaining 40.4 percent.

93 Héctor Rodríguez, "Dos caminos ante los sindicatos," *Marcha*, January 11, 1963, p. 10.

94 See, among other works, Magdalena Broquetas, "Los frentes del anticomunismo. Las derechas en el Uruguay de los tempranos sesenta," *Contemporánea. Historia y problemas del siglo XX*. 3:3 (2012); Mauricio Bruno, *La caza del fantasma. Benito Nardone y el anticomunismo en Uruguay (1960–1962)* (Montevideo: FHCE, 2007); Gabriel Bucheli, "Organizaciones 'demócratas' y radicalización anticomunista en Uruguay, 1959–1962," *Contemporánea. Historia y problemas del siglo XX*. 3:3 (2012); Roberto Garcia Ferreira, "El Cine Trocadero: un testigo de la Guerra Fría," *Contemporánea: Historia y problemas del siglo XX* 1:1 (2010); and Mariana Iglesias, "En procura del orden interno: sentidos y estrategias en torno a la sanción de medidas de excepción en el Uruguay de mediados del siglo XX," *Nuevo Mundo Mundos Nuevos* (2009).

95 See "El gobierno contra el derecho de reunión. Decretó medidas de seguridad. Quieren el golpe," *Época*, April, 9, 1965, cover; and "Dictadura legal," *Época*, October 8, 1965, cover. For a general overview of the period, see Rosa Alonso Eloy and Carlos Demasi, *Uruguay, 1958–1968: crisis y estancamiento* (Montevideo: Ediciones de la Banda Oriental, 1986).

96 For bibliography on the Brazilian influence see: Ananda Simões Fernandes, "Quando o inimigo ultrapassa a fronteira: as conexões repressivas entre a ditadura civil-militar brasileira eo Uruguai (1964–1973)," (MA thesis, Historia Universidade Federal do Rio Grande do Sul, Porto Alegre, 2009); and Gissele Cassol, "Prisão e tortura em terra estrangeira: a colaboração repressiva entre Brasil e Uruguai (1964–1985)" (MA thesis, Universidade Federal de Santa Maria 2008).

97 See, for example, the events prompted by Brizola's confinement. *Época*, "Brizola fue internado sin pruebas," back page, March 23, 1965.

98 American Embassy Montevideo, "Joint Week no. 19," May 15, 1965. Uruguay, Box 2791, RG 59, NARA, College Park, Maryland.

99 See *Época*, "Entrevista Onganía-Costa: 'Uruguay, un grave peligro'," September 1, 1965, 7. *Época*, "¿Otra vez la Cisplatina?," September 6, 1965, 7. The news raised concern among Uruguayan diplomats in Argentina and Brazil. See "Declaraciones General Juan Carlos Onganía," Argentina, Confidential Folder no. 20, 1965. Archive of the Ministry of Foreign Affairs, Uruguay.

100 See González Sierra, *Los olvidados*, p. 218.

101 For a biography of Sendic, see Blixen, *Sendic*.

102 Clara Aldrighi, *La izquierda armada: ideología, ética e identidad en el MLN-Tupamaros* (Montevideo: Ediciones Trilce, 2001); Andrés Cultelli, *La revolución necesaria, contribución a la autocrítica del MLN Tupamaros* (Buenos Aires: Colihue, 2006); Eleuterio Fernández Huidobro, *Historia de los Tupamaros*, 3 vol. (Montevideo: Tupac Amaru, 1986); Hebert Gatto, *El cielo por asalto: el Movimiento de Liberación Nacional (Tupamaros) y la izquierda uruguaya (1963–1972)* (Montevideo: Taurus, 2004); Maria Esther Gilio, *La guerrilla tupamara* (La Habana: Casa de las Américas, 1970); José Harari, *Contribución a la historia del MLN (Tupamaros)* (Montevideo: Editorial Plural, 1987); Alain Labrousse, *Una historia de los Tupamaros: De Sendic a Mujica* (Montevideo: Editorial Fin

de Siglo, 2009); Alfonso Lessa, *La revolución imposible: los tupamaros y el fracaso de la vía armada en el Uruguay del siglo XX* (Montevideo: Editorial Fin de Siglo, 2002); Eduardo Rey Tristán, *A la vuelta de la esquina: la izquierda revolucionaria uruguaya, 1955–1973* (Montevideo: Fin de Siglo, 2006). On the "coordinator," see Nicolas Duffau, *El coordinador (1963–1965) La participación de los militantes del Partido Socialista en los inicios de la violencia revolucionaria en Uruguay*, Colección Estudiantes (Montevideo: Universidad de la República, FHCE, 2008), and Rolando Sasso, *Tupamaros, los comienzos* (Montevideo: Editorial Fin de Siglo, 2010).

103 For a reflection on the methodological dilemmas involved in the reconstruction of this process, see Marina Cardozo, "'El cordero nunca se salvó balando': reflexiones acerca de los relatos de un militante de la izquierda armada," in several authors, *Recordar para pensar. Memoria para la democracia. La elaboración del pasado reciente en el cono sur de América Latina* (Santiago de Chile: Ediciones Böll Cono Sur, 2010).

104 "In the so-called national and traditional Left, the communist and socialist parties, the anarchists, etc. (a very long etcetera, as even Blancos [National Party members] and Colorados play at being leftists) compete against each other over who is more revolutionary, but if there is one feature that stands out in this Left is the dualism between thinking and acting, between ideology and commitment.

For self-proclaimed Uruguayan revolutionaries, defining themselves as such does not seem to entail an ethics, an imperative to guide their actions and their lives, but rather a vaguely critical and/or analytical intellectual attitude.
Revolution is doing – and naturally – with some knowledge and idealism, even if that bothers the orthodox Marxist-Leninists. By idealism we mean man's influence on reality, changing it according to his ideas.
That is our barricade." "Ser y hacer," *Barricada*, no. 1, September 1964, 3.

105 "La marcha de los cañeros y la reordenación de la izquierda uruguaya," *Barricada*, no. 1, September 1964, 4.

106 By Arismendi-Quijano line he meant the position held by the general secretary of the Communist Party, Rodney Arismendi, and by Carlos Quijano, the director of the weekly newspaper *Marcha*.

107 Rey Tristán, *A la vuelta de la esquina*, 112.

108 See Ciro Bustos, "El sueño revolucionario del Che era Argentina," interview by Jaime Padilla, Malmö, Sweden, 1997, available in Archivo Cedinci and Bustos, *El Che quiere verte*, 231–239. For the reactions to the EGP in Uruguay, see the articles featured in *Marcha*. Rogelio García Lupo, "Masetti, un suicida," *Marcha*, May 14, 1965, 18; Rodolfo Walsh, "Masetti, un guerrillero," May 14, 1965, 19.

109 See Eduardo Pérez, "Una aproximación a la historia de las Fuerzas Armadas Peronistas," in Eduardo Duhalde and Eduardo Pérez, *De Taco Ralo a la alternativa independiente. Historia documental de las Fuerzas Armadas Peronistas y del Peronismo de base* (La Plata: De la Campana, 2003); Alejandra Dandan and Silvina Heguy, *Joe Baxter, del nazismo a la extrema izquierda La historia secreta de un guerrillero* (Argentina: Editorial Norma, 2006), chapter 7; and Bustos, *El Che quiere verte*.

110 For an example of Cooke's activities in Montevideo, see "Carta a Héctor Tristán," in Eduardo Luis Duhalde (comp.), *John W. Cooke. Obra completa. Artículos periodísticos, reportajes, cartas y documentos*, vol. 3 (Buenos Aires: Ediciones Colihue, 2009), 45.

111 For an overview of Guillén's biography, see Guillermo Daniel Nañez, "Abraham Guillén: Los remotos orígenes de la guerrilla peronista 1955–1960," in *Historia, Publicación del Instituto Superior de Formación Docente (Berazategui)*, no. 50, year 4, no. 3; Hernán Reyes, "Abraham Guillén: teórico de la lucha armada," *Lucha Armada* no. 4, September–November 2005; interview with Abraham Guillén, *Bicicleta, Revista*

de comunicaciones libertarias, October 1978, Spain; and "¿Quién es Abraham Guillén?" interview in Carlos A. Aznarez and Jaime E. Cañas, *Tupamaros? Fracaso del Che?* (Buenos Aires: Ediciones Orbe, 1969) 167–77.

112 Eduardo Pérez, "Una aproximación a la historia de las Fuerzas Armadas Peronistas," 48, 51.

113 For a biography of Joe Baxter, see Heguy and Dandan, *Joe Baxter. Del nazismo a la extrema izquierda*. On Nell Tacci's imprisonment, see John Willam Cooke, "El caso Nell, clave para el proceso político argentino," *Marcha*, May 31, 1968, and Ariel Collazo, "La extradición de Nell no debe ser concedida," May 24, 1968. See also the initial accounts of *Al Rojo Vivo*, January 31, 1967.

114 See *Época*, "Chispa guerrillera en Brasil," March 27, 1965, 5.

115 See Denise Rollemberg, *O apoio de Cuba à luta armada no Brasil: o treinamento guerrilheiro* (Rio de Janeiro, RJ: Mauad, 2001), chapter 2; Jose Caldas, *Caparaó, a primeira guerrilha contra a ditadura* (Sao Paulo: Boitempo Ed., 2007). See also the account by Flavio Tavares, *Memorias do Esquecimento* (Sao Paulo: Globo, 1999), 173–205. On the coordination with Guevara in Bolivia, Manuel "Barbarroja" Piñeiro indicates that support groups were being formed in Argentina and Brazil when Guevara began his campaign. See Manuel Piñeiro, *Che Guevara y la revolución latinoamericana* (Colombia: Ocean Sur, 2006), 97–98. For the links between exiles in Montevideo and the planning of Caparaó, see Artigas Rodríguez Devicenzi "Asunto: Actividades del ex-diputado Leonel Brizola" (May 8, 1967), Brazil, box 169, Archive of the Foreign Affairs Ministry, Uruguay.

116 Envar El Kadri and Jorge Rulli, *Diálogos en el exilio* (Argentina: Forosur, 1984), 178.

117 Leibner, *Camaradas y compañeros*, 481.

118 Blixen, *Sendic*, 108.

119 See *Época*, "Castelo nos gobierna internaron a Brizola" January 30, 1965, 1.

120 See Correspondence of Pablo Vicente, in Juan Domingo Perón Papers, Box 6 and 7. Hoover Institution Archives.

121 See Fernández Huidobro, *Historia de los Tupamaros.* vol. 2, 69–71, and Blixen, *Sendic*, 122–4.

122 In this sense, one of the most quoted works by some Tupamaros was *The Revolt* by Menachem Begin. See Rey Tristán, *A la vuelta de la esquina*, 173.

123 See Blixen, *Sendic*, 123; Jorge Torres, *Tupamaros: la derrota en la mira* (Montevideo: Editorial Fin de Siglo, 2002), 114, 184, 347–60.

124 Abraham Guillén, *Estrategia de la guerrilla urbana* (Montevideo: Manuales del pueblo, 1966).

125 No copies of Torres' text have survived but several of his fellow militants say it was the basis for the MLN-T's Document No. 1, which was adopted by the organization in June 1967. The document has some aspects that are indeed very similar to Guillén's 1966 book (Blixen, *Sendic*. 139–140). Abraham Guillén became an influential urban guerrilla thinker, publishing books on the subject in Latin America, Spain, and the United States. He even described himself as "the tactical and strategic inspiration" of the Tupamaros, although he did not identify with them politically because of his "libertarian background." See *Bicicleta, revista de comunicaciones libertarias*, year 1, no. 9, October 1978.

126 It is likely that both Torres and Guillén were aware of the text of Bengochea's *Guerra de guerrillas* conference, or knew at least of his discussion with Guevara, where he argued that guerrilla operations could be based in the city, the countryside, or border areas. See Bengochea and López Silveira, *Guerra de guerrillas*, 67–73.

127 Documento I, in INDAL, *Movimiento de Liberación Nacional (Tupamaros): documentación propia* (Belgium: Heverlee-Louvain: Information documentaire d'Amérique latine, 1973).

128 *Punto Final*, "30 preguntas a un tupamaro," July 2, 1968, no. 58, document section.

129 See *Cristianismo y Revolución*, October 1968, no. 10.

130 Jorge Chagas and Gustavo Trullen, *Pacheco, la trama oculta del poder* (Montevideo: Rumbo, 2005), 172.

131 *Punto Final*, "30 preguntas a un tupamaro," 7–8. The reference to "creating many Vietnams" is taken from Guevara's Message to the May 1967 Tricontinental Conference.

132 Francisco Panizza, *Uruguay: Batllismo y después. Pacheco, militares y tupamaros en la crisis del Uruguay Batllista* (Montevideo: Banda Oriental, 1990), 152.

133 "Respuesta del MLN al semanario Al Rojo Vivo," in Omar Costa (comp.), *Los Tupamaros* (Mexico: Ediciones Era, 1971), 139.

134 Carlos A. Aznarez and Jaime E. Cañas, *Tupamaros: Fracaso del Che? Un análisis objetivo de la actualidad uruguaya* (Buenos Aires: Ediciones Orbe, 1969).

135 Guillermo Caviasca, *Dos caminos. ERP-Montoneros en los setenta* (Buenos Aires: Centro Cultural de la Cooperación Floreal Gorini, 2006), 67.

136 "The *foco* is a generator of conscience and is in no way a specific combat unit, existing in a specific strategic framework in a given national society. The Tupamaros have no rural guerrilla column, they have cells (or "columns," as they call them) that carry out urban guerrilla actions, but that doesn't mean they don't have a *foco*. They most certainly do." *Cristianismo y Revolución*, no. 28, April 1972, 58.

137 See Juan Carlos Cibelli, "Orígenes de la FAL," *Lucha Armada en la Argentina*, no. 1; Gabriel Rot, "Notas para una historia de la lucha armada en la argentina. Las Fuerzas Argentinas de Liberación," *Políticas de la Memoria*, no. 4, Summer 2003, 2004.

138 Taken from Pablo, "Informe y propuesta a los militantes," in Rot, *Notas para la historia de una lucha armada*, 153. This organization did not survive the polarization that divided Peronists and anti-Peronists in Argentina's armed organizations.

139 Daniel de Santis, "Carta a un tupamaro. Desde el alma y con dolor. Carta abierta a Eleuterio Fernández Huidobro," in Daniel de Santis, *Entre tupas y perros* (Buenos Aires: Ed. R y R, 2005).

140 See Guillén, in *Bicicleta, revista de comunicaciones libertarias*, year 1, no. 9, October 1978.

141 Marlon Aseff, *Retratos do Exilio, Solidariedade e Resistencia na Fronteira* (Santa Cruz do Sul: EDUNISC, 2009), 122.

142 The MIR was particularly concerned with the coverage that these actions would have in the press and engaged a large number of its leaders in them. See Andrés Pascal Allende, *El MIR Chileno, una experiencia revolucionaria* (Argentina: Ediciones Cucaña, 2003), 39; Interviews with Andrés Pascal Allende conducted by the author and Max Marambio, *Las armas de ayer* (Santiago: La Tercera, Debate, 2007), 67.

143 See Regis Debray, *Los Tupamaros en acción* (Mexico: Editorial Diógenes, 1972), 8.

II

The Subjective Bonds of Revolutionary Solidarity. From Havana to Ñancahuazú (Bolivia), 1967

How far my land is / And, yet, how close / or is there a territory /
    where our bloods mingle as one /
So much distance, so many roads / such different flags /
    yet poverty is the same / and the same men are waiting.
I want to tear up my map / draw up a map of everyone /
    mestizos, blacks, and whites / linking their arms together.
The rivers are like bloodstreams / running through a vast,
    sprawling body / and the scarlet color of the land is / the blood
    of the fallen.
We are not the foreigners / the foreigners are others /
    they are the merchants / and we the slaves.
I want to tear up life / change it completely / give me your
    hand, *compañero* / come help me, don't be long / a drop alone
    is nothing / but with others it becomes a downpour.

These verses, sung to the tune of a *milonga* – an urban music genre typical of the Río de la Plata region, were penned by Daniel Viglietti during his first visit to Havana, Cuba, in the months of July and August 1967. This young guitarist and singer-songwriter was in Cuba participating in the First International Protest Song Meeting, one of the many activities organized under the Conference of the Organization for Latin American Solidarity. The song begins on a melancholic note with the traditional yearning for one's homeland. However, it quickly veers toward other views of distance and cultural and political borders.

Havana in 1967 was the "territory where our bloods mingle as one," where far became near, and where one was no longer a foreigner. Besides the concrete experience of being in Havana at a time when the city was receiving thousands of militants, artists, and intellectuals from across Latin America who engaged in stimulating cultural and political discussions, Viglietti expressed how distances and geographies were changing in the perspectives of some sectors of Latin America's Left. The impression was that maps were being torn up and the "map of everyone" was being drawn from the different revolutionary experiences that were taking place in Latin America: a drop alone is nothing / but with others it becomes a downpour.[1]

The search for new political strategies, languages, and practices that signified a relative departure from the initial ideas of the Cuban revolutionaries did not mean that the activists of the new Southern Cone Left no longer acknowledged the Cuban Revolution as having spearheaded a new path for Latin America, nor did it entail their adoption of a more local perspective.[2] On the contrary, the defense of specific conditions was inextricably linked to a strategy that could only be continental, and which the Cuban Revolution radicalized in 1967.[3]

Starting in 1966 a change began to take place in the way these Southern Cone groups interpreted the discourse of the continental strategy of the revolution. Until that year most of the initiatives promoted by the Cuban Revolution were connected with other regions of Latin American, with the exception of the EGP in Argentina, which appears to have been a personal project of Guevara's. Three developments in the years 1966 and 1967 led these nascent organizations to view the issue of continentality differently from how they had viewed it until then: the Conference of the Organization of Solidarity with the People of Africa, Asia, and Latin America, held in January 1966; Guevara's Bolivia campaign, carried out from 1966 to 1967; and the Conference of the Organization for Latin American Solidarity, held in July 1967. These events were pivotal in helping to build this notion of subjective closeness in the map of the Latin American revolution. It was an identity that went beyond a mere political declaration of solidarity and touched on emotional aspects associated with the idea of belonging to a movement whose collective action transcended borders and was coordinated in a unified manner.

A Territory Where Our Bloods Mingle as One: The Tricontinental and the OLAS

In January 1966 Cuba hosted the Tricontinental Conference. This event sought to reactivate the Third World movement that had been launched in Bandung in 1956. But the aim was not just to revitalize that movement; it was also to redefine it by giving it new contents that entailed an even greater convergence of the idea of Third Worldism and the various socialist projects that were being attempted in different parts of the world. This explains the changes proposed with respect to previous experiences, like Bandung or the movement of non-aligned countries. The aim was to incorporate Latin America into what until then had been a series of Afro–Asian conferences. The Tricontinental Conference did not only invite states to participate, it also engaged political movements that were fighting for national liberation in different countries of the Third World. With respect to previous experiences, the host of this conference expressed a series of changes that had occurred in the last decade, shifting the focus from the issues of development and independence to the language of revolution and socialism.[4] Besides these changes, the conference showed a wide variety of positions within and outside the so-called communist camp. In contrast to earlier conferences, in this case the Soviet Union had been invited, causing much friction with China. There were also many other clashes, most notably around the Israel question, the tensions between China and India, and a range of regional conflicts. As host, the Cuban government tried to maintain a neutral stance, which at times was seen by the new Southern Cone Left as ambiguous, or as evidencing a proximity to the Soviet Union. This alignment with the Soviet Union, along with the fact that the Cuban government chose primarily Soviet-leaning communist parties to extend its invitations to Latin American delegations and Ernesto Guevara's absence from the conference prompted multiple critical readings by members of the New Left, in particular those with Trotskyist and Maoist tendencies in various places of Latin America.[5] Others, however, viewed the conference favorably; they saw it as an initial step in the construction of a common global language for the revolutionaries of the world.

The conference had significant repercussions in Latin America. The leader of Chile's Socialist Party, senator Salvador Allende, said, almost prophetically:

The Johnson Doctrine constitutes for the Chilean people, as for all the countries of Latin America, an explicit declaration that imperialists will respond with violence to any popular movement that has any chance of coming into power. This has made the Chilean popular movement – which has achieved notable gains expanding and deepening democracy in our country – clearly realize that the United States will use force to prevent it from accessing power by democratic and legal means.

It also means that, consequently, we have an obligation to intensify our struggle; mobilize the masses, link anti-imperialist actions to the everyday demands of the population: strikes, land occupations, collective mobilizations, and the awareness that we will meet with opposition from reactionary violence and we will oppose it with revolutionary violence.

It will be the people of Chile and our country's conditions that will determine what method we use to defeat the imperialist enemy and its allies. We know that this struggle is extremely harsh and difficult for one country to take on by itself, and that to make it easier we will need to be backed by international support and solidarity.[6]

Based on these arguments, Allende called for the creation of an "initiative aimed at permanently connecting and coordinating the anti-imperialist actions of the Latin American people." That an emblematic advocate of the peaceful and electoral path to socialism was warning of the risks of reactionary violence, and the need to consider revolutionary violence, reveals the fluidity of a historical period in which, as we will see in later chapters, the two paths were not viewed as necessarily antagonistic in terms of political principles, but rather as strategic dilemmas connected with the struggle for social change, which admitted different stances depending on the place. This is evident in the close relationship between Allende and Castro, who voiced their differences publicly but also made it clear that they believed they were both part of the same historical movement, and in the Chilean case, in the talks that Allende had with groups that questioned the electoral path.[7]

According to Richard Gott, Latin America's communist parties and Fidel Castro himself were initially against Allende's position.[8] It is likely that they had assessed the risks that such an initiative would entail, as it would evidence all the conflicts that were emerging at the local level. However, in the days immediately following the conference the delegations of Peru and Venezuela – which represented armed groups that at that moment generated great expectations in Cuba – also raised the need to create a body to coordinate anti-imperialist actions in Latin America. This, combined with Allende's proposal, led the Latin American sectors that had participated in the Tricontinental Conference to agree to create the Organization for Latin American Solidarity (OLAS). The document containing the decision to create the OLAS stated that an examination of organizational problems and a general review of strategic and tactical issues had suggested that a continental body should be created to unite, coordinate, and further the struggle against U.S. imperialism.[9]

The Tricontinental meeting, and the call for the OLAS conference that followed, had strong repercussions in the United States and some Latin American governments. In the same month as the Tricontinental Conference, the Peruvian government convened an extraordinary meeting of the OAS to consider what it claimed was the Soviet Union's active role in support of "subversive movements" in Latin America.[10] Venezuela joined in denouncing Cuba's intervention in the continent. Both governments were facing guerrilla movements that were supported explicitly by Cuba. In the case of Venezuela it was an organization – the Fuerzas Armadas de Liberación Nacional (National Liberation Armed Forces), formed primarily by members of the Venezuelan Communist Parties and activists who had broken away from Acción Democrática (Democratic Action); in Peru, it was the Movimiento de Izquierda Revolucionario (Movement of the Revolutionary Left), founded initially by former APRA members. Both movements received different forms of support from the Cuban Revolution.

In 1963, the OAS had established a special security committee to counter the subversive action of international communism.[11] Through this

Figure 2.a. Illustration on the impact of OLAS´ Conference. Back cover of Magazine Punto Final. N. 35. Second fortnight of August 1967.

committee, the OAS closely monitored the development of the international solidarity conferences promoted by Cuba in 1966 and 1967. Three special meetings of foreign ministers were also convened to examine the resolutions of the Tricontinental and OLAS conferences. These actions of the OAS entailed a new level of open confrontation with Cuba and the political forces of the Left in the region.

In 1966, the Soviet Union tried to dispel the accusations regarding its role in Latin America, declaring in numerous occasions that its participation in the Tricontinental Conference in no way questioned its amicable relationship with the different governments of Latin America.[12] Generally speaking, the Soviets were not looking to support these guerrilla groups. However, according to research by Daniela Spenser, while the Soviet Union did not appear to back such initiatives, it did ultimately provide assistance through Czechoslovakia. The main aim of the Soviets was to maintain a good relationship with Cuba due to the symbolic prestige that such an

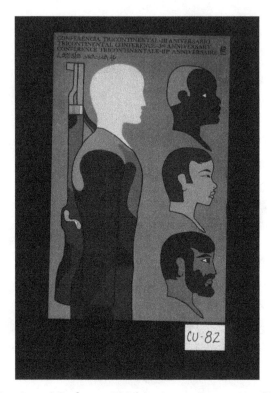

Figure 2.b. Tricontinental Conference, Third Anniversary Poster. 1970. Hoover Archives.

alliance gave them, in a context of profound divisions within the communist world. That aim led them, at times, to disregard some of the principles of peaceful coexistence in its foreign policy in order to make concessions to the Cubans, such as providing modest economic aid to some guerrilla organizations.[13]

In contrast to the Soviet Union, Cuba stepped up its aggressive foreign policy in the region. The concerns that Cuba would adopt the peaceful coexistence policy proposed by the Soviet Union in Latin America began to diminish in the months following the Tricontinental Conference. On July 26, 1966, Fidel Castro delivered a speech that dispelled some of the previous uncertainties. Among other things, he denounced the "pseudo-revolutionaries" who argued that conditions were not ripe in Latin America to launch an armed struggle, and accused them of being "the best allies of imperialism and exploitation," as:

they try to hold back the revolutions, [they are] the defeatists, those who don't want to fight [...] But one thing we are certain of is that in the vast majority of the countries of Latin America the conditions for a revolution are superior to the conditions that existed in Cuba, and if these revolutions do not happen it is because in those countries many of the self-proclaimed revolutionaries lack conviction (applause) [...] And it is a mistake to believe that conscience comes first and only then the struggle. The struggle has to come first, and once the struggle begins, a growing surge of revolutionary conscience will inevitably follow!"[14]

Castro's speech contained a strong criticism of the Latin American communist parties aligned with the Soviet Union, which had for the most part opposed the armed strategies furthered by Cuba. The key points of the speech were communicated by the media of the Southern Cone New Left that expressed that same view. In Uruguay the speech was published in full by the newspaper *Época*. The magazine *Punto Final* summarized the impact of the speech stating, "In Chile's case the choice is simple: reformism or revolution."[15] What the reactions to this speech clearly revealed was the belief that regardless of the conditions that existed in each country, initiating a revolutionary struggle could bring about subjective conditions faster, and the Cuban Revolution would support those who took that approach on a national level, even if it meant going against the position of the communist parties that followed the Soviet line.[16]

In April 1967, Guevara, whose whereabouts were unknown since 1965, published a powerful manifesto in the first number of the *Tricontinental* magazine, in which he defended the idea of a "global war against imperialism" strategy developed by the "exploited and backward peoples of the world" whose "strategic objective, then, will be the real liberation of the peoples; a liberation that will be achieved through armed struggle, in most cases, and which in America will be, almost inevitably, a Socialist Revolution."

The text confirmed two issues that were important for the sectors of the New Left. First, it put to rest the rumors of possible disagreements between Castro and Guevara. Guevara appeared once again in a publication of the revolution with a message that ran counter to the peaceful coexistence policy of the Soviet Union. Second, the text went beyond a mere declaration of continentality to propose certain notions of what a strategy of global struggle against imperialism would be. The military strategy consisted in "draw[ing] the enemy out of his natural environment, forcing him to fight in places where his living habits clash with the existing reality," leading to "two, three, many Vietnams sprouting around the globe." Militants had to be inspired by proletarian internationalism, as "[e]very drop of blood spilled in a land under whose flag one was not born in is experience gained by the survivor to be applied later in the struggle for liberation of one's own country."[17]

By June 1967 that declaration was spreading across the Southern Cone. Among other things, Guevara's article enabled a reading that belied the exceptionality that some Southern Cone elites claimed for their countries. Images portraying the exceptionality of these countries – such as those describing Chileans as "English," or Uruguay as the "Switzerland of America," or Argentines as the "Europeans" of the continent – had been used repeatedly to highlight the differences that set them apart from the rest of Latin America. It is true that, as noted in the introduction, these countries had attained privileged levels of development in comparison to other areas of Latin America. However, that tended to obscure the situation of rural lower classes living under conditions comparable to those in the rest of the continent, including similar levels of poverty, marginalization, and racism, as was denounced by these groups. Moreover, these claims tended to overlook the geopolitical situation of subordination to the United States in the context of the Cold War. As the Cold War advanced in Latin America, bringing with it a growing influence of the United States, it relativized those national exceptionalities.

The logic of the Cold War explained "the global war against imperialism," proposed by Guevara, in which national differences were blurred and subsumed into a conflict that was to be international and would affect the entire continent. The MIR put it clearly: "Chile will not be an exception."[18] An early 1968 text by Argentina's PRT interpreted Guevara's message along the same lines. This document asked:

Why does Che say two, three, many Vietnams, and not two, three, many Cubas? Because he recognizes the exceptional nature of the Cuban Revolution, which will not come again. Because the strategic assessment of the global revolution as a whole foresees the inevitable intervention of imperialism before the revolution can seize power.[19]

In that interpretation, the global conflict erased national particularities as, sooner or later, the conflict would be reduced to a conflict between "popular" forces and the empire, which would intervene in the different national territories.

In July 1967, Uruguay's MLN-T published its *Documento 1* (Document No. 1), which included a chapter devoted to the continental scope of the revolution that "endorsed Guevara's document in all its terms." It argued that if "repression and counterrevolution are taken to a continental scale, revolution should not stop at the national border." It also proposed a strategy aimed at wearing down imperialist forces, which involved attacking them on various fronts in different places of Latin America.[20]

The *Message to the Tricontinental* was published at the same time as rumors of Guevara's possible involvement in a guerrilla movement in Bolivia began to circulate. As many have noted, Guevara's plan to act in

South America was not limited to a specific country but was instead based on a continental conception of revolutionary strategy, which had points in common with the *Message to the Tricontinental*.

The OLAS Conference was held while Guevara's Bolivia campaign was underway. In July 1967, members of different organizations of Latin America's Left met in Havana for the first time ever to collectively discuss political strategies. The conference was attended by 164 leaders from twenty-seven Latin American countries, and one of the leaders of the Black Power Movement, Stokeley Carmichael, as guest participant from the United States. Participants were divided into four working committees to discuss: (1) the anti-imperialist revolutionary struggle in Latin America; (2) a common stance and actions against the political and military intervention and economic and ideological penetration of imperialism in Latin America; (3) the solidarity of the peoples of Latin America with national liberation struggles; and (4) the statutes of the OLAS.

Pressure from the Cuban hosts and the general desire that the conference be held in an atmosphere of unity enabled agreements in three of the four committees. However, the greatest differences arose in the third committee, which dealt with the more sensitive issues of Latin American solidarity, pitting the Cubans against the communist parties aligned with the Soviet Union. A motion condemning the Soviet Union for its technical aid to the governments of Chile, Brazil, and Colombia received fifteen votes in favor, eight abstentions, and the negative votes of the Salvadorian, Bolivian, and Uruguayan communist parties. The same occurred with a motion to censure the Venezuelan Communist Party for abandoning the guerrilla movement. This situation led some communists to threaten to walk out of the conference as a form of pressure. However, as the communists met the intransigency of the Cubans with their decision to stay, the disagreements continued until the end of the conference.[21]

OLAS discussions focused on how to provide effective solidarity to countries that, like Cuba, had defeated imperialism, or those that, like Venezuela, Colombia, Brazil, Bolivia, Guatemala, and Peru, had launched "a final battle" against it. In this sense, there were two positions: while the Cubans argued that the only way to promote solidarity was to deploy a strategy of continental armed struggle, the pro-Soviet communist parties held a more moderate view, which did not discard the possibility of armed struggle, but considered it only one of many forms of political activism, together with electoral confrontation and unionism.

By the end of the conference the Cuban position had prevailed. According to the Cubans, the series of U.S. interventions that followed after the fall of Árbenz in Guatemala in 1954 – including the Bay of Pigs invasion to Cuba, the military intervention in the Dominican Republic, and a total of ten coup d'états staged from 1961 to 1966 and enthusiastically supported by the United States – provided the most conclusive evidence that the United States would crush any possibility of social change attempted through legal and peaceful means.[22] The OLAS response to this process of "continentalization" from above through imperialist means would be a "continentalization" from below through revolutionary means. The conference concluded that:

(1) Revolution constitutes a right and a duty of the peoples of Latin America....
(2) All other forms of struggle must further, and not delay, the development of the essential form, which is armed struggle.
(3) For most countries in the continent the problem of organizing, initiating, developing, and concluding an armed struggle is today the most pressing and fundamental task of the revolutionary movement.
(4) Those countries in which this task is not yet seen as an immediate one may nonetheless consider it as an inevitable perspective in the development of their national revolutionary struggle.[23]

Such continentalization from below was based, not only on present political reasons, but also on historical grounds connected with the continent's political tradition. In multiple discourses an analogy was made between the early nineteenth century independence wars against the Spanish empire and current political struggles. The former were conceptualized as an armed struggle to which the peoples had adhered and some elites had betrayed. Moreover, both past and present struggles were continental. The general declaration said:

Simón Bolívar, the epitome of the liberators of that time, declared: "For us, the homeland is America." These men who embodied the revolutionary vanguard of the movement for emancipation were not only conscious that the struggle was one and the same, from the Río Bravo to the Patagonia, they also set out together to free the common homeland with actions that were also common and transcended borders."[24]

Regardless of whether these analogies were historically accurate or not, the option for the revolution manifested through these statements also involved establishing a nationalist legitimacy in a Cold War context in which the OAS was trying to present the revolution as something that was foreign to the Latin American tradition because of its ties to the Soviet Union. That discourse was also connected with various popular nationalist movements of the 1940s and 1950s, which in the early 1960s were sympathetic toward the revolution. In the Southern Cone these movements were important in the groups studied here. Mario Roberto Santucho, the future leader of the PRT-ERP, originally began his political activism in the Frente Revolucionario Indoamericano Popular (Popular Indo-American

Revolutionary Front, or FRIP), an Indo-Americanist group with ties to Peruvian leader Víctor Raúl Haya de la Torre. Santucho's group took up the figure of Argentine liberator José de San Martín, and chose the colors of the national flag for the design of their own flag. In Uruguay, the MLN-Tupamaros had links to the Latin Americanist third line and in the 1960s they took up the figure of José Gervasio Artigas, who led the fight against Spanish domination in the territory of what is now Uruguay.

Although the conclusions of the OLAS were adopted by unanimous vote, Fidel Castro's closing speech at the Chaplin Theater again reflected the differences between the pro-Soviet communist parties and the majority position backed by Cuba. An important part of the speech focused on criticizing the position of the Venezuelan Communist Party, which had decided to abandon armed struggle to become an electoral force. To refer to that party he used terms such as "team of traitors" or "enemies of the revolution." Castro also took the opportunity to question the Soviet Union's role in Latin America in supporting such positions adopted by the communist parties, as well as its technical aid to regimes that combated guerrilla movements in their countries. As Castro said this, he received a resounding ovation, which made the differences all the more obvious. While six of the seven participants on the conference platform stood up to applaud, Uruguayan communist leader Rodney Arismendi remained seated with his arms crossed. Communist delegations, Soviet reporters, and the Soviet ambassador, who was sitting in the box reserved for distinguished guests, did the same. When their attitude was perceived by the rest of the theater the applause became louder, spurred by Raúl Castro who from his place in the platform encouraged participants to keep clapping.[25]

The definitions adopted by the OLAS Conference were actually aimed at building a new international that would dispute Moscow's influence without joining any of the other international alignments (Maoism, Trotskyism). In the words of Chilean socialist senator Carlos Altamirano:

The contradiction in our time is no longer formed by the terms 'imperialism-socialist countries' but rather by the terms 'imperialism-periphery countries.' The third world, through the Tricontinental and now through the OLAS, seems ready to take over this task. Havana has become as of now the capital of the new international that will process the liberation of Latin America.[26]

The OAS reaction to the OLAS Conference increased the international expectations placed on it. By June 1967 Venezuela had convened a conference of foreign affairs ministers to denounce the "disembarking of an expedition of aid and support commandos that have been publicly recognized by the Cuban government."[27] Venezuela's conflict with Cuba dated back to 1963 when the government had found a shipment of weapons from

Cuba. From then on Venezuela had taken an active role in international forums, denouncing Cuba's foreign policy, and in June 1967 it organized a meeting to assess the impact of the OLAS Conference and set up a committee to study Cuba's foreign policy.[28] This attention from the OAS gave Cuba a central importance that paradoxically enhanced its global role. This was even pointed out in press accounts that were not sympathetic to the revolution.[29]

The Cuban Revolution cleverly used to its advantage the spotlight turned on it by the OAS, the United States, and some Latin American governments. Although the repeated failures of the guerrilla movements supported by Cuba from 1962 to 1967 revealed the limitations and weaknesses of its foreign policy, Cuba again took center stage in Latin America, as had occurred with the missile crisis and its suspension from the OAS in 1962. Moreover, the region's supposedly unanimous backing of the OAS anti-communist stance enabled Havana to emerge as the only alternative for the whole of Latin America's Left. While some governments, like Chile's, had a somewhat different view from the majority position in the OAS, these nuances did not fit the general picture painted by the OLAS, where there were only governments aligned with U.S. imperialism, on one side, and governments aligned with the peoples of Latin America, on the other.

The idea that the Cuban Revolution expressed the sentiments of the Latin American peoples led to the hosting of multiple cultural activities in Havana in 1967, thus reinforcing the centrality of the revolution in that context. The First International Protest Song Meeting was held in the framework of the OLAS with the participation of major Latin American singer-songwriters.[30] In addition, the renowned Salon de Mai of the Musée d'Art Moderne de la Ville de Paris moved to Havana in July 1967 after its exhibition in Paris.

As mentioned in the previous chapter, in the conference's discussions the situations in Chile and Uruguay were considered relatively exceptional. According to the conference's initial report, "to speak today of armed struggle in Chile or in Uruguay is as absurd as denying that possibility in Venezuela, Colombia, Brazil, Guatemala, or Peru."[31] Following the debate, that paragraph was removed and the final resolutions reflected a view that upheld the inevitability of armed struggle throughout the continent.

Paradoxically enough, the Southern Cone groups that were closer to the Cuban position did not participate officially in the OLAS. The armed organizations that in the coming years would become the leading representatives of the armed struggle strategy were not part of the local committees in Chile and Uruguay. The Chilean delegation was monopolized by socialists and communists, and the Uruguayan committee was also formed primarily by these two forces. In both cases, the socialists tried to propose a more heterogeneous makeup for the national OLAS committees, while the communists opposed the inclusion of a number of new groups that were emerging in the mid-1960s with more radical profiles.

The discussion over which groups could join the national committees was not just about how they should be formed, but also about what they would represent. While socialists and other groups proposed that, without relinquishing their political independence, the national OLAS committees should become the commanding units of a unified struggle against imperialism spearheaded by Cuba, the communists tended to defend a version closer to the classic role of solidarity with Cuba or with any revolutionary groups active in the region.[32]

Argentina's delegation was formed primarily of members of the Peronist Left, and a sector of the Socialist Party. Argentina's Communist Party, which at the Tricontinental Conference had been the staunchest opponent of the creation of the OLAS, decided not to participate. It was the Movimiento Revolucionario Peronista (Peronist Revolutionary Movement, or MRP) – headed by John William Cooke, who spoke on behalf of the Argentine delegation – which, upon returning from the OLAS Conference, began forming the first group of the second wave of Argentine guerrilla organizations that emerged in the late 1960s: the Fuerzas Armadas Peronistas (Peronist Armed Forces), founded in 1968. This decision seemed to be legitimized by the leader of the Peronist movement himself, Juan Domingo Perón, who in September 1967, in line with the atmosphere at the OLAS, told *Marcha*, "right now, a pacifist revolutionary is like a vegetarian lion."[33] With the exception of the Peronists, the groups that in the following years would become major players in the development of guerrilla warfare in the Southern Cone did not have the opportunity of joining the OLAS committees, even though they identified with the conference's cause. Argentina's PRT – an organization from which the ERP would later emerge – applied to join the OLAS committee but received no answer.[34] The Chilean MIR, like the Uruguayan Tupamaros – still a nascent organization – were not invited to join the national committees.

Those who were unable to attend the conference still tried to find a way to participate. MIR activist Miguel Enríquez, the organization's future leader, was in Havana during the conference.[35] In Uruguay, a group of new organizations, including the MLN-Tupamaros, sent a special statement through journalist Carlos María Gutiérrez to be read at the conference.[36]

All the Southern Cone parties that participated in the OLAS declared that they backed the resolutions, but paradoxically the groups that capitalized on these results in the following months were groups that had not officially participated. Although the communists parties tried to minimize the differences with Cuba and emphasized its active solidarity with the revolution, the divisions that arose in the conference and which were amplified by the press of the Southern Cone New Left were difficult to hide.[37] These disagreements had a strong impact on sectors that were drawn by what the Cuban Revolution proposed, and they aggravated the rifts that had been forming, especially within the Left.

The region's socialist parties welcomed the OLAS resolutions with enthusiasm. However, their political practice put into question the definitions adopted by the conference, as they were not planning on becoming clandestine organizations and continued to aspire to hold seats in parliament. Although they backed the OLAS resolutions and were persecuted in Argentina (Coral), Chile, and Uruguay as a result of that support, their organizational model associated with traditional electoral practice was not the best instrument for the "era of armed struggle" heralded by the OLAS.

The OLAS definitions were best capitalized on by groups that in 1967 were only beginning to emerge and which proposed and called for concrete forms of armed struggle in their respective countries, as they seemed to be the best suited for the new scenario opened up by the conference. These groups – which, as shown in the previous chapter, were attempting to build a strategy that would adapt armed struggle proposals to the conditions of the Southern Cone – also had serious doubts about the opportunity of launching such actions. The definitions adopted at the OLAS Conference, along with the reactions they prompted in national spheres operated as incentives for these groups to push forward with a number of ideas they were developing.

In Argentina and Chile, two groups that were moving away from Trotskyism fully embraced the armed struggle option after the OLAS Conference. There was a shift in certain Trotskyist sectors of Argentina's PRT and Chile's MIR toward more Latin Americanist alternatives that opened the door for new organizations to be formed by merging with other political organizations of the Left. In the case of the MIR, even though the vast majority of its initial leaders had a Trotskyist background, the movement did not have an explicitly defined identity, and neither did it adhere to the Fourth International. As for the PRT – an organization formed through an alliance between Nahuel Moreno's Trotskyist group Palabra Obrera and the FRIP, a small group from northern Argentina headed by the Santucho brothers, with an initially nationalist Indo-American profile – it maintained its alignment with the Fourth International.[38]

The Cuban Revolution had been the change that had made this new framework of alliances and this re-conceptualization of international politics within Trotskyism possible. All of these groups had declared themselves firm supporters of the Revolution. But their relationship with the Revolution was problematic, due primarily to two reasons: the constant suspicions of bureaucratization and Sovietization of the Revolution raised by the Trotskyist press at different stages of Cuba's political development;

and Cuba's critical view of certain insurrectional traditions that dismissed the role of the rural *foco*. These differences were proved by the divisions that arose over the strategies proposed by Hugo Blanco's MIR in Peru and Yohn Sosa's MR-13 in Guatemala.[39] This context of tensions gave way to the emergence of sectors within the PRT and Chile's MIR that leaned more decidedly toward a pro-Cuban position, thus clashing with the old leadership in both organizations.

In Argentina's case, the new coup d'état staged in June 1966 radically altered previous political conditions. This time the armed forces were proposing a new kind of dictatorship – the "Argentine revolution," which, in line with the 1964 coup in Brazil, entailed a drastic transformation of the economy, society, and politics. Its leading aim involved a conservative modernization that would ensure growth at the expense of abandoning certain protectionist policies, banning political parties, and imposing cultural controls that included taking over universities to "wipe out Marxism."[40]

In a climate of banned political parties, anti-communist laws, and book-burning in the University, the dictatorship's reaction to the OLAS Conference did not come as a surprise. After the conference, the government launched police actions to arrest any Argentines who had participated in the conference. It was in this context that in its fourth congress, held in January 1968, the PRT adopted a document entitled *The Only Road to Power and to Socialism*. This document, written for the most part by Roberto Santucho, with contributions from Helios Prieto and Sergio Prada, marked the starting point for the development of an armed organization.[41] After reviewing the different Marxist traditions, the document proposed a unique synthesis of Trotskyism and Maoism, arguing that the former had best contributed to understand the contemporary world but had failed to provide appropriate strategies for the revolution, while the political and military reflections of the latter had provided essential elements to further revolutionary processes. It went on to claim that this synthesis had been achieved in the Cuban Revolution through a new doctrine: Castroism. The document demanded that the party abandon the ambiguous attitude it had toward Castroism, and called for an explicit commitment with the continental and international strategy it proposed. What the PRT needed to do was to drop the debates raised by Nahuel Moreno (the organization's traditional Trotskyist leader) and immediately declare its intent to initiate an armed struggle under the continental strategy proposed by Castroism. The document argued that the rural *foco* debate was no longer that relevant, and that Cuba was now more open to the strategies of others, who sought to actively form a revolutionary army, rather than leave such a task to be carried out spontaneously by the masses.[42]

In Chile, a new generation also emerged within the MIR in opposition to the old guard of Trotskyist activists, countering their insurrectional methods with Guevara's ideas. The change of direction in this organization also occurred after the OLAS Conference, in late 1967. In its third congress, held that year, the MIR adopted the political and military theses that marked the beginning of a new stage in the organization, which included taking its operations underground.

This shift in the MIR occurred at a particular moment of the "revolution in freedom" of Eduardo Frei Montalva's Christian Democratic government. In 1967, the resurgence of inflation, with its effect on wages and government spending, coupled with the delays in the agrarian reform and the implementation of the nationalization policy fueled discontent. The leftist sectors in the Christian Democratic Party (PDC) and the FRAP called for a radicalization of the reform programs. Social organizations that had been formed in the countryside and in urban peripheries and which had close ties to the Christian Democrats also radicalized their demands.[43] The government responded to this social unrest by adopting a confrontational discourse aimed at the Left and stepping up state repression with new specialized riot-control squads within the police force. The increase in repressive actions against social mobilizations stirred an unprecedented number of clashes in the streets.[44]

One of the moments in which the government adopted this confrontational discourse was during the public debate surrounding the local OLAS committee and the conference's definitions. By doing so it revealed signs of polarization within both the governing party and the Left. In August 1967 the leaders of the PDC declared that the party "is not against the OLAS operating in Chile.... The PDC maintains that democracy is the best way to achieve ... development.... However, in line with its principles, it admits that in cases where the government does not respect the fundamental rights of individuals and of the people, and where no democratic solution is possible, armed insurrection is a legitimate means of defending those rights." This declaration attracted international attention. *The New York Times*, spokespersons of the U.S. State Department, and the governments of Colombia and Venezuela questioned such position.[45]

After these reactions, President Frei adopted a belligerent attitude toward the Chileans who had participated in the event, and declared, "I have no legal means of preventing institutions such as the OLAS from being established in Chile, but morally I condemn them."[46] In the days that followed the government brought a criminal action against socialist senator Carlos Altamirano – which would result in his imprisonment – because of his statements in support of the OLAS, and established a permanent "antisubversive" committee controlled by the military.[47]

It is against this backdrop of social unrest and political polarization that the MIR discussed its strategic issues. There are no surviving internal documents of the MIR from 1967, but some insight into the debate can be drawn from texts featured at the time in the magazine *Estrategia* and some articles published by *Punto Final*, which mark the beginning of that discussion, as well as the memoirs of Miguel Enríquez and Luis Vitale that touch on this period.[48] While Vitale cautioned that Enríquez had *foquista* deviations, Enríquez described the MIR as "a grab bag" of groups, factions, and disputes, not even "minimally structured," "isolated from the masses," with no "strategy and much less tactics," and where "armed actions were never seriously attempted, even though there was much talk of them and the movement defined itself as an armed organization."[49] Vitale, in turn, notes that during this period the MIR discussed its founding documents, including the declaration of principles, the program, and the insurrectional and political theses that called for the penetration of trade unions and popular sectors. The differences were in the strategies defined by each leader. Vitale was closer to insurrectional practices that were typical of a form of radical unionism associated with Trotskyism and anarchism. Enríquez, on the other hand, represented a different trend that had emerged after the Cuban Revolution, associated with the development of an armed structure that would promote the radicalization of popular sectors. They were both radically critical of the "bourgeois legality" of the reformist sectors of the Left, but the methods they chose to defy it were completely different.[50] Both trends had coexisted in the MIR since the organization was founded in 1965. The first trend represented sectors of the labor movement that had become politically active in the 1950s. The second represented mostly student groups that began to have a major influence in radical leftist organizations in the mid-1960s.

The leading figure in the December 1967 congress was Miguel Enríquez, a 23-year-old student of the University of Concepción and the son of a Radical Party senator. Enriquez arrived straight from Cuba, one day into the congress, with a reformulated version of the political and military theses drafted in 1965, and was welcomed with applause.[51]

The new definitions reflected the movement's far Left, represented by a group of young people connected with the Universities of Concepción and Santiago, which had grown significantly in the organization through the work conducted in student and popular sectors.[52] This change brought a new direction to the MIR, which focused on working more intensely with the masses and adjusting the party with the aim of generating conditions for armed struggle. Thus the definitions adopted by the MIR in its third congress, held five months after the OLAS Conference, also provided guidance for the armed struggle strategy proposed at the conference.

Although the MLN-Tupamaros had been founded in January 1966, the year 1967 was marked by a great uncertainty about the future of the movement, as a result of police persecution and the decision of almost thirty of its members to go underground. It was not until late 1967 that the

MLN-T resurfaced publicly in a particular context of political polarization, as authoritarian measures were first implemented under the government of Óscar Gestido, and then stepped up by his successor, Jorge Pacheco Areco, after Gestido's death in December 1967. On October 9, a day after Guevara was killed, the government issued a decree implementing prompt security measures (a limited form of state of emergency). Under these measures, over 400 people were arrested, most of them labor activists, and left-wing newspapers were shut down. The aim of the measures was to send out a clear signal – directed at the labor movement and the internal opposition within the governing party – that protests against the attempts to resume negotiations with international financial bodies (the International Monetary Fund, the World Bank, and the Inter-American Development Bank) would not be tolerated. The government would continue to implement authoritarian measures over the coming months. On December 12, a week after Gestido's death, in an attempt to clearly mark the shift that the government was to take under his administration, and in line with regional discussions concerning the OLAS Conference, Pacheco decided to ban a number of left-wing political groups that had adopted the OLAS definitions and to close down the newspapers *Época* and *El Sol*, which represented such groups.[53] For some members of the MLN-T, this new context was a decisive factor that helped determine the organization's orientation and contributed to its explosive growth in the year 1968.[54]

The Revolution Is Coming. Guevara in Bolivia

As these processes were unfolding in each country, a new development – the arrival of Guevara to Bolivia – added unique elements to the regional dynamics. Guevara's arrival was preceded by a wave of rumors that put him in the country or claimed he had delegates traveling around South America seeking support for his project. The Tupamaros, still a small organization, discussed the possibility of giving up on armed struggle in Uruguay and going instead to Bolivia. Another group of Uruguayan activists, who were members of a minor group allied with the Communist Party – the Movimiento Revolucionario Oriental (Eastern Revolutionary Movement, or MRO) – also received military training in Cuba to fight in Bolivia.[55] As Guevara began organizing his guerrilla campaign, in Chile a sector of the Socialist Party formed a group under the name Ejército de Liberación Nacional (National Liberation Army, or ELN), and in Argentina a new group was created primarily with former communists who in 1967 had traveled to Cuba for training to support Guevara in Bolivia.[56] The goal of both groups was to prepare the rearguard for the Bolivian ELN. In addition to the support network built by people close to Guevara in Chile and Argentina, the Cuban Revolution also maintained political relations with the traditional Left. In Uruguay's case, contacts were established by members of the Communist Party or allied groups. In Chile, most contacts were made through the Socialist Party. While the Tupamaros were invited to participate in this campaign, MIR and PRT members were not, due most likely to the Cuban government's reservations about Trotskyism, as noted above. Also, as shown in the previous chapter, as Guevara was carrying out his campaign in Bolivia, a military *foco* was being formed in Brazil.[57]

In May 1967, some months before the OLAS Conference, guerrilla activities in Bolivia were attracting the attention of media that sympathized with the Southern Cone New Left. One of the reasons for such interest was that on April 20 Regis Debray had been captured along with another three members of the ELN in Bolivia. This prompted Carlos María Gutiérrez to write an article in *Marcha* establishing a clear link between *Revolution in the Revolution?* and the guerrilla campaign in Bolivia.

The journalist had great intellectual respect for Debray and described the guerrilla organization as the practical application of his theory. In his opinion this guerrilla campaign entailed a qualitative leap from other experiences attempted by Latin American revolutionaries since January 1959, and was the result of the reflection and systematization work carried out by Debray and the Cubans, which would lead to positive outcomes.[58] Lastly, Gutiérrez noted that as the "country and the area selected fit the general scheme of the Latin American insurrectional thesis" it was quite plausible that the rumors that put Guevara there were accurate.

As a bordering country, Chile was closer to the guerrilla group in Bolivia, so that the impact in this Southern Cone nation was even greater. On guerrilla presence in Bolivia, the magazine *Punto Final* noted: "Revolutionary war is no longer a distant matter for Chileans. It's right across the border from us, in Bolivia."[59]

The support expressed for this venture in the region was an important factor because, as Gutiérrez indicated, the guerrilla campaign had regional aspirations that dated back to pre-Guevara projects. The guerrilla *foco* sought to expand from Bolivia to other countries. As Manuel "Barbirroja" Piñeiro would later recall in the 1990s, "Che wanted to personally launch a revolutionary armed struggle in Latin America's Southern Cone."[60]

However, the situation of the guerrilla movement in Bolivia was much more uncertain than what was described by the press that sympathized with the New Left. Guevara had arrived in November. In late December, Guevara's group consisted of twenty-four guerrillas, of whom only nine were Bolivian. It is in that context that Guevara disputed the group's leadership with the general secretary of the Bolivian Communist Party. Guevara wanted to retain control over the group's military direction, and the Communist Party reacted by withdrawing its support for the guerrilla group. Over the coming months, the group began to receive some local support. But in March the first guerrillas were captured and confessed that Cubans were involved in the campaign. At this time the farm that operated as the group's guerrilla center was also detected.

These developments attracted the attention of the Bolivian army, the United States, and the Brazilian and Argentine dictatorships, which offered their support to track down the guerrillas. Ciro Bustos and Debray, the leading contacts of the guerrilla group, were captured in April. Debray confessed that Guevara was in Bolivia.[61] As of that moment, the search was intensified and morale among ELN members declined until they sought only to escape without being detected by the army.

Guevara's Bolivia campaign ended with a resounding defeat, marked by its failure to establish contacts with popular sectors in the area and by conflicts with the Bolivian Communist Party. In less than a year the guerrilla campaign had been crushed. Most of the forty-seven members who had participated throughout the campaign were killed. Five survivors fled across the border to Chile where they were captured. Through the support efforts of Chilean activists, the government finally agreed to turn the guerrillas over to Cuba.[62]

The first reports that Guevara had been found and killed by Bolivian Rangers came on October 10, and by October 11 the news had traveled around the world. Pictures of Guevara's dead body were featured in national and international media. The photos had been taken by Freddy Alborta, a renowned Bolivian photographer who had been called expressly to Vallegrande to record Guevara's death in images. When he photographed Guevara, Alborta chose the angle and composition of the images with a clear intent:

They had left his eyes open, to better identify him, but that helped me to photograph not a common corpse but a person who seemed to be alive and I had the impression I was photographing a Christ, and it wasn't just me but many people who compared him to the body of a Christ.[63]

The photographs of Guevara's naked body laid out on display with a military officer standing over him pointing at a bullet wound on his chest, his eyes open, giving the impression that he was alive, enabled symbolic readings of his death that were quickly picked up by all those around the world who sympathized in some way with Guevara.[64] On the one hand, the open eyes challenged the main purpose of the photographs, which was to prove his death. On the other, Guevara's death was likened over and over to the death of Jesus Christ. The image of the officer pointing to the wound on his chest evoked the episode in the gospel where an apostle puts his fingers on Jesus' chest. The way Guevara's body was positioned and the expression on his face recalled classical paintings depicting the death of Jesus, such as Andrea Mantegna's *Lamentation over the Dead Christ*.[65]

The interpretation of the photographs foreshadowed the strongly emotional reading that Guevara's death would have among the groups of the Southern Cone Left. His death was not seen as a failure of his continental strategy but as one of the possible outcomes of the choices Guevara had made, as he himself had said in his *Message to the Tricontinental*, which now became a sort of political testament.[66]

Overcoming Guevara's death meant carrying on his struggle. Guevara was not dead if others continued to fight. Nonetheless, Guevara's followers were far from unaffected by his death. Although Guevara's fate was not a surprise given the risks he had taken, his death forced his followers to face the reality of the dangers that revolutionary commitment involved. While this was evident in other regions of Latin America, for activists in the Southern Cone it was still not all that clear in 1967. The nascent groups in the Southern Cone countries had yet to suffer the savage repression seen in other parts of Latin America.

While internally the Southern Cone groups could acknowledge that there were errors in the implementation of Guevara's strategy, and, as shown in the previous chapter, his death reinforced the need to search for alternatives to the rural *foco*, publicly his fate was explained by the isolation that Bolivia's other left-wing parties, in particular the Bolivian Communist Party, had subjected the ELN guerrillas to, and by the involvement of the CIA and the Rangers in the activities of the Bolivian army.

But along with the political reading of Guevara's death there was also what could be called a sentimental reading of his death. Multiple oral history accounts evidence the emotional impact that his death had on the political lives of activists of the 1960s.[67] This sentimental reading was not removed from political discussions and neither did it entail a contradiction. The same magazines examined in this and the previous chapter featured poems about Guevara's death in their October and November issues, which illustrate the outpouring of emotion triggered by his death.

The debates on political strategy were characterized by a neutral and often "technical" language that advocated the need to resort to violence as a rational matter, devoid of romantic subjectivity or sentimentality and based on an objective reality, which could only be changed through illegal practices that entailed putting your life at risk. Poetry, in contrast, enabled a different way of addressing the issues of revolution, sacrifice, death, and violence. It boosted a subjectivity that stressed the ethical value of sacrifice in opposition to the comfort offered by consumer society and assigned an emancipating role to violence.[68]

As historians, we are not used to working with poetry as a historical source. The literality with which we tend to approach sources goes against the polysemy of poetical language. In this sense, what I will do below is to simply transcribe two poems and look at some ideas that arise from them, but recognizing that there are other possible readings. I selected two poems published in different magazines and which illustrate some of the emotions and perceptions that were experienced by those who were affected by Guevara's death in the initial aftermath.

In the poem *Che*, by the Argentine Julio Huasi, which was first published in *Punto Final* and later in *Cristianismo y Revolución*, a great variety of images emerge, expressing the vitality of a figure that seemed untouched by his tragic fate.[69] A universe of images, which range from the cosmic to the biological and the everyday, are interspersed with a tense language that seeks to attribute a religiousness close to Catholicism to the iconic figure of Che Guevara, with constant allusions to Jesus Christ and the Our Father prayer: "Let the sweet war of the people – not peace – be with you." The eyes of Guevara are like "burning lights in every hunger-stricken hut," his heart will beat in every child that is born and in every woman who gives birth. In the last verses this tension between the rupture signified by the figure of Che Guevara and the attempt to establish a new kind of sacred language is particularly evident:

> Our Father who are in war,
> Glory be to America for giving birth to you.
> From matter you will continue firing,
> love or death, Ernesto, look over us,
> love or death, Ernesto, we will avenge your love,
> love or death, eternal lover,
> you have not fallen, you have merely emerged forever
> to lead us always to victory
> for ever and ever in our America, thus it shall be
> with you we shall overcome.

Throughout, the poem several images evoke the materiality of violence: bones, blood, "Ravens and doves are now fighting over your flesh," bullets. But at the same time the rawness with which violence is described is always associated with oxymorons, such as "the sweet war of the people" or "gunpowder caresses." This device responds to a striking intersection between two languages that were common among young people in the Southern Cone during that period. One was the language of love, associated with sectors of North American counterculture, and the other was the language of Latin American revolutionary violence. In Huasi's poem, Che Guevara combined both:

> You were overflowing with love, your love burned history,
> with golden testicles, you furiously loved liberation,

> you gave America your smoldering love, your gunpowder,
> you woke her in the night with your burning, armed kiss,

However, Guevara's love also had its limitations, which were shaped by the demands of the revolutionary struggle:

> I cried with my bones sunken in America
> I didn't want you to see me because you'd have me shot,
> Che has no need for tears, he needs concrete bullets,
> weeping in your name is a great betrayal,

Lastly, Guevara's death meant not defeat but the beginning of victory:

> Let no one cry or pray, your emerald legacy
> bestows us your mighty rifle to fight with,
> let no one lower their flags, but raise them higher than ever,
> let no one take your name in vain
> let only murderers wear mourning clothes,
> to mourn their own unquestionable and very real death,
> Ernesto, you will go with us to their funerals,
> We'll be there with brilliant candles, with firm triggers.
> Jesus comes down from the cross, the suffering is over,
> Pick up the gun, Camilo, leave the nails and shoot,
> The time for turning the other cheek is over.

In his poem *In Grief and Rage*, first published in *Punto Final* and later in his own country, Uruguayan writer Mario Benedetti explores the feelings triggered by Guevara's death, "even though this death may be one of those foreseeable absurdities."[70] What surrounds much of the poem are feelings of shame and guilt:

> ashamed of feeling cold
> and warming ourselves by the fireplace as always
> of being hungry and eating
> such a simple act
> opening the record player and listening in silence
> especially if it's a quartet by Mozart
>
> ashamed of our comfort
> and asthma shaming us
> as you, *comandante*, are falling
> gunned down
> fantastic
> pure
>
> you're our bullet-riddled conscience

Both feelings are associated with the comfort that consumer society offers the middle classes. The fireplace, the record player, a quartet by Mozart, all represent objects that tie the poet to comfort at the very moment Guevara was giving his life.

In the last verses we again see that tension between religiousness and the search for other absolutes in the face of death:

> wherever you are
> if you are there
> if you're getting there
> it'll be a shame to find there is no God
>
> but there'll be others
> of course there'll be others
> worthy of receiving you
> *comandante.*

Both poems condense some of the emotions most strongly felt among those who had followed Guevara's experience in Bolivia closely. The guilt, the fascination with violence as an emancipating practice, the feeling of living in a new historical era, the loyalty to Guevara, and the quest for a transcendental subjectivity other than religion. In a way, the reading of these poems has certain points in common with Raymond Williams' concept of "structure of feelings," as it refers to a sense of generational identity in the way beliefs, values, and emotions were expressed, which precedes politics through art, and which is not yet able to take formal shape in the field of politics.[71] Those feelings, together with the reports blaming Guevara's death on the betrayal by the Bolivian Communist Party and the reformist sectors, led young people who were attracted by the discourse of the Left to lean toward the New Left. While this New Left was not yet able to develop a fully articulated proposal by re-interpreting Guevara's death in terms of the future, it did constitute an alternative to the traditional methods of the Left.

Several conservative press media, however, rushed to predict the demise of the New Left and proclaimed that "The death of Ernesto Guevara demolishes the myth of the efficacy of his action and becomes a symbol of the painful sterility of using force against the law."[72] Other, more observant analysts noted that his death signified a new beginning. Mariano Grondona, a young lawyer who served as advisor in Onganía's military dictatorship, published a column entitled *The Heirs of Marx* in Argentina's most popular magazine. There he described Guevara and Debray as Castro's "sword" and "pen," who had met the end of their careers in "the Bolivian jungles." After reviewing the different Marxist theories, from Marx to Mao, he found continuity with Marxist thought in Debray and Guevara's "attempt to

Figure 2.c. Cover of Marcha. Guevara un libertador de América. Marcha n. 1375. 10/20/20/1967. (CEIU Archive).

rationally channel the frustration of the disadvantaged and give it a program of action." And he finished his analysis with a warning:

The world today is not facing the discontent of industrial workers in the heart of every European society, but the despair of almost all the nations that span the torrid and southern regions of the earth. The revolutionary leaders of these peoples, those who have lost faith in the possibility of a peaceful reform, do not yet have a Marx of their own, which is why they resort to the old arsenal of ideas of he who, more than a hundred years ago, formulated the doctrine of a different resentment. This adaptation is not achieved without increasing distortions, but if the gap between the developed world and the underdeveloped world continues to grow at such rapid speed, new combatants and new thinkers, who we have yet to meet, will stir up humanity with a long period of conflicts and violence. Guevara's death and Debray's imprisonment do not, in this sense, mark the end of a revolutionary situation, but are, instead, its first signs.[73]

Grondona was right. The publication of *The Bolivian Diary of Ernesto Che Guevara* graphically illustrates the way his death turned into a new beginning. In March 1968, when the Bolivian army was considering selling the *Diary* to United States or British publishing houses, Bolivian interior minister Antonio Arguedas decided to secretly give the text to the Cuban government. In March 1968, Arguedas sent a friend to Chile with the *Diary*. There the text was delivered to the offices of *Punto Final* magazine, and from there it was sent to the government of Cuba. Arguedas' gesture caused a political scandal that forced him to request asylum in Chile.[74] In July 1968, the diary was published almost simultaneously around the world in book form. The Cuban government granted *Punto Final* publishing rights for the entire Southern Cone region.[75]

What the *Diary of Ernesto Che Guevara in Bolivia* depicted was a complex and difficult series of events marked by the guerrilla group's increasing political and social isolation during the year that the campaign lasted.[76] Although the text could be read as the confirmation of Guevara's defeat, it was re-interpreted in epic terms.[77]

Conclusion

The OLAS Conference and the arrival of Guevara to Bolivia came at a time of growing social unrest, repressive reactions from democratically-elected governments, and the intensification of dictatorial solutions in the Southern Cone. In this context, several activists of the New Left, who were exploring new forms of political struggle in which violence would play a pivotal role, viewed the policy furthered by the Cuban Revolution in 1967 as an encouragement to their own local definitions.

The resolutions adopted at the OLAS Conference, regarding the inevitability of armed struggle in the continent, strengthened the positions of the groups of the New Left in the debates with the traditional Left that were being held in the countries of the Southern Cone. Moreover, the international impact of the conference sparked intense discussions in national public spheres over what positions the governments should take with respect to the OLAS. In a framework of increasing local polarization, the conflict between the OAS and the OLAS redefined local situations in terms of continental meanings. For sectors of the Left, it meant taking the revolution to the continental level. For government sectors, it was a subversive threat brewed in Cuba that had to be contained even if the measures required to do so went against freedom of expression and freedom of association in democratic countries such as Chile and Uruguay.

Guevara's campaign in Bolivia added new elements to this political reading of the process of continentalization of the revolution. On the one hand, the high expectations placed on the military and political capacity of Guevara in Bolivia fueled the actions of these groups in the region and their gathering efforts. On the other hand, paradoxically the sentimental reading of Guevara's death contributed to encourage the conviction among Southern Cone militants that armed struggle was the only way forward.

In terms of the political culture that these groups were building, the OLAS and Guevara's idea of a continental strategy for the revolution contributed to strengthen the Latin American identity that could already be found in the political history of some of these organizations. Latin Americanism was now not just a question of the past, a cultural issue, and a geopolitical place in the global order, it was also a common political and military strategy. The figure of Guevara had symbolized that strategy and generated a type of identification that went beyond the merely political to create a type of subjective, sentimental identification with Southern Cone militants. Latin Americanism thus became a political, military, and also subjective project.

In short, the geopolitical definitions adopted by the Cuban Revolution in 1967 and its implications encouraged emerging groups of the Southern Cone New Left to continue developing the armed struggle proposals they had been discussing for some years. The conference did not live up to the expectations it had raised among friends of the Cuban Revolution, but it also failed to prove the fears of its enemies. The revolution did not take on continental dimensions after the conference. The guerrilla groups that the Cubans had set their hopes on and supported in other regions of Latin America did not prosper. However, the OLAS did have an unexpected result. Regis Debray described it clearly seven years later:

The OLAS emerged at a time when the center of gravity of revolutionary struggle was shifting from north to south, from the Caribbean region (Guatemala, Venezuela, Santo Domingo, Colombia) to the "Southern Cone" (Chile, Argentina, Uruguay): it expressed the tendencies of that past while, at the same time, the tendencies of the future were stamping their mark. Geographically and historically, Bolivia served as nexus between the two eras and the two regions, a thoroughfare for revolutionary influx.[78]

The revolution had moved from countries with low socioeconomic development, characterized by the presence of the rural world, to countries that were considered the most modern in Latin America, with a greater development of urban middle classes.[79] By the start of the new decade, Chile had acquired a unique singularity.

Notes

1 Mario Benedetti, *Daniel Viglietti* (Madrid: Ediciones Júcar, 1974).
2 The Montoneros and the path they took after Perón's return in 1973 may be considered an exception to the process of continentalization. However, the close relationship that this organization had with the Cuban Revolution would appear to contradict that.

3 Tanya Harmer, "Two, Three, Many Revolutions? Cuba and the Prospects for Revolutionary Change in Latin America, 1967–1975," *Journal of Latin American Studies*, vol. 45, issue 01, February 2013, 61–89.

4 See Odd Arne Westad, *The Global Cold War: Third World Interventions and the Making of Our Times* (Cambridge, New York: Cambridge University Press, 2005).

5 See the debate between Gilly and Castro mentioned in Chapter 1; see also "Cuba, la tricontinental y la revolución latinoamericana. Resolución de la III Sesión Plenaria del C.C. del MIR chileno verificada el 17 de abril de 1966," *Estrategia*, no. 4 (June 1966), Santiago de Chile.

6 "Discurso en la Primera Conferencia Tricontinental, La Habana, 5 de enero de 1966," in Frida Modak (coord.), *Salvador Allende: pensamiento y acción* (Buenos Aires: CLACSO – FLACSO- Brazil, 2008), 289–90.

7 On the relationship between Allende and Castro and the debates on the paths to revolution, see Tanya Harmer, *Allende's Chile and the Inter-American Cold War* (Chapel Hill: University of North Carolina Press, 2011).

8 Richard Gott, *Guerrilla Movements in Latin America* (Oxford, New York, Calcutta: Seagull Books, 2008), XLVIII.

9 Carlos María Gutiérrez, "Los oleajes de la Olas," *Marcha*, March 10, 1967, 14.

10 *The New York Times*, January 22, 1966, 11.

11 It understood international communism as "any act of aggression or subversion or other act that may endanger the internal security of the American republics and the political defense of the hemisphere, as well as the preparation of such acts that may arise from the continued intervention of the countries of the Sino-Soviet bloc in this hemisphere." Council of the Organization of American States, *Special Consultative Committee on Security. Statutes*, April 23, 1963.

12 Plutarco, "Informe especial: la diplomacia y los países socialistas," *Punto Final*, no. 18, 2nd fortnight of December 1966, 12–13.

13 Daniela Spenser, "La crisis del Caribe: catalizador de la proyección soviética en América Latina," in Daniela Spenser (coord) *Espejos de la guerra fría. México, América Central y el Caribe* (México DF: CIESAS-Porrua, 2004), 281–319.

14 "Fidel Castro: El primer deber de todo revolucionario es hacer la revolución," *Época*, July 29, 1966, 5.

15 "Actualidad nacional," *Punto Final*, no. 10, 2nd fortnight of August 1966, 4.

16 Carlos María Gutiérrez, "Fidel: nuevas condiciones, nuevos lenguajes," *Marcha*, August 5, 1966.

17 Ernesto Guevara, "A crear muchos Vietnam," *Punto Final*, no. 27, 2nd fortnight of April 1967, 20–6.

18 "Apoyo del MIR de Chile a la carta del Che Guevara," *Estrategia*, no. 9, July 1967, 1–7.

19 Sergio Domecqu, Carlos Ramírez, and Juan Candela (pseudonyms), *El único camino para la toma del poder y el socialismo*, 22.

20 "Documento I," in INDAL. Movimiento Liberación Nacional Tupamaros.

21 See Carlos María Gutiérrez, "OLAS, nace una nueva internacional," *Marcha*, August 11, 1967, 20–1, and the article on the position of the secretary general of the Uruguayan Communist Party, Rodney Arismendi. At the end of the article, Gutiérrez included a photograph in which Arismendi was the only participant on the platform who was not applauding the closing address, while all the other members of the conference bureau were shown fervently applauding Castro's final words. See Carlos María Gutiérrez, "Con Rodney Arismendi," *Marcha*, September 15, 1967, 21.

22 OLAS, *Actuación de la OEA: Guatemala (1954), República Dominicana (1965), Cuba (1959–1967), Intervencionismo y Fuerza Interamericana de Paz* (Havana: Primera Conferencia de Solidaridad de los Pueblos de América Latina, 1967).

23 OLAS, *Primera Conferencia de la Organización Latinoamericana de Solidaridad* (Montevideo, Uruguay: Nativa Libros, 1967), 103.
24 Ibid., 96.
25 Gutiérrez, "Con Rodney Arismendi," and Fidel Castro, "Discurso pronunciado en el acto clausura de la Primera Conferencia de la Organización Latinoamericana de Solidaridad (OLAS), celebrada en el Teatro Chaplin, La Habana, 10 de agosto de 1967." http://www.cuba.cu/gobierno/discursos/
26 See Carlos María Gutiérrez, "OLAS, nace una nueva internacional," *Marcha*, August 11, 1967, 21.
27 "Reunión Consulta solicitada por Venezuela," 1967, Oficios y ordenanzas, 101–358, Ministry of Foreign Affairs Archive, Chile.
28 "Discurso del Doctor Pedro Paris Montesino, Delegado especial de Venezuela, pronunciado en la sesión de apertura celebrada el 19 de junio de 1967," Duodécima reunión de consulta de ministros de relaciones exteriores, June 19, 1967, Ministry of Foreign Affairs Archive, Chile.
29 "El Mundo: OLAS vs. OEA," *Confirmado*, July 20, 1967, 20.
30 Casa de las Américas. "Encuentro de la Canción Protesta. 1967," Havana, 45 (November–December 1967), 143–4.
31 Carlos Jorquera, "Lucha armada y lucha guerrillera," *Punto Final*, no. 35, 2nd fortnight of August, 1967.
32 "Conversaciones entre PC y PS," *Punto Final*, no. 15, 1st fortnight of November 1966, 25.
33 Eduardo Galeano, "Con Perón en puerta de hierro. El caudillo, los gorriones y la providencia," *Marcha*, September 8, 1967, 21.
34 Although the PRT had ties with certain Trotskyist sectors that had thus far had a very positive opinion of the Cuban strategy, the Revolution viewed Trotskyism with distrust. See Ernesto González (coord.), *El trotskismo obrero e internacionalista en la Argentina. Tomo 3: Palabra Obrera, el PRT y la Revolución Cubana (vol. 2: 1963–1969)* (Buenos Aires: Antídoto, 1999), chapter 21.
35 Avendaño and Palma, *El rebelde de la burguesía*, 67.
36 Juan Carlos Mechoso, *Acción directa anarquista. Una historia de la FAU* (Montevideo: Recortes, 2002), 61.
37 See Carlos María Gutiérrez, "El discurso de Fidel, Mensaje a los neo socialdemócratas," *Marcha*, August 26, 1967, 19, and "Con Rodney Arismendi."
38 For the Chilean case see Luis Vitale, *Contribución a la historia del MIR* (Santiago: Ed. Instituto de Investigación de Movimientos Sociales "Pedro Vuskovic," 1999), and a text attributed to Miguel Enríquez, "Algunos antecedentes del Movimiento de Izquierda Revolucionaria. 1965/1971," published in several compilations. See also Miguel Enríquez, *Con vista a la esperanza* (Santiago: Escaparate Ed., 1998) and Alfonso Valdés Navarro, Pedro, "Elementos teóricos en la formación y desarrollo del MIR durante el período 1966–1970" (undergraduate memory, Universidad de Valparaíso, 2006). Archivochile.com. For the Argentine case, see Ernesto González (coord.), *El trotskismo obrero e internacionalista en la Argentina*, vol. 3, *Palabra Obrera, el PRT y la Revolución Cubana* (Buenos Aires: Ed. Antídoto, 1999), 269–315.
39 See the episode mentioned in endnote 58 in Chapter 1.
40 For an overview of the recent debates and research on the tension between modernization and conservatism during the Onganía dictatorship, see Valeria Galván and Florencia Osuna (comp), *Política y cultura durante el "Onganiato." Nuevas perspectivas para la investigación de la presidencia de Juan Carlos Onganía (1966–1970)* (Rosario, Prohistoria, 2014).
41 Sergio Domecqu, Carlos Ramírez, and Juan Candela (pseudonyms), *El único camino para la toma del poder y el socialismo* (Ediciones Combate, 1969).

42 The term spontaneity was used in reference to the insurrectional strategy advocated by Moreno. For a different view on the Cuban position, see Simón Torres and Julio Aronde, "Debray and the Cuban Experience," *Monthly Review* 20, no. 3 (July–August 1968). In that article two Cuban officers, writing presumably under pseudonyms, criticized Debray's position.

43 Faúndez notes that left-wing parties used this critical period in the Frei administration to expand their influence in sectors where Christian Democrats had a large following: peasants, including Mapuche people; women workers; and the recently organized poor in the cities. Julio Faúndez, *Izquierdas y democracia en Chile, 1932–1973* (Santiago: Ediciones BAT, 1992), 159.

44 After discussing three massacres (El Salvador mines, 1966; Santiago de Chile strike, 1967; Puerto Montt, 1969) and other isolated incidents, the magazine *Punto Final* concluded that in such a repressive scenario with an unequal balance of powers (no policemen had been killed) legality no longer offered guarantees for social mobilization. "El costo de la vía pacífica," *Punto Final*, no. 109, July 1970, 3.

45 See *Punto Final*, no. 34, 1st fortnight of August 1967, 2, 4; *Confirmado*, July 20, 1967, 20–21; "Gobierno venezolano deplora creación de la 'OLAS' en Chile," *El Mercurio*, July 16, 1967, 53.

46 "No aceptaremos la violencia dentro de Chile ni acciones que perturben a otros pueblos," *El Mercurio*, July 17, 1967, 1.

47 "El poder Burgués," *Punto Final*, no. 38, 2nd fortnight of September 1967, 1.

48 See Luis Vitale, *Contribución a la historia del MIR* and Miguel Enríquez, "Algunos antecedentes del Movimiento de Izquierda Revolucionaria. 1965/1971," published in several compilations. See Miguel Enríquez, *Con vista a la esperanza* (Santiago: Escaparate Ed., 1998). The value of these two texts is that they provide opposing views of the process experienced by the MIR from 1965 to 1967 written by people who were direct participants in these events.

49 Miguel Enríquez, "Algunos antecedentes del Movimiento de Izquierda Revolucionaria. 1965/1971," 72–5.

50 In the first issues of the magazine *Estrategia*, without directly criticizing Guevara, a piece under the title "The Current Stage of Latin American Revolution" explicitly adhered to the insurrectional movement that had emerged across Latin America. It identified two moments: a first period, from 1960 to 1962, in which "the political work with the working people and even the peasant masses was neglected" to focus instead on the construction of a guerrilla *foco*; and a second period, from 1963 to 1965, which had brought renewed hopes, as "we are now beginning to understand that to create a guerrilla *foco* it is first necessary to have the support of significant sectors of the peasant population, who need to be politicized with genuine peasant leaders and not just with students. 'It is the party that guides the rifle,' and, therefore, armed struggle must be guided by a revolutionary Marxist party." *Estrategia*, no. 1, November 1965, Santiago. As representatives of this second moment, the author mentions the MIR of Hugo Blanco and Yon Sosa, both with close ties to Trotskyism and who would later be harshly criticized by Castro and Debray.

51 Most of the central committee (10 in 15), the entire national secretariat (5), and the position of general secretary were filled with representatives of "non-traditional" sectors that had been a minority until then.

52 See Avendaño y Palma, *El rebelde de la burguesía: la historia de Miguel Enríquez*, García Naranjo, *Historias derrotadas: opción y obstinación de la guerrilla chilena (1965–1988)*. Chapter III, Pedro Alfonso Valdés Navarro, "Elementos teóricos en la formación y desarrollo del MIR durante el período 1966–1970" (Universidad de Valparaíso, 2006). Archivochile.com.

53 The banning of political parties was an unprecedented event in Uruguay's political history of the second half of the twentieth century. In contrast to most countries of Latin America, Marxist parties had yet to be banned in Uruguay. In fact, Pacheco did not ban the Uruguayan Communist Party. The measure only targeted the parties that had stated their support for the OLAS majority declaration.

54 See interview with Efraín Martínez Platero conducted by the author, and "La militancia tupamara," in Rey Tristán, *A la vuelta de la esquina, la izquierda revolucionaria uruguaya, 1955–1973.*

55 See Federico Leicht, *Cero a la izquierda. Una biografía de Jorge Zabalza* (Montevideo: Letraeñe Ediciones, 2007) 43–55.

56 In Chile, the ELN was created as a secret organization within the Socialist Party. See Cristián Pérez, "El Ejército del Che y los Chilenos que continuaron su lucha," *Estudios Públicos* 89 (Summer 2003), and Patricio Quiroga Zamora, *Compañeros: el GAP: la escolta de Allende* (Santiago de Chile: Aguilar, 2001). In Argentina there was a short-lived ELN, from which the Revolutionary Armed Forces were later formed. See "Reportaje a la guerrilla argentina: FAR los de Garín," *Cristianismo y Revolución*, no. 28 (1971). On the former communists who participated in these activities, see Mora González C., "Modelo para armar: itinerarios y ámbitos disidentes del Partido Comunista Argentino en la gestación de uno de los grupos fundadores de las Fuerzas Armadas Revolucionarias (1960–1967)," *Izquierdas*, no. 12, www.izquierdas.cl, April 12, 2012, 111–42.

57 See chapter 2.

58 Carlos María Gutiérrez, "Bolivia, otra forma de la guerrilla," *Marcha*, May 12, 1967.

59 "Ayudemos a las guerrillas bolivianas," *Punto Final*, no. 28, 1st fortnight of May 1967, 1.

60 Manuel 'Barbarroja' Piñeiro, *Che Guevara y la Revolución Latinoamericana* (Colombia: Ocean Sur, 2006), 98.

61 Jon Lee Anderson, *Che Guevara: A Revolutionary Life* (New York: Grove Press, 1997), 71.

62 See Pérez, "El ejército del Che y los Chilenos," and Quiroga," *Compañeros*.

63 Transcribed from the video by Leandro Katz, *El día que me quieras* (New York: First Run/Icarus Films, 1997).

64 For an overview of the ways in which the photographs of his death were read by artists, see David Kunzle, *Che Guevara. Icon, Myth, and Message* (Hong Kong: Regents of the University of California, 1997), and John Berger, "Che Guevara: The Moral Factor," *The Urban Review* vol. 8, no. 3 (September 1975), 202–8.

65 See Kunzle, 91.

66 "Wherever death may surprise us, we will welcome it, provided our battle cry has been heard by at least one receptive ear and another hand has reached out to take up our weapons, and other men are preparing to chant our funeral songs to the rattling sound of machine guns and new cries of war and victory." Ernesto Guevara, "A crear muchos Vietnam," *Punto Final*, no. 27, 2nd fortnight of April 1967, 20–26.

67 See, for example, Pablo Pozzi, *Por las sendas argentinas. El PRT-ERP. La guerrilla marxista* (Buenos Aires: Eudeba, 2001), 167–83, and Clara Aldrighi, *Memorias de insurgencia. Historias de vida y militancia en el MLN Tupamaros. 1965–1975* (Montevideo: Ediciones de la Banda Oriental, 2009).

68 The play *Marat/Sade*, written by Peter Weiss in 1963, which proposed an imaginary dialogue on revolutionary violence between the Jacobin Jean-Paul Marat and the Marquis de Sade, illustrated the tensions between a discourse that calls for violence from a rational perspective as a necessary instrument for the emancipation of popular sectors, as defended by Marat, and another perspective that explores the instinctive and subjective forces that drive the violent practices defended by Sade. It is no coincidence that various versions of this play were put on stage in Argentina, Chile, and Uruguay

during this period. See, also, Peter Weiss, "Testimonio: Che Guevara," *Punto Final*, no. 45, January 2, 1968, 22–3.

69 Julio Huasi, "Che," *Punto Final*, no. 40, October 24, 1967, Document 2, 15, and *Cristianismo y Revolución*, no. 5, November 1967.

70 Mario Benedetti, "Consternados, Rabiosos," *Punto Final*, no. 42, November 21, 1967, 33.

71 On the concept of "structure of feelings," see Raymond Williams, *Marxism and Literature* (Oxford: Oxford University Press, 1977), 128–36.

72 "Lección de las guerrillas bolivianas," El Mercurio, October 13, 1967, 4.

73 Mariano Grondona, "Los herederos de Marx," *Primera Plana*, year 5, no. 252, October 24, 1967, 11.

74 "'Punto Final' y el Diario del Che," *Punto Final*, no. 648, September 28, 2007.

75 "El diario del Che en Bolivia," *Punto Final*, no. 59, 1st fortnight of July 1968.

76 Ibid., 91.

77 See Fidel Castro, "Una introducción necesaria," in ibid.

78 Regis Debray, *La Crítica de las Armas* (Mexico D.F.: Siglo Veintiuno Editores, 1975), 13.

79 On the role of the middle classes in Southern Cone societies, see John J. Johnson, *Political Change in Latin America: The Emergence of the Middle Sectors* (Stanford, California: Stanford University Press, 1958).

III

Dependence or Armed Struggle. Southern Cone Intellectuals and Militants Questioning the Legal Path to Socialism. Santiago de Chile, 1970–1973

On November 4, 1970, Salvador Allende was sworn into office as president of Chile. His government promised a revolution that raised expectations across the globe. His political project involved bringing together the best of the two worlds of the Cold War by achieving socialism through democracy. Apart from the differences with the Cuban Revolution, this process was conceived as a new step in the road to Latin America's liberation. Among the possibilities that the electoral victory of Unidad Popular opened up, it provided a place of refuge for many militants of the region. From the start, Allende's solidarity with political refugees from Latin America was a key aspect of his government and one of the most heated issues of public debate. In the first weeks of his presidency alone Allende granted political asylum to seventeen Bolivians, seven Brazilians, nine Uruguayans, and twelve Mexicans.[1]

While Chile had a long-standing tradition of political asylum, during this period the number of refugees grew, as many left-wing organizations from the region saw in socialist Chile a safe haven from the persecution they were suffering in their own countries. Often there was no official request for asylum and instead refugees were taken in as a result of the support that certain Chilean left-wing parties provided other Latin American parties, in some cases even against Allende's wishes or without his knowledge.

This was a source of many international problems for the government of Allende, who had to strike a delicate balance between upholding the principles of revolutionary continental solidarity advocated by the OLAS – an organization of which he had been vice president – and maintain good relations with the other governments of the region, which were for the most part right-wing.[2] This was done in the framework of an ideologically pluralist policy furthered by the government, which involved promoting Latin Americanism and calling for a greater role for the global South in world affairs.[3]

It was in that situation that many militants of the Southern Cone armed Left came together, engaged in discussions, and began to conceive political action in the region in a coordinated way. There, a number of academics connected with these political experiences developed the more radical lines of the dependency theory, offering frameworks for interpreting the regional political process through intense public involvement. This context of political meetings and academic discussions was also what led militants of Chile's MIR, Argentina's ERP, Uruguay's MLN-Tupamaros, and Bolivia's ELN to create the Revolutionary Coordination Board (JCR).

By examining these exchanges, this chapter will show how such experiences helped strengthen a transnational network of political activists connected with different organizations of the New Left that had been developing in Argentina, Brazil, Bolivia, Chile, and Uruguay since the mid-1960s, and which had influenced the political process in Chile and in other Southern Cone countries, and how such experiences had led to a common interpretation of the historical process underway.

Argentines, Uruguayans, Brazilians, and Bolivians in Allende's Chile

After the 1964 coup in Brazil a number of political activists and academics who were persecuted by the dictatorship turned to Chile as a place of refuge.[4] Initially these constituted only a small group, because, as seen in Chapter I, most of the early exiles settled in Montevideo. However, as of 1968, when the Brazilian dictatorship introduced a more authoritarian policy with Institutional Act No. 5 and Uruguay began to suffer the repressive measures of the government of Pacheco Areco, a second wave of exiles sought refuge in Santiago.[5]

This second wave was for the most part connected with some twenty guerrilla organizations that had been visibly active since 1968. These predominantly urban groups advocated guerrilla warfare as the way to overthrow the dictatorship, and denounced left-wing and nationalist parties for their failure to stop the advancing authoritarianism.[6] The members of the majority of these groups were recruited from urban sectors linked to the student movement and, to a lesser extent, the working classes. Many of them sought to bring together the various organizations that existed, as they more or less shared a common diagnosis of the Left as a whole, as well as a similar political strategy.[7] These guerrilla groups sought to reconcile Guevara's rural guerrilla orthodoxy with the new urban guerrilla tactics.[8]

All of these organizations sought to develop a rural guerrilla movement as a strategic goal, but they understood that to achieve that goal an initial stage was necessary to build up material and human resources in the cities. Expropriation actions were accompanied by kidnappings used to pressure the government into liberating political prisoners. The setting for this initial stage was urban. The year 1969 was the year of "general immersion in armed struggle," extending into 1970.[9] Although some actions were successful, the effectiveness of repression, with its systematic use of torture, meant that by 1972 most organizations had been defeated. Most of these groups never achieved their goal of developing a rural guerrilla movement, with the exception of Guerrilha do Araguaia, which had sent members to the Araguaia region, in the state of Pará, to initiate a rural guerrilla movement, which survived until 1974.

Many of the militants in these organizations ended up seeking refuge in Chile, where by 1973 they had formed a community of as many as 1,200 Brazilian exiles.[10] Some fled to Chile escaping persecution, others requested asylum, and others arrived through different means. For example, between 1969 and 1971, the Swiss, United States, and British ambassadors to Brazil were kidnapped by Brazilian guerrilla groups and were liberated in exchange for the release of a total of 125 political prisoners who were sent directly to Santiago.[11] These kidnappings in Brazil inspired similar actions by other guerrilla groups in Latin America.[12] According to the accounts of several of these exiles, the experience in Chile changed the way Brazilians perceived Latin America. In the words of José María Rabelo:

This experience was very humbling, as even though we were leftist we felt – I repeat – kind of superior, we had an almost colonialist attitude with respect to the rest of Latin America. When we left Brazil we thought we were going to teach everyone else, and we quickly realized that we had a lot to learn. And, you see, in that whole universe of Latin American heroes, of Guevara, Allende, Bolívar, Camilo Torres, Artigas, Tupac Amaru, and all the great leaders of the first and second independence, there aren't many Brazilian names that can be counted among them, no matter how much we love and respect them. What we had seen as Latin America's instability, was actually just the result of a greater degree of development in political struggles. That explains, to a great extent, the troubled history of these peoples who, perhaps even more than us, never passively accepted the domination of the diverse interests that came to our continent to exploit and impoverish us.[13]

The impact of the Chilean experience also stemmed from the social involvement generated by the political process of the Unidad Popular government. As Marijane V. Lisboa recalls, Chile was "a laboratory of Marxism" where "everything was new, and I wanted to experience it all."[14]

Far from being idle during this period, the Brazilian exiles continued their activism in Chile. One of the leading activities of the organized exile community was the denunciation of what was happening in Brazil. From 1969 to 1973 the Comitê de Denuncia à Repressao no Brasil (Committee for Denouncing Repression in Brazil) published the *Frente Brasileira de Informações* bulletin in Algeria, France, Italy, and later Chile, to report the

authoritarian measures adopted by the Brazilian government and the use
of torture in that country. The publication heralded what was to come in
the rest of the region.

In addition to denouncing the violations committed by the dictatorship, certain sectors of the Brazilian exile community tried to continue their revolutionary project through various means. According to
Denise Rollemberg, a minority of these exiles even carried out robberies in Chile with the aim of maintaining and supporting a military
infrastructure. Some of them were jailed during the UP government,
and even reported having been tortured by a police officer connected
with the Communist Party.[15] There were also exiles who, believing they
would soon be returning to Brazil, decided to join the working classes,
performing manual tasks that would put them in touch with the idealized world of labor and prepare them for their work with the masses
once they were back in Brazil. This practice was in line with the idea
of proletarianization upheld by several Southern Cone organizations at
the time.[16]

For most armed group militants it was an opportunity to reflect on the
increasing isolation that armed left-wing organizations were experiencing
in Brazil.[17] This was played out through debates in magazines. As many
as ten different magazines were published in Chile by Brazilian activists,
including *Resistencia*, *Campanha*, and *Debate*.[18] Among the recurring issues
discussed in these publications were the risk of isolation caused by "militarist deviations" and the need to form a party with a firm ideological commitment to Marxism–Leninism. These debates and reflections involved
exchanges with other Latin American left-wing organizations. An example
of this openness to dialog with organizations from the rest of Latin America
is the fact that the magazine *Debate* – published in Paris in February 1970,
and released in Santiago as of June 1972 under the name *Teoría y práctica* –
was written in Spanish and not Portuguese.[19]

As for the influx of Bolivian militants to Chile, this country was already
a well-known territory for the members of the ELN organized by Guevara.
In 1966, while Guevara was still alive, several Chilean activists, mostly
connected with the Socialist Party, including Beatriz Allende (daughter of
Salvador Allende), Elmo Catalán, and Arnoldo Camú, had formed one of
the leading rearguards of the Bolivian ELN. In addition to taking care of
such tasks as sending resources to the Bolivian guerrilla movement, after
Ñancahuazú these activists tried to ensure that the guerrillas could escape
through Chile. The Chilean activists also played a leading role during the
stage of reorganization of the ELN in 1968 and 1969, following the first
defeat suffered by Guevara. Inti Peredo, who had been appointed second-
in-command under Guevara, took refuge in Chile and planned the ELN's
reorganization from there. A number of Chilean activists joined these

efforts. The journalist Elmo Catalán, of *Punto Final*, was one of the Chileans who traveled to Bolivia and became a major leader of the Bolivian ELN.[20]

Guevara's role in the founding of the ELN gave a markedly internationalist character to the organization. For example, of the sixty-seven militants who participated in the second military campaign, whose aim was to take the town of Teoponte, seven were Chilean, two were Argentine, one was Brazilian, one Peruvian, and one Colombian.[21] For that reason, the reorganization efforts of the ELN received significant support from other countries in the region. Following a contact with the Uruguayan Tupamaros through a *Prensa Latina* journalist, the MLN-T offered a large part of the British pounds obtained in the Sucesión Horacio Mahilos S.A. heist in Uruguay.[22] Also, in 1969, Inti Peredo had met in La Paz with Alejandro Dabat of the PRT.[23]

The internationalist dimension of the ELN was used by Bolivia's military forces to discredit the organization, using the long-standing conflict with Chile to its advantage. In 1968, in reaction to the publication of Guevara's Bolivian diary in Chile and the asylum request by Minister Arguedas, President Barrientos declared, "Insurgency and treason go through Chile."[24]

In July 1970, the mining town of Teoponte was taken over by sixty-seven ELN activists, for the most part young middle-class men.[25] The aim of this group, which was divided into three platoons, was to build a military force that would later advance on Alto Beni, tropical Chapare, and the jungle area of Santa Cruz. In Teoponte they planned to kidnap U.S. Ambassador Ernest Siracusa, who was expected to visit the town. But due to last minute changes in the ambassador's plans, he was not there when the ELN arrived. They decided, instead, to kidnap two German managers of the mining company located there, asking in exchange for the release of jailed ELN activists.[26] After seizing the town, the activists hid in the mountains. Initially the campaign appeared to have been successful, as President Ovando agreed to the exchange and liberated ten activists. However, the military campaign would be short-lived. By late September, thirty guerrillas had been executed, nine had been killed in combat, and the rest had been captured. Only some ten activists were still holding back the army. Of the handful of starving and weakened guerrillas, two activists tried to leave, taking some of the scarce food with them. The rest saw this attempt as desertion and executed them.

In 1970, after the Teoponte campaign failed, Chile again became a place of refuge for Bolivians. On November 4, 1970, the same day that Salvador Allende took office, Chile's new socialist government took in eight survivors of the Bolivian guerrilla movement who were fleeing from Teoponte. One of these guerrillas was Osvaldo "Chato" Peredo, who had taken the helm of the ELN after his brother Inti Peredo – the leader originally appointed by Guevara in 1967 – was murdered. The eight survivors traveled by plane to Arica, where they were welcomed by a mass rally of students.[27] A month earlier, three survivors of the same campaign had also crossed the border into Chile with the support of members of the Chilean Socialist Party, just as members of Guevara's campaign had done in 1967.

This time, however, the political developments in Bolivia brought innovations. In 1971, Rene Zavaleta Mercado – an intellectual originally with the Movimiento Nacionalista Revolucionario (Revolutionary Nationalist Movement, or MNR) who had moved increasingly closer to the ELN – wrote an article for *Punto Final* where he said that while the Ñancahuazú and Teoponte campaigns had been an initial political and military failure, they had achieved a "deferred political success." In his view, the radicalization of these nationalist youths and their shift to the left entailed "a key tactical opportunity," that helped explain General Juan José Torres' rise to power.[28] The situation that triggered the internal coup within the military regime and brought Torres to power was, in fact, shaped by the Teoponte actions, the university occupation, and a general strike staged on October 7 by students, workers, and peasants, which swayed military support in his favor.

Torres – a left-wing nationalist general who had participated in the nationalization policies of the Ovando government and had a favorable opinion of the reformist process promoted by Velasco Alvarado in Peru – furthered some of the policies that had been initiated in the previous administration. In addition to continuing with the process of nationalizations and implementing an independent foreign policy, Torres introduced an innovation with respect to the Peruvian process by calling for the establishment of a popular assembly that would lead the process of change. One of the first measures of the new government was to offer ELN militants the chance to go into exile, while promising a fair treatment to those who were still on the run.[29]

During the early months of 1971 the ELN placed a greater emphasis on urban guerrilla warfare. They had received assistance from the Uruguayan Tupamaros, who instructed ELN members on how to build underground hideouts and taught them other techniques for city fighting.[30] They committed political assassinations, which they called executions, targeting members of the repressive forces who had played a significant role in the persecution of the ELN.[31] Simultaneously, members of the ELN moved closer to the government. Major Ruben Sánchez – a military office who had been captured by Guevara and as a result of that experience had become more sympathetic to the Left – was instrumental in initiating contacts between the government and the guerrillas.[32] Ten months later, when the government was toppled by a conservative military conspiracy, ELN members and some military officers convened by Sánchez played a major role in the only attempt to resist the coup, known as the "Laikakota Battle."[33]

After the resistance was defeated and Hugo Banzer took office as president in August 1971, Chile became for the third time a place where ELN activists could seek refuge and reorganize the resistance. During this period, Torres increased his contacts with Latin American leftist groups and continued his Marxism studies. It was in that context that he published *Dinámica nacional y liberación* (National Dynamics and Liberation), an interpretation of Bolivian history from a dependency theory perspective.[34] In Chile he also tried to form a left-wing front, bringing together the various groups that had participated in or had supported Torres' Popular Assembly. The result of these efforts was the Frente Revolucionario Antiimperialista (Anti-Imperialist Revolutionary Front, or FRA) made up of most of the legal left-wing parties (PCB, MIR, PRIN, POR-Combate, POR-Masas, PSB), and armed groups, including the ELN and a new armed organization formed by military officers and headed by Major Sánchez. The goal of this front was to organize the resistance from Chile. But multiple internal conflicts would cut this initiative short.[35]

According to Ruben Sánchez, he toured Europe to raise funds for the resistance, with the support of Debray and in contact with Torres. The tour was a success, raising US$100,000. Contributors included Pablo Picasso and Yves Montand. However, when the fundraisers returned, the FRA had already disbanded due to differences over the assessment of the Popular Assembly experience.[36] Meanwhile, ELN members made contact with Cuba again to resume plans for a new armed incursion. These plans, however, would be frustrated by the coup d'état in Chile, and in September 1973, the militants who were still in Chile fled quickly to Buenos Aires, which became the new operations center.

Another group of exiles who found refuge in Allende's Chile were the Uruguayan Tupamaros.[37] Although no clear records exist, some 1,500 to 3,000 Uruguayans – the vast majority of them formal members of the organization or sympathizers – are said to have passed through Chile from 1971 to 1973 fleeing the persecution unleashed by President Juan María Bordaberry.[38]

From the small group of no more than forty people who in 1966 had started thinking about urban guerrilla warfare, in less than two years the MLN-T had become one of the most popular guerrilla movements of the continent's Left. The year 1972 would turn out to be a paradoxical one for this organization, as the realization of its growth led it to take its military confrontation with the state to a different level.[39] This change in strategy resulted in a resounding military defeat from which the MLN-T would not recover in the coming years. During 1972, thirty-seven people were killed in armed force operations and seven were tortured to death in prison. By

October of that year, the armed forces issued a statement informing that the MLN-T had been dismantled. At the end of the year, the armed forces reported that there were 5,000 prisoners awaiting trial by military courts on charges of sedition.[40] In this context, Chile was the main destination for activists and militants who were able to flee the country.

While the first Tupamaros arrived in Chile in 1971, the MLN-T had already established relations with the Chilean Socialist Party. Previous contacts had been made in order to channel funds to the Bolivian ELN (the British pounds that had been stolen by the MLN-T) and also during the kidnapping of Britain's ambassador to Uruguay, as Salvador Allende had offered to act as mediator.[41] Activists who were part of the leadership of the MLN-T recall several meetings with Salvador Allende, in which he had appeared very willing to grant asylum, but had asked that exiles refrain from interfering in domestic politics and from associating with the MIR, which Allende considered Unidad Popular's leading opposition in the Left.[42] Of this first group of no more than seventy activists who arrived in the year 1971, the vast majority returned to Uruguay, after going to Cuba to receive military training, and were arrested in early 1972.[43]

As of April 1972, the number of Uruguayan exiles in Chile grew significantly as the organization received increasing blows in Uruguay. That year, MLN-T members decided to come out of their isolation in Chile and become more involved in the country's politics and the spaces for interaction with other Latin American organizations that were opening up in Allende's Chile. In the words of Jorge Selves, one of the leaders who was in Chile during that period:

Exile in Chile gave members of the Latin American Left the first opportunity to become familiarized with each other, meet, and engage in exchanges ... We realized the significance of what the MLN had achieved, especially for those groups in the Left that have adopted an armed or revolutionary stance. [...] Seen today from a distance it may be difficult to appreciate. But in less than two years we built a network of relationships that spanned all of Latin America, with some groups that were reorganizing themselves and had some representatives left.[44]

It is in this context that the MLN-T chose to prioritize its relationship with the Chilean MIR. This was the organization that in Chile had the greatest ideological and political affinities with the MLN-T. The MIR offered logistic support for the growing needs faced by the MLN-T as a result of the increasingly larger group of militants arriving from Uruguay, while the MLN-T offered the MIR technical and operational advice in exchange.[45] The Tupamaros held workshops where they explained their *berretines* (urban hideouts) techniques and began working on designing a homemade machine gun and explosives.[46] Some MLN-T militants participated in President Allende's security team – the Grupo de Amigos

Personales (Group of Personal Friends, or GAP) – initially formed by social-ists and MIR members. They advised the team in technical aspects of the president's security and used part of the GAP's infrastructure to transport weapons and supplies to Uruguay.[47] In other cases, MLN-T rank-and-file members participated in land "seizures" and workplace "occupations."[48]

As the number of exiles continued to grow it became increasingly dif-ficult to provide shelter for all of them. The thirty houses that the MLN-T had in Santiago were no longer enough to absorb the influx.[49] According to some accounts, MLN-T leaders, in coordination with the MIR and Unidad Popular, decided to set up campsites in the Andes, for twenty to thirty militants each. These campsites turned into a proletarianization experi-ment, where young and mostly urban activists had to adapt to a new way of life marked by the austerity and isolation of rural environments, which the writer Fernando Butazzoni describes as something of a cross between a "military training camp and [a] hippie commune. It was a sort of Guevara Woodstock."[50]

A major concern during this period was explaining the MLN-T's defeat in Uruguay. This was discussed internally in different instances that cul-minated in February 1973 with a symposium held in Viña del Mar in which some fifty militants participated, representing members who were in Chile, Argentina, and Cuba, and a small group of Tupamaros who were still in Uruguay. The self-criticism was strongly influenced by the debates in Chile among the different armed organizations of the Southern Cone.

The document adopted in this symposium had certain points in com-mon with some of the issues that were being discussed by the Brazilian exile community. On the one hand, the document criticized the mili-tarist tendencies that had been stressed in the year 1972 and which had enabled a new scenario where the "enemy moved into a counter-offensive."[51] The explanation given for this was the ideological weak-ness of the movement and the emergence of multiple contradictions within it that had to do with generational and "class" conflicts. Unlike most armed organizations in the Southern Cone, which had adopted an ideological definition like the political parties of the Left   for the most part Marxism–Leninism – the Tupamaros had resisted any form of ideological definition. While this was initially seen as a refreshing and heterodox approach in a context marked by the ideological debates of Latin America's Left, in Chile it was reinterpreted as a weakness that explained the Tupamaros' defeat.[52]

The solution to these problems was to be found in transforming the MLN-T into a Marxist–Leninist party, with a strong ideological training of its officers.[53] This had to be an ideological but also a moral transformation. In addition to their training, militants had to follow the guiding principles of proletarianization, which the Tupamaros termed *peludización* in honor of the sugarcane workers of Bella Union, who were known as *peludos* (or hairy ones).[54]

Another issue debated at the symposium was whether they should return to Uruguay or not. In Chile, everyone seemed to agree on the need to wait some time before preparing the return. In early 1973, the Uruguayans in Chile cautioned that an authoritarian backlash was inevitable, and they predicted that foreigners would be the first to be targeted as they had been the subject of right-wing campaigns that undermined the president's public image. In talks with the MIR and members of the president's team it was decided that most MLN-T militants would be evacuated through Cuba, and then to Argentina.[55] According to an internal document, by June 1973 most MLN-T militants had been sent either to Cuba or to Argentina, and a small core group of no more than fifty Tupamaros remained in Chile carrying out logistical and military coordination tasks with the MIR. At that time, ties with the MIR were strengthened through the work of several Tupamaros in certain central organizational tasks of the MIR.[56]

As for Argentina, in comparison to the other communities, there were fewer Argentines who were organized and connected to some form of exile. A number of academics had moved to Chile as a result of the repressive policies implemented in Argentina's universities after the Onganía coup in 1966. Although some retreated to private centers in Argentina, others were attracted by the situation in Chile.[57] This second group included intellectuals such as Marcos Kaplan, who was a researcher at FLACSO from 1967 to 1970, and Sergio Bagú, also with FLACSO from 1970 to 1973.[58]

Kaplan, who was the leading collaborator of Silvio Frondizi – one of the most representative intellectuals of Argentina's New Left in the 1960s – decided to settle in Chile, where he worked in the University of Chile and FLACSO's Latin American School of Political Science.[59] There he published his most influential work, *Formación del Estado Nacional en América Latina*, where he reflected on the processes of dependent growth, oligarchic hegemony, and the construction of the national state. Bagú was already a well-known intellectual before going to Chile to work in FLACSO. He was one of the most innovative economic and social historians of the 1950s. In Chile, he began a rich exchange with both ECLAC structuralists and dependency theorists.[60]

Another Argentine intellectual, sociologist Juan Carlos Marín, who had been connected with the Partido Socialista de Vanguardia (PSV) (Vanguard Socialist Party), was working as researcher and professor at the University of Concepción since the mid-1960s. He forged a close relationship with the new generation of students, who, as of 1967, would form the leadership of the MIR.[61]

The cycle of urban uprisings, that began in 1969 in Argentina, had eroded the stability of the dictatorial regime. A deep political crisis opened up promising opportunities for the New Left that was emerging among armed political groups and social movements (rank-and-file unionists, youth movements, revolutionary Christians). From 1969 to 1971, these groups capitalized on the clash between the dictatorship and society, undermining other identity-based divisions, such as the Peronist/anti-Peronist opposition and the working class/middle class opposition. Following the dictatorship's decision to call elections in 1971, the development of that social movement and the leadership of these sectors began to be disputed. As of that moment, traditional political leaders, and in particular Perón, took on a new role in the opposition movement, competing with the role of the armed groups. In that context, the dictatorial regime stepped up its repressive policies against these organizations, seeking a transition to democracy in which these new actors would be relegated to a marginal role in national politics.

This led some Argentine armed groups to look to Chile as a potential rearguard, where militants wanted by the police could hide. They also saw Chile as a place to develop political contacts and as a stopover on their way to Cuba, as Chile's resumption of diplomatic relations with Cuba enabled, among other things, direct flights from Chile to Cuba. The PRT-ERP was particularly alert to what was happening in Chile. According to a document issued by the leadership of that organization at the time, "[t]he establishment of the people's government in Chile, a country that borders Argentina along more than 3,000 kilometers, gives our revolutionary war a friendly frontier, a significant political and military need that we did not have before."[62]

PRT members Enrique Gorriarán Merlo and Joe Baxter encouraged by the impact that Allende's victory had had in the region, decided to visit Chile.[63] In his memoir, Gorriarán Merlo describes the contacts established with the MIR and the discussions with Regis Debray during that trip. Through agreements with the MIR they began a formal relationship with the Chileans that would later be strengthened as a result of the incidents connected with the Rawson prison escape in Trelew in 1972. The meeting with Debray – who had settled in Chile after his release through an amnesty granted by the Torres government – confirmed Gorriarán Merlo's doubts regarding the ideas set out by the French militant in *Revolution in the Revolution?*

Academic and Militants Thinking about Revolution

In the 1960s, Santiago became one of South America's most important centers of production in the field of social sciences. A number of elements converged to contribute to this academic development. In 1957, a UNESCO conference held in Rio proposed the creation of two research and teaching centers to promote and modernize social science studies in Latin America. The initiative to establish a center in Brazil was cut short by the 1964 coup. By contrast, the Facultad Latinoamericana de Ciencias Sociales (Latin American School of Social Sciences, or FLACSO) established in Chile continued in activity throughout the 1960s, attracting social scientists from Chile, the rest of South America, Europe, and North America to its academic programs.[64] The Economic Commission for Latin America and the Caribbean (ECLAC) was established in Chile in the 1950s and became a space for reflecting on development issues. Also, a number of research and academic centers connected with the Catholic Church were created in the country (CIAS, DESAL, ILADES). Besides these international organizations, the process of transformation and renovation of the country's universities gave rise to research centers in the field of social sciences, which drew intellectuals from across the region.[65] Lastly, the development of certain state institutions under programs of the Christian Democratic government and the role played by the Chilean Socialist Party in Latin America also brought many Latin American intellectuals and technical experts to the country.[66]

These spaces generated a steady flow of academics, technical experts, and intellectuals coming into Chile from different parts of Latin America. The fact that Chile avoided the authoritarian processes that swept the region (Brazil, 1964; Argentina, 1966; Bolivia, 1971) also acted as an incentive for several academics who were fleeing their own countries to choose Chile as their destination. It was in these spaces that a significant number of exiles were active, working and contributing to issues that were key for political and academic thinking during that period. In addition, in the 1970s, Allende's victory in the elections increased the influx of a range of academics from different parts of the world who flocked to Chile to witness the UP experience firsthand. They were welcomed by the government and offered a space to collaborate with the process under way, allowing them to exercise complete intellectual independence.

Brazil had a major presence in this wave of academic exiles that began arriving in the mid-1960s as a result of that country's dictatorship. This group represented a diversity of academics that also expressed different approaches within the field of politics. By way of example, Chile became a very important place for three Brazilian intellectuals that achieved renown in the 1960s. Following the coup in Brazil, educator Paulo Freire traveled to Chile to work with sectors of the Christian Democratic government in literacy programs. There his thinking was radicalized as he questioned the experiences of reformist and developmentalist governments. This led him to propose a more radical literacy program, which was set out in his *Pedagogia do Oprimido* (*Pedagogy of the Oppressed*), where he suggested the need for a more organic link with the subordinated sectors of society. The aim would no longer be development but the promotion among these sectors of a critical conscience of their social conditions, as a way of ensuring their liberation.[67]

Fernando Henrique Cardoso, a Brazilian social scientist who had begun his academic training as a Marxist, moved to Chile after remaining in his country for two years following the coup.[68] It was in Santiago, while working at ECLAC, that he met sociologist Enzo Falletto from the University of Chile, with whom he wrote *Dependencia y Desarrollo en América Latina* (*Dependency and Development in Latin America*), published in 1969. In this book they set forth a critical view that described the limits of the developmentalist project in the region. The text had a strong influence in academic circles, eroding the foundations of developmentalism and introducing a more political approach that focused on the study of the state. This gave way to a new generation of economists and sociologists who had originally embraced developmentalism but were starting to move away from it.

Theotônio dos Santos was another Brazilian academic who relocated to Chile, after suffering persecution at the University of Brasilia. From there he contributed to the development of another school of thought within the so-called dependency theory, but in this case closer to certain political ideas of the far Left.[69] The most radical version of the dependency theory was expressed by the works of Theotônio dos Santos, but also of other Brazilian intellectuals such as Vania Bambirra and Ruy Mauro Marini, who were strongly committed to the ideas proposed by the groups of the New Left, as well as the works of German academic André Gunder Frank. These academics, who had been working at the University of Brasilia, came to Santiago escaping the persecution of the Brazilian dictatorship. Sociologists dos Santos and Bambirra had been involved in the creation of Política Opéraria (POLOP) in the early 1960s. This small political organization, primarily linked to university circles, had a major influence in the debates of the Brazilian Left, as it provided theoretical inputs from Trotskyism (law of uneven development) to criticize the theory of development in stages (*etapista*), which was furthered by the Communist Party, regarding the democratic bourgeois nature that the revolution should have in Brazil. In the framework of this debate they introduced some of the aspects that would later be developed academically in the dependency theory. In the early 1960s, dos Santos and Bambirra entered a master's program in the University of Brasilia, where dos Santos would later teach. Also there during those years was Marini, a young sociologist who had been involved in the POLOP and had been invited by Darcy Ribeiro to teach sociology in this brand new university.[70] Lastly, André Gunder Frank, a German economist who had studied in the United States, joined the University of Brasilia in 1964 as visiting professor. Although his training was neoclassical and he had politically conservative views, Frank was seduced by the intellectual and political debates under way in the Left at the time.[71] These intellectuals held a regular seminar on Marx's Capital at the University of Brasilia, where they drew on their shared political experience and began forming a clearer view in academic terms.

The first to leave Brazil for Chile after the 1964 coup was dos Santos, who, following a period underground in Brazil, decided to seek asylum in Chile in 1966.[72] There he was appointed director of the new social studies research center that was being formed in the University of Chile under the name Centro de Estudios Sociales (CESO). Bambirra and Frank would join the center in 1967. In 1970, Ruy Mauro Marini traveled from Mexico to the University of Concepción, invited by Nelson Gutiérrez, a student and MIR leader. And, in 1971, Marini also became involved in the activities of the University of Chile and of CESO in Santiago.

This group's works were made public through a University of Chile publication – *Los Cuadernos del Centro de Estudios Socioeconómicos* – that came out from 1966 to 1968, which had a significant influence in academic circles both in Chile and in the region.[73] This was an interdisciplinary journal that covered a range of subjects, but was to a certain extent focused on the analysis of the structures of dependency in Latin America's history. CESO was also a space for rich exchanges among intellectuals who were active in Latin America's Left. Some of these intellectuals included: Tomás Vasconi, André Gunder Frank, Marta Harnecker, Cristian Sepúlveda, Jaime Torres, Marco Aurelio García, Álvaro Briones, Guillermo Labarca, Antonio Sánchez, Marcelo García, Emir Sader, and Jaime Osorio; Regis Debray, who joined the center after being liberated in Bolivia; the Cubans Germán Sánchez and José Bell Lara, who had drifted apart from Havana after the constraints placed on *Pensamiento Crítico*; and the Mexican Luis Hernández Palacios.[74] In this sense, CESO could be said to have been this group's political and academic platform.

The first book to set out the group's program was written by André Gunder Frank and published initially in English in 1967 as *Capitalism and Underdevelopment in Latin America*.[75] That same year Frank arrived in Chile. The book, which was a compilation of essays written in Latin America during the 1960s, became one of the leading reference works for dependency theory thinkers. There Frank identifies three contradictions that had shaped capitalist development in Latin America in the last four centuries:

These contradictions are: the expropriation of economic surplus from the many and its appropriation by the few; the polarization of the capitalist system in a metropolitan center and peripheral satellites; and the continuity of the basic structure of the capitalist system throughout the history of its expansion and transformation, as a result of the persistence or recreation of these contradictions everywhere and throughout time. My thesis is that these internal contradictions of capitalism and the historical development of the capitalist system have generated underdevelopment in the peripheral satellites whose economic surplus was expropriated, while generating economic development in the metropolitan centers, which appropriate that surplus – and, further, that this process still continues.[76]

For Frank, the continuity of the economic structures of dependency over four centuries was so strong that it precluded the possibility of any independent economic development processes. That is, these countries' satellite condition prevented any form of national capitalist development. In Latin America, "a bourgeoisie cannot be expected to emancipate the economy and the people from underdevelopment."[77] The popular sectors, which have no ties with the central countries, are the only ones that can break dependency. And in his view, the only way to break that dependency was through a socialist revolution.

In his arguments, he repeatedly challenged two perspectives that had begun to be questioned by academic and political approaches since the mid-1960s. On the one hand, the more classic perspective of Latin American development theory that held that autonomous capitalist development was possible with certain levels of social integration; on the other, the theses that the communist parties had defended since the 1950s that propounded a revolution by stages, which involved a first stage of alliance with the national bourgeoisie to develop a national capitalism that would break feudal vestiges.

The book was very well received throughout the continent. A middle-class readership connected with the university expansion process and the development of the social sciences that was looking for political answers in the discourses of the social sciences felt represented by the approach proposed in Frank's essays.[78] In his writings these readers found scientific arguments for certain political commitments that they were simultaneously embracing.

Theotônio dos Santos, as noted above, was another important figure in this group of radical dependency theorists. In addition to acting as coordinator of these debates due to his institutional position as CESO director, dos Santos played a major role by offering a version of the dependency theory applied to the specific historical situation that Latin America was experiencing in the 1960s. Of his works, perhaps the most significant in this sense was *Socialismo o Fascismo, el nuevo carácter de la dependencia y el dilema latinoamericano* (Socialism or Fascism. The New Face of Dependency and the Latin American Dilemma). This book, completed in 1966 and published in 1969 in Santiago, was his most influential in political terms, as it combined structural aspects of political economics with the specific situation of advancing authoritarianism in dictatorial Brazil, which was a premonitory sign of what would later happen in Chile and the Southern

Cone. In Chile he worked on a revised version, which he published in 1972 in Buenos Aires.[79]

In both works the key argument was the idea that political radicalization in Latin America was inevitable, as the only way that capitalism could survive in a context of political and economic crisis was to resort to a new form of fascism, different from European fascism. Fascism was the result of the new nature of dependency, determined by processes of economic transnationalization. These processes were gradually destroying national economies, undermining national bourgeoisies and the political regimes that these social sectors had implemented in the 1940s and 1950s.

In dos Santos' perspective, the economic and social crisis that shaped the new form of dependency generated a "revolutionary situation" in which reformist, developmentalist, and popular nationalist alternatives encountered deep limitations: the structural limitation of dependant development, and the political limitation of the contradictions of the demands of the social masses aggravated by the crisis. In this scenario only two paths were open: socialism or fascism.

As another major exponent of this group, Ruy Mauro Marini proposed a "theory of overexploitation" in his book *Subdesarrollo y revolución* (Underdevelopment and Revolution), published in Mexico in 1969 when he was already in Chile. There he argued that in dependent or peripheral countries the tendency to over-exploit is greater than in central countries, due to the fact that the extraction of surplus is intensified as a result of unequal international trade relations.[80] In contrast to developmental theorists, Marini posited that economic development in dependent countries led to increasing inequality. The "overexploitation theory" offered a new justification for the idea of continentality of the revolution, which in this case was redefined as proletarian internationalism of dependent countries.

Aside from their writings and the political repercussions these had, the commitment that the three foreign academics had with Chilean politics was very significant. Dos Santos served as an advisor to some sectors of the Socialist Party and the MIR. Frank and Marini, for their part, publicly declared their support for the MIR.[81] In Marini's case, this support led him to assume an even greater commitment and join the organization. He served on the MIR's central governing committee as of 1972 and was in charge of foreign relations after the coup.[82]

These academics also played an important role in *Chile hoy*, a magazine meant for the general public, for which they were regular contributors. The idea for the magazine was proposed by Marta Harnecker, who would become the magazine's director, while the position of assistant director would be filled by José Manuel Quijano, a young economist who was the son of Carlos Quijano, the director of Uruguay's prestigious weekly publication *Marcha*. The magazine tried to develop a more theoretical reflection on

Figure 3.a. Martha Harnecker gives an interview to Miguél Enriquez for Chile Hoy, 1973. Armindo Cardoso Collection. Biblioteca Nacional de Chile.

the political process, in dialog with the issues of dependency, imperialism, the duality of power, and the construction of a new popular non-bourgeois institutional structure, the rise of fascist authoritarianism, and the threat of a potential civil war.

Martha Harnecker's work in *Chile hoy*, and in other ventures, is representative of a cultural and political climate marked by a great social demand for literature connected with Marxism. These products, in the form of magazines and various types of publications, went beyond the academic sphere and were aimed at bringing Marxism to popular sectors. In addition to her involvement in the *Chile hoy*, Harnecker played a very important role as a promoter of Marxism – in particular in its Althusserian version – among the new generation of Chilean activists and foreign activists who were in Chile at the time of Allende.

Harnecker had been a Catholic activist – having headed the Catholic University group Acción Católica Universitaria – and in the late 1950s began developing a social awareness, attracted by the works of Jacques Maritain. In 1963 she won a scholarship to study in Europe. There she became familiarized with Marxism. Initially, Harnecker formed part of a group of Latin Americans who studied the writings of Regis Debray. It was through Debray that she met French philosopher Louis Althusser, who invited her to participate in a reading group that studied Marx's

Capital. Althusser, a member of the French Communist Party who felt seduced by the Maoist experience, was one of the leading figures of structural Marxism of that time, and he created a space formed by young philosophers who abandoned the Communist Party and would ultimately lean toward Maoism. Althusser was a proponent of an anti-humanist Marxism, that rejected the historicist and idealistic traditions and focused on the epistemological break of the historical materialism of the mature Marx, with *Capital* as his most significant work. This conception offered a scientific method that enabled an understanding of the hidden social structures of domination that went beyond historicist versions.[83] Harnecker was inspired by his teachings and abandoned the profession she had initially-chosen – psychology – to devote herself fully to Marxist studies. She was the first to translate Althusser's *Pour Marx* into Spanish (translated as *La teoría revolucionaria de Marx*), in 1967, and she began drafting the outline of what would later become her classic book *Los conceptos elementales del materialismo histórico* (The Basic Concepts of Historical Materialism).[84] Some of these ideas were published by her as an article, featured in the Tribuna Ideológica section of *Punto Final*, under the pen name Neva.[85] These ideas were also discussed in Chile, in CESO and the Sociology Department of the University of Chile, both of which she joined upon returning from France.

The first edition of *Los conceptos elementales* was published in 1968. The book sought to incorporate and disseminate the leading Marxist categories in light of Althusser's interpretation and to describe the construction of a theoretical model for interrelating these categories. The attempt to provide a rational structure and a system of scientific categories to explain social structure, social classes, and change was what motivated this popular version of Althusser produced by Harnecker, in which the formalist language of structuralism seemed to offer the region's militants scientific certainties.

By 1971, the book was in its seventh edition. In 1972, Harnecker and Gabriela Uribe undertook the *Cuadernos de Educación Popular* (CEP) project, a collection of booklets that were intended to serve as an activist handbook for the masses. The collection was divided into two series: *Por qué socialismo?* (Why Socialism?) and *Para luchar por el socialismo* (Fighting for Socialism). The first was a simplified version of *Los conceptos elementales*, written in a more didactic style, with illustrations and outlines. The second series described the "conditions of organization, class awareness, planning, and leadership of mass struggle."[86] In Harnecker's own words both initiatives had the same goal: "The truth is that the essential purpose of all my work is and has been pedagogical."[87]

Her works were immensely popular. *Los conceptos elementales* became a key manual for activists throughout Latin America. The book's publishing success was due, among other things, to the intellectual sponsorship of Louis

Althusser, who wrote a prolog to the first edition, and later another prolog to the sixth edition.

Punto Final reviewed it, calling it an obligatory reference work for revolutionary activists: "For revolutionary activists whose theoretical and political training is acquired in the struggles of revolutionary parties, Marta Harnecker's book will usefully guide the experience they gain and further it through the application of Marxist–Leninist theory."[88]

There were some, however, who questioned her work from a radical perspective, criticizing the strong formalization of the French structuralist influence against which they upheld the Gramscian historicist tradition.[89] The influence of Harnecker's work spread rapidly among militants of various organizations who were in Chile at the time. Tupamaro leader Eleuterio Fernandez Huidobro recalls that she made a great impact on the Tupamaros who were in Chile.[90] In Argentina, the magazine *Nuevo Hombre*, which had ties to the PRT-ERP, informed in an article entitled "Culture as a Weapon of Liberation," that Harnecker's *Cuadernos* would be published locally in a version adapted to Argentina "specific characteristics."[91]

There were other undertakings that also expressed these intellectual exchanges among Chileans, exiles, and visiting academics, which expanded during the Unidad Popular government. Another research center, created much later than the CESO, the Catholic University's Center for Studies on National Reality also influenced political and academic discussions significantly.[92] Although at a reduced scale, the arrival of Bolivian militants also had an intellectual impact. Rene Zavaleta Mercado, one of Bolivia's most renowned intellectuals who had been a supporter of revolutionary nationalism and had veered to the left in the late 1960s, backing Torres' government, had been exiled in Chile since 1971.[93] He was the coordinator of the National Situation Studies Center at Chile's Catholic University where he published the first version of *Poder dual, problemas de la teoría del estado en América Latina*, where he draws on Lenin and Trotsky to examine the duality of power in the Bolivian and Chilean processes.[94] Also, Belgian sociologist Armand Mattelart worked on perspectives of cultural dependence and imperialism in Chile, where he published *How to Read Donald Duck*, coauthored with Ariel Dorfman. Other magazines, such as *Cuadernos de Documentación Tercer Mundo*, *Marxismo y Revolución*, published by Ruy Mauro Marini in 1973, the second era of the magazine *Estrategia*, and the already-mentioned *Punto Final*, also provided major inputs for discussion in this area of debate where pressing political matters met intellectual reflection.

The works reviewed here reveal a singular moment in the relationship between academic production and political commitment, where certain actors of academia legitimized their studies by adopting certain political stances, while political actors looked to academic work as a way of legitimizing their practices. It helped build academic careers while strongly influencing left-wing politics. The coming together of these academics in the highly unique historical circumstances that existed in Chile in the early 1970s entailed that their intellectual reflection had multiple political implications.[95]

Revolutionary Solidarity under the UP government

Because of its political ideology, the Chilean MIR was the organization that was in closer contact with a large number of these exiles, who, moreover, came from organizations in the region which had similar backgrounds. As of 1969, the MIR had adopted an armed struggle strategy. Many of its rank-and-file members focused on promoting "direct actions" among the masses – such as land seizures and occupations – as part of the growing mobilization of peasants, settlement dwellers, and students, which had been on the rise since 1968.[96] A smaller group, connected with the leadership, focused on developing a military force, by staging bank heists and other robberies. The "bank expropriations" were armed propaganda actions that exposed part of the organization's leadership. This forced many leaders to go underground. Elections were not part of that strategy, as is obvious in an early 1969 document entitled *No Elections! Armed Struggle Is the Only Way.*[97]

When in 1970 the victory of the Unidad Popular coalition became a real prospect, the MIR seemed to temper its attitude with respect to elections. Without abandoning its skepticism toward elections as a way of seizing power, the MIR acknowledged that the possibility of an electoral triumph of the Left had generated expectations in various popular sectors, which saw such an event as part of a more general process of social mobilization. The MIR sought to work with these popular sectors and the more radical sectors of the UP coalition in order to channel their mobilization toward a revolutionary strategy.

Just as the MIR moved closer to the UP experience, the presidential candidate also became interested in integrating the MIR in some way into the campaign and later into the new government. During the campaign, Allende and the MIR engaged in talks. The MIR decided to suspend its armed propaganda actions as of June, so that they would not be used against the UP coalition in the run-up to the election. Shortly after taking office, Allende granted amnesty to some thirty MIR activists who had been imprisoned during the Frei administration, and he dropped the charges against another group of leaders. Allende had invited the MIR to form part of his personal security team during the campaign and the MIR had accepted, joining members of the Socialist Party connected with the Chilean ELN and three members of Cuban intelligence in Allende's

Group of Personal Friends (GAP).⁹⁸ Although the MIR maintained its distance with the Unidad Popular coalition, the GAP offered it a privileged space for political interaction with Allende, the Socialist Party, and Cuba. Allende, for his part, viewed this space as a way of being in close contact with and having a relative control over a force that could potentially generate greater problems within the Left. However, the agreement implicit in the GAP was short-lived, as in mid-1971 the MIR activists abandoned the group, taking half of its weapons with them. The victory of the UP coalition sparked multiple debates within the MIR, with tensions arising between the more militaristic positions that called for the consolidation of a guerrilla group and other positions that called for furthering the work with the masses.⁹⁹ The latter appeared to have prevailed. In any case, the victory in no way changed the MIR's more general interpretation of the inevitability of armed struggle in the process toward socialism. In an October 1970 document the MIR stated that the general diagnosis of the correlation of forces between imperialism and its native allies, on the one hand, and popular forces, on the other, had not changed. Rather, it said, "the clash has merely been delayed, and when it comes, it will be more legitimate and will take on a more massive dimension, thus making the strategy of armed struggle more relevant than ever."¹⁰⁰

This diagnosis inspired the MIR's strategy during the UP government. In an interview with Andrés Pascal Allende he described this strategy as having three main goals: working with the masses; working within the armed forces; and building a central military force.¹⁰¹ During this period, the MIR developed what it called "middle fronts," which contributed to give an enormous boost to the number of activists and of supporters in the fringes of the movement.¹⁰² According to Pascal, while in 1970 the MIR had no more than 3,000 members, by March 1973, the party's membership was nearing 10,000, and over 30,000 more activists formed part of its middle fronts.¹⁰³ The MIR also tried to conduct intelligence work within the armed forces, with the aim of detecting possible conspiracy attempts and building political awareness among subordinate officers in preparation for a potential counter-revolutionary strike.¹⁰⁴ Lastly, the MIR made efforts to develop a central military force that would be tasked with combating any coup attempts. This preparation also entailed, as the MIR had stated, a strategy that would necessarily be continental. In this context, the relationship with militants from neighboring countries gained new significance in the planning of a military rearguard. Within this strategy, the interaction with exiles from the region and the protection of these exiles went beyond mere declarations.

The event that best describes the position of the MIR regarding how the government should address the issue of solidarity with "Latin American revolutionaries" and the role that the MIR played in that process are the incidents surrounding the Rawson prison break in Trelew, in southern Argentina. In June 1972, some MIR members were instructed to prepare an alternative landing strip near the Linares airport.[105] At the same time, members of Argentina's FAR also contacted the Tupamaros to ask them to provide a pilot.[106] Although the plan was called off in Chile and the Tupamaros were unable to collaborate as requested, in Argentina the plans for a prison break from the Rawson penitentiary continued. On 25 August, a group of twenty-five political prisoners, members of three armed groups – the FAR and the Montoneros, both left-wing Peronist groups, and the ERP – succeeded in breaking out of the jail they were being held in. They fled to a nearby airport, in the city of Trelew, where a group of guerrillas had hijacked a plane to fly the escaped prisoners to safety. The escape did not go as planned, however, and only six prisoners made it to the plane. These six prisoners were responsible for the escape committee and were also top leaders of the organizations involved. The other nineteen were delayed: by the time they reached the airport the airplane had already taken off. They immediately held a press conference, put down their weapons, and surrendered to navy forces.[107]

The six who had been able to escape joined five militants who were already on the hijacked plane, with its ninety-six passengers. On Wednesday, August 16, 1972, the plane landed in Pudahuel, Chile at 1:25 a.m., sparking a heated debate in the country. The Argentine dictatorship demanded that the guerrillas be returned to their country, the Chilean Right denounced the risks of granting asylum to "terrorists," the government hesitated, and certain sectors of the Left declared their full solidarity with the "revolutionaries."[108]

The arrival of the Argentine guerrillas occurred in a climate of growing differences between rupturists and gradualists in the UP, which had been brewing since June, when a meeting of high government officials revealed disagreements within the coalition. While the Communist Party and Allende urged the coalition to implement the UP program and initiate conversations with the Christian Democratic Party, the other sectors pushed to "move forward without compromise."

In addition, a series of street clashes in Concepción culminated in a demonstration in support of the government, which was, paradoxically, repressed by the government, leaving one UP activist dead. These incidents led to the forming of the "People's Assembly" in Concepción in July 1972, with the support of all UP parties except the Communist Party. The Assembly appealed to the president, proposing a shift in the government's political direction, with the dissolution of the current "counter-revolutionary" parliament and the establishment of the "people's assembly" that had been part of the UP platform.[109] Along the same lines as the

People's Assembly in Concepción, labor sectors launched the "Cordón Cerrillos" initiative, spurring a major social mobilization that pressed for results in the process of expropriation. This coordination of workers from more than 200 companies played an increasingly important role in the staging of political events that questioned the president's politics.

Lastly, another high point of the conflict between rupturists and gradualists was the Lo Hermida raid. On August 5 the police stormed into the Lo Hermida settlements of Lulo Pinochet, Asalto al Cuartel Moncada, and Vietnam Heróico looking for a member of an allegedly extremist organization. The raid generated resistance among settlement dwellers, and left one civilian dead, eleven wounded, and 160 arrested. That same day there was an explosion in the locality of Ventanas. Various press media blamed the radical Left, using different arguments. The MIR – and, in some cases, their connection to foreigners – became the main issue of contention between the Left and the Right and the leading source of internal tension between gradualist and rupturist sectors on the Left.

The opposing right-wing press denounced the role that these groups were playing in the radicalization of certain social sectors that had been growing since Allende took office.[110] Chile had a long tradition of political asylum in Latin America, which dated back to the nineteenth century and had gained renewed relevance in the 1960s.[111] However, what in the mid-1960s, during the government of the Christian Democratic Party, was seen as a humanitarian issue, under Allende's government took on new meanings.[112] The arrival of new refugees was denounced by the opposition's press media as part of an international conspiracy carried out by the most radical Left, a group that had ties with Cuba and through which Cuba was seeking to interfere in Chile's political life. The U.S. State Department was also worried. A 1971 report called Chile a "Mecca for the left," with some 1,500 exiles from other countries living in Chile at that moment. While expressing concern, the document admitted that thus far these groups' interest in exporting the revolution had not been contemplated by the Unidad Popular government, whose foreign policy was aimed at strengthening relations with its neighboring countries, even those ruled by conservative governments.[113]

The MIR was also questioned by gradualist groups in the Left. In a highly critical statement, the Communist Party described the organization as "a group devoted to the task of clearing the way for reactionary sedition through political provocations and irresponsible aggression. Its leaders fluctuate between vileness and paranoia, between despicableness and madness."[114]

Despite the criticism from the Communist Party, the "move forward without compromise" approach brought the MIR close to important sectors of the UP. Starting in 1972, most of the Socialist Party and the MAPU joined the MIR in calling for the construction of popular power, challenging institutional government and the limits of the reform processes implemented by the government.[115] Because of their material resources, large membership, and widespread political involvement, the Socialist Party was the force that most interfered with the government's plans. Criticism, however, fell primarily on the MIR, as it was the only sector involved in these efforts that was not part of the UP coalition. The MIR tried to capitalize on this criticism by turning into the Left's most visible challenger of the government's policies.

It was amidst such a climate that Chile received the escaped prisoners from Rawson. Disregarding any tactical considerations, the MIR took a principle-based approach that focused on revolutionary solidarity: "What 'tactical consideration' could we give the Argentine people to justify sacrificing the freedom and perhaps the lives of its most valuable and capable revolutionary leaders in the name of 'good diplomatic relations' with a military clique whose days are numbered?"[116]

The MIR quickly activated its various mechanisms for mass mobilization with the aim of demanding asylum and calling attention to the human rights abuses committed by the Argentine dictatorship. From the pages of its official newspaper *El rebelde*, it demanded "Asylum for the Argentine Revolutionaries," and featured Che Guevara's image and the phrase "There are no borders in this fight to the death."[117] The editorial piece argued that this case offered a good opportunity to back with actions the ideal of proletarian internationalism, and it questioned the government's attitude thus far. Lastly, it called for a mobilization in support of the Argentine revolutionaries. The Christian Left and some far Left sectors of the Socialist Party joined the mobilizations of the MIR.

Initially, the Chilean government decided to leave the decision to the courts. It was a particularly sensitive problem for the government. Even though Argentina was under a conservative military dictatorship, the two governments had maintained very good relations up until that moment. Argentina needed allies to contain the growing presence that Brazil was acquiring as it furthered its sub-imperial designs. For Chile, Argentina represented an exception in a context of increasing regional hostility.[118] The Argentine Embassy in Chile asked the government to hold the escaped prisoners under preventive detention while the Argentine government prepared the formal extradition request. President Allende told the press that the matter would be resolved by the justice system.[119] But as the Argentine courts were preparing the extradition request, a tragedy occurred that would alter the course of the events. On August 22, members of the Argentine armed forces executed the prisoners who had surrendered after the failed attempt to escape from Trelew. Of the nineteen prisoners,

Figure 3.b. Cover of Magazine: El Rebelde. n. 44, 22/08/1972. CEDINCI Archive.

only three survived. The official story was that the prisoners were killed while trying to escape again.

The news had a major impact in Chile. A day after the executions, the Socialist Party asked the president to grant the escaped prisoners safe conduct, allowing them to travel to Cuba: in view of the massacre, extradition would mean certain death for these militants.[120] After the Trelew executions, a large part of the sectors that formed the UP coalition agreed with the MIR that asylum or safe conduct should be granted. On August 25, the government issued the order of safe conduct, allowing them to travel to Cuba. According to the memoirs of his brother Julio Santucho, the president's daughter, Beatriz Allende, visited Mario Roberto Santucho, the PRT-ERP leader, who was among the escaped militants, to express her condolences for the death of his wife, killed in the massacre, and to give him a gun on behalf of her father.[121] Some 300 people – militants from the MIR and its mass fronts, members of the Socialist Party, and some fellow Argentine militants who were living in Chile – gathered at the airport to see them off.[122] In Cuba, they were welcomed by Interior Vice Minister Manuel Piñeiro.[123] The episode culminated with a letter from the guerrillas thanking the Chilean people, and another letter in which Juan Domingo Perón expressed his gratitude for the treatment given to the Peronist militants.[124]

After the crisis was over, in an interview in Cuba, Santucho gave special thanks to the MIR, the Christian Left, and the far-left sectors of the Socialist Party for their efforts against the extradition. His statements expressed the internationalist tone that was shaping the relationships among the organizations of the Southern Cone in Chile.[125]

The Trelew episode showed a series of contacts that, in 1972, were being forged among different armed groups of the Southern Cone as a result of the presence of various militants on Chilean soil. Although some personal memoirs, and the documents of the JCR, mark the Rawson prison escape as the starting point of the collaboration efforts that would culminate in the creation of the JCR, a number of isolated elements indicate that during that year, if not earlier, different exchanges had already been under way among the organizations that would later form the JCR.

On April 16, 1972, the Buenos Aires daily newspaper *La Nación* reported that according to intelligence sources a meeting had been held on February 20 in Santiago with the participation of leaders of the ERP, the MIR, the MLN-T, the ELN, and the Marighela and Lamarca command units.[126]

The renewal of diplomatic relations with Cuba, which entailed Cuba's deployment of a large diplomatic staff to Chile, and the resumption of flights between Santiago and Havana turned Santiago into an ideal place for these groups to establish contacts with Cuba. This is corroborated by the Cuban officials assigned to that embassy.[127] Fidel Castro's visit also set the atmosphere for conversations among Southern Cone groups.

The contacts with the ERP had begun in the year 1971, with two visits by ERP leaders to Chile – the first by Enrique Gorriarán and Joe Baxter, and the second by Gorriarán and Roberto Santucho.[128] Guillermo Rodríguez, a member of the Chilean MIR, recalls that he was part of the security team in a house in Chile, where some thirty ERP militants were staying before going on to Cuba for training, prior to the Trelew events. He remembers that he was also on the security team of a group of Bolivian MIR militants that same year.[129]

As for the Tupamaros, contacts had begun as early as the year 1971, with the Uruguayan exiles who came to Chile, and as of 1972, they came into greater contact with the MIR. A 1972 document seized by the armed forces in Uruguay revealed how important international contacts had become for the organization and particularly the activities that were being conducted in Chile, which they considered a "logistics channel and a base of operations for our fellow militants."[130] However, it noted that such a task had been questioned by Cuba, thus posing the need for the Tupamaros in Chile to work within the strategic framework of the MIR and the Chilean Socialist Party.

Besides the contacts among militants, the debates in the newspapers of these organizations proved an increasing regional convergence. In 1971, *El Combatiente*, the PRT-ERP's mouthpiece, devoted its front page to the MLN-T, with the headline: "Uruguay: Only One Way, Revolutionary War." The article expressed its "support for the MLN-T alternative."[131] An article featured in July 1972 in the MIR paper *El Rebelde* defined the Tupamaros as "a sister organization to which we are linked by similar ideological and political beliefs."[132] For their part, in their *Carta del Uruguay*, published in Chile during 1972, the MLN-T members who were outside Uruguay provided an almost weekly and very positive coverage of PRT-ERP actions, and were strongly supportive of the Chilean MIR. The issue of *El Rebelde* that covered the Trelew events featured an article on the ERP, which foresaw the establishment of the coordinating body:

We – the ERP says – call ourselves internationalists because we understand that our struggle, the struggle of the Argentine people, against imperialist domination is the same struggle waged by Uruguayans, Chileans, Cubans, Vietnamese, and all peoples. [...] In this sense, we're willing to help one another, to share and collaborate with other revolutionary peoples, especially with our Latin American brothers.[133]

These organizations were so in tune with each other that whenever certain tactical options could be interpreted as disagreements, they saw the need to explain the reason for the differences in tactics. For example, before the 1973 elections in Argentina, the PRT-ERP felt it had to explain its position with respect to elections, which differed from the "critical support" of the MIR for the Unidad Popular coalition in Chile in 1970, or the Tupamaros' position with respect to the Frente Amplio (Broad Front, or FA) coalition in Uruguay's 1971 elections.[134]

While in the cases of Uruguay and Argentina these discussions can be found in the internal documents of their armed organizations, in Chile they were debated more openly, as the MIR had a public voice that the other groups lacked in their countries due to the fact that they operated underground. Through *Punto Final* and *El Rebelde*, the MIR defended the PRT-ERP and the MLN-T against the accusations of extreme Left deviations hurled by the press of the Chilean Communist Party.[135]

The concept of "sister" organizations that was being used increasingly by these publications presupposed affinities that were different from those that had served as common ground for previous international groupings of the Left. In this case the agglutinating factor did not appear to be associated with the ideological definitions (communism, socialism, Trotskyism, Maoism) that brought left-wing groups together on an international level. Within these "sister" organizations there were groups with different ideological backgrounds, ranging from Catholicism and nationalism to Marxism–Leninism. While the Tupamaros refused any of the traditional ideological definitions and described themselves as a nationalist leftist group, the MIR and the ERP defined themselves as Marxist–Leninists. Their military development was also different. The MLN-T was a fully formed guerrilla organization, which had earned certain international renown due to its unique urban guerrilla strategy. The ERP had a somewhat shorter history, but it was already proving its effectiveness in its first kidnapping actions. The MIR, for its part, had certain particularities: it was not, strictly speaking, a guerrilla organization. Although from 1969 to 1970 the MIR had conducted certain underground actions, the new political scenario after Allende's victory had boosted its activities among the masses. What all of these organizations seemed to have in common was that in local contexts they supported the idea that social and political conflicts would ultimately lead to armed struggle.

Moreover, this affinity was developed amidst growing authoritarianism and the resulting waves of exiles who poured into Chile, which seemed to confirm the OLAS' thesis of the inevitability of armed struggle and the need to coordinate a continental revolutionary strategy. The interpretation put forward by MIR leaders was very similar to what dos Santos posited, but with more explicit political consequences than those described by the sociologist.

In September 1971, Bautista van Schouwen, a member of the MIR's political committee, gave a speech in the Santiago popular settlement of La Victoria in honor of Commander Carlos Lamarca, a Brazilian military officer who had deserted to join the Vanguarda Popular Revolucionária (Popular Revolutionary Vanguard, or VPR). After describing Brazil's dictatorship as the most hideous in Latin America, Van Schouwen noted that its "sub-imperialist delusion" had become a threat to its neighboring peoples, turning it into the "support base and coordinating center of counter-revolutionary reaction in the Southern Cone."[136] According to Van Schouwen, "the reactionary and counter-revolutionary dynamics of the Brazilian dictatorship is today the mandatory reference point for devising the strategy for Latin America's continental revolution." In view of that threat, proletarian internationalism and revolutionary solidarity were no longer a question of principles, they were a matter of objective necessity.[137] Lastly, van Schouwen listed the places in which these processes were unfolding in Latin America: Bolivia, Uruguay, Brazil, and Argentina.

The "ominous" nature of the Brazilian dictatorship seemed to generate a regional scenario with very limited options, which was clearly condensed in the "fascism or socialism" antinomy posed by some dependency theorists and MIR leaders as of 1971.[138] In the other countries of the region "counter-revolution" appeared to be on the rise. In 1971, the Brazilian dictatorship had played an active role in the coup staged against progressive military officer Juan José Torres in Bolivia, and it had influenced the elections in Uruguay to prevent the victory of the Frente Amplio left-wing coalition.[139] In 1972, the repressive crackdown on guerrillas, social organizations, and left-wing groups by the conservative government of Juan María Bordaberry in Uruguay was also openly backed by Brazil. In 1973, the private sector and the extreme Right group Patria y Libertad (Fatherland and Freedom) received explicit support from the governments of Brazil, Bolivia, Argentina, and Paraguay, as well as from investors in those countries. In 1973, Roberto Thieme, the leader of Patria y Libertad, returned to Chile through Bolivia, after visiting Argentina and Paraguay with the aim of raising funds to organize an urban guerrilla group in Chile.[140]

The new face of authoritarianism that was emerging in Brazil was characterized by the systematic torturing of social and political activists. *Punto Final* regularly featured reports denouncing the various science-based torture techniques that were designed to break activists physically and mentally. The new forms of torture that were introduced in Brazil with the wave of repression unleashed in 1968 were copied in Bolivia in 1971 under the Banzer government. Argentina also evidenced the influence of Brazilian interrogation methods, and in 1972 the Bordaberry government in Uruguay adopted some of the same techniques.[141] Activists from these countries gave detailed firsthand accounts of long torture "sessions" in which prisoners were repeatedly beaten and subjected to near drowning (a water-based torture known as the "submarine"), hanging by limbs, prolonged standing, mock executions, electric shocks to the genitals, and countless other torments. These reports appealed to the readers' empathy with the victims.

These descriptions were not meant to discourage militants, as the reports claimed that torture had not achieved its goal of destroying guerrilla movements. While admitting that it had indeed affected the organizations, the reports offered optimistic examples of militants who had been able to withstand the terrible series of physical and mental torments without giving away any relevant information to the enemy.[142]

As of the late 1960s, Brazilians played a key role in denouncing these abuses. Some of the sources interviewed remember how the denunciation activities of the Brazilians had impacted them and their perception of an increasing authoritarianism.

A MIR militant recalls how, a few days after the coup, she had participated in a meeting with Brazilian activists, who explained in detail the torture methods employed in Brazil and gave them handbooks with instructions on how to be prepared, telling them that "that was what was coming." She remembers that, after the Brazilians left the meeting the MIR militants voiced their skepticism about the possibility of that happening in their country. They argued that Chile was very different from Brazil. In her words, "it took us a long time to realize everything. Well, in truth we had been told all there was to know, but we just didn't want to listen."[143]

The region's rising authoritarianism pushed these groups to find concrete ways in which to coordinate their actions. In November 1972, the MIR, the MLN-T, and the PRT-ERP began discussing the possibility of establishing an international organization. After spending two months in Cuba, the leaders of the PRT- ERP returned secretly to Argentina through Chile. Once in Argentina they met with the leaders of the MLN-T stationed outside Uruguay, as well as with the MIR leadership. A 1975 document of the JCR describing its origins indicates that a major meeting was held in the month of November in Santiago with the participation of the MIR's political committee, three top leaders of the MLN-T, and some leaders of the PRT-ERP.[144] According to this document, Miguel Enríquez proposed holding a "small Zimmerwald" of the Southern Cone, in allusion to the 1915 meeting in Switzerland convened by socialists opposed to World War I, where the foundations for the Third International were laid. In the text this goal was posed as a necessary step: "Uniting the revolutionary vanguard that has embarked decisively on the path of armed struggle against imperialist domination and toward the establishment of socialism is an imperative at this moment."[145]

Besides the continental strategy defined by Guevara in his message to the Tricontinental and which these groups felt they represented, there were concrete needs that demanded the forging of alliances between the region's groups. From the MIR's perspective the possibility of an authoritarian reaction in Chile, which seemed increasingly imminent, entailed the need for a strategic rearguard that would make it possible to organize the resistance. In this sense, the relationship with the Argentine organizations became key because of the extensive border shared by the two countries.[146]

In the PRT-ERP's case, the year 1972 represented the consolidation of a significant shift in its international relations. Besides considering Chile as a potential strategic rearguard, other aspects helped strengthen the need for an alliance. After Cuba but before returning to Chile, the PRT-ERP leadership traveled to Europe. There, Santucho decided that the PRT-ERP would leave the Fourth International due to the latter's accusations against Cuba, the withdrawal of its support to the Latin American guerrillas groups, and the "entryism" attempts within the PRT-ERP by members of the Fourth International.[147] In this context, the need to create a regional organization that was more in line with Guevara's strategy and Fidel Castro took on renewed importance for a party that had put great care into its international relations.

Lastly, with no MLN-T leaders left in Uruguay and the organization's defeat, the steering committee that the MLN-T had established outside of Uruguay needed to increase its international contacts in the region, as they were key for ensuring their survival in Chile and Argentina, the two places that were chosen at different times as possible rearguards. It was in this context that certain agreements were discussed at the November 1972 meetings. The first joint activities had to do with the incorporation of militants from the different organizations through an international leadership training school and the forming of committees tasked with military infrastructure and logistic matters.[148]

According to a former MIR member, Osvaldo Torres, who participated in the school's activities, it operated in the outskirts of Santiago in early 1973. He remembers them as an experience of about one week in which theoretical and political issues were discussed.[149] The school had a very intense schedule, with classes in the morning and in the afternoon. All activities took place in a summer house with facilities that were inadequate for the number of participants. At night, socialization activities were held in an atmosphere of open camaraderie. Participants included MIR members, PRT-ERP militants who traveled from Argentina especially for the activities, and Tupamaros who were exiled in Chile. The instructors were political leaders from the three organizations and some academics who supported or were members of the MIR, including, according to Torres's recollections, Tomás Vasconi, Andres Cultelli, and Ruy Mauro Marini, who was one of the organizers.

In Torres' view, besides discussing specific issues, the overall aim was to promote solidarity and political relations among militants from the different organizations. In his account he describes the differences and similarities between the organizations. With respect to the PRT, Torres remembers that they "were leaders from the PRT structure who were also workers. That was very unusual, because in general the MIR's organizational structures were headed by university students, who had become professional militants but with a petit-bourgeois background." The Tupamaros, by contrast, were somewhere in the middle in both age and class origins. They were about "twenty-five to thirty-five" years of age. As for ideological aspects, Torres recalls that the MIR was closer to the PRT-ERP militants, while they saw the Tupamaros as "good for action" but "very lacking in ideological terms" and affected by the defeat that they were still trying to process.

Other tasks conducted in Chile during this period had to do with the production of homemade weapons. Initially, these tasks were carried out by MIR militants from its core force, who were later joined by Tupamaros. Joint tasks were later undertaken under the JCR. In 1973, some of these workshops had produced grenades and had also begun designing parts of a machine gun that could later be assembled by militants. According to Pascal Allende, they had already begun testing a standardized production of these parts using the machinery that the MIR activists had access to in industrial units, but the coup interrupted such developments.[150]

By mid-1973, the situation in Chile had become extremely complicated, which made coordination activities difficult. The June 29 "Tanquetazo" – a failed coup attempt that took place two days after the coup in Uruguay – was the first real military insurrection attempt against the government of Salvador Allende. Although it failed, several of the officers who had opposed it were known to have acted for opportunistic reasons. The coup was seen as imminent.[151] Meanwhile, the democratic transition in Argentina was turning the neighboring country into a safer place for many of these foreign activists. The March 1973 elections, Cámpora's inauguration as president (supported by Peron) in May, the amnesty granted to political prisoners, and the return of Perón, who appeared closer to the Left, were all signs of a new historical moment in Argentina, which could also have a regional impact.[152] The left-wing press in Chile reported that during Cámpora's inauguration ceremony crowds could be heard chanting "Allende and Perón, together as one," and that Salvador Allende and Osvaldo Dorticos, in representation of Cuba, had been at the ceremony. The magazine *Chile hoy* headlined that fortnight's issue with "Santiago-Buenos Aires-Lima-Havana: the New Axis."[153]

In June 1973, according to a former member of the MLN-T, Efraín Martinez Platero, the second meeting of the JCR was held in Rosario, Argentina. MIR, PRT-ERP, and MLN-T delegations were present at the meeting, in which Bolivia's ELN formally joined the JCR, after a series of bilateral conversations with the member organizations.[154] According to the account of one of the participants, the event lasted several days and strengthened the relationship among the organizations.[155] Each group presented a long self-criticism report, which was discussed openly by the other participants. The members of the Bolivian ELN received the loudest applause because of the symbolic meaning represented by their struggle, as it was Che Guevara's organization. As for practical matters, the meeting discussed the plans of the PRT-ERP to create a guerrilla *foco* in Tucumán, a border team was formed and tasked with purchasing means of transportation (cargo trucks, small aircrafts, motorboats) and investing in transportation companies to ensure the movement of militants from one country to the other, and the search for contacts abroad was launched.

By 1973 exchanges among militants from these organizations had already begun. The murder of PRT-ERP member Gerardo Alter in 1973 in the Florida barracks in Uruguay, and the death a year later of Uruguayan militant Hugo Cacciavilliani in 1974 in Tucumán, are just two examples that prove that these exchanges existed.[156] Bolivian militant Chato Peredo also claims to have been involved in the Samuelson kidnapping perpetrated by the PRT-ERP in Argentina.[157]

The Tupamaros realized that their members faced a great risk if they remained in Chile, so they started to evacuate them to Cuba and to a lesser extent to Argentina. Only a few stayed in Chile after the coup. The PRT-ERP then focused its attention on the events that were unfolding at home. The MIR began to prioritize its preparations for the coup resistance in a much more adverse scenario than had originally been expected. Some Brazilian militants started leaving for Europe or Argentina.

Cuba also began sending home many of its diplomatic officials and their families. The Cuban advisors were worried about the direction that the UP government was taking, as they believed a coup was imminent and feared the Allende administration was too passive to put up an adequate resistance.[158]

The Cubans and the foreign militants in Chile had reasons to fear the outcome. On September 11, 1973, when the coup was finally staged, foreigners were among the most vulnerable as they had less chances of surviving underground and, at the same time, were singled out as scapegoats by the new regime, which saw them as the most flagrant expression of the international subversion to which Allende had opened the country's doors. On the day of the coup, the Cuban Embassy was attacked by extreme Right groups, and then remained surrounded by military forces until an agreement was reached to allow the diplomatic staff to leave the country. Two orders were issued on the day after the coup summoning all foreigners to the nearest military headquarters or posts. In the first three months, nine Uruguayans, eight Argentines, four Brazilians, four Ecuadorians, two French citizens, two U.S. citizens, and eleven other foreigners of different nationalities were executed.[159] Foreigners flocked to different diplomatic headquarters seeking refuge after the coup. Certain international organizations and diplomatic personnel were instrumental in saving the lives of many who were unable to reach the embassies on their own.[160] According to a report by the Inter-American Commission on Human Rights, 688 Brazilians, 619 Uruguayans, 582 Bolivians, and 352 Argentines left Chile by means of diplomatic asylum.[161]

Nobody had foreseen the savageness and magnitude of the repression unleashed by the military on September 11. Starting with the air attack on the presidential palace of La Moneda, the new regime was letting anyone close to the ousted government know that they would be treated as war enemies, who – in the regime's particular view – could be legitimately

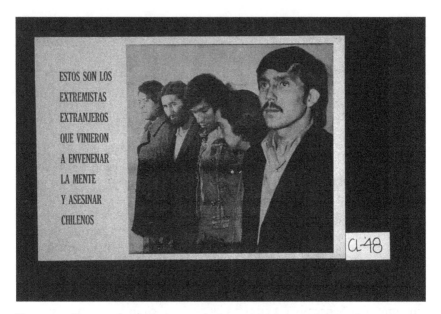

Figure 3.c. "Estos son los extremistas extranjeros que vinieron a envenenar la mente y asesinar Chilenos." Poster of Chilean Dictatorship. Hoover Archives.

subjected to torture, various abuses, prison, and execution. In the three months that followed, 1,261 people were executed or forcefully disappeared. This figure represents fifty-five percent of all the people who were executed or disappeared during the entire dictatorship.[162] The Left and the social movement were completely overtaken by the magnitude of the military actions. The research by Mario Garcés and Sebastián Leiva on one of the few armed resistance efforts reveals that the actual outcome exceeded what both gradualists and rupturists expected.[163]

The leadership of the Communist and Socialist Parties met on September 15; both parties decided to instruct their most widely-known leaders to seek asylum in an embassy. MAPU activists made a similar decision.[164] The MIR took a different stance. Although it admitted that the situation called for a retreat, it decided to keep all its militants and leaders in the country and penalize anyone who decided to seek asylum, with some exceptions, such any foreigners among their ranks. The MIR felt that its political stance had been proven right by events. According to Beatriz Allende's account, on the day of the coup, as the armed forces were closing in on him at La Moneda, the president told Enríquez on the telephone: "It's your turn now."[165] This was read by the MIR as a confirmation of its ideas. The time had come to fight for what they had been advocating. A month after the coup, Miguel Enríquez declared:

The Left has not failed in Chile, and neither has socialism, nor the revolution, nor the workers. What has ended tragically in Chile is the reformist illusion that social and economic structures can be changed and revolutions can be made with the passive compliance and the consent of those affected: the ruling classes.[166]

In his view, the coup confirmed once and for all the unfeasibility of the peaceful road to socialism and opened up the way for a revolutionary strategy. The events that followed, however, would confirm that neither strategy had the resources to confront the state violence that would be unleashed by the dictatorial regime.

Conclusion

The presence of exiles in Chile, during the Unidad Popular government, had multiple impacts both inside and outside the country. Their presence was an issue of contention between the Right and the Left. By exaggerating the influence that foreigners exerted in local left-wing organizations, the conservative press sought to further its claims that the government was at the mercy of radical foreign leftist groups.[167] The presence of exiles also affected the debate within the Chilean Left. It could even be maintained that their mere presence weakened Allende's assertion of the feasibility of the peaceful road to socialism. These exiles were themselves proof of the authoritarian reaction that was spreading across the region. Brazilian, Uruguayan, and Bolivian exiles represented the tragic culmination of different processes of political reform. What the inflow of exiles to Chile also showed, in addition to the rise of authoritarianism, was the resounding defeat of the region's guerrilla groups, although the MIR failed to perceive this.

Besides the influence it had in the national political process, the Southern Cone exile experience in Chile marked a major moment in the construction of a transnational network involving the various armed left-wing groups in the region, which had begun earlier and would have its most concrete expression from 1974 to 1976 with the establishment and actions of the JCR in Argentina and in other parts of the world. These groups found, in Chile, a place for in-depth political exchanges. Up until that point these militants had only gathered occasionally. The Chile experience, however, provided the opportunity for both leaders and rank-and-file members of these groups to come into contact regularly in various instances connected with the political process that unfolded in Chile under the UP government.

The political situation in the region tended to strengthen Guevara's call for a continental revolution. Independently of these countries' shared traditions, a continental revolution strategy was justified by the very real "continental counter-revolution strategy" deployed from Brazil since 1964. The interpretation that these actors made of the new authoritarianism, from the perspective of the dependency theory, helped strengthen this transnational network and some pillars of the already mentioned transnational political culture.

This context fostered a process of political and ideological "homogenization" of these organizations. This homogenization was ideological but it also had to do with a historical and structural interpretation. The organizations of the New Left had been formed with activists coming from a range of ideologies: including, indo-Americanism, left-wing nationalism, Catholicism, and the various branches of Marxist thought, such as Leninism, Trotskyism, Maoism, etc. However, during the period of exile in Chile all of these groups started to veer toward a specific ideological definition, which could be described as a non-Soviet Marxism–Leninism. The organizations that still had ties to international Trotskyism severed those ties completely in 1972. The Tupamaros, who had traditionally resisted an ideological definition, declared in 1973 that they were Marxist–Leninists. Bolivia's ELN embarked on an ideological discussion that culminated in 1974 with the establishment of a Marxist–Leninist party. The reasons for such an alignment had to do with the influence of Harnecker's writings, which offered a new canon for understanding Marxism–Leninism that claimed to distance itself from communist orthodoxy but which, through a rigidly structuralist and supposedly scientific language, provided certainties to members of relatively new organizations. In some cases, these organizations had been weakened by repression, and were in need of firm ideas to debate with the traditional Left. The process of ideological development of the Cuban Communist Party also influenced Southern Cone militants.

Harnecker's own experience illustrates this evolution, which took her from Catholicism to the New Left, and finally to embrace non-Soviet Marxism–Leninism with the emergence of the Cuban orthodox line. After abandoning her Catholic activism, Harnecker began working with Jacques Chonchol, one of the founders of the MAPU. Upon returning from Europe, where she had adopted Althusser's theories, she became involved with the more rupturist sectors of the Socialist Party. In 1972 she met Manuel Piñeiro, the director of Cuba's Americas Department. In 1973, after requesting asylum in the Venezuelan Embassy, she left for Cuba where she married Piñeiro. As of that moment she became one of the leading intellectuals of the pro-Cuban Latin American Left.

The other aspect that contributed to this "homogenization" was a common interpretation of the historical process that Latin America was going through, which was very close to some versions of the "dependency theory." As shown above, some of the most renowned dependency theorists had very close ties to these organizations. Regardless of how this theory was received academically, politically it was interpreted as a justification for the most radical options. This is illustrated by a review quoted on the back cover of André Gunder Frank's *Capitalism and Underdevelopment in Latin America*, which read: "This book is enormously important because it provides, like no other, the economic and social basis that completes the political conclusions of Regis Debray."[168]

In addition to the network that began to be formalized, the horizontal meeting of militants, the theory of dependency, Harnecker's version of structural Marxism, and a shared political interpretation, strengthened aspects seen in previous chapters, as well as incorporating new ones to the political culture discussed above. On the one hand, the meetings among militants of the region enhanced the feeling of belonging to a transnational community that had specific dimensions that were expressed in emotions: friendship, camaraderie, and even love. On the other, this period provided a more systematic framework of ideas that made it possible to begin developing ideas connected with the dependency theory and an interpretation of what was happening in the region, a political ideology of sorts, which these groups felt they were lacking as compared to the traditional Left.

In the end, the magnitude of repression after September 1973 was so great that it demolished the initial arguments of "reformists" and "revolutionaries" alike. The Left as a whole suffered the repressive onslaught of the Chilean dictatorship and all initial resistance projects failed. The dialog maintained by the MIR with the other organizations of the region served to warn them of the possibility of a repressive reaction. But the MIR was unable to draw on past experience to foresee the magnitude of repression and the ways in which it would affect its members. The MIR expected a much more moderate scenario than what eventually occurred. The belief in Chile's unique political culture had permeated even its staunchest detractors.

The "revolutionaries" were once again on the move. Now Argentina would become the rearguard for Bolivians, Chileans, and Uruguayans, and the dying hope of South America's revolution.

Notes

1 Patricio Quiroga, *Compañeros, El GAP: la escolta de Allende* (Santiago: Aguilar, 2001), 108.
2 See Tanya Harmer, *Allende's Chile and the Inter-American Cold War* (Chapel Hill: University of North Carolina Press, 2011), and Joaquín Fernandois, *Chile y el mundo, 1970–1973, La política exterior del gobierno de la Unidad Popular y el sistema internacional* (Santiago: Ediciones Universidad Católica de Chile, 1985).
3 Bureau of Intelligence and Research, State Department, "Chile: A Precarious Search for Good Latin American Relation", 6/4/1971 (Chile Declassification Project).
4 See Denise Rollemberg, *Exílio: entre raízes e radares* (Rio de Janeiro: Editora Record, 1999).

5 Rollemberg, *Exilio*, 50. Arquidiocese de São Paulo1985, *Brasil Nunca Mais* (Petrópolis: Ed. Vozes, 1985). Elio Gaspari, *As ilusões armadas. A ditadura envergonhada* (Sao Paulo: Companhia das Letras, 2002), 333–43.

6 For an overview of these groups, see: Jacob Gorender, *Combate nas trevas*; Marcelo Ridenti, *O fantasma da revolução brasileira* (Sao Paulo: UNESP, 1993); Marcelo Ridenti, "Esquerdas armadas urbanas: 1964–1974," in Marcelo Ridenti and Daniel Arao Reis (comp.), *Historia do Marxismo no Brasil* (Campinas: Unicamp, 2007); and Daniel Aarao Reis Filho, *Ditadura militar, esquerdas e sociedade* (Rio de Janeiro: Zahar, 2000).

7 See "La unidad de las izquierdas revolucionarias," *Pensamiento Crítico* 46 (November 1970), 72.

8 "Entrevista a Joaquín Cámara Ferreira Toledo, dirigente de Acción Libertadora Nacional," in *Pensamiento Crítio* 46 (November 1970), 130. Also featured in *Cristianismo y Revolución* 26 (November–December 1970), 130.

9 Gorender, *Combate nas trevas*, 153–60.

10 Rollemberg, *Exilio*, 169. Information obtained from Cátia Cristina de Almeida Silva, "Resistencia no exterior: os exilados brasileiros no Chile (1969–1973)," paper presented in the conference *Usos de Pasado: XII Encuentro Regional de Historia*, ANPUH-RJ 2006, 4.

11 See: "Exilio, pasaporte a la angustia," *Ercilla*, January 26, 1971; "El horror de las torturas y los crímenes en Brasil," *Punto Final*, February 2, 1971, 8–15; Jacob Gorender, *Combate nas trevas: a esquerda brasileira: das ilusões perdidas à luta armada* (Editora Atica: Sao Paulo, 1987); Flávio Tavares, *Memórias do Esquecimiento* (Globo: Sao Paulo, 1999), 19–33; Elio Gasparri, *A ditadura escancarada* (Sao Paulo: Editora Schwarcz, 2005), 202–4

12 Various press media would later describe 1970 as the year of kidnappings in Latin America. See "Secuestros: epidemia para un continente," *Ercilla*, December 20, 1970.

13 Pedro C. Uchoa Cavalcanti and Jovelino Ramos (comp.), *Memórias do exílio, Brasil 1964/ 19?? De muitos caminos*, vol. 1 (Sao Paulo: Livramento, 1978), 148.

14 Cavalcanti and Ramos, *Memórias do exílio, 1964/19??*, 182.

15 Rollemberg, *Exilio*, 156.

16 Rollemberg, *Exilio*, 163.

17 See Denise Rollemberg, "Debate no exilio: Em busca da Renovação," in *Historia do Marxismo no Brasil*, Marcelo Ridenti and Daniel Arao Reis (comp.) (Campinas: Unicamp, 2007).

18 Thatiana Amaral de Barcelos; Ana Paula Goulart Ribeiro, "Militantes e jornalistas: A imprensa editada por exilados políticos brasileiros durante a ditadura," paper presented at Intercom – Sociedade Brasileira de Estudos Interdisciplinares da Comunicação: XIV Congresso de Ciências da Comunicação na Região Sudeste – Rio de Janeiro – May 7–9, 2009.

19 Rollemberg, *Debate no exilio*; Rodrigo Pezzonia, "Revolução em DEBATE: O grupo DEBATE, o exílio e a luta armada no Brasil (1970–1974)" (Master's diss.: Universidad Estadual de Campinas, 2011).

20 "Carta de Elmo Catalán," *Punto Final*, June 23, 1970, 2–4.

21 *Punto Final*, December 8, 1970, 16, 119.

22 For information on how these pounds were channeled, see chapter 3 in Clara Aldrighi, *La intervención de Estados Unidos en Uruguay (1965–1973)*, vol. 1 (Montevideo: Ediciones Trilce, 2007), and Gustavo Rodríguez Ostria, *Sin tiempo para las palabras, Teoponte, la otra guerrilla guevarista en Bolivia* (Cochabamba: Grupo Editorial Kipus, 2006), 263. See Letter from Commander Osvaldo Chato Peredo thanking Tupamaros for their collaboration. Omar Costa, *The Tupamaros* (Mexico: Ediciones Era, 1971), 170.

23 Rodríguez Ostria, *Sin tiempo para las palabras*, 269.

24 Dirección de Asuntos Internacionales, Departamento de Asuntos Americanos (Bolivia), Aerograma RIA: 348, 12/5/1968, AGHMRREE (Santiago, Chile).
25 For information on the Teoponte campaign, see the thorough study by Gustavo Rodriguez Ostria, *Sin tiempo para las palabras*. See also the account by Osvaldo Peredo, *Volvimos a las montañas*, 53–106, and the document compilation by Hugo Assman, *Teoponte. Una experiencia guerrillera* (Oruro: CEDI, 1971).
26 Rodríguez Ostria, *Sin tiempo para las palabras*, 360.
27 Osvaldo Peredo Leigue, *Volvimos a las montañas* (Santa Cruz: Fernando Valdivia Editor, 2003), 94.
28 Rene Zavaleta Mercado, "Porque cayó Bolivia en manos del fascismo," *Punto Final Documentos*, December 21, 1971, 13.
29 For an account of the Torres government, see Jorge Gallardo Lozada, *De Torres a Banzer: diez meses de emergencia en Bolivia* (Buenos Aires: Ediciones Periferia, 1972). For the historical context, see James Dunkerley, *Rebellion in the Veins, Political Struggle in Bolivia, 1952–1982* (Verso: London, 1984).
30 Rodriguez Ostria, *Sin tiempo para las palabras, Teoponte*, 574.
31 "Bolivia: El MIR construye una vanguardia," *Punto Final*, May 9, 1972, 22–4.
32 Gallardo, *De Torres a Banzer*, 392
33 Gallardo, 491.
34 Ibid., 78.
35 See: Correspondence of René Zavaleta Mercado and Rubén Sanchez with Elisabeth Burgos, in *Elisabeth Burgos-Debray Papers*. Hoover Institution Archives. Box/Folder 4:10, 4:47.
36 Martin Sivak, *El asesinato de Juan José Torres: Banzer y el Mercosur de la muerte* (Buenos Aires: Ediciones del Pensamiento Nacional, 1998), 77. And Sánchez, Rubén 1998 January 13 – February 13. Interviewed by Elisabeth Burgos in *Elisabeth Burgos-Debray Papers*. Hoover Institution Archives Box/Tape: 20: 37
37 For a complete review of the experience of Uruguayan exiles in Chile, see Clara Aldrighi and Guillermo Waksman, "Chile, la gran ilusión," in *El Uruguay del exilio, gente, circunstancias, escenarios*, Silvia Dutrenit Bielous (ed.) (Montevideo, Uruguay: Trilce Ediciones, 2006). For a testimonial account of several of these exiles, see Graciela Jorge and Eleuterio Fernández Huidobro, *Chile roto* (Santiago: LOM Ediciones, 2003). Astrid Arrarás, "Armed Struggle, Political Learning and Participation in Democracy: The Case of the Tupamaros" (Princeton, 1998); "Breve síntesis histórica de la organización," (1976) in ADLADC (Montevideo, Uruguay); Alfonso Lessa, *La revolución imposible: los tupamaros y el fracaso de la vía armada en el Uruguay del siglo XX*; Andrés Cultelli, *La revolución necesaria, contribución a la autocrítica del MLNT* (Buenos Aires: Colihue, 2006); Clara Aldrighi, *Memorias de insurgencia, historia de vida y militancia en el MLN Tupamaros, 1965–1975* (Montevideo: Ediciones de la Banda Oriental, 2009).
38 Ministerio de Relaciones Exteriores, Chile, Santiago, 12/14/1972, Uruguay Box, 1972, EMBACHILE OFICIOS Y ORDENANZAS in AGHMRREE (Santiago, Chile). Aldrighi and Waksman, who interviewed many exiles in Chile, estimate the number of Uruguayan exiles in "two to three thousand." See Aldrighi, "Chile, la gran ilusión," 35.
39 "Plan de marzo de 1972," in "Anexo Documental," in José Harari, *Contribución a la historia del MLN-Tupamaros* (Montevideo: Editorial Plural, 1987), 404–12.
40 See Ministerio del Interior, *7 meses de lucha antisubversiva; acción del Estado frente a la sedición desde El 1° de Marzo al 30 de setiembre de 1972* (Montevideo: Ministerio del Interior, 1972). For testimonial accounts by some of the victims who suffered this repressive onslaught, see Carlos Rovira and Filomena Grieco, *Veinte años después del 14 de abril de 1972* (Montevideo: Ediciones de la Plaza, 1993); Virginia Martínez, *Los fusilados de*

abril: ¿Quién mató a los comunistas de la 20? (Montevideo: Ediciones del Caballo Perdido, 2002). See also Serpaj, *Uruguay, Nunca Más* (Montevideo: Serpaj, 1989), 67–80.

41 See Aldrighi and Waksman, "Chile, la gran ilusión," and Raúl Elgueta, "El caso Jackson, reflexiones y enfoques," Confidencial RIA N. 404/99, June 30, 1971, Uruguay Box, AGHMRREE (Santiago, Chile).

42 Interview with Jorge Selves conducted by Clara Aldrighi and contributed by her.

43 Aldrighi, Waksman, "Chile, la gran ilusión," 39. A report of the Chilean embassy in Uruguay gives a figure of "approximately 60." See Raúl Elgueta, "Embajador de Chile en Uruguay, El Poder Ejecutivo procura frenar salida del país de procesados políticos," Montevideo, September 1, 1971. Confidencial RIA N. 606/145, Uruguay Box, AGHMRREE (Santiago, Chile).

44 Interview with Jorge Selves conducted by Clara Aldrighi and contributed by her.

45 Ibid.

46 A Tupamaro militant died while working on the production of explosives. "Entrevista a Efraín Martínez Platero," in Aldrighi, *Memorias de insurgencia*, 366.

47 Jorge and Fernández Huidobro, *Chile roto*, 19.

48 Ibid.

49 Aldrighi, *Memorias de insurgencia*, 350.

50 Interview with Fernando Butazzoni in Jimena Alonso, "Tupamaros en Chile. Una experiencia bajo el gobierno de Salvador Allende," in *Encuentros Uruguayos, Revista Digital*, 3rd year, number 3 (2nd part), September 2010. http://www.encuru.fhuce.edu .uy/index.php?option=com_content&view=article&id=59:tupamaros-en-chile-una-experiencia-bajo-el-gobierno-de-salvador-allende&catid=22:seccion-documental

51 Simposio de Viña del Mar (Montevideo: MLNT) 15, ADLADC (Montevideo, Uruguay).

52 Ibid., 11.

53 Ibid., 19.

54 On the role of the "peludos" in the history of the MLN-T, see Chapter II. See "Simposio de Viña," in MLN-Tupamaros, "La carta de los presos y otros documentos" (undated), ADLADC (Montevideo, Uruguay)

55 Jorge and Fernández Huidobro, *Chile Roto*, 39. Interview with Efraín Martínez Platero conducted by the author. Interview with Jorge Selves conducted by Clara Aldrighi.

56 *Balance partidario del Regional Santiago*, September 1973, 3, ADLADC (Montevideo, Uruguay).

57 For the relationship between Chilean and Argentine academics during this period, see María Agustina Diez, "El dependentismo en Argentina, una historia de los claroscuros del campo académico entre 1966 y 1976" (PhD diss., Universidad Nacional del Cuyo, 2009).

58 See Manuel Becerra Ramírez, "Marco Kaplan, un científico social," biographical sketch in http://www.bibliojuridica.org/libros/4/1785/4.pdf. For a review of Kaplan's role in the new Argentine Left, see Horacio Tarcus, *El marxismo olvidado en la Argentina. Silvio Frondizi y Milcíades Peña*. Also Luis Gómez, "Entrevista con el profesor Sergio Bagú, El periplo intelectual de un científico social latinoamericano," in *La Insignia*, Mexico, February 2006, http://www.lainsignia.org/2006/febrero/cul_015.htm

59 On the relationship between Marcos Kaplan and Silvio Frondizi, see Tarcus, *El marxismo olvidado en la Argentina* (Buenos Aires: El Cielo por Asalto, 1996).

60 Gómez, "Entrevista con el profesor Sergio Bagú."

61 See Juan Carlos Marin, *El ocaso de una ilusión* (Buenos Aires: Colectivo ediciones, 2007) and personal interview by me.

62 "Resoluciones del Comité Central, Marzo de 1971," in Daniel de Santis, *A vencer o morir: PRT-ERP, Documentos*, vol. 1, 133 and 134.

63 Enrique Gorriarán Merlo, *Memorias de Enrique Gorriarán Merlo: de los sesenta a La Tablada* (Argentina: Planeta, 2003), 132–4.

64 See Fernanda Beigel, "La Flacso chilena y la regionalización de las ciencias sociales en América Latina (1957–1973)," *Revista Mexicana de Sociología* (Mexico) 71, no. 2 (April–June 2009), 319–49.

65 Inés Cristina Reca, "El movimiento estudiantil y el proceso de reforma de la Universidad de Chile," *Revista Mexicana de Sociología* 32, no. 4 (July–August 1970), 893–947; Manuel Antonio Garretón and Javier Martínez (dir.), *La reforma en la Universidad de Chile*, vol. 3 (Santiago: Ediciones Sur, 1986).

66 Eduardo Devés-Valdés, *Redes intelectuales en América Latina, hacia la constitución de una comunidad intelectual* (Santiago: Universidad Santiago de Chile, IDEAS, 2007), 180.

67 See Andrew J. Kirkendall, *Paulo Freire and the Cold War Politics of Literacy* (Chapel Hill: The University of North Carolina Press, 2010) chapter 3, and Paulo Freire, *Pedagogía del Oprimido* (Buenos Aires: Siglo XXI, 1972).

68 Fernando Henrique Cardoso, *The Accidental President of Brasil. A memoir with Brian Winter* (New York: Public Affairs, 2006) chapter 5.

69 For a review of the commitment of various academics from Chile and the region with Chile's radical Left, as well as the space and value that the MIR attributed to that space of critical thought, see the insightful and thorough PhD dissertation by Ivette Lozoya. *Pensar la revolución: Intelectuales y Pensamiento Latinoamericano en el Mir chileno (1965–1973)*, IDEA-Universidad de Santiago de Chile.

70 *Memoria, Ruy Mauro Marini*, in Ruy Mauro Marini Escritos website, at http://www.marini-escritos.unam.mx/002_memoria_es.htm. On dos Santos, see Martins Carlos Eduardo, "Theotônio dos Santos: introducción a la vida y obra de un intelectual planetario," in Francisco López Segrera (ed.), *Los retos de la globalización. Ensayo en homenaje a Theotônio dos Santos* (Caracas: UNESCO, 1998), and "Discurso do profesor Theotônio dos Santos na Cerimonia de Recepção do título de profesor emérito de Universidade Federal Fluminense (UFF)," 12/17/2010, in the Theotônio dos Santos blog, at http://theotoniodossantos.blogspot.com/2010/12/discurso-do-professor-theotonio-dos.html

71 For biographical information on Frank, see Theotônio dos Santos, "André Gunder Frank – recordatorio", in e-l@tina, vol. 3, no. 11 (April–June 2005); André Gunder Frank, "Latin American Development Theories Revisited: A Participant Review," *Latin American Perspectives* 19, no.2 (1992); and the text "The Cold War and Me" and "A letter to several friends written by Andre Gunder Frank in Santiago, Chile, July 1, 1964," in the André Gunder Frank official website http://rrojasdatabank.info/agfrank/index.html

72 See safe conduct request for Theotônio dos Santos, in Aerograma no. 79, Rio de Janeiro, April 5, 1966. AGHMRREE, (Santiago, Chile).

73 *Cuadernos del CESO*, Vol. 1–10, (1966–1968).

74 See Ruy Mauro Marini, "Memoria," at http://www.mariniescritos.unam.mx/002_memoria_es.htm

75 For an analysis of the impact of Frank's works, see Aldo Marchesi, "Imaginación política del antiimperialismo: intelectuales y política en el Cono Sur a fines de los sesenta," *E.I.A.L.* 17.1 (2006–2007).

76 André Gunder Frank, *Capitalismo y subdesarrollo en América Latina* (Havana: Instituto del Libro, Editorial de Ciencias Sociales, 1970), 29.

77 Ibid., 158.

78 On the repercussions of Frank's work, see Tulio Halperín Donghi, "Dependency Theory and Latin American Historiography," *Latin American Research Review* 17 (1982), 1.

79 Theotônio dos Santos, *Socialismo o fascismo, el dilema latinoamericano* (Santiago: Prensa Latinoamericana, 1969). Theotônio dos Santos, *Socialismo o Fascismo, el nuevo carácter de la dependencia y el dilema latinoamericano* (Argentina: Ed. Periferia, 1972).

80 Ruy Mauro Marini, *Subdesarrollo y Revolución* (Mexico: Siglo Veintiuno Editores, 1969).

81 The dependency theory also had some impact in Argentina. See María Agustina Diez, *El dependentismo en Argentina*. This literature had important points in common with the ideas raised by Argentina's armed organizations. For example, Luis Mattini recalls that Santucho used Agustín Cepeda's *Crisis de una burguesía dependiente* to criticize the role of the national bourgeoisie in the national liberation movement. Luis Mattini, *Hombres y mujeres del PRT-ERP de Tucumán a La Tablada* (Argentina: Ed. De la Campana, 1995), 195.

82 He wrote for the magazine *Correo de la Resistencia*, published abroad in late 1973, signing his articles with the pseudonym "Luis Cerda." See "Ruy Mauro Marini, Escritos," at http://www.marini-escritos.unam.mx/

83 For a biographical overview of Althusser see: Louis Althusser, *The future lasts forever: a memoir* (New York: New Press,1993).

84 For a biographical overview of Harnecker, see "El marxismo un anti dogma," an interview with Harnecker featured in Marta Harnecker, *Los conceptos elementales del materialismo histórico (versión corregida y ampliada)* (Mexico, Spain, Argentina: Siglo XXI Editores, 1985), and "Tras las pistas de Althusser. Entrevista a Marta Harnecker de Nestor Kohan" (Brancaleon Films, 2014) in youtube.com https://www.youtube.com/watch?v=YnGdv8D55pM

85 Information extracted from the review of "Los conceptos elementales del materialismo histórico," *Punto Final no. 95, Sección Documentos,* 6.

86 Introduction in Marta Harnecker, Graciela Uribe, *Cuaderno de Educación Popular (CEP) no. 8: El partido vanguardia del proletariado. Segunda serie. Para Luchar por el socialismo* (Santiago: Quimantú, 1972). The other numbers had titles such as *CEP, no. 9: El partido: su organización, CEP, no. 10: Dirigentes y masas, CEP, no. 11.*

87 Harnecker, "El marxismo como un antidogma."

88 See "Reseña," *Punto Final, Sección Documentos,* no. 95, 1970, 7.

89 See Pilar Campaña, Rigoberta Rivera, "El reformismo instantáneo," *Punto Final,* December 5, 1972, 23; and Marta Harnecker, "Aprender a leer, Marta Harnecker responde a críticos de Punto Final," *Chile hoy,* 1972. Harnecker also recalls that while teaching at the University of Chile she initially experienced some resistance from MIR students, but that at the end of the year those same students came up to her to apologize. See "Marxismo y desafíos actuales. Entrevista a Martha Harnecker," November 2000, Antonio Castañeda and Sergio Quiroz. *Cuadernos de Marxismo,* in Archivo Chile: http://www.archivochile.com/Ideas_Autores/harneckerm/8otros/harneotros0007.pdf

90 "All those youths had read Martha Harnecker and were mesmerized when they heard Santucho or Enríquez speak, and they repeated what they heard like parrots. In Chile that was all very popular, don't forget that the Chilean experience was dazzling." "Entrevista a Eleuterio Fernández Huidobro," Clara Aldrighi, *Memorias de la insurgencia, Historias de vida y militancia en el MLN Tupamaros (1965–1975)* (Montevideo: Ediciones de la Banda Oriental, 2009), 76.

91 The notebooks were published by Carlos W. Vila of the Centro de Estudios Políticos de Córdoba. Information from "La Cultura como arma de liberación," *Nuevo Hombre,* May 2, 1973, 15.

92 Andrés Pascal Allende, a sociology student and member of the MIR's steering committee, described his involvement in the efforts to establish the center. See interview by me.

93 For a review of Zavaleta Mercado's writings, see Luis Tapia, *La producción del conocimiento local. Historia y política en la obra de René Zavaleta,* (La Paz: Muela del Diablo, 2002).

94 The first edition was published as a working document by the studies center (Centro de Estudios de la Realidad Nacional, Universidad Católica). See René Zavaleta Mercado, *Documentos de trabajo n. 8: El poder dual (contribución a un debate latinoamericano)* (Santiago: Universidad Católica de Chile, 1973). Later editions were published in book form by the publishing house Siglo XXI, starting in 1974.

95 See Diez, *Los dependentistas argentinos*, 99–102.

96 Pedro Naranjo Sandoval, "La vida de Miguel Enríquez y el MIR," in Miguel Enríquez, *Miguel Enríquez y el proyecto revolucionario en Chile: discursos y documentos del Movimiento de Izquierda Revolucionaria* (Santiago: LOM Ediciones: Centro de Estudios Miguel Enríquez, 2004), 63.

97 "Documentos," *Punto Final*, February 11, 1969.

98 For testimonial accounts of the GAP, see Patricio Quiroga, *Compañeros, El GAP*, Max Marambio, *Las armas de ayer* (Santiago: La Tercera, 2007). See, also, Christian Pérez, "Salvador Allende, apuntes sobre su dispositivo de seguridad: el Grupo de Amigos Personales," *Estudios Públicos* 79 (Winter 2000). On the Cuban involvement in this group, see Harmer, *Allende's Chile and the Inter-American Cold War.*

99 Pedro Naranjo Sandoval, "La vida de Miguel Enríquez y el MIR," 67.

100 "El MIR y el resultado electoral (octubre de 1970)," in Miguel Enríquez, *Con vistas a la esperanza* (Santiago: Escaparate Ediciones, 1998), 53. For a study by the MIR on the UP period, see Carlos Sandoval Ambiado, *Movimiento de Izquierda Revolucionaria, 1970–1973* (Concepción: Ediciones Escaparate, 2004).

101 Interview with Andrés Pascal Allende conducted by the author.

102 For a study on the middle fronts, see Sandoval, *Movimiento de Izquierda Revolucionaria, 1970–1973*, 233–49.

103 Andrés Pascal Allende, *El MIR Chileno, una experiencia revolucionaria, a los 36 años del surgimiento del MIR* (Argentina: Cucaña, 2003), 70.

104 On the relationship between the Left and the armed forces, see Verónica Valdivia, "'Todos juntos seremos la historia': La vía chilena al socialismo," in Pintos, *Cuando hicimos historia*, 177–206; Jorge Magasich A., *Los que dijeron "No". Historia del movimiento de los marinos antigolpistas de 1973*, vol. 1 and 2 (Santiago: Lom Ediciones, 2008).

105 Avendaño y Palma, *El rebelde de la burguesía: la historia de Miguel Enríquez*, 151.

106 "22 de agosto de 1972: Hablan protagonistas de la fuga: Teníamos que liberar a los compañeros," at http://www.pagina12.com.ar/1999/99-08/99-08-22/pag19.htm

107 For an overview of the events connected with the Trelew prison escape, see Tomás Eloy Martinez, *La pasión según Trelew* (Buenos Aires: Granica Editor, 1973); *Trelew*, DVD, directed by Mariana Arruti (Argentina: Fundación Alumbrar, 2004).

108 The events connected with the guerrillas' arrival and subsequent stay in Chile are covered by Chilean daily and weekly press media.

109 "Asamblea del Pueblo: respuesta al parlamento burgués," *Punto Final*, August 1, 1972, 6, 7. "El Presidente Allende rechaza la 'Asamblea del Pueblo'," *Punto Final*, August 15, 1972, 23.

110 "Crisis del Orden Público," *El Mercurio*, 8/8/1972.

111 On Chile's role in Latin America during the nineteenth century, see Mario Sznajder, Luis Roniger, *The Politics of Exile in Latin America* (Cambridge University Press, 2009), 93–105.

112 See, for example, the debates that the establishment of a local OLAS committee prompted in the governing Christian Democratic Party. See Chapter II.

113 Bureau of Intelligence and Research, Department of State, *Chile: A Precarious Search for Good Latin American Relations, Intelligence Note* (June 4, 1971) NARA. See online at: http://foia.state.gov/Search/results.aspx?

114 "El fracaso de una provocación," *El Siglo*, 8/9/1972.

115 With respect to the dilemmas generated by this controversy, the works by Valenzuela and Winn provide two paradigmatic looks at the limitations and possibilities of both strategies.

116 See "Declaración del Secretariado Nacional del MIR frente al problema de los revolucionarios argentinos," in Miguel Enríquez, *Con vistas a la esperanza*, 156.

117 *El Rebelde*, 8/22/72.

118 Fernandois, *Chile y el Mundo, 1970–1973*, 123–34.

119 *El Mercurio*, 8/19/1972, 1.

120 *El Mercurio*, 8/24/1972, n/a.

121 Julio Santucho, *Los últimos guevaristas*, 139.

122 *El Mercurio*, 8/26/1972, 1, 12.

123 *El Mercurio*, 8/28/1972, 1.

124 "Secuelas de un asilo," *Chile hoy*, September 1, 25.

125 José Carrasco Tapia, "La fuga que conmovió al continente," *Punto Final, Documentos*, no. 166 (1972).

126 Chilean Embassy in Buenos Aires, "Extrañas versiones en caso Sallustro," 04/18/1972, Argentina vol. 1806, AGHMRREE (Santiago, Chile).

127 Interview with Luis Fernandez Oña, in Tanya Harmer, "The Rules of the Game: Allende's Chile, the United States and Cuba, 1970–1973,"(PhD diss., London School of Economics and Political Science, 2008), 103.

128 Gorriarrán, *Memorias*, 132.

129 Email correspondence with me.

130 "Descubrimiento del CAI (Comité de Asuntos Internacionales) y su misión de lograr apoyos de movimientos extremistas internacionales," in Ministerio del Interior, *7 meses de lucha antisubversiva*, 134.

131 "Uruguay: un solo camino, la guerra revolucionaria," *El Combatiente*, no. 65, 12/19/1971.

132 "Chile, la posición del MIR," *El Combatiente*, no. 70, 7/30/1972.

133 "ERP, Guerra de Masas," *El Rebelde*, year 6, no. 44, 8/22/1972.

134 "In recent years, in our neighboring countries of Chile and Uruguay there have been electoral processes without banned parties, with a strong participation of popular and reformist anti-imperialist sectors, processes that were gradual but at the same time rendered the continuation of guerrilla warfare actions somewhat pointless, thus posing the need for a truce and forcing the MIR and the Tupamaros to momentarily suspend their operations." "Nuestra posición en la situación política actual," *El Combatiente*, no. 70, 7/30/1972.

135 The MIR defended these organizations against the Communist Party's criticism, stating, for example: "They haven't stopped there. Not content with slandering Chilean revolutionaries within and outside Unidad Popular, they have gone as far as gratuitously insulting the Argentine revolutionaries of the Ejército Revolucionario del Pueblo (ERP), while others have accused such heroes of the Latin American revolution as Uruguay's Tupamaros of being extreme Left terrorists." Miguel Enríquez, "La posición del MIR," in *Documentos. Punto Final*, May 9, 1972, 11–16.

136 "En homenaje a Lamarca el MIR plantea sus lineamientos políticos," in *Documentos. Punto Final*, October 17, 1971, 28–9.

137 Ibid.

138 See Miguel Enríquez, "La alternativa de Chile es socialismo o fascismo," in *Documentos. Punto Final*, November 9, 1971. See Edgardo Enríquez, "La conciliación: Caldo de cultivo del fascismo," *Punto Final*, October 10, 1972, 5–7.

139 "Bolivia: Golpe Fascista, última advertencia para Chile," *El Rebelde*, year 5, no. 5, August 28, 1971, 11. Rene Zavaleta Mercado. "Brasil y Estados Unidos. Porque cayó

Bolivia en manos del fascismo," *Documentos. Punto Final*, November 23, 1971, 1–16; Eleno, "Bolivia. El botín de los gorilas brasileros," *Punto Final*, November 7, 1972, 22–6.

140 Tanya Harmer, *Allende's Chile and the Inter-American Cold War*, 228.

141 "El horror de las torturas y los crímenes en Brasil," *Punto Final*, February 2, 1971, 8; "Uruguay. El ejército a cargo de las torturas," *Punto Final*, June 20, 1972, 20; "Las torturas en Argentina," *Punto Final*, July 2, 1972, 12; "Bolivia: desde las cárceles se sigue luchando," *Punto Final*, December 19, 1972, 10.

142 "Uruguay: Los ensayos del pentágono," *Punto Final*, December 5, 1972, 11.

143 Interview with Hilda Amalia Garcés conducted by the author.

144 The recollections of the participants at these meetings are not very clear. To date, I have consulted two of the three participants who have survived the dictatorships and the passage of time: Andrés Pascal Allende of the MIR, and Efraín Martínez Platero of the MLN-T. I tried to interview a third participant, Luis Mattini of the PRT-ERP, but have had no response from him. Of the list of participants given by John Dinges in *The Condor Years*, only these three leaders are still alive. Mario Roberto Santucho and Domingo Menna of the PRT-ERP, Miguel and Edgardo Enríquez and Alberto Villabela of the MIR, and William Whitelaw of the MLN-T were all killed in different repressive actions. Enrique Gorriarán Merlo of the PRT-ERP and Nelson Gutiérrez died recently. For the list, see Dinges, *The Condor Years*, 51.

145 JCR, "Editorial: Junta de Coordinación Revolucionaria. Orígenes y perspectivas," *Revista Che*, no. 2, February 1975.

146 Interview with Andrés Pascal Allende conducted by the author.

147 Maria Seoane, *Todo o nada. La historia secreta y pública de Mario Roberto Santucho, el jefe guerrillero de los años setenta* (Buenos Aires: Ed. Sudamericana, 2003), 184; Eduardo Weisz and José Luis Bournasell, *El PRT-ERP: nueva Izquierda e Izquierda tradicional* (Buenos Aires: Centro Cultural de la Cooperación, Dep. de Historia, 2004), 69–73.

148 See JCR, "Orígenes," and interviews with Pascal Allende and Martínez Platero conducted by the author. Also, Dinges, *The Condor Years*, 41–63.

149 Interview with Osvaldo Torres conducted by the author.

150 Interview conducted by the author.

151 For an overview of the situation of the military in the UP period, see Verónica Valdivia Ortiz de Zárate, *El golpe después del golpe. Leigh vs. Pinochet. Chile 1960–1980* (Santiago: LOM Ediciones, 2003), chap. 2, and Verónica Valdivia Ortiz de Zárate, "'Todos juntos seremos la historia: Venceremos.' Unidad Popular y Fuerzas Armadas," in Julio Pinto Vallejo (coord.) (Santiago: LOM Ediciones, 2005), 177–206.

152 On the expectations raised by the Cámpora administration among certain sectors of the Left, see Maria Laura Lenci, "Cámpora al gobierno, Perón al poder. La tendencia revolucionaria del peronismo antes de las elecciones del 11 de marzo de 1973," in Alfredo Puciarelli (editor), *La primacía de la política. Lanusse, Perón y la nueva izquierda en tiempos del GAN* (Buenos Aires: Eudeba, 1999), 167–205. For an overview of testimonial accounts of the "Peronist Spring," see Eduardo Anguita and Martín Caparrós, *La voluntad. Una historia de la militancia revolucionaria en la Argentina. La patria socialista*, vol. 3/ 1973–1974 (Argentina: Booket, 2006).

153 "El grito de Buenos Aires, Allende y Perón, un solo corazón," *Chile Hoy*, June 1, 1973.

154 See interview with Efraín Martínez Platero conducted by the author, and JCR, "Orígenes y perspectivas."

155 Ibid.

156 In a joint statement, the PRT-ERP and the MLN-T explained that Gerardo Alter "had been sent to Uruguay in an exercise of proletarian internationalism, a

concept shared by both organizations. [...] The presence of our fellow activist Alter in Uruguay is the product of the increasingly close and fraternal relations between our organizations."Lastly, they expressed their rejection publicly, "vehemently [denouncing] the counter-revolutionary coup of the Chilean army, orchestrated by the CIA, [we] declare our utmost solidarity with the Chilean people. [...] The MLN-T and the ERP are absolutely confident that the Chilean workers, led by the MIR, will successfully wage a guerrilla war and a political struggle of the masses against Pinochet's savage fascist dictatorship. MLN-Tupamaros and Political Leadership of the PRT-ERP, "Ante el asesinato en la tortura de los compañeros Gerardo Alter y Walter Arteche" (1973), ADLADC (Montevideo, Uruguay). Hugo Cacciavilliani died in an action against the army while participating in the PRT-ERP guerrilla unit Compañía de Monte Rosa Giménez, in Tucumán. See "Hugo Cacciavilliani"(1974), in ADLADC (Montevideo, Uruguay).

157 Peredo, *Volvimos a las montañas*, 120; Rodríguez Ostria, *Sin tiempo para las palabras, Teoponte, la otra guerrilla guevarista en Bolivia*, 588.

158 To understand Cuba's position under these circumstances, see Harmer, *Allende's Chile and the Inter-American Cold War.*

159 Manuel Antonio Garretón and Carmen Garretón Merino, *Por la fuerza sin la razón. Análisis y textos de los bandos de la dictadura militar* (Santiago: LOM Ediciones, 1998), 35, 73, and 75.

160 On the role of the embassies in protecting refugees after September 11, see Héctor Mendoza y Caamaño, *Chile surgimiento y ocaso de una utopía, 1970–1973. Testimonio de un diplomático mexicano* (Mexico: Secretaría de Relaciones Exteriores, Acervo Histórico Diplomático, 2004). Different accounts highlight the key role played by Swedish Ambassador Harald Edelstam in aiding numerous Southern Cone refugees. See, among others, Marambio, *Las armas de ayer*; Jorge and Fernandez Huidobro, *Chile Roto.*

161 Aldrighi and Waksman, "Chile, la gran ilusión," 80.

162 Information extracted from Comisión Nacional de Verdad y Reconciliación, *Informe Rettig* (Santiago: Ed. del Ornitorrinco, 1991).

163 Mario Garcés and Sebastián Leiva, *El golpe en La Legua. Los caminos de la historia y la memoria* (Santiago: LOM Ediciones, 2005), 38–40, 110.

164 Jorge Arrate, Eduardo Rojas, *Memoria de la izquierda Chilena,(1970–2000)*, vol. 2 (Santiago: Javier Vergara Editor, 2003), 189.

165 Pedro Naranjo Sandoval, "La vida de Miguel Enriquez y el MIR" in Pedro Naranjo, et alters, *Miguel Enríquez y el proyecto revolucionario en Chile* (Santiago: LOM, 2004), 83.

166 "Reportaje al MIR," transcript of an October 8, 1973 interview with MIR General Secretary Miguel Enríquez. *Resistencia, vocero de los comandos de apoyo a la Resistencia Revolucionaria Chilena*, year 1, no. 2; CEDINCI, Buenos Aires.

167 "Intervención extremista extranjera," *El Mercurio*, 11/17/1973. A few days after the coup, journalists with ties to the Secretaría General de Gobierno of the new regime published the *Libro Blanco del cambio de gobierno en Chile* (Santiago: Editorial Lord Cochrane, 1973), which, among other things, denounced the existence of the so-called Plan Z. This was an alleged plan of the UP government to organize a self-coup to justify a purge of top-ranking military commanders and civilian opposition leaders, that would be followed by a foreign invasion

168 In Frank, *Capitalismo y subdesarrollo*, 399.

IV

"The Decisive Round in Latin America's Revolution" – Bolivian, Chilean, and Uruguayan Militants in Peronist Argentina. Buenos Aires, 1973–1976

On September 16, 1973, thousands of demonstrators took to the streets of downtown Buenos Aires to protest the coup d'état in Chile. Some 20,000 people marched to the intersection of Callao and Las Heras Avenues, filling over twenty blocks. Among the demonstrators were activists from various Peronist and left-wing organizations, including the Juventud Peronista (Peronist Youth, or JP) and the Federación de Jóvenes Comunistas (Federation of Communist Youths, or FJC), as well as armed groups, such as the Grupo Obrero Revolucionario (Revolutionary Workers' Group, or GOR), and the Fuerzas Armadas de Liberación (Liberation Armed Forces, or FAL). According to the coverage by the PRT-ERP newspaper *El Combatiente*, there was also a large number of militants and supporters waving PRT-ERP flags and carrying a banner that read: "Chile, Uruguay, and Argentina Fighting for Latin America's Liberation." The slogans they chanted all echoed the same interpretation of what had happened on the other side of the Andes: "Chile, Chile, Chile, Teaches Us a Lesson / There Will Only Be a Revolution When the People Take Up Arms!" According to the reporter, this slogan was heard alongside others chanted by the crowd that reflected a similar assessment of the recent outcome: "Out of Chile! Out of Argentina! Yankees Out of Latin America!" "We Must Join Together and Arm Ourselves to the Teeth!" "Tupas, MIR, ERP, Together We Will Seize Power!" The *Combatiente* reporter noted that even the communist demonstrators of the FJC joined in these slogans: "Allende Will Not Be Mourned! Allende Will Be Avenged! Avenged with Machine Guns!"; "If They Don't Leave, If They Don't Go, They'll Get Another Vietnam!" Two days later, at a public tribute to Salvador Allende held in front of the seat of the national congress, groups of demonstrators shouted: "No More Words! The People Want Arms!"[1]

As we saw in Chapter III, after the coup in Chile the Southern Cone groups on the radical Left felt that their thesis of the inevitability of armed struggle gained new ground on the Left. In their view, what had been defeated in Chile had not been a revolution but a particular way of leading

Figure 4.a. "Las enseñanzas del Proceso Chileno" (The learnings of Chilean process). Cover of El Combatiente. N. 91. 9/29/1973. (David Cámpora Collection. CEIU Archive, FHCE.)

the Left and steering popular movements: reformism. Chile had to be a lesson for the political processes that were still standing.

The year 1973 came to a close with a state of affairs that was far from the expectations that had been raised at the beginning of the decade. The 1971 Banzer coup in Bolivia, the authoritarian reaction of President Bordaberry in 1972 in Uruguay and the subsequent dissolution of parliament in 1973, and the military coup in Chile in September 1973 had dashed those expectations.

For the militants of the armed Left, however, the Southern Cone was still a "key zone" where the fate of Latin America's revolution would finally be decided. In 1975, writing in *Correo de la Resistencia* under the pseudonym "Luis Cerda," Brazilian sociologist Ruy Mauro Marini – who was at the time head of the MIR's foreign committee – argued that while there were countries in Latin America with nationalist reformist projects

(Peru, Panama, Venezuela, Mexico) that were a source of concern for the United States. The Southern Cone was the "key zone" where the future of revolution in Latin America would be disputed:

What is clearly plain to see now is that there has been a shift in Latin America's revolutionary focal point, both in terms of geography and in terms of class and program content. The main factors that are furthering Latin America's revolutionary process today are not to be found therefore in countries ruled by bourgeois reformism, but precisely in those countries where counter-revolution has succeeded in seizing power (a typical example is Chile) or where it is fighting to do so (Argentina). Counter-revolutionary violence in those countries, as well as in Bolivia and Uruguay, is precisely how bourgeois and imperialist forces are responding to revolutionary movements whose growth jeopardizes the very survival of their domination. Which is why we can say that it is in those countries where the decisive round in Latin America is being played out.... Where the revolutionary movement succeeds in stopping [authoritarianism] (as may be the case today with Argentina) and, more so, where the proper means are found to bring down those regimes (as is the case mainly with Chile, but also with Uruguay and Bolivia), that is where we will have taken a decisive step, a major step in paving the way for the downfall of bourgeois and imperialist domination in our continent.[2]

In Marini's view, which expressed the sentiment of the recently created Junta de Coordinación Revolucionaria, after 1973 Argentina had become a critical place for the final outcome of the confrontation between revolution and counter-revolution. Counter-revolutionary forces had not yet established themselves firmly in Argentina and the country's geographical location made it a strategic site for revolutionary militants from neighboring countries (Uruguay, Chile, Bolivia, Brazil) to regroup and form a rearguard. But the situation in Argentina was also changing rapidly. The coup in Chile had even impacted Perón, who was elected president in September 1973.

In November, Perón wrote General Prats – the former commander-in-chief of the Chilean army who had sought asylum in Argentina – telling him that in Latin America "reactionary forces have shown revolutionaries how dearly they would be made to pay for their humanitarianism." He then went on to describe how Argentina would respond to imperialist plans: "The entire Nation will stand up against them. Every Argentine will rise up to defend national sovereignty. All our fellow peoples of America will support us."[3] A month later, however, the new Chilean Ambassador to Argentina reported back to the military junta expressing his satisfaction over the warm welcome he had received from Perón. In welcoming the ambassador, Perón referred to the problem of the exiles who had sought refuge at the Argentine Embassy in Chile as a "curse in disguise." He noted that both governments had emerged from the need to put a stop to rising

polarization and that "since he [had taken] office his main concern had
been to restrain the excesses of extreme leftist groups and that he would
not cease in that effort."[4] Two weeks later, the Chilean Ambassador met
with Argentine Foreign Minister Alberto Vignes and as they discussed
the death on Chilean soil of Argentine citizens linked to Unidad Popular,
Vignes conveyed the pressure that parliament was putting on him to investigate those cases, and he immediately declared that "it would be deplor-
able if this sort of people were to ruin our relations."[5]

Despite the growing relationship between Perón and the Chilean dictatorship, Uruguayan, Chilean, and Bolivian militants flocked to Argentina,
as they saw it as the only safe place left in the region that still offered certain freedom for political activities.

This period of Peronist Argentina, spanning 1973 to 1976, marked a
new moment in the history of the JCR organizations. On the one hand,
as noted above, the Allende experience strengthened the radical positions
that posited the inevitability of armed struggle and those that expressed
most firmly the concern over the expansion of the military infrastructure
of armed left-wing groups. On the other hand, the geopolitical situation turned Argentina into a safe place that offered these organizations
refuge and a rearguard base. During this period, the JCR gained certain institutional autonomy with respect to its founding organizations;
it developed a significant propaganda, logistics, and weapons infrastructure. It was also at this time that it implemented an international policy
through which it expanded its contacts, reaching out to different regions
of the world.

The PRT-ERP – the only non-Peronist armed left-wing organization –
had a complicated relationship with the new democratic government that
took office in May 1973. In the months of May through August 1973, the
PRT engaged in legal political activities and called a truce with the new
government. As of September, following its strike on the Army Health
Command, the ERP went back underground and stepped up its armed
actions. In a communiqué published in its newspaper *Estrella Roja* under
the title "The ERP Will Continue Fighting," it justified its return to
armed struggle arguing, "[t]he existing democracy is highly relative and
a harsh repression is being prepared to finish it off."[6] Its documents and
actions expressed a profound disillusionment with the democratic process
that had been opened with the Peronist government.

Since mid-1973 both the armed organizations of the Peronist Left and
the PRT-ERP had been denouncing the emergence of far Right organizations that had perpetrated a number of attacks against individuals and
institutions, with the support of the government. Throughout 1974 and
1975 these groups expanded their actions, attacking and killing intellectuals, artists, and social activists who sympathized or had ties with the

Peronist and non-Peronist Left. These groups also targeted exiles. By September 1974 these organizations had murdered some 200 people.[7]

Several documents described Peronism as a form of Bonapartism that was starting to be surpassed by social and, primarily, labor mobilization, which could not be contained by the old style of populist leadership.[8] The PRT-ERP also repeated the arguments already put forward by other organizations in the region regarding the authoritarian solutions that national elites in alliance with imperialist forces and national armies were imposing in the countries of the region, and the impossibility of furthering reformist programs in this context.[9]

The armed organizations of the Southern Cone all stated in their documents that their strategic goal was the construction of a people's revolutionary army. But the ERP was the organization that took this approach most seriously. From 1973 to 1975 it staged seven attacks against military barracks and garrisons.[10] While most of these actions were not considered a success in military terms, they were viewed as extremely positive by the ERP because of their ability to challenge the army.[11] Moreover, this line of action did not entail any loss of support among their sympathizers. During these years, the number of PRT-ERP militants grew and the organization expanded its area of influence. While in 1970 the PRT consisted of 250 militants, by 1975, according to María Seoane, its membership had grown to 600 militants and 2,000 supporters, and according to Pablo Pozzi it had reached some 5,000 to 6,000 militants and supporters combined.[12]

This military strategy against Perón's government was launched in January 1974 with an attack on the C-10 Armored Cavalry Regiment in the locality of Azul. Three months after Perón had become president with sixty-two percent of the votes, the PRT-ERP staged an action involving eighty to 100 guerrillas. Targeting one of the country's most important military regiments entailed a clear defiance of the president's authority.[13] The action failed and fourteen guerrillas were arrested, three were killed in the crossfire, and two were captured and disappeared. The following day, Perón gave a press conference, dressed for the first time in many years in his military uniform, and declared his intention to "wipe out terrorism."[14]

Besides the chorus of conservative voices supporting the measures proposed by Perón to "wipe out" this organization, several sectors of the Peronist and communist Left questioned the PRT-ERP's action, as it gave the executive branch an excuse to speed up its plans to implement a stricter criminal code and involve the armed forces in the political conflict.

The leaders of the PRT-ERP were relatively aware of how isolated this action had left their organization.[15] In that context, the PRT-ERP turned to its regional allies. It is not by chance that, while contacts had begun in 1972, the first public appearance of the Junta Coordinadora Revolucionaria occurred in 1974 with a press conference held by the ERP after the events at Azul, where the joint declaration "A los pueblos de América Latina" (To the Peoples of Latin America) was read.[16]

The declaration was a call to implement one of the "leading strategic ideas of Commander Che Guevara" and renew the tradition of "our peoples" who joined together against the "Spanish colonialists." In this organization's view the question was how to lead that "awakening of the peoples."[17] There were two lines of thinking that "conspired" against revolutionary efforts: "These are an enemy – bourgeois nationalism – and a mistaken notion among those on the side of the people – reformism."[18] Against these, the declaration optimistically saw "the armed pole, the revolutionary pole ... growing stronger and stronger among the masses."[19]

The fact that it was the ERP that first presented this declaration indicates the new stage that the coordination efforts among armed left-wing groups had entered in 1972. The ERP harbored militants of JCR member organizations from neighboring countries and provided the necessary material and human resources for them to plan rearguard operations from Argentina into bordering countries. The PRT-ERP was also instrumental in the network's maintenance, as it was the only organization that was able to increase its capacity for armed actions from 1973 to 1975, through successful kidnappings that brought in significant funds, while the other organizations suffered major defeats during that same period.[20]

The military campaign in Tucumán was perhaps the most ambitious military project taken on by the Southern Cone guerrilla groups. The campaign was a PRT-ERP initiative that involved forming a specialized military group known as "Compañía de Monte Ramón Rosa Jiménez," whose aim would be to establish a liberated zone in the province of Tucumán, extending some 350 km into Bolivian soil. It was actually only able to cover some thirty to forty kilometers, with about fifty to 100 guerrillas who, dressed in soldiers' uniforms but with *alpargatas* on their feet, sought to turn that stretch of land into a liberated area.[21]

Some accounts by PRT-ERP militants insist that the aim of this rural guerrilla was to create, not a *foco* to raise awareness through armed action, but a "liberated territory" that would support the political work that was being carried out in other areas. In this case the *foco* was not meant to lay the groundwork for a party that would later step in, as the territory where these actions were planned was located near sugar mills that had a long tradition of trade union action, and in which the PRT had been conducting union organization efforts since the 1960s. Moreover, rural guerrilla actions were considered as complementing urban guerrilla warfare.[22] The territory chosen was similar in some senses to the sites of the campaigns attempted in the early 1960s, discussed in previous chapters.[23] Despite this attempt to move away from *foquismo*, the military strategy had many aspects in common with Che Guevara's campaign in Bolivia. Argentina's northern region had been a focus of attention for Guevara since Masetti's incursion and it had continued until his Bolivia campaign. The ERP's campaign also had aspirations of continentality that were similar to Guevara's project in Bolivia. Like Guevara, who intended to cross over to Argentina from Bolivia with a group of 200 guerrillas, the ERP planned to expand its liberated zone into Bolivian territory, more specifically into the Bolivian Yungas.[24]

Moreover, according to the hypothesis underlying the ERP's strategy, a liberated zone in Tucumán would spark a counterinsurgent reaction that would internationalize the conflict. In a public document issued in January 1976 the group stated that if it succeeded in forming a guerrilla army the area would be invaded by a regional force backed by the United States. As will be shown below, the Tucumán campaign did not reach such dimensions – and, in the end, the internationalization was processed elsewhere.[25]

Throughout the campaign there were attempts by both the ERP and the national army to turn the scenario of the conflict into a dramatization of a formal war. While the army sought to exaggerate the characteristics of the guerrilla group, the guerrillas tried to give the idea that they were turning into a regular army, in the manner of the Vietnamese or Chinese experience.[26] The ERP implemented a persuasive communicational strategy through its newspaper, focusing particularly on all aspects connected with the supposed formalization of the revolutionary army. Relations among Compañía de Monte guerrillas were meant to reproduce the ranks, aesthetics, and rituals of a regular army, and this was conveyed and amplified by *Estrella Roja*, which reported on the awarding of medals, promotions in rank, and daily rituals, in which the ERP's anthem was sung and the guerrillas marched dressed in their military gear and bearing ERP badges. All of this information played up the features of the ERP, giving an exaggerated idea of the military dimensions that this guerrilla group was achieving.[27]

It was in this context that the other member organizations of the JCR began to think about how they could use to their advantage the situation of the Argentine guerrilla group. They saw in the supposed military development of the ERP a significant support they could draw on to plan actions that would be launched from Argentina into their respective countries.

In its internal bulletins, the PRT-ERP featured accounts of Latin American militants who were participating in Argentine experiences. A piece featured in Internal Bulletin No. 42, for example, under the heading "Letter from a Latin America Revolutionary," a member of a "sister organization" described his experience in the PRT's school of leaders and in ERP actions, and expressed his admiration for the organization's development. He admitted that in the beginning of the decade "the vanguard of the war was with the MLN-Tupamaros, but we believed that couldn't last for long. Because the MLN was not a Marxist–Leninist party and it was formed by all sorts of ideologies, both revolutionary and pseudo-revolutionary." Even at that stage there were already indications that the PRT-ERP "would one day occupy the position that the MLN-T had then, if that fellow movement did not embrace Marxism–Leninism." The author of the letter then went on to convey his experience in the "school of leaders," showing his admiration for the "high level of political and ideological development and how concerned everyone was with furthering their Marxism–Leninism education." In his activities in the ERP he had been able to "confirm that much progress had been achieved in terms of political and ideological development since 1971." He also perceived the "great spirit of sacrifice" and "high fighting morale" of ERP combatants.[28]

Chilean and Uruguayan militants are known to have participated in the Compañía de Monte in Tucumán.[29] The involvement of militants from other countries occurred in the framework of the strategic projects of each of the groups that were part of the JCR.

The MIR had furthered the creation of the JCR to ensure a strategic rearguard in the event of a coup d'état in Chile.[30] However, after the coup these plans were limited when the group's leaders decided to stay in Chile and proposed the "No Asylum!" policy to give a different image from that of most of the Left, whose activists started going into exile. While some MIR militants did flee from repression and made it to Buenos Aires, they were not admitted back into the organization because they had questioned its No Asylum! decision.

Carmen Castillo remembers that the first MIR leader allowed to leave Chile was Edgardo Enríquez, brother of the movement's general secretary. The reasons for his departure were both political and personal.[31] In March 1974 he traveled to Buenos Aires from where he left for Paris to establish a number of contacts with European and Latin American left-wing organizations.[32] Beyond Enríquez's movements and the statements of support to the JCR, the MIR had not defined how the rearguard would operate in Argentina. Throughout 1974, even as Chile's intelligence services (the Dirección Nacional de Inteligencia, or DINA) captured most of its members, the MIR persevered in its decision not to send militants abroad.[33]

The MIR's failure to reach out to the JCR for support led PRT-ERP leader Domingo Menna, head of foreign affairs, to travel to Chile in July 1974, where he met for several days with the MIR's political committee. The differences between the MIR and the PRT-ERP revolved around three issues: the lack of coordination with the JCR in the activities that MIR delegates conducted outside Chile, a biased view on the part of the PRT-ERP regarding the low levels of proletarianization in the MIR, and the delay in the initiation of armed propaganda actions in Chile.[34] This last issue later prompted an epistolary discussion between Miguel Enríquez and Roberto Santucho. While the PRT-ERP questioned the MIR's delay in launching armed propaganda actions, the MIR militants doubted the degree of military development claimed by the PRT-ERP.[35] The PRT-ERP's response is not fully known, although in Internal Bulletin No. 65 of August 1974 it reaffirms its political position.[36] In later visits by MIR militants to Argentina the differences were gradually overcome as it became clear that the MIR had the firm intention of carrying out armed propaganda actions, and the two organizations began conducting joint efforts in Europe.[37]

The assassination of MIR general secretary Miguel Enríquez on October 5, 1974 proved just how far the dictatorship's repressive actions were advancing on the organization's leadership. Many of its top leaders had either been captured or disappeared. By mid-1975, around ninety percent of the original members of the central committee had fallen.[38] A year after Enríquez was killed, the other two top leaders of the MIR – Andrés Pascal Allende and Nelson Gutiérrez – sought refuge in the Costa Rican Embassy and the Apostolic Nunciature, respectively. Their request for asylum evidenced the end of the No Asylum! strategy.[39]

According to journalist Nancy Guzmán, Miguel Enríquez's death led his brother Edgardo to return to Buenos Aires and take a more proactive attitude with respect to the JCR. The catastrophic situation within the MIR meant that support from Argentina was critical. Before Argentina, Edgardo made a stop in Cuba where he organized an MIR training school. In May 1975, Enríquez left Cuba for Buenos Aires with the aim of preparing a return operation with a group of MIR militants.[40] A few militants were selected to participate in JCR activities in Argentina. Most of them had been in Cuba and traveled to Buenos Aires in early 1976 to receive specific training within the structure of the PRT-ERP.[41]

The plans that were underway in Argentina in the years 1975 and 1976 did not prosper. In addition to the difficulties they had in making contact with militants who were inside Chile, in Argentina these militants were being watched by several state and parastatal intelligence organizations, both Chilean and Argentine.

The Tupamaros had also left Chile for Buenos Aires, even before the coup. The democratic government in Argentina coupled with the worsening situation in Chile had led a significant number of Uruguayan militants to leave Chile, with some going to Cuba, to prepare their return to Uruguay, and others to Buenos Aires, to plan logistic aspects of possible incursions into Uruguay.

In 1973, the MLN-T had been unable to overcome the internal crisis it had suffered after its defeat in 1972. In early 1973, several militants had organized the Viña del Mar Symposium, where, in line with the intellectual and political climate that prevailed in Chile at the time, they had explained their defeat as a result of "petit-bourgeois deviations" and "ideological weakness," and had called for the creation of a "Marxist–Leninist party" as a way of solving those problems. The adoption of a new language and a new ideological paradigm generated a superficial consensus in the context of the crisis and aligned them with their regional (the MIR and the PRT-ERP) and continental (the Cuban Communist Party) allies, which had also adopted such definitions.[42] However, this language and ideological definition meant different things to the different sectors of the MLN-T.

The Tupamaros in Chile, Cuba, and Argentina devised a military plan to return to Uruguay. A military committee would be in charge of training some sixty militants in Cuba, obtaining weapons and personal identification documents in Uruguay, and preparing the infrastructure in Buenos Aires and the Argentine and Uruguayan coasts.[43] The coup in Uruguay altered that plan. After the coup, the MLN-T could not set up a solid and stable base of militants on Uruguayan soil. Every group of militants that returned to Uruguay was immediately detected by the dictatorship.

In that context, the MLN-T leadership began to have increasing doubts as to the feasibility of organizing an armed resistance within the country. The differences that had been emerging since 1972 were aggravated in 1974, finally leading the organization to split at the end of the year. Most leaders concluded that, given the defeats of 1973 and 1974, there was no choice but to suspend any plans for an armed comeback; they decided instead to focus on a political strategy of denunciation of the dictatorship and strengthening alliances with Uruguayan politicians who had been exiled in Buenos Aires after the coup.[44]

Several militants who were in Argentina reacted to this decision by insisting on the continuation of armed action in Uruguay. A small group of unionists – who had recently arrived from Montevideo, together with Andrés Cultelli, an old militant who was in charge of the school of leaders – formed Tendencia Proletaria (Proletarian Tendency), which focused on political work in factories, in line with the PRT's political agenda in Argentina's trade union movement, as a jumping board for generating a military strategy for the masses.[45] That was the line that prevailed in the central committee meeting held in October 1974 in Argentina. A new leadership was established there, whose aim would be to build a "proletarian, clandestine, and armed" Marxist–Leninist party.[46]

This internal conflict was marked by accusations that confused personal matters and political issues and which went as far as death threats. Each side accused the other of being responsible for the disappearance of the one million dollars that the PRT-ERP had entrusted them with delivering to the MIR. Rank-and-file members also questioned the "bourgeoisified" lifestyle of the leaders, who justified it as a way of misleading repressive forces.[47]

The concept of proletarianization is key to understanding many of the transformations that the Tupamaros underwent in Argentina.[48]

The PRT-ERP had a major influence throughout this process. While the definitions regarding proletarianization were connected with the 1972 experience in Chile, coming into closer contact with the PRT-ERP heightened that perspective.[49]

In addition to this intellectual influence, the PRT-ERP also intervened in the internal conflicts of the Tupamaros. The member of the PRT-ERP's political committee mentioned above, Domingo Menna, participated in the MLN-T's central committee meeting in the framework of the reciprocity that had been decided by the JCR leaders. These interventions reveal a clear influence on the decisions that the weakened Tupamaros were adopting in Argentina, setting forth the strongest arguments for the *peludos* to take over the leadership and for the Tupamaros to return to Uruguay.[50] Menna's assessment of the situation of the Southern Cone was very far removed from the reality that several militants from these organizations were suffering in neighboring countries: "We are moving toward a new Vietnam and the four organizations [of the JCR] have the responsibility of turning this new hope in Latin America into a real and concrete possibility."[51]

"Domingo" – one of the leaders who left the MLN-T after the central committee meeting and who disagreed with Menna's positions there – recalls that while there were differences of opinion, discussions were conducted in an atmosphere of utmost respect and a certain admiration for the role that the PRT-ERP was playing at that moment in the context of the Southern Cone.[52]

Another group in which the PRT-ERP had some bearing was the Bolivian ELN (ELN-B). In this case the influence was much stronger, to the point that in 1975 the organization changed its name to "Bolivian PRT." Most members of the ELN-B fled to Argentina from Chile after the September 11 coup. This organization had been severely hit. Despite the prestige it had earned as the guerrilla group founded by Guevara, its strategic plans had proven ineffective and had revealed its inability to remain in Bolivia for any substantial period of time. Its two attempts at establishing an armed *foco* had failed, and its incursions into urban areas after the Banzer coup had not lasted more than a year.[53]

The members of the ELN were not the only Bolivians who were flocking to Buenos Aires. Many of Bolivia's leftist activists were there too, seeking to coordinate actions against the Banzer dictatorship. After the first attempt to forge an alliance of left-wing groups was frustrated in Chile, former president General Torres tried again to create a leftist front in Argentina. He formed the Alianza de la Izquierda Nacional (Alliance of the National Left, or ALIN) to prepare his return to Bolivia.[54]

One of Torres's closest allies during his exile in Chile and Argentina was Major Ruben Sánchez. This Bolivian military officer – who had been captured by Guevara and later joined the revolutionary cause under Torres's popular government – formed a small armed group in Chile, made up mostly of former members of the military (FAR). After establishing this group he came into contact with the armed organizations of the Southern Cone: in particular the PRT-ERP (through which he joined the JCR) and, as of 1973, the ELN-B.[55]

After the coup in Chile, the ELN-B moved most of its military and logistic apparatus and maintained some safe houses in Argentina. There, several of its members participated in PRT-ERP activities. To a great extent, the ideological priorities of the PRT also permeated the ELN-B's agenda of ideological discussions, sparking some internal conflicts. Issues that had already been discussed in Chile, such as proletarianization and the construction of a Marxist–Leninist party, were brought up again by ELN-B members in Argentina. Much criticism was directed at historical leader Chato Peredo because of his militarist deviations. His main opponent was Sánchez, who had the support of the PRT-ERP.[56]

It was in that context that the ELN convened its first congress, held in Lima in 1975, and the organization split into two factions. One faction, formed by a minority headed by historical leader Chato Peredo – associated with the *foquista* strategy that had resulted in the Ñancahuazú and Teoponte defeats – was removed from steering positions and put to work as rank-and-file members. The other faction, formed by those who called for the construction of a Marxist–Leninist party and were in favor of proletarianization, took the helm of the organization. Thus, the transformation of the ELN into the PRT also entailed a shift in its leadership, as Major Rubén Sánchez took over, along with his daughter and son-in-law. Although Sánchez had only recently joined the ELN, he had forged close ties with the high-ranking members of the PRT-ERP and that relationship most likely helped him rise within his group.[57]

This second faction was the one that prevailed.[58] A "euphoric" message to the PRT-ERP was issued at the end of the congress, announcing the transformation of the ELN into the Partido Revolucionario de los Trabajadores de Bolivia (Workers' Revolutionary Party of Bolivia, or Bolivian PRT) and acknowledging that the participation of "*compañero* N" of the JCR had been decisive in the new direction of the organization.[59]

These congress resolutions were in line with those adopted a year earlier by the MLN-T. They were even viewed by Argentine intelligence as a sign of the interference of the Argentine PRT in the Bolivian organization.[60] The tasks set out were also similar to those planned by the MLN-T: "Proletarianize our organization, systematically study Marxist–Leninist theory – the party's ideological line – , and improve practical activities based on the concrete engagement in criticism and self-criticism." As with the MLN-T and the PRT-ERP, adopting an ideological definition was seen as an almost magical solution to the political analysis issues they had experienced in the past.

While Torres sent out messages announcing his return and operated politically through the ALIN, the Bolivian PRT (PRT-B) tried to initiate armed actions in southern Bolivia. After the PRT-B congress, Sánchez returned to Bolivia to begin establishing a network to re-launch actions.[61] The PRT-B's plans were linked to the ERP's Compañía de Monte efforts in Tucumán, and they were backed by the JCR. Two key participants in this operation were Luis Stamponi, an Argentine activist who had joined the ELN-B in the late 1960s, and the Uruguayan Enrique Lucas, a former MLN-T member who had joined the ELN-B during his stay in Argentina in the framework of JCR activities.[62] The 1976 coup in Argentina cut these plans short, with the ensuing assassination of Torres in Argentine soil and the disappearance of Stamponi and Lucas in Bolivia in joint operations staged by the dictatorships of the Southern Cone.

The documentation found in the files of the Dirección de Inteligencia de la Provincia de Buenos Aires (Intelligence Bureau of the Province of Buenos Aires, or DIPBA) reveals that, in parallel to the efforts undertaken by each organization in Buenos Aires, the JCR was developing joint propaganda mechanisms and logistic activities to support the organizations' armed actions in their countries. Among the activities projected were the production of films, the establishment of a news agency, and the publication of a political theory magazine.[63]

A number of documents discovered in the DIPBA mention the filming project, which included a full-length film and four short films on Vietnam. The movies were to be shot in Argentina, sponsored by the Grupo Cine de la Base and partially financed by the Cuban–Argentine Cultural Exchange Institute.[64]

In 1974, the political theory magazine was launched under the name *Che Guevara*, with the first number coming out in November–December of that year, and the second in February 1975. The magazine was intended as a way of introducing the organization to the world. The idea was to publish the magazine in several languages, and it did come out in at least three (French, Portuguese, and Spanish). It featured essays penned by members of each organization, giving a historical account of their actions, describing the situation in each country, and outlining the JCR's involvement in the future plans of the individual organizations. Each number also included joint documents issued by the JCR and some pieces that mentioned the coordinating body's Guevarista definition. As early as March 1975 the continuity of the project was jeopardized and the third number of *Che Guevara* magazine was not published until October 1977.[65]

The logo of the organization, featured on the back cover of the magazine, condensed the meanings that the coordinating body sought to build.[66] It

Figure 4.b. Cover of Magazine: Che Guevara. No. 1, November 1974. (David Cámpora Collection. CEIU Archive.)

shows the silhouette of a man holding a rifle high above his head, over a map of Latin America. Behind the shape of the continent is a five point star that serves as background for the badge, and it is surrounded by a circle with the name of the JCR and its member organizations. The overlapping of these different images (the man, the continent, the star) symbolizes how the identity of these groups had been shaped. In the center was a man with his rifle, thus highlighting the core element that had brought these organizations together: armed struggle. The continent was the territory on which their actions unfolded, and the star, already used by some of the member organizations (the ERP, the MLN-T), conveyed a number of meanings associated with the international communist movement and with Latin American unity.

It is still hard to determine the degree of development that the JCR attained in terms of infrastructure in Argentina because many of the militants involved in such tasks were kidnapped and disappeared, and because

Figure 4.c. Logo of JCR in Che Guevara, No. 2, February 1975. (David Campora Collection. Archive CEIU Archive, FHCE.)

of the compartmentalization of information that characterized these actions, which meant that logistic information had to be kept secret. One of the few surviving leaders of the JCR, the Tupamaro Efraín Martínez Platero, recalls that the members in charge of logistics had used JCR funds to enter into agreements with land transportation companies that were critical for distributing various supplies across borders.

Many DIPBA documents from early 1975 describe several raids of JCR houses where important conspiratorial activities were conducted. A report entitled "Procedure and Detentions of Tupamaro Elements" documents thirteen house raids involving sites linked to JCR activities and the arrest of foreign militants, linking the tools and materials seized in those raids to two activities that were dubbed "Plan Conejo" and "Plan 500" by the Buenos Aires police.[67]

The aim of "Plan Conejo" was to provide forged identity documents (IDs, passports, driver's licenses, police and military service cards, etc.) for the members of all the JCR organizations. The forged documents found were Argentine, but also from bordering countries, the United States and Canada, and Europe. Two houses were set up for forgery activities. Various materials used for such purposes were found in both houses, including a "very expensive modern photographic enlarger."

"Plan 500" involved the production of 500 homemade machine guns. This project had been initiated in Chile, where the industrial units had begun experimenting with homemade weapon production, and it continued in Argentina. A month before these workshops were discovered in the raids, the ERP reported in its paper *Estrella Roja* that a machine gun that could shoot more than 500 rounds had been designed. This machine gun was the result of two previous attempts by a Bolivian ELN militant and by an ERP militant. *Estrella Roja* featured an image of the "JCR 1" machine gun, as it was called, and presented it as a weapon that could be made at a non-industrial workshop, although it informed that there were also efforts underway to mass produce the different parts of the machine gun. The raids were most likely connected with the announcement of the weapon's development in this publication. The tasks involved in "Plan 500" were conducted in three sites: two fully-equipped shops and an indoor firing range. A fourth site was used to assemble FM devices to intercept police taps.

Weapons, explosives, weapon production shops, houses used for document forgery, and people's jails were found in these raids conducted by Argentine police forces. They reveal that in early 1975 the coordination efforts between the member organizations of the JCR were reaching a significant level of development in terms of infrastructure.[68] During the raid operations, two Uruguayans were gunned down, and twenty-six Uruguayan, three Argentine, and two Chilean militants were captured.

While the raids showed the coordination capacity of these organizations, they also exposed the increasing difficulties that the JCR was beginning to face in Argentina as repression was stepped up and the intelligence services of the Southern Cone enhanced their own coordination. In 1974 Perón started to suggest that the armed forces should be involved in the "fight against subversion." Although some sectors of the military were initially against this involvement, the ERP attacks appear to have persuaded them.[69] According to historian Marina Franco, in the months of August, September, and November the army participated in different repressive actions in the provinces of Catamarca and Tucumán.[70] During this period the government also passed the State Security Act, which expanded the concept of subversion and provided legal mechanisms to widen the scope of political persecution. It was no longer just members of clandestine organizations that were targeted, but also members of any social, political, and cultural organizations that were critical of the status quo. Lastly, in early 1975, the army launched an attack on the ERP's military campaign

Figure 4.d. Note of the homemade machinegun made by the JCR in *Estrella Roja*, No. 49. 08/22/1972. (David Campora Collection. Archive CEIU Archive, FHCE.)

in Tucumán, in what was known as "Operation Independence." This consolidated the army's involvement and leading role in the fight against subversion.

In addition to growing repression and state control, exiles had to face the enhanced coordination among the region's armies, police forces, and intelligence services. The most significant example of coordination among the various repressive agencies of the region's dictatorships is what is known as Operation Condor. Most of the literature on Operation Condor points to a meeting organized in November 1975 by DINA chief Manuel Contreras as the origins of the regional coordination of the Southern Cone's military intelligence services. In his final speech at this meeting Contreras proposed a plan to defeat Marxism in the region once and for all, which would be deployed in three phases (or levels). The first phase consisted in the development of a multilateral intelligence system in the region; in the second phase, the governments would conduct joint operations in Latin

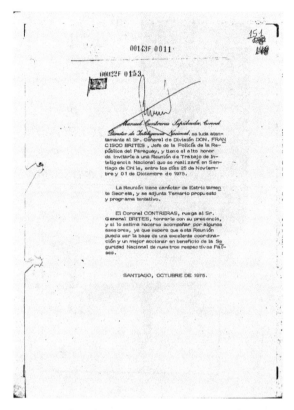

Figure 4.e. First meeting of Condor Plan in *National Security Archive* Electronic Briefing Book No. 239 – Part II.

America; and in the last phase, joint commands would carry out operations in the United States and Europe. The following meeting was also held in Santiago, in May 1976, and it included a new member: Brazil. Participants discussed infrastructure issues and planned the beginning of phase three. Less than a year after the first meeting, actions were being conducted under Operation Condor at the three levels mentioned above.[71]

Besides Operation Condor, there is evidence of earlier cooperation efforts that are relevant for this study. Patrice McSherry cites a declassified CIA document that reveals that in February 1974 Perón had begun promoting coordinated actions between the intelligence services of the region with the aim of persecuting members of the armed left-wing organizations of the Southern Cone. As with Chile before, concerns began to be raised about Argentina's safety as a conspiratorial center for left-wing activists. But this was very different, as Perón was not Allende, and he had no sympathy for these sectors, which he saw as supporting the elements he had vowed to "wipe out." It is in this context that Perón authorizes the federal police to cooperate with the security services of Brazil, Bolivia, Chile, and Uruguay. This authorization included permission for the services of neighboring countries to operate in Argentine territory, as well as to arrest individuals and take them out of the country without due process. These decisions were made after a meeting held in Buenos Aires in February 1974 with the participation of the region's police chiefs.[72]

This context explains a number of actions perpetrated against Uruguayan and Chilean militants in Argentina in the years 1974 and 1975 before Operation Condor had fully crystallized.[73] As the March 1975 raids were being conducted, Jorge Isaac Fuentes – a member of the Chilean MIR – and Amílcar Santucho – brother of the ERP leader – were captured in Paraguay as they were carrying out a JCR mission aimed at expanding the organization's political contacts in Peru and Venezuela. The trip had attracted the attention of Paraguayan intelligence, and in May 1975 it informed the Argentine and Chilean intelligence services of the presence of these militants on Paraguayan soil. Although the region's intelligence services were already aware of the JCR's actions – as in February 1974 the organization had announced its existence – the documents seized from these two militants revealed the many international contacts that were being pursued by this coordinating body.[74]

According to John Dinges, the information seized in Paraguay catalyzed the need to enhance mechanisms for coordinated action between the military intelligence services of the region.[75] This led Lt. Col. Manuel Contreras, head of the Chilean DINA, who was in close contact with the CIA, to convene a working meeting of the region's military intelligence services. The invitation to the meeting was accompanied by a document providing a general diagnosis of the continentalization of the political conflict, which had points in common with the assessments made by the Left. Just as the Left denounced the hand of the United States in the continentalization of the political repression furthered by the OAS and similar bodies, Contreras' document described a similar, but inverted, version of continentalization:

Subversion recognizes no Borders or Countries, and infiltration permeates all areas of National life.

Subversion has developed Intercontinental, Continental, Regional, and Subregional Commands, centralized to coordinate dissociative actions. By way of example we can mention the Tricontinental Conference in Havana, the Junta Coordinadora Revolucionaria para el Sur, etc.... Thus, we have come to the conclusion that to face this Psycho-Political War what we need on an international level is not a domestically-centralized Command but an efficient Coordination that will enable a timely exchange of information and experiences, in addition to a certain degree of personal knowledge among the Heads of Security.[76]

In contrast to the "battle cry against imperialism" proposed by Guevara and taken up again by the JCR, Contreras' war was waged against international subversion and it was a psycho-political war. The conflict was not limited to armed groups that challenged state power, but extended to the Left as a whole, regardless of its forms of expression. Although some authors have stressed the role of the JCR as the trigger for the development of Operation Condor, this document would appear to disprove that assertion, as the JCR is only mentioned as one example of the various international activities conducted by left-wing groups. The range of political affiliations of the victims of Operation Condor also seems to refute that assertion. As will be shown below, this regional operation targeted a wide spectrum of political dissidents.

While Contreras' call was written with a sense of urgency and presented as an original idea, the truth is that, as shown in previous chapters, there had been coordination efforts and training experiences among the different national police and military forces since the mid-1960s. In some cases, these activities were sponsored by the United States, as is proved by the School of the Americas experience. In others, they were the result of joint actions conducted under the OAS. And lastly, some were prompted by specific situations, such as Che Guevara's Bolivia campaign.

The New Left had been aware since the mid-1960s of the risks that these coordinated actions would pose for political processes in the Southern Cone. While the JCR continued along this line, denouncing the process of internationalization of repression, surprisingly enough it highlighted aspects that had little to do with what was really happening. In a document entitled "Military Pact Against the Peoples of Latin America," written in Paris in January 1976, the JCR warned about the 11th Conference of American Armies, which was aimed at "organizing counter-revolutionary actions in Latin America." After observing that "hatred toward the peoples [had] prevailed throughout this conference" and citing Videla's warning that "it did not matter how many people had to die to attain the goal of restoring peace" in his country, the text informed of a counter-revolutionary plan, promoted by the United States, with the aim of creating regional forces that would be more powerful than the national armies. These regional forces would be formed by the armies of several countries and would act as counterinsurgency forces, with the United States as a strategic reserve. This example appears to have more to do with its strategic expectations than with reality. According to the document, if rural guerrilla forces were able to recruit more than 1,000 men in the region of Tucumán, Argentina, the counter-revolutionary armies of Argentina, Chile, Bolivia, Paraguay, and Uruguay would be called into action to combat them. If the guerrilla forces reached 2,000 regular members, the U.S. armed forces would step in and intervene directly. The text reported that this plan was already in motion: "We have accurate information that allows us to assert that the paramilitary gangs that are operating in Tucumán are under the technical direction of the CIA. The peoples of the world know these methods well and the example of Pinochet's brutal rule in Chile is all the proof we need of them."[77]

Although the text was right in detecting the convergence of the Southern Cone armies in the fight against guerrilla groups and the Left in general, it revealed gross misinformation regarding, or disinterest in, the reconstruction of the coordinated actions that were being conducted by the intelligence services since 1975. Captured militants had already been illegally moved across borders, from Argentina to Chile and Uruguay, and Chilean and Uruguayan agents were operating freely in Argentine soil. This information was not unavailable to the JCR. But in early 1976 this JCR document chose to denounce something that played to the expectations that the Argentine PRT-ERP still had for its Tucumán campaign, even though it had little to do with the actual persecution that its "sister" organizations were suffering right there in Argentina.

The coordination between the region's intelligence services had been extremely effective in its actions against the JCR. Before the meeting that marks the official beginning of Operation Condor, the JCR's activities in Argentina had been greatly curtailed as a result of the raids described above and the capturing of Fuentes and Santucho's brother in Paraguay. By mid-1975 Argentina was becoming a dangerous territory for the JCR's projects. A DIPBA report drafted after the Conejo and 500 Plan operations stated: "This second stage of operations allows us to assert that this subversive apparatus, formed primarily by Uruguayan, Chilean, and other foreign elements, has been almost totally destroyed".[78] In that context, the JCR entered a period of more intense work abroad (in Europe, Africa, and Latin America) and cut down its activities in Argentina. In July 1975, a resolution of the expanded PRT-ERP central committee stated that the JCR was a "small embryo of an internationalist organization" that was important "as an instrument to move forward in the construction of international revolutionary forces.... [O]nce we have liberated zones, the JCR will play a much bigger role."[79]

Although in mid-1975 the PRT-ERP still had high hopes for its Tucumán campaign, when military troops were deployed to the area it realized that its goal of establishing a liberated zone would be a long-term goal, and therefore the JCR would have to focus on its activities abroad.

The political crisis and the power vacuum created by Perón's death in July 1974 fueled the expectations of the PRT-ERP. The organization saw 1975 as the year of great definitions and the final battle. In the PRT-ERP's view, the lack of political leadership of the president, the conflicts between different Peronist factions (Lopez Rega's circle, the CGT, and political sectors from the party's center), the army's increasing involvement in the actions against guerrilla groups, and growing social discontent due to the more liberal economic shift were all elements that proved the need to accelerate the revolutionary process.[80]

While a range of analysts who have studied this period agree on the political crisis diagnosis, what is not so clear is how the armed Left could capitalize on that crisis.[81] During that year some 800 people were killed, mostly as a result of actions by the military and the death squads; to a lesser extent, by left-wing guerrilla groups. Most studies of this period note that, neither the PRT-ERP nor the Montoneros factored in the drop in mobilization when they decided to focus on military actions in 1975, and so they continued their guerrilla actions, thus aggravating their political isolation.

The ERP's response to the ebb in social mobilization in the second half of the year was to strengthen its focus on armed actions. Although it was beginning to feel the effects of Operation Independence in Tucumán, the PRT-ERP decided to maintain the Compañía de Monte Rosa Jiménez, and in January 1976 it even tried to set up another armed *foco* in the area of Cardillal, to take the pressure off other areas of Tucumán.[82]

In December 1975, amidst rumors of a coup, the PRT-ERP planned an ambitious military operation that was meant to have a "psychological impact" on the public, as the organization wanted to show the military strength it had achieved. The plan was to take Arsenal Battalion 601 in Monte Chingolo, which was one of the Argentine army's most important arsenals.[83] The PRT-ERP was defeated in the action. Of the seventy-seven guerrillas who participated directly in the operation, fifty-one were killed, twenty-three were captured and later killed, and only three were imprisoned.[84] After the action, the ERP blamed the defeat on the betrayal by Rafael de Jesús Ranier, known as "Oso," who a month later was captured by the ERP, interrogated, put on trial by the "revolutionary court," and "sentenced" to death.[85] The ERP's losses as a result of these two operations (Tucumán and Monte Chingolo) weakened its material infrastructure and human resources, as well as what was left of the JCR in Buenos Aires.

On March 24, 1976 the coup cancelled once and for all any possibilities of action for the JCR in Argentina. The margin of action of the organizations was further limited as there were no more places where they could take refuge, and the coordination of repression in the region meant that security forces could act freely. The Argentine coup was a golden moment in the development of Operation Condor. The repression against all of the Left and the anti-dictatorial forces that were still in Buenos Aires was intensified, targeting leaders across a range of anti-authoritarian movements, such as the former president of Bolivia, General José Torres, and four Uruguayans – Senator Zelmar Michelini, Congressman Héctor Gutiérrez Ruiz, and the Tupamaros William Whitelaw and Rosario

Barredo – who were murdered only days after the coup. The persecution of militants of JCR member organizations was also stepped up. After the kidnapping of Fuentes, of the MIR, and Amílcar Santucho, of the ERP, in Paraguay, Chile's security services confirmed the plans that were being carried out from Argentina and Edgardo Enríquez' involvement in those plans. From then on, Argentina's security forces began to follow Enríquez, in coordination with Chilean intelligence. This, too, was intensified after the coup. The Chilean MIR, which had been virtually dismantled in Chile, suffered the disappearance of ten of its members in Argentina, including Enríquez, who was the top political representative of the MIR in the JCR.[86] This group of militants was the last hope that the MIR had outside Chile. By 1978, some 1,000 MIR militants would be living in exile, mostly in Europe and Cuba.[87] Thirty-seven Uruguayan members of the MLN-T – which had split into two factions and been practically wiped out inside Uruguay – were abducted and disappeared in Argentina between March 1976 and the year 1979.[88] The vast majority of the 2,000 who had initially gone to Chile in 1971 were no longer with either faction of the organization and were in exile in Europe, Mexico, or Cuba.[89] Lastly, in less than a year the PRT-ERP was practically dismantled, and many of its leaders, including its general secretary Roberto Santucho, were killed or disappeared.

A document of the Argentine Intelligence Agency SIDE noted that the coup in Argentina had altered "the balance of geopolitical power between subversive and counter-subversive forces." The document examined the "escalation in the concentration of efforts and the generation of right-wing reactions that led to the displacement of pseudo-leftist or leftist governments or governments that were too weak to decisively deal with the actions of armed underground groups (AUG) that were already operating in their respective countries." The last stage in that process had been closed with the seizing of power in Argentina, but now the conflict was expanding into other regions of the world where subversive forces would continue their political struggle, as the margin for action within Argentine borders was very limited. This prompted the following reassessment:

The traditionally-accepted notion of "territoriality" is no longer valid in this revolutionary-type war that [Latin] America is suffering. Therefore, in the current circumstances it is imperative to achieve a unity of action that sets aside traditional borders but is respectful of the incorporeal concept of sovereignty.

For the enemy, the loss of Argentina as a theatre of war entails losing the whole area of the "Southern Cone of the American continent," and thus its actions will be confined to countries outside the area with scarce local, and even less international, repercussion. They will direct their actions toward territories outside the continent, much likely in Africa and Europe, in that order.[90]

The JCR in the World. Between Solidarity, Internationalism, and Survival

The possibility of focusing on political actions abroad that had been suggested in mid-1975 had turned into the only viable option after the March 1976 coup in Argentina. JCR members left Buenos Aires mostly for Europe, Cuba, and Mexico, with a smaller group traveling to Algeria. The activities that had begun in France in 1974 continued in 1975, with the establishment of a Latin American news agency (APAL), the publication of the *Che Guevara* magazine, the promotion of an association of Latin American students in Europe, and various political contacts with different left-wing organizations of Europe and the Third World, that were head-quartered in France. From there it spread its activities to Italy, Sweden, and Portugal through communities of Uruguayan, Chilean, Bolivian, and, later, Argentine exiles, who arrived fleeing the escalation of repression in their countries.[91]

One of the leading concerns of JCR militants was the establishment of political contacts in order to foster solidarity with the Southern Cone.[92] The organization's documents highlighted two levels of solidarity efforts. First, what they called "broad democratic solidarity," based on the denunciation of human rights abuses. One document noted that "in the hands of reformists, the struggle for democracy does not go beyond the narrow framework of opportunism, it never truly lives up to its principles and, therefore, it can never be the vanguard of the solidarity movement," so that, "as the Vietnamese say, legal movements are not reformist if they are framed in a revolutionary strategy." For this it was necessary for the JCR to have its own democratic solidarity team that at certain moments "would have to conduct its activities carefully masked."[93]

The JCR's activities involved supporting solidarity and denunciation campaigns, funding lawyers appointed to defend cases connected with human rights abuses, and appealing to a range of solidarity bodies that gradually emerged in the late 1970s in Europe.[94] The documents found convey a utilitarian view of the concept of human rights. In contrast to research by Vania Markarian, in this case there is little evidence of a shift from the revolution paradigm to the human rights paradigm. On the contrary, what these documents reveal is a markedly instrumental use of the concept of human rights that is subordinated to a revolutionary strategy.[95]

In this sense, there was a level above this "democratic solidarity," which was "revolutionary solidarity," consisting in the "moral support provided to organizations that, like those who are part of the JCR, are fighting for liberation and socialism in a people's war." The highest level of revolutionary solidarity was proletarian internationalism, which consisted in "moral and material solidarity that can take the form of assistance with combatants and weapons in the war for liberation."[96]

In a document that is most likely from 1976 the JCR poses the need to establish relations with the following parties, in order of priority: the Cuban Communist Party, the People's Movement for the Liberation of Angola, Palestine groups, and the Workers' Party of Vietnam. However, it warned that the Cuban Revolution's failure to recognize the JCR would hinder its contacts with other organizations. In the JCR's words:

[We need to] start forging relations with Cuba, between the party and the JCR, to help neutralize the reformist pressures of the communist parties of Latin America. Let us not forget that as long as Cuba does not recognize us as a body, we will have fewer chances of furthering relations in Europe, Africa, and even Asia.[97]

The document observed that the first congress of the Cuban Communist Party (PCC), held in December 1975, entailed the consolidation of a new foreign policy with respect to Latin America. Starting in 1967, Cuba moderated its foreign policy, shifting from a revolutionary approach to focus on forging alliances with new nationalist governments of military (Peru, Bolivia, Panama) or populist (Argentina, Mexico) origin, whose agendas had nationalist and Latin Americanist elements that had points in common with Cuba and which offered some hope of easing the embargo.[98] In this sense, in the resolutions of its first congress, the PCC declared: "We will be friends of our friends, we will respect those who respect us, and our weapons will always be used to defend ourselves against anyone who decides to attack us."[99] In the Southern Cone this new situation gave rise to conflicts with the ELN in Ovando's Bolivia and with the ERP in Peron's Argentina.[100]

The critical situation in which most of the guerrilla groups of the Southern Cone found themselves in the mid-1970s also gave the Cubans – who had been following these processes closely – little hope for a renewal of armed struggle, at least not in the form that had been previously conceived. The Bolivian Chato Peredo and the Uruguayan Efraín Martínez Platero recall that in discussions they had with Fidel Castro during this period Castro suggested that they intensify their work with the masses and reduce their emphasis on armed struggle.[101] Since the Chilean UP experience, Cuba was also concerned over the growing conflicts between the communist parties and armed groups of the Southern Cone.[102]

The first congress of the PCC also sealed once and for all "the unbreakable alliance that unites the parties, peoples, States, and Governments of Cuba and the Soviet Union." In the context of Latin America this definition meant adhering to the orthodoxy of the Latin American communist parties. In contrast to heterodox positions and the debate sparked in Cuba in the late 1960s over such diverse issues as cultural policies, guerrilla warfare strategies, or the dependency theory, the congress' ideological chapter called for a sole interpretation of Marxism–Leninism and highlighted the threats posed by those who proposed interpretations of Marxist–Leninist theory that deviated from the "correct" interpretation of the international communist movement. Although no organization in particular was mentioned, the tone of the accusations was similar to that of the accusations that had been directed by Southern Cone communists at JCR member organizations since the late 1960s, as seen in previous chapters.[103]

In addition to these shifts in foreign policy that explain the change of focus in the relationship between the Cuban government and the armed groups of the Southern Cone, there were other political reasons that made the Cubans wary of the JCR. The JCR had been very vague in the definition of eligibility conditions for joining it, reflecting its intention of coordinating efforts with a wide range of Latin American organizations and even with radical Left groups in Europe.[104] Although these ideas were never implemented, some groups were invited to various events held by the JCR.[105] In what seems to be a reasonable conjecture, some militants have suggested that this intention of expanding beyond the Southern Cone may have upset Cuba, as to a certain extent it meant disputing Cuba's influence over the continent's revolutionary Left.[106]

A number of documents from the 15th session of meetings of the JCR held in June 1977, which were found in the Archivo de la Lucha Armada David Cámpora (David Cámpora Armed Struggle Archive, or ADLADC), reveal a clear interest in furthering the JCR's international position and in consolidating its institutional structure. At those meetings the JCR adopted its provisional bylaws and a work plan, which was intended to tell the world about the JCR.[107]

Although this meeting's resolutions and the documents published by the JCR in 1977 gave an image of relative strength, the truth was that the situation of the participating organizations was marked by a profound weakness. In 1977 all the member organizations of the JCR had been defeated and forced to leave their respective countries. As long as there were countries in the region that could be used to organize a rearguard there could still be hope for a revolution. The movement of militants within the Southern Cone helped postpone the final defeat and expand the military plans of the organizations. But after the coup in Argentina the situation changed and the militants were forced to flee to faraway lands. This situation sparked serious internal crises given the impossibility of continuing with armed actions in the short term. In every organization the main discussions revolved around the return to armed actions. While some considered that the prevailing conditions did not allow for such a return in the near future given the magnitude of the repression unleashed by the new authoritarian regimes, others proposed plans for re-launching armed propaganda actions in each country.

The debates within the JCR were limited by the fragmentation within its member organizations and by the geographic distances imposed by exile. The ELN and the MLN-T had split into factions and each faction no longer felt represented by the others in the JCR. In fact, the MLN-T did not participate in the June 1977 meetings discussed above. In addition to internal disagreements, national differences began to emerge in a context of profound defeat. The following example shows how the crisis of the organizations combined with national differences and the geographical distances created by exile hindered the work of the JCR. An article published in *El Rebelde* by the MIR on the issue of Bolivia's lack of access to the sea, prompted by a meeting between Pinochet and Banzer, sparked protests from some members of the Bolivian ELN who were in France. The ELN-B delegate in France threatened to quit the JCR if the MIR did not retract. This was followed by a member of the Argentine PRT informing the *compañera* who had voiced the complaint that the ELN-B no longer existed, as it had been turned into the PRT-B, information that she had not yet received from her own organization.[108] This incident illustrates the difficulties faced by reorganization attempts in a large exile community marked by political and territorial fragmentation and poor communication.

In Europe the great issues of debate within the JCR had to do with the assessment of the situation in the Southern Cone and the policy of alliances. The MIR and the PRT-ERP – the two organizations whose core structures were stationed abroad – had different views on each of those issues. It was not until 1977, with the publication of its Manifesto, that the JCR was able to fully grasp the impact that the "counter-revolutionary dictatorships" had had on the Southern Cone Left as a whole, and to focus on the Left's unity issues.[109]

The other issue of debate had to do with determining the JCR's international scope. The question was whether the coordination efforts of the JCR would be limited to Southern Cone organizations or whether it should open itself up to organizations from other continents. From what can be gathered from the 1976 documents, everyone seemed to agree on the JCR's Latin American projection, but there were disagreements with respect to the relationship with certain sectors of the "European far Left."[110] While the PRT-ERP was reluctant, the MIR publicly acknowledged its contacts with some organizations such as Lotta Continua and Manifesto in Italy, Ligue communiste révolutionnaire in France, and Student League and KB in West Germany, which, it said, opened up "a channel for mutual knowledge and for sharing experiences and opinions that contribute to strengthen and harmonize the world's revolutionary Left."[111]

El Correo de la Resistencia, a publication of the Chilean MIR, reported on multiple events and meetings that were staged or held in solidarity with the Chilean people in 1974 and 1975. These included various public meetings with the Italian groups Lotta Continua, the Partito di Unità Proletaria (PdUP), and Avanguardia Operaia, the German Kommunistischer Bund (KB), and fellow militants from the French magazine *Politique Hebdo* or from the Ligue communiste. In a speech delivered in Italy in 1974, Edgardo Enríquez referred to this explicitly:

How deeply moved my comrades who are fighting in Chile would be if they could see the red and black flags of the MIR waving in the streets of Rome alongside the red flags of the Italian revolutionaries, united by a revolutionary passion that transcends borders and continents ... How moved the workers and rural laborers of Chile would be if they could see their working class brothers furthering Chile's struggle in Italy with the enthusiasm that overflows these demonstrations.

Enríquez acknowledged that "the vanguard workers of Europe," particularly in Italy, France, and West Germany, "have made major efforts in solidarity with their working class brothers in Latin America and other underdeveloped and dependent regions of the world." Lastly, he saw the revolutionary Left as a global movement:

This movement is forging more and more international solidarity ties and calling on the proletariat of Latin America to sever all ties with the parties of the big bourgeoisie, to build the revolutionary party of the proletariat ... Everywhere, this revolutionary Left is gaining in political consistency every day, overcoming its original weaknesses little by little ... It is the revolutionary Left and the most combative proletariat of Europe that have stepped forward with greater determination and fighting spirit in solidarity with the Chilean resistance ... It is now, then, when international labor and revolutionary inspired solidarity is more needed than ever to support the Chilean resistance.[112]

Enríquez's words could not have been any clearer and straightforward. They were certainly in line with what Wallerstein and others have posited with respect to the revolutionary dimension of the global sixties.

However, others questioned this initial view, most notably those close to the PRT-ERP. In one of their monthly meetings, Raúl, a leader of the Argentine PRT, noted that JCR actions in Latin America and Europe had to be qualitatively different. While in the Latin American continent member organizations had to fight against reformism and nationalism, the JCR had no business giving its opinion on the policies of Europe's communist parties.[113]

Not expressing an opinion did not mean it did not have an extremely critical view of Europe's New Left, in line with the view of communists themselves. For Raúl:

The European far Left does not support a revolutionary strategy for Latin America. Its class make-up, its methods, its fighting experience, all lead it to make unilateral, non-scientific analyses, that are vitiated by petit-bourgeois impressionism. This means, at best, that from it we can only expect to receive support for an anti-imperialist and anti-capitalist combatant democratic solidarity, which is distinguished by its methods and goals and its broad democratic solidarity supported by reformism and social democracy, but does not go as far as providing moral and material support for a revolutionary strategy that sees war as the only path for achieving socialism across the continent.[114]

Not everyone in the JCR agreed with Raúl's assessment. Militants of the Chilean MIR suggested an alternative view that differed from the PRT's, which seemed to be the predominant view in the JCR. Pablo, an MIR leader, held that in practice what was happening in Europe was that: (1) in terms of revolutionary solidarity, the far Left was the force that contributed the most, even though other sectors participated at specific moments; and (2) while broad sectors were involved in democratic solidarity, the far Left is also the most active force in these actions.[115]

What this MIR leader expressed was very much in line with what many Southern Cone militants saw in Europe. Although ostensibly most of the European Left supported the cause of Southern Cone militants, it was the members of the non-parliamentary Left who played a very active role in the various solidarity activities.

The difference in views regarding relations with the European Left also had to do with the history of some of the JCR member organizations and their situation when they reached Europe. The MIR had been receiving enormous support from these sectors since 1974. But the situation of the PRT was somewhat different, as the Argentine process was much harder to understand for Europeans and there was a prior relationship with sectors of European Trotskyism that had been eroding since the 1960s as the PRT moved closer to Cuba.

However, despite these differences, the PRT's view appears to have prevailed, with the MIR also leaning toward it. As of 1976, less and less mention is made of the European Left, even in the *Correo de la Resistencia* of the MIR. From that year on, the JCR's international relations were focused on a framework of alliances that had little to do with European organizations. Vietnam, Cambodia, Cuba, Palestine, Angola, and the communist world were among the priorities on its agenda, and it was clear to the JCR members that Cuba, with its pro-Soviet communist party stance, was the key to approaching those places.[116]

Conclusion

In late 1977, the JCR had apparently been left entirely to the PRT-ERP. None of the other organizations could deposit much hope in the JCR's coordination efforts. By 1978, the JCR had disappeared. The PRT was divided, the MIR was busy with Operation Return that was to be launched from Cuba without JCR support, the Tupamaros were fragmented and with a small, much weakened group still in Buenos Aires trying to return to Uruguay, and the Bolivians joined new organizations after dissolving the PRT-B in 1979.[117] Although these militants continued their political activity through different paths – including continuing with armed struggle, becoming involved with the human rights movement, and shifting to political projects on the center-left – the dream of a continental revolution had been crushed by the triumph of the continental counter-revolution.[118]

Both the armed left-wing groups and the armed forces of the Southern Cone seemed to share the idea that, from 1973 to 1976, a conflict unfolded in Argentina that was critical for the future of the Southern Cone, and which transcended national politics. In the words of the guerrillas, the conflict was between revolution and counter-revolution, while for the armed forces it was "the geopolitical balance of powers between subversive and counter-subversive forces."[119] But while the members of the JCR saw themselves as authentic revolutionaries, as opposed to other leftist forces that in their view were slowing down the revolutionary process, the armed forces made no such distinctions when it came time to deploy their repressive practices, which they unleashed equally across the full spectrum of the region's social and political Left.

The ousting of Torres in Bolivia and the coup against Allende in Chile, as well as the escalation of authoritarianism in Uruguay, were read by these groups as the confirmation of their hypothesis of the impossibility of implementing gradualist change, the inevitability of authoritarianism, and the need to be prepared for such scenarios. The response to growing authoritarianism was to reaffirm the goal of establishing the people's revolutionary armies that these groups had been proposing in their documents since the late 1960s.

The fact that it was the PRT-ERP that took the lead within the JCR in focusing on military action can be explained, among other things, by a particular historical circumstance. The military development of the PRT-ERP occurred in a context of democracy, even if it was a limited one, which contrasted with the situation in neighboring countries, where dictatorial regimes had succeeded in halting any attempt at armed resistance. Although initially the PRT-ERP's military development met with objections within the JCR, by 1975 all its member organizations had embraced that strategy.[120]

In Argentina, this emphasis on military action furthered by the PRT-ERP has been explained by what is known as "militarist deviation." This expression, which was part of the discourse used by militants in the 1960s, has been taken up again in many of the academic studies that focus on the actions of the PRT-ERP in the years 1973–6, which use it to describe the result of the emphasis placed on the confrontation with the army and the failure to politically analyze the democratic situation that began in 1973 and Perón's leadership in that process.[121]

Recently, historian Vera Carnovale has proposed an alternative explanation that argues that this "militarization" was not the result of a failure to understand the political process, or of an alienation generated by armed practice, but a foreseeable outcome of the political definitions, meanings, and imaginaries that guerrilla groups had been developing since the late 1960s.[122] Carnovale's approach is relevant as it shows that there was no contradiction between the political project that made these armed groups popular during the dictatorship and the political project that made them unpopular during the democratic period.

However, the existing literature has paid no attention to something that is quite evident in the documents and political actions of this organization from late 1973 and early 1974: the regional justification of its domestic actions. As discussed above, the coup in Chile was read as a confirmation that armed struggle was the right path and as a forewarning of what could come in Argentina and had to be avoided. The justification for armed struggle under a democracy, according to the PRT-ERP's interpretation, had to do with stopping a coup that seemed highly likely given the advancing authoritarianism in the region from 1973 to 1976 and Argentina's condition as the only non-dictatorial regime in the region. The reaction to this advancing authoritarianism had to be regional. It was not by chance that the JCR was publicly launched at a press conference held after the attack on the Azul cavalry regiment, which marked a qualitative leap in the ERP's confrontation with the Argentine army.

In this sense, the military strategy deployed by the ERP from 1973 to 1976 should not be read as merely the result of local circumstances, but as the consequence of a regional assessment shared with its "sister" organizations, which gradually started to converge in a common strategy. By 1975, what remained of the other member organizations of the JCR seemed to agree that the strategy implemented by the ERP was the right one, and so they implemented similar strategies in their countries.

During this period the defeats suffered by the MIR, the Tupamaros, and the Bolivian ELN increasingly isolated the survivors of these organizations. In this sense, emphasizing military action was the most obvious way of continuing a struggle that from a political and moral point of view seemed more than justified as it was a fight against dictatorships.[123]

Although the exchanges among armed organizations had served to alert each other to the growing authoritarianism in the region, they were no use in assessing the chances that the PRT-ERP could have of resisting a coup.

Of a structure of 1,500 militants and 2,200 sympathizers and collaborators that the party had in March 1976,[124] only about 300 members remained by mid-1977, spread throughout Italy, Spain, and Mexico. As in Uruguay and Chile, the same militants who had accurately foreseen the emergence of new authoritarian regimes had failed to adequately prepare themselves for the political and military challenges posed by such regimes.

Notes

1 See "El pueblo argentino con Chile" and Mario R. Santucho, "Las enseñanzas del proceso chileno," *El combatiente*, no. 91, September 21, 1973, 2, 12.

2 Luis Cerda "Aspectos internacionales de la revolución latinoamericana," *Correo de la Resistencia*, no. 9, July–August 1975, 60–1.

3 Letter from Perón to General Prats, November 11, 1973, www.elortiba.org/cs_doc3 .html#Carta_al_General_Prats_

4 "Telex 909, Embachile Baires," December 14, 1973, in Colección Argentina, vol. 1837, Archivo General Histórico, Ministerio de Relaciones Exteriores, Santiago, Chile, AGHMRREE (Santiago, Chile).

5 "Telex 937, Embachile Baires," December 28, 1973, in Colección Argentina, vol. 1837, AGHMRREE (Santiago, Chile).

6 "El ERP seguirá combatiendo," *Estrella Roja*, no. 25, November 21, 1973, 6.

7 Pilar Calveiro, *Política y/o violencia. Una aproximación a la guerrilla de los años 70* (Buenos Aires: Norma, 2005), 137. For figures on the violent actions perpetrated from 1973 to 1976, see Inés Izaguirre and others, *Lucha de clases, guerra civil y genocidio en la Argentina. Antecedentes, desarrollos y complicidades* (Buenos Aires: Eudeba, 2009), and María José Moyano, "Argentina: guerra civil sin batallas," in *Sociedades en guerra civil. Conflictos violentos de Europa y América Latina*, Peter Waldmann and Fernando Reinares (comp.) (Barcelona, Buenos Aires: Paidós Ed., 1999). One of the members of the PRT-ERP leadership observed self-critically that its actions did not target these parapolice groups. In his opinion, the organization's highly ideological structure hindered its understanding of the greatly repressive nature of these groups. See Luis Mattini, *Hombres y mujeres del PRT-ERP. De Tucumán a la Tablada* (La Plata, Argentina: Ed. de la Campana, 1995), 246–51.

8 See PRT, *El Peronismo ayer y hoy* (Mexico: Editorial Diógenes, 1974), and "El PRT a los compañeros del peronismo revolucionario," *El combatiente*, no. 81, July 16, 1973, 7.

9 See, for example, Mario R. Santucho, "Las enseñanzas del proceso chileno," and "El ERP seguirá combatiendo."

10 For an overview of the PRT-ERP's actions, see: Mattini, *Hombres y mujeres del PRT-ERP*; Vera Carnovale, *Los combatientes, historia del PRT-ERP* (Buenos Aires: Siglo XXI, 2011); Gustavo Plis Stenberg, *Monte Chingolo. La mayor batalla de la guerrilla argentina* (Buenos Aires: Booket, 2006); Pablo Pozzi, *"Por las sendas argentinas ..." El PRT-ERP. La guerrilla marxista* (Buenos Aires: EUDEBA, 2001); María Seoane, *Todo o Nada. La historia secreta y pública de Mario Roberto Santucho, el jefe guerrillero de los años setenta* (Buenos Aires: Editorial Sudamericana, 1991); and Daniel de Santis, *La historia del PRT-ERP por sus protagonistas* (Buenos Aires: Estación Finlandia, 2010).

11 Information extracted from Pablo Pozzi, *"Por las sendas argentinas ..." El PRT-ERP. La guerrilla marxista*, 81.

12 Ibid.

13 De Santis, *La historia del PRT-ERP*, 100; Seoane, *Todo o nada*, 80.

14 Liliana de Riz, *La política en suspenso, 1966–1976* (Buenos Aires: Paidós, 2000), 148–9.

15 Mattini, *Hombres y mujeres del PRT-ERP*, 256.

16 "Hechos de Azul. Recortes periodísticos. Tomo III, 19/1/1974," MDS, Legajo 1453, Archivo DIPBA, La Plata, Argentina.

17 Junta de Coordinación Revolucionaria, "A los pueblos de América Latina. Declaración Conjunta," *Estrella Roja*, no. 31, March 4, 1974, 10–14.

18 Ibid.

19 Ibid.

20 In the years 1973 and 1974, the ERP raised large sums of money through kidnapping operations that targeted important businessmen and whose primary aim was, in most cases, extorting money as a means of "compensating the people" for the "crimes" committed against workers by the businesses they represented. One of the most spectacular was the kidnapping of ESSO executive Victor Samuelson in December 1973. See "Recuperado algo de lo mucho que ESSO le debe al pueblo," *Estrella Roja*, no. 28, January 7, 1974, 4–6. The ERP obtained US$14 million in ransom for Samuelson's release. JCR activists were also involved in that action. ELN member Osvaldo Peredo recalls that he participated in the planning of the kidnapping, and an anonymous MLN source claims to have participated in the negotiations. See Osvaldo "Chato" Peredo, *Volvimos a las montañas* (Santa Cruz, Bolivia: Editor Fernando Valdivia, 2003), 120, and Clara Aldrighi, *Memorias de insurgencia. Historias de vida y militancia en el MLN-Tupamaros, 1965–1975* (Montevideo: Ediciones de la Banda Oriental, 2009), 347–8. In August 1974, the MIR's paper *Correo de la Resistencia* reported that US$5 million of the ransom money would be divided among the four organizations of the JCR. See "ERP, Internacionalismo proletario," *Correo de la Resistencia*, no. 2, August 1974, 22. A political problem was sparked within the JCR when it came time to divide the ransom money, as the million dollars that were to go to the MIR were given to members of the MLN-T who were in turn supposed to give the money to the Chileans but never did. The incident has been mentioned in several accounts. See Gorriarán, *Memorias*, 203–6.

21 See de Santis, *La historia del PRT-ERP*, 473–503, and Mattini, *Hombres y Mujeres del PRT-ERP*, 285–99.

22 See "La guerrilla rural y urbana," *Estrella Roja*, no. 35, July 1, 1975, 2–3. This position has certain points in common with the ideas posited by Ángel Bengochea in the early 1960s. See Juan José López Silveira and Ángel Bengochea, *Guerra de guerrillas* (Montevideo: Editorial Uruguay, 1970), and chapter 2.

23 Bengochea was one of the four honorary presidents elected for the Fourth Congress of the PRT (the other three were Guevara, Trotsky, and Nguyen Van Troi), held in 1968, in which the party decided to take up arms. See *El Combatiente*, no. 1, March 6, 1968.

24 de Santis, *La historia del PRT-ERP*, 498.

25 JCR, "Pacto militar contra los pueblos de América Latina," January 1976, Paris, Archivo ADLADC, Montevideo, Uruguay.

26 See Santiago Garaño, "El monte tucumano como 'teatro de operaciones': las puestas en escena del poder durante el Operativo Independencia (Tucumán, 1975–1977)," *Nuevo Mundo Mundos Nuevos*, Cuestiones del tiempo presente, 2011 [online], published online on September 29, 2011, www.nuevomundo.revues.org/62119

27 See, for example, "Condecoraciones," *Estrella Roja* no. 40, 20, "Grados y reglamentos en el ERP," *Estrella Roja*, no. 42, 20, and "Numero especial: La verdad sobre Tucumán," *Estrella Roja*, no. 63, November 2, 1975.

28 "Carta de un revolucionario latinoamericano," *Boletín interno*, no. 42, April 27, 1973.

29 The ERP documents that refer to the participation of foreigners in the Tucumán Compañía de Monte feature contradictory information. While there are internal documents and reports in *Estrella Roja* that mention the participation of Chileans and Uruguayans in Tucumán, in response to accusations that the guerrillas were receiving support from outside the country, "Lieutenant Armando" emphasized the presence of local Tucumán activists in the group. "Reportaje al teniente Armando," *Estrella Roja* no. 63, November 2, 1975, 9.What perhaps best illustrates the proletarian internationalism behind the Tucumán strategy is the involvement of Swedish national Svaente Graende, a forestry technician who traveled to Chile in 1972 to work in the south. In 1973 he joined the MIR and after the coup he headed the "Panguipulli guerrilla" resistance attempt. After the resistance attempt failed, Graende crossed the Andes into Argentina with five other activists. In Buenos Aires they contacted the ERP and two of them joined the Compañía de Monte. "Chile. La guerrilla de Panguipulli," *Estrella Roja*, no. 71, March 14, 1976, 4–6, 16.The Uruguayan Tupamaros were Rutilio Bentancourt and Hugo Cacciavillani. For biographical information on both militants see: List of Persons Killed at the Rosario Chapel Massacre, www.desaparecidos.org/arg/victimas/listas/capilla.html; "Galería de nuestros mártires," *Correo Tupamaro*, year 1, no. 6, October 1976, Archivo ADLADC, Montevideo, Uruguay; and Álvaro Rico (coord.), *Investigación Histórica sobre la dictadura y el terrorismo de estado en el Uruguay (1973–1985)*, vol. 1 (Montevideo, UDELAR-CSIC), 144–5.

30 For a historical overview of the MIR's actions during the Chilean dictatorship, see: Julio Pinto Vallejo "¿Y la historia les dio la razón? El MIR en dictadura, 1973–1981," in Verónica Valdivia, Rolando Álvarez, and Julio Pinto, *Su revolución contra nuestra revolución. Izquierdas y derechas en el Chile de Pinochet (1973–1981)* (Santiago: LOM, 2006); and Carlos Sandoval Ambiado, *Movimiento de Izquierda Revolucionaria. Coyunturas y vivencias (1973–1980)*, (Concepción, Chile: Escaparate Ediciones, 2011).

31 See account by Carmen Castillo, *Un día de octubre en Santiago* (Mexico: ERA, 1982), 117.

32 *Correo de la Resistencia*, no. 3–4, September–October 1974, 31–2.

33 See "Texto de Carta de Gabriel," *La situación de los derechos humanos en Chile*, vol. 2 (Santiago: Talleres Gráficos La Nación, 1975), 255.

34 PRT-ERP leader Arnol Kremer recalls that when Edgardo Enríquez, a civil engineer from Chile's upper classes, went to Argentina to participate in the JCR as an MIR representative some activists were wary of him for what they considered his "class weaknesses," and put him up in a prefabricated house with no hot water in the outskirts of Greater Buenos Aires. This hindered most of the activities that Enríquez had planned to carry out in the Argentine capital, because of the distance. Luis Mattini, *Los perros. Memorias de un combatiente revolucionario* (Buenos Aires: Continente-Pax, 2006), 116–25.

35 Comisión Política (MIR), "La táctica del MIR en el actual período" (December 1973), in Miguel Enríquez, *Con vista a la esperanza* (Concepción, Chile: Escaparate Ediciones, 1998), 314.

36 *Boletín interno*, no. 65, August 1974. Mattini reconstructs some aspects of this discussion in *Hombres y mujeres del PRT-ERP*, 300–7.

37 To review some aspects of these later talks between the two organizations, see Mattini, *Hombres y Mujeres del PRT-ERP*, 378, and John Dinges, *The Condor Years* (New York: The New Press, 2004), 84. In 1975 the dictatorship published a compilation of documents of left-wing organizations. The aim of this compilation was to show the OAS the magnitude of "subversive actions." One of the texts featured there contains interesting information on the MIR's contacts with the ERP. I have not yet been able to confirm whether that document is authentic. See "Texto de Carta de Gabriel," *La situación de los derechos humanos en Chile*, vol. 2 (Santiago: Talleres Gráficos La Nación, 1975), 255.

38 "Debimos detener las acciones armadas antes," interview with Hernán Aguiló in *La Nación*, February 4, 2007, www.lanacion.cl/noticias/site/artic/20070203/pags/200702 03235146.html

39 These leaders' decision to abandon the No Asylum! call sparked a heated internal discussion in the MIR. See Sandoval, *Movimiento de Izquierda Revolucionaria. Coyunturas y vivencias (1973–1980)*, 337–80.

40 Nancy Guzmán, "Edgardo Enríquez fue asesinado en Buenos Aires," *La Nación*, December 20, 2009, www.lanacion.cl/edgardo-enriquez-fue-asesinado-en-buenos-aires/noticias/2009-12-19/220604.html

41 In the year 1975, Domingo Villalobos (known as "Sargento Dago") and Svaente Graende, two MIR activists who were participating in the Compañía de Monte in Tucumán, are murdered. That same year, Jorge Isaac Fuentes is kidnapped in Asunción as he returns from a JCR mission in Peru. In March 1976, Jorge Ángel Machuca Muñoz, Claudio Melquíades, and Heriberto Leal are kidnapped. A month later Edgardo Enríquez is also kidnapped and disappeared. Patricio Biedma, Mario René Espinoza, Homero Tobar Avilés, and Miguel Orellana are disappeared in mid-1976. See Comisión Nacional de Verdad y Reconciliación, Chile, *Informe Rettig: informe de la Comisión Nacional de Verdad y Reconciliación*, vol. 1 (Santiago: La Nación: Ediciones del Ornitorrinco, 1991), and "Desaparecidos chilenos en Argentina," www.desaparecidos.org/arg/chile/

42 Simposio de Viña del Mar (Montevideo: MLNT), Archivo ADLADC, Montevideo, Uruguay; Clara Aldrighi. *Memorias de la insurgencia.* 245–456.

43 "Breve síntesis histórica de la organización" (1976), Archivo ADLADC, Montevideo, Uruguay; Astrid Arrarás, "Armed Struggle, Political Learning and Participation in Democracy: The Case of the Tupamaros" (Dissertation Thesis, Princeton, 1998), Archivo ADLADC, Montevideo, Uruguay.

44 See Carta de renuncia, "Las razones de nuestra ruptura," Archivo ADLADC, Montevideo, Uruguay; "Entrevista a Luis Alemany," in Aldrighi, *Memorias de insurgencia.* 317–43. Jimena Alonso and Magdalena Figueredo, "El caso de los 'renunciantes'," *Cuadernos de la historia reciente.* no. 6, 2010.

45 See "Desgrabación de Gabriel hoja 9," in *Descasetamiento*, Archivo ADLADC, Montevideo, Uruguay. For a view of the internal conflict from this faction's perspective, see Andrés Cultelli, *La revolución necesaria* (Montevideo: Colihue, 2006).

46 "Tupamaros. Documentos y comunicados. 1974–1975," Archivo ADLADC, Montevideo, Uruguay.

47 See "Desgrabación de Gabriel hoja 9," in *Descasetamiento*, Archivo ADLADC, Montevideo, Uruguay. For a view of the internal conflict from this faction's perspective, see Andrés Cultelli, *La revolución necesaria* (Montevideo: Colihue, 2006).

48 For a discussion on the issue of proletarianization, see "Debate en el Comité Central," *Descasetamiento*, Archivo ADLADC, Montevideo, Uruguay, and MLN-Tupamaros, "MLN (Tupamaros): Balance, situación actual y perspectivas," *Che Guevara, Revista de la Junta de Coordinación Revolucionaria.* no. 2, February 1975.

49 See the influential PRT-ERP document by Luis Ortolani, "Moral y proletarización," *Políticas de la memoria*, no. 4, Summer 2004–2005, 96.

50 "Menna cassette 18," *Descasetamiento*, Archivo ADLADC, Montevideo, Uruguay.

51 "Cassette N. 6, hoja 6," *Descasetamiento*, Archivo ADLADC, Montevideo, Uruguay.

52 See "Entrevista a Domingo," in Clara Aldrighi, *Memorias de insurgencia.*

53 Gustavo Rodríguez Ostria, *Sin tiempo para las palabras, Teoponte, La otra guerrilla guevarista en Bolivia* (Cochabamba: Grupo Editorial Kipus, 2006).

54 Martín Sivak, *El asesinato de Juan José Torres: Banzer y el Mercosur de la muerte* (Buenos Aires: Ediciones Colihue, 1997), 81.

55 For the relationship between Torres and Sánchez, see Jorge Gallardo Lozada, *De Torres a Banzer: diez meses de emergencia en Bolivia* (Buenos Aires: Ediciones Periferia, 1972), and for Sánchez' relationship with the PRT-ERP, see Gorriarán, *Memorias*, 235–7, and Sivak, *El asesinato de Juan José Torres: Banzer y el Mercosur de la muerte*, 83.

56 See Peredo, *Volvimos a las montañas.*

57 Peredo, *Volvimos a las montañas*, 132.

58 Peredo, *Volvimos a las montañas*, 133.

59 ELN Bolivia, "Nace el PRT de Bolivia" (April 6, 1975), Archivo ADLADC, Montevideo, Uruguay.

60 "Parte información procedente de SIDE, *Asunto: Ingerencia del Partido Revolucionario de los trabajadores (PRT) de Argentina en la promoción del similar boliviano,*" MDS, Legajo 3393, Archivo DIPBA, La Plata, Argentina.

61 There are different interpretations of this moment. For historian Gustavo Rodríguez Ostria, the party no longer had any weight and the emergence of groups such as the MIR and the PS1 offered alternatives for renewal of the armed Left. By late 1975 and early 1976, a large part of its network of militants was dissolving. John Dinges has a somewhat positive view, as he says Sánchez is believed to have gathered 150 armed militants who were preparing General Torres' return, working in different mining areas and in Bolivia's leading cities. Rodríguez Ostria, *Sin tiempo para las palabras*, 569–99; Dinges, *The Condor Years*, 150–5.

62 Dinges, *The Condor Years*, 150–5.

63 See "Relaciones (1974)," Archivo ADLADC, Montevideo, Uruguay.

64 "Participación clandestina de un equipo técnico argentino de una filmación de películas subversivas," MDS, Legajo 29775, Archivo DIPBA, La Plata, Argentina, and "Pautas de discusión de objetivos y tareas del frente de cine de la JCR, 1977," Archivo ADLADC, Montevideo, Uruguay.

65 The three numbers are available in Archivo ADLADC, Montevideo, Uruguay.

66 Image taken from *Che Guevara, Revista de la Junta de Coordinación Revolucionaria*, n. 2, February, 1975.

67 See MDS Legajo 15174, and MDS Legajo 3010, Archivo DIPBA, La Plata, Argentina. Also, "Memorándum I-09/975, Junta de Comandantes en Jefe, Servicio de Información de Defensa, Departamento III-Planes-Operaciones-Enlace," in *Movimiento de Liberación Nacional-Tupamaros (MLNT-T), Índice cronológico de documentos, Actualización histórica sobre detenidos desaparecidos* (Uruguay: Presidencia de la República, 2011) (pdf) 80–4, www .presidencia.gub.uy/wps/wcm/connect/presidencia/portalpresidencia/comunicacion/ informes/investigacion-historica-sobre-detenidos-desaparecidos.

68 A Uruguayan intelligence document that describes the objects found in these raids lists fifty-six FAL rifles, forty-eight sub-machine guns, fifty rifles, 120 pistols and revolvers, 150 hand grenades, one ton of gelignite and assorted ammunition, two trucks, four cars, one motorboat, and four workshops (carpentry, construction, weaponry, documents). See "MLNT Documento 9," *Anexos, Actualización histórica sobre detenidos desaparecidos*, 6, www .presidencia.gub.uy/wps/wcm/connect/presidencia/portalpresidencia/comunicacion/ informes/investigacion-historica-sobre-detenidos-desaparecidos.

69 Rosendo Fraga, *Ejército: del escarnio al poder (1973–1976)* (Buenos Aires: Planeta, 1988), 276.

70 Ibid.

71 Samuel Blixen, *El vientre del cóndor: del archivo del terror al caso Berríos* (Montevideo, Uruguay: Brecha, 1994), and John Dinges, *The Condor Years: How Pinochet and His Allies Brought Terrorism to Three Continents* (New York: New Press, 2004), and Peter Kornbluh, *The Pinochet File: A Declassified Dossier on Atrocity and Accountability* (New York: New Press, 2003), and Patrice McSherry, *Los estados depredadores: la operación Cóndor y la guerra encubierta en América Latina* (Uruguay: Ediciones de la Banda Oriental, 2009).

72 Patrice McSherry, *Los estados depredadores*, 121, and Martin Edwin Andersen, *Dossier Secreto. Argentina's Desaparecidos and the Myth of the Dirty War* (Boulder, Colorado: Westview Press, 1993), 108. On the foundational meeting of Operation Condor, see Kornbluh, *The Pinochet File*, and Dinges, *The Condor Years*. For updated information on the criminal trials concerning Operation Condor, see IPPDH, *A 40 años del condor. De las coordinaciones represivas a la construcción de las políticas públicas regionales en derechos humanos* (Buenos Aires: IPPDH, 2015).

73 These include, among others, the murder of General Carlos Pratt and the counter-information operation dubbed "Colombo," whose objective was to falsely report that the 119 MIR activists killed by the Chilean dictatorship had been killed by their own comrades in Argentina and Europe as a result of internal disputes. See Kornbluh, *The Pinochet File*. In Uruguay's case, the government also began coordinating operations with the Argentine government in 1974. On September 13, five Tupamaros were detained on Argentine soil, and a month later three of them were found dead. The operation that culminated with the detention of Washington Barrios in Argentina in September 1974 and his subsequent disappearance in 1975 was also launched in Uruguay. Lastly, in November 1974, six MLN-T activists and a child were detained in Argentina. On December 20, the bullet-riddled bodies of five of the six were found in the locality of Soca, in the Uruguayan department of Canelones. See Álvaro Rico (coord.), *Investigación histórica sobre la dictadura y el terrorismo de estado en el Uruguay* (Uruguay: UdelaR, 2008), 94–103, 686–93. Lastly, the process that ended with the March 1975 raids was the result of mutual contacts between the intelligence services of Argentina and Uruguay. Cultelli, *La revolución necesaria*, 145.

74 Most of the relevant information on these kidnappings is found in what are known as the "Archivos del Terror." Centro de Documentación y Archivo para la Defensa de los Derechos Humanos (CDYA), Asunción, Paraguay, at www.gwu.edu/~nsarchiv/CDyA/index.htm. For a compilation of these documents, see Alfredo Boccia Paz, Myriam Angélica González, and Rosa Palau Aguilar, *Es mi informe. Los archivos secretos de la policía de Stroessner* (Asunción: CDE, 1994). And for a reconstruction of the operation, see Dinges, *The Condor Years*.

75 Dinges, *The Condor Years*, 82–126.

76 "Primera reunión de inteligencia nacional," in *Operación Condor en el Archivo del Terror*, on the website of the National Security Archive, www.gwu.edu/~nsarchiv/NSAEBB/NSAEBB239b/index.htm

77 JCR, "Pacto militar contra los pueblos de América Latina," January 1976, Paris, Archivo ADLADC, Montevideo, Uruguay.

78 MDS, Legajo 3010, Archivo DIPBA, La Plata, Argentina.

79 Comité Central Ampliado, "Vietnam Liberado," *El Combatiente*, no. 175, July 30, 1975, 4.

80 Ibid., 2.

81 See: Calveiro, *Política y/o violencia*; Liliana de Riz, *La política en suspenso, 1966–1976* (Buenos Aires: Paidós, 2000), as well as Juan Carlos Torre, *Los sindicatos en el gobierno, 1973–1976* (Buenos Aires: CEAL, 1989), and Andersen, *Dossier Secreto*; Alfredo Puciarelli (comp.), *La primacía de la política* (Buenos Aires: Eudeba, 1999), and Richard Gillespie, *Los soldados de Perón* (Buenos Aires: Grijalbo, 1982), Maristella Svampa, "El populismo imposible y sus actores, 1973–1976," in Daniel James (dir.) *Nueva Historia Argentina, Violencia, proscripción y autoritarismo (1955–1976)* (Buenos Aires: Sudamericana, 2003), María José Moyano, "Argentina: guerra civil sin batallas," in Peter Waldmann and Fernando Reinares (comp.), *Sociedades en guerra civil. Conflictos violentos de Europa y América Latina* (Barcelona, Buenos Aires: Paidós Ed., 1999).

82 On the military's view of Operation Independence, see Acdel Vilas, *Tucumán, enero a diciembre de 1975*, www.nuncamas.org/investig/vilas/acdel_00.htm, and FAMUS,

Operación independencia (Buenos Aires: FAMUS, 1988). On the PRT-ERP's view of that experience, see "Número especial: La verdad sobre Tucumán," *Estrella Roja*, no. 63, December 10, 1975, and de Santis, *La historia del PRT-ERP*. On the human rights abuses committed during "Operation Independence," see *Informe de la Comisión Bicameral Investigadora de las Violaciones a los Derechos Humanos de Tucumán* (Madrid: IEPALA, 1991). On the interpretation of Operation Independence as the prelude to state terrorism, see Pilar Calveiro, *Poder y desaparición*. For approaches on the Tucumán campaign, see: Santiago Garaño, "El monte tucumano como 'teatro de operaciones': las puestas en escena del poder durante el Operativo Independencia (Tucumán, 1975–1977)", and Andersen, *Dossier Secreto*, 124–57, as well as de Santis, *La historia del PRT-ERP*, 473–503.

83 For the reconstruction of this action, see Gustavo Plis-Sterenberg, *Monte Chingolo. La mayor batalla de la guerrilla argentina* (Buenos Aires: Booket, 2006).

84 *Boletín Interno*, no. 98, December 27, 1975, 2.

85 "Ajusticiamiento de un traidor," *El combatiente*, no. 200, January 21, 1976, 3–4.

86 Comisión Nacional de Verdad y Reconciliación, *Informe Rettig: informe de la Comisión Nacional de Verdad y Reconciliación, 2 vol.* (Santiago: La Nación: Ediciones del Ornitorrinco, 1991).

87 Patricio Rivas, *Chile, un largo septiembre* (Santiago: LOM Ediciones, 2007), 119.

88 Madres y Familiares de Detenidos Desaparecidos (Uruguay), *A todos ellos: informe de Madres y Familiares de Uruguayos Detenidos Desaparecidos*.

89 Cultelli, *La revolución necesaria*, 147–54.

90 SIDE, "Parte de inteligencia n. 06/76. Asunto: Modificación del equilibrio de fuerzas subversivas contrasubversivas en el plano geopolítico," MDS, Legajo 22851, Archivo DIPBA, La Plata, Argentina.

91 "Boletín del secretariado europeo. Información estrictamente reservada a los equipos centrales de cada país," and "Carta de Pepe," Stockholm, 3/1976, Archivo ADLADC, Montevideo, Uruguay.

92 "Relaciones," undated; JCR, "Acuerdo sobre relaciones políticas (junio 1977)," and JCR, "Criterios para trabajo de solidaridad (junio 1977)," Archivo ADLADC, Montevideo, Uruguay.

93 "Relaciones," undated, as well as JCR, "Acuerdo sobre relaciones políticas (junio 1977)," and JCR, "Criterios para trabajo de solidaridad (junio 1977)," Archivo ADLADC, Montevideo, Uruguay.

94 "Boletín del secretariado europeo. Información estrictamente reservada a los equipos centrales de cada país," 6, Archivo ADLADC, Montevideo, Uruguay, and SIDE, "Identificación del abogado argentino que gestionó en Suiza la intervención de una misión extranjera en nuestro país," January 16, 1976, MDS, Varios, Legajo 4384, Archivo, DIPBA, La Plata, Argentina.

95 See Vania Markarian, *Idos y recién llegados. La izquierda uruguaya en el exilio y las redes transnacionales de derechos humanos* (Montevideo: Ediciones de la Vasija/Correo del maestro, 2006).

96 "Relaciones," undated, Archivo ADLADC, Montevideo, Uruguay.

97 Ibid., Archivo ADLADC, Montevideo, Uruguay.

98 For an excellent overview of these transformations, see Tanya Harmer, *Allende's Chile and the Inter-American Cold War* (Chapel Hill: The University of North Carolina Press, 2011).

99 Primer congreso del Partido Comunista de Cuba, *Tesis y Resoluciones* (Havana: Editorial Ciencias Sociales, 1978), 523. By 1975 the following countries had resumed diplomatic relations with Cuba: Argentina, Bahamas, Barbados, Colombia, Guyana, Panama, Peru, Trinidad and Tobago, and Venezuela.

100 Luis Mattini, *Los perros. Memorias de un combatiente revolucionario* (Buenos Aires: Continente-Pax, 2006), 179–83, as well as Rodríguez Ostria, *Teoponte*, 221–3.

101 Some of the existing accounts of discussions between leaders of these organizations and Fidel Castro give the impression that Castro was trying to play down the impact that Cuba's revolutionary model of armed struggle had had in the region. Peredo recalls that in 1972 Castro said to him, "in light of the current experience, I would not repeat the assault on the Moncada or the Granma landing," thus distancing himself from the previous rhetoric and mystical aura that had surrounded guerrilla warfare. Peredo, *Volvimos a las montañas*, 118. Martínez Platero recalls that Castro suggested that there had already been enough armed struggle: "Fidel did say that ... the Tupamaros had achieved something in their country that nobody in Latin America or the world had, but [he also said] 'if you stay put, one day the people will vindicate you ... stay on the path of calmness, serenity." Interview with Efraín Martinez Platero conducted by the author on January 25, 2008. In 1978, according to a report by Paraguayan army commanders, JCR representatives met in Africa with Raúl Castro and complained about the little support they were receiving from Cuba. Raúl Castro promised them that they would have Cuba's full support provided they met certain conditions, namely "(1) Irrefutable proof of the existence, organization, operations, and strength of these groups, ... and (2) The revitalization of their combat leaders and the establishment of liberated territories." If both objectives were met, then Cuba would send advisors and military supplies. In 1978 such conditions were unattainable for any of the organizations in the region. See Asunción Embajada del Uruguay, "Informe periódico de inteligencia N 001/78," (1978/6/5). DNII, Ministerio del Interior, Montevideo, Uruguay.

102 See Harmer, *Allende's Chile and the Inter-American Cold War.*

103 Primer Congreso PCC, *Tesis y resoluciones*, 514, and Fidel Castro, *Informe del Comité Central del PCC al Primer Congreso* (Ciudad de La Habana: Editorial de Ciencias Sociales, 1978), 233.

104 An Interpol report mentions an event that was planned for early 1974 in Argentina to which more than fourteen organizations from Latin American countries would be invited. Interpol Ministerio de Justicia, "JCR," (1975), Archivo CDYA. Also, a JCR document from 1977 informed that there was a significant number of "organizations that have reached an important level of agreement with the JCR, to the point of considering the possibility of jointly carrying out activities to further that process.... These organizations are the Venezuelan MIR, the Socialist Party of Puerto Rico, Nicaragua's Frente Sandinista, Guatemala's Ejército Guerrillero de los Pobres, El Salvador's Frente de Liberación Nacional Farabundo Martí, Costa Rica's Movimiento Revolucionario del Pueblo and Socialist Party, Chile's MAPU, Brazil's MR8, Colombia's Movimiento Revolucionario 19 de Abril (M-19), ELN and FARC, and Argentina's Movimiento Montonero." JCR, "A los secretarios de Argelia, Francia y Mexico. Líneas de acción y plan de trabajo JCR," Archivo ADLADC, Montevideo, Uruguay, 5.

105 In October 1977, the JCR planned a meeting of revolutionary movements in Venezuela. "Plan de tareas del Secretariado Ejecutivo de la JCR," Archivo ADLADC, Montevideo, Uruguay.

106 Patricio Rivas, *Chile, un largo septiembre* (Santiago: LOM Ediciones, 2007), 164–7.

107 JCR, "A los secretariados de Argelia, Francia, y México. Líneas de acción y plan de trabajo," Archivo ADLADC, Montevideo, Uruguay.

108 Secretariado de la JCR Filial Europa, "Informe al Buró Central de la JCR sobre el abandono por parte del ELN del trabajo de la Junta en Europa, problemas derivados y necesidad de que se implemente una rápida solución (febrero 1976)," Archivo ADLADC, Montevideo, Uruguay.

109 "Manifiesto JCR," *Revista Che Guevara*, no. 3, October–December 1977, 18.

110 "Sesión Ordinaria 25/6/76," Archivo ADLADC, Montevideo, Uruguay.
111 *Correo de la resistencia, Edición especial no. 3*, 63. For earlier attention to the Third World by the European New Left, see Quinn Slobodian, *The Foreign Front. Third World Politics in Sixties West Germany* (Durham, London: Duke University Press, 2012). Although this study does not focus significantly on the case of Latin America it helps understand the political climate that prevailed when these Southern Cone militants began arriving.
112 Enriquez, Edgardo, "Discurso del compañero Edgardo Enriquez. Roma 14 de setiembre de 1974," *Correo de la Resistencia*, nos. 3–4, September–October 1974.
113 Sesion ordinaria 12/04/1976. Secretariado Zonal Europeo. Carpeta JCR 3. Archivo ADLADC.
114 Ibid.
115 Sesión del 6/2/1976. Secretariado Zonal Europeo. Carpeta JCR 3. Archivo ADLADC.
116 See "Relaciones," ADLADC Archive.
117 For historical approaches on Operation Return, see Julio Pinto Vallejo "¿Y la historia les dio la razón? El MIR en Dictadura, 1973–1981," and Carlos Sandoval Ambiado, *Movimiento de Izquierda Revolucionaria. Coyunturas y vivencias (1973–1980)* (Concepción, Chile: Escaparate Ediciones, 2011). In the last number (3) of *Che Guevara* magazine there are no articles on the situation in Chile. In the January 1978 document on the international policy of the MIR, the JCR is mentioned as a precedent but not with the emphasis it had been given earlier. MIR, "Política internacional del MIR," *Correo de la Resistencia. Edición especial no. 5*, March–April 1978, 23–4. Regarding the MLNT in Buenos Aires, see "Sección II. Cronología documental y anexos. MLNT-II-1976–1978," in *Actualización de la investigación histórica sobre detenidos desaparecidos* (November 2011), www.presidencia.gub.uy/wps/wcm/connect/presidencia/portalpresidencia/comunicacion/informes/investigacion-historica-sobre-detenidos-desaparecidos. For different approximations to the PRT division, see: Mattini, *Hombres y mujeres del PRT-ERP*; Carnovale, *Los combatientes*; Daniel de Santis, *La historia del PRT-ERP*. On the end of the PRT-B, see Rodríguez Ostria, *Sin tiempo para las palabras, Teoponte, La otra guerrilla guevarista en Bolivia*.
118 Although intelligence reports inform of coordination activities among guerrilla groups and in some cases describe them as JCR activities, these meetings were no longer connected with an organizational structure. Government reports inform of meetings held in different places among "extremists" who for the most part belonged to the organizations that had formed part of the JCR and others.
119 See: SIDE, "Parte de inteligencia n. 06/76. Asunto: Modificación del equilibrio de fuerzas subversivas contrasubversivas en el plano geopolítico," MDS, Legajo 22851, Archivo DIPBA, LA PLATA, ARGENTINA, and Luis Cerda "Aspectos internacionales de la revolución latinoamericana," *Correo de la Resistencia*, no. 9.
120 A document of the Chilean MIR put it as follows: "The ERP has succeeded in consolidating and expanding its influence among the masses, strengthening urban armed actions, and initiating armed struggle in periphery areas and in the north." Comisión Política del MIR, "La situación internacional," last quarter of 1975, in MIR, *MIR, dos años en la lucha de la resistencia popular del pueblo chileno, 1973–1975* (Madrid, Ed. Zero, 1976), 93.
121 These approaches share a meta-narrative of armed struggle that posits the idea that the movement was going in the right direction until the reinstatement of democracy, and that after 1973 military inertia led them to ignore the opinion of the population, even of those sectors that had sympathized with the guerrilla. One of the more paradigmatic approaches of this perspective is the work by Pilar

Calveiro, who in countering politics to violence in her book *Política y/o violencia. Una aproximación a la guerrilla de los años 70* suggests a view in which the emphasis on military actions in the years 1973–1976 negated the political dimension of these organizations. In her view, "Weapons are potentially 'maddening': they can be used to kill and, therefore, they create the illusion of having control over life and death. Obviously they are not in themselves political, but placed in the hands of very young people, the majority of whom also lacked any consistent political experience, they were turned into a wall of arrogance that in a sense masked a certain political naivety." Pilar Calveiro, *Política y/o violencia*, 135. See, also, Svampa, "El populismo imposible y sus actores, 1973–1976." Pablo Pozzi explains the concept by suggesting that the "political situation, and in particular its military victories, led it to be constantly moving forward, so that the military did not follow the political but tended to become more and more autonomous." This approach is somewhat different from the more widespread notion of militarism. Pozzi, *Por las sendas argentinas*, 271.

122 Carnovale, *Los combatientes*, 99.
123 Many social scientists have studied the effects of state terrorism on individuals and society as a whole. However, there are very few studies that delve into the political dimension of state terrorism, the impact that state terrorism had on the armed or legal Left it sought to wipe out. There are very few studies that look at the transformations that occurred in left-wing organizations as democratic or dictatorial states developed illegal repressive practices against them. In my opinion, this aspect is key to understanding the behaviors of the organizations considered in this chapter.
124 de Santis, 625.

V

Surviving Democracy. The Transition from Armed Struggle to Human Rights, 1981–1989

By 1978, the PRT had been decimated and the members who were left had split into two bitterly opposed groups, one in Europe and the other in Central America. The Tupamaros had practically disintegrated and its members were scattered in a large diaspora across various European countries, Cuba, Mexico, and a few in other parts of the world. The ELN had more or less disappeared as a group and some of its members were attempting new political projects. Only the Chilean MIR had survived without rupturing and had begun preparing a return operation that would engage them into the first years of the 1980s. Other than appealing to some individual militants from other groups, the MIR did not coordinate this operation with the JCR, or with any of the other members. By the early 1980s, none of the surviving militants of the 1970s saw the JCR or the possibility of developing a regional project to promote armed struggle in the region as feasible endeavors, as they focused their efforts in reorganizing their own organizations, which had been harshly hit by the dictatorships. The future of the other organizations appears to have been constrained by their need to survive and rebuild themselves in national scenarios that would be shaped by the transitions to democracy.

The dream of a continental revolution was no longer a persuasive idea for the surviving members of these organizations. The revolution traveled once again up north. In an open letter published in 1981 the MIR looked to developments in Central America as a reference for the coming struggles against the Chilean dictatorship:

If we look at the countries of Latin American where revolutionary struggle has been taken to its maximum expression, socialist Cuba, Revolutionary Nicaragua, and El Salvador today – which has launched the final battle to topple its dictatorship – we will see that the development of revolutionary democratic struggle imposes the need for popular forces to reach a higher degree of unity as a decisive factor.[1]

The document recognized the new state of affairs in Latin America, where revolutionary struggles were being played out primarily in Central America, and it viewed those struggles as marking a unique way of combining armed struggle and democracy. Nicaragua impacted in many ways on several of the militants who had been close to that experience during their exile. On the one hand, in terms of the military strategies furthered by the Frente Sanidinista de Liberación Nacional (Sandinista National Liberation Front, or FSLN) there was an insurrectional approach, which had been an element that had been neglected by the Southern Cone experiences. On the other, the diversity of actors involved in the process allowed for a more pluralistic view than that which had created the political movements of the Southern Cone. Moreover, the revolutionary model that incorporated elections, the acknowledgement of liberal rights, political party freedom, and a mixed economy model entailed a major innovation with respect to the Cuban Revolution. Lastly, several Southern Cone militants had been closely connected to the Nicaraguan Revolution, as they had participated in the pre- and post-revolutionary process. Although the most notable of these was the ERP faction headed by Enrique Gorriarán Merlo, Chilean and Uruguayan militants were also involved.[2]

The international context also experienced certain changes that had an effect on these militants. On the one hand, the shift in Cuba's foreign policy, with its alignment with the Soviet Union, its campaign in Africa, and the end of its support to revolutionary armed struggle in the Southern Cone, made it difficult for the region's organizations to resume certain initiatives. On the other, a number of studies, such as Samuel Moyn's and Barbara J. Keys', have shown how the way in which opposition movements positioned themselves with respect to the dictatorships of the Southern Cone was shaped by the international context of the late 1970s. This context was characterized by a new sensitivity, promoted by the Jimmy Carter administration, toward defending a particular notion of human rights, the efforts of international organizations such as Amnesty International and Human Rights Watch, and greater attention to these matters by international bodies, such as the United Nations and the Organization of American States.[3]

Lastly, the processes of renovation in left-wing thinking eroded the way of conceiving the revolutionary political culture of the previous decades. Several intellectuals and militants in the exile diaspora, who were in contact with other experiences, made a variety of proposals, ranging from: a revalorization of democracy and human rights with respect to the views that had prevailed in the 1970s – which had been more tied to criticism of liberalism; the acknowledgement of various emancipation causes – such as the rights of women and indigenous groups; and lastly, a more pluralistic approach to social change that incorporated Christian sectors, democratic sectors from the center of the ideological spectrum, and sectors from Latin America's populist and nationalist traditions. In terms of theory, this renewal involved a rereading of the works by Italian communist intellectual Antonio Gramsci (1891–1937). In particular, the concept of cultural hegemony, and his view of political conflict as a war of position, enabled them to rethink collective action by moving away from a military political approach to focus especially on the mobilization of civil society and the role of intellectuals and culture producers.[4] This renovation permeated discussions in exile communities in various cities, from Mexico City and Managua to Rome, but also in the Southern Cone countries, where emerging social movements, much less ideological than those of the 1970s, were starting to strike a new tone in the way political action was approached.[5]

The 1980s were marked by new social movements that produced a shift in the focus of public debates. These groups – which consisted of citizens, women, and victims of human rights abuses – were more horizontally structured than the traditional left-wing organizations; they proposed an agenda that was more in line with the everyday demands of urban popular sectors, moving away from the great revolutionary goals of the previous decade.[6] The incorporation into these movements of some of the earlier militants opened up alternative paths for activism, which during the transitions to democracy gradually emerged as more effective in the fight against the dictatorship than the older models of armed struggle.

In this sense, the period that begins in the 1980s was characterized by a political geography that differed from the previous decades. The agenda of the new movements, the international support they received, and the places where they gathered in exile all determined a more decentralized reality. The various political and social movements engaged in horizontal exchanges involving actors from the region, but they did not seek to develop centralized strategies. Moreover, the struggles in Central America, and in particular the triumph of the revolution in Nicaragua, served as inspiration for several of these organizations but they were never seen as part of a continental strategy. These changes revealed a more dramatic change of era than what many of these militants were willing to admit: a transition to a form of collective action that was no longer conceived as a continental revolution but as diverse local struggles without a common revolutionary goal.

Several of the armed organizations from the previous period participated in the anti-dictatorship struggle by supporting the development of a human rights movement within and outside the Southern Cone that denounced the situation of political prisoners and the disappearance of individuals. They participated in this movement with a degree of ambiguity that allowed them to report human rights abuses to international organism while at the same time positing in their publications the idea that the only way of putting an end to such abuses was through a revolutionary change that would topple the dictatorships. The prevailing atmosphere of renovation put into question some of the principles on which the political culture of the armed groups had been built. Many associated this renovation with the end of the armed experience of the 1970s. In a context of harsh persecution against armed groups by the region's dictatorships, diminished support from the Cuban Revolution as Havana aligned itself more closely with the Soviet Union, and the possibilities being opened up by the human rights movements, these discourses of renovation emerged as an alternative to the revolutionary discourses. Although the paths taken by each of these groups gradually diverged and the elements that united their actions in the 1970s grew less significant over time, those that attempted to act in the 1980s faced the same dilemma: namely, finding a way to reconcile a tradition of insurgent political culture with the climate of renovation.

All the groups grappled with the tension between the past of the 1970s and the present of the 1980s. For some this entailed abandoning armed struggle for the time being, while for others it meant rethinking the ways in which armed struggle would be developed in a new context. With the exception of Chile, none of the countries of the region – neither Argentina nor Uruguay nor Brazil – saw their militants resuming armed struggle after democracy was restored. All of the militants who remained organized as a group, however, viewed armed struggle as a possibility that could not be ruled out. Even those who became legal organizations maintained armed groups for security and finance issues.

Their appropriation of the climate of renovation will be full of contradictions, uncertainties, inertias, and reinterpretations of the ideas signified by the very notion of human rights and democracy. In more than one case their adaptation will not stem from an ideological transformation and will result instead from the inevitable and harsh acceptance of historical circumstances marked by a change of sensitivity toward political violence among important sectors of the population, a re-legitimizing of the values of democratic liberalism, and the situation of the armed forces of the dictatorships, which remained untouched.

This chapter will look at the processes of disaggregation of these regional spaces and the implications for the transnational political culture that had been developing. For that reason, it will follow a different structure. Instead of focusing on one city in the region like the previous chapters, it will review the efforts undertaken in this period to reorganize and adapt to the new political circumstances of each country's transition to democracy. While I will consider the exchanges that in some cases continued within the region and in other parts of the world, such as Nicaragua, the chapter will be structured primarily around national political processes into which what was left of the various organizations tried to incorporate.

Chile: The Continuation of Armed Struggle

While armed groups in Argentina, Uruguay, and Brazil had suffered multiple internal fractures that hindered their actions abroad, as of 1978 MIR militants operating mostly from Cuba were planning an action aimed at reestablishing the organization's presence in Chile.[7] That year, the top leaders of the MIR who were in Cuba began to design what they dubbed Operation Return, which involved positioning the MIR in political struggles within Chile. This operation was part of the so-called Plan 78, under which the MIR acknowledged the resurgence of social mobilization in the country and posed the need to accompany that mobilization with armed actions staged by revolutionary organizations. These actions were to be deployed on multiple fronts, ranging from cities and their peripheries with semi-permanent urban guerrilla units and popular militias to permanent rural guerrilla units in southern Chile. According to this plan's strategy, all of these actions would contribute to form a revolutionary army in the framework of the long-term people's war that had been the MIR's goal since it was formed but which in this new context appeared more feasible.[8] Chile's Left was unique in the region in that it had no fully consolidated armed organizations in the period prior to the dictatorship. While the Uruguayan dictatorship in 1973 and the Argentine dictatorship in 1976 succeeded in dismantling armed organizations that had been suffering defeats prior to the coups, in Chile armed militants had not reached a significant level of development in terms of military actions against the state, although in their political statements they claimed they had. They began developing such actions during the dictatorship, with very limited results in the first years. Moreover, a new aspect that was specific to Chile gave armed struggle a different dimension. Certain sectors of the Chilean Communist Party gradually began to consider the possibility of creating an armed front to combat the dictatorship. By the late 1970s the traditional divide between communists and armed groups that had prevailed in the 1970s across the Southern Cone began to disappear in Chile with the emergence of the Frente Patriótico Manuel Rodríguez (Manuel Rodríguez Patriotic Front, or FPMR).[9]

The MIR's military strategy was linked to a political strategy that sought to build an opposition front against the dictatorship, headed by revolutionary leftist groups and sustained by a broad and diverse social movement representing various sectors of Chilean society through the establishment of anti-dictatorship resistance committees. This social movement would deploy a variety of tactics, including conducting lawful protests and forming popular militias.

Putting this plan in motion required significant support from outside the country, as MIR forces within Chile were practically decimated as a result of the harsh blows suffered in the years 1975 and 1976. MIR leader Patricio Rivas recounts that some 2,000 MIR militants exiled in countries around the world, including France, Spain, Sweden, Mexico, Panama, Costa Rica, and Cuba, were asked if they would participate in the operation. Of the total consulted, 400 were selected and began some form of training in clandestine schools, with 200 of them making their way back to Chile between 1979 and 1986.[10]

According to former MIR militant Hernán Vidal, Cuba's support in the preparations for Operation Return was key. Despite the shifts within the Cuban Communist Party noted in Chapter IV, which entailed a certain distancing from the policies of the Southern Cone groups, the Americas Department maintained good relations with the MIR. That explains the support in the form of military training provided by Cuba to many of the militants who were preparing their return in guerrilla camps on the island. Cuba's support, however, came after the MIR had finally abandoned the already moribund JCR project in 1978. The MIR's withdrawal from the JCR had been a condition since 1976 for having the support of the Americas Department. In any case, Cuba applied different criteria when it came to its support for the MIR and the Chilean communists. While MIR militants were trained in guerrilla camps, the Chilean Communist Party received military training in the military schools of the Cuban government.[11]

By August 1979 the MIR was announcing in its clandestine press media the arrival of its top leader Andrés Pascal Allende. In an interview, Pascal Allende called on the Chilean people to establish a "democratic, popular, and revolutionary government" by way of a struggle against the dictatorship combining legal, semi-legal, and illegal means, gathering in a common front all the sectors of the Left and even Christian Democrats who truly upheld democratic values.[12] As worthy examples of this strategy, Pascal Allende cited the cases of Nicaragua, El Salvador, and Guatemala, where anti-dictatorship fronts appeared to be achieving significant results. These experiences were not new for several MIR militants who had been immersed in the struggles in Central America. A group of MIR militants in Costa Rica had joined the southern front of the FSLN to fight in the Nicaraguan revolution.[13]

During the first two years the operation in Chile appeared to have a major impact in the cities. Both the MIR's clandestine newspaper *El rebelde en la clandestinidad* and its news agency *Agencia Informativa de la Resistencia* reported on a series of armed actions – including bank expropriations, attacks on dictatorship officials, sabotages, and street barricades – which revealed an increase in armed activity. Analysis by the MIR press suggested that this was in line with a growth in social mobilization connected with the human rights movement, the student movement, sectors of the labor movement, and the popular settlement movement. According to Pinto and Leiva, such attempts would turn these years into the MIR's most successful period of military activity, which had been greatly weakened after the coup.[14]

The MIR's military expansion, however, did not follow the same path as the social protests. While in late 1981 an economic crisis caused a deep impact among popular sectors, by mid year the military apparatus of the MIR had began to be detected and destroyed by the Central Nacional de Informaciones (National Information Agency, or CNI, which replaced the DINA in 1977). By 1983, when social mobilization expanded in a cycle of large protests that challenged the dictatorship's capacity to control the opposition, the MIR's military force had already been greatly diminished. The CNI first cracked down on the MIR military force in 1980 in reaction to the MIR's assassination of Roger Vergara, the director of the intelligence school. This brought major changes within the CNI, leading it to step up its persecution of the MIR.[15]

The initial attacks on MIR forces were followed by strikes against the rural guerrilla *focos* in the Andean area of southern Chile's Neltume region. These places were associated with earlier Mapuche peasant struggles during the Unidad Popular period and armed resistance attempts against the coup. The Neltume military camp was discovered and raided, leaving eleven MIR militants dead.[16] This was the beginning of a string of defeats and reactions that ended in 1983 with the fall of the top military leaders of the MIR, Arturo Villabela and Hugo Ratier, and a series of actions against the organization in the year 1984 that left it severely weakened for years to come.[17]

According to historian Steve Stern, the conspiratorial nature of the MIR's actions, especially with respect to Neltume-related events, helped bring back the so-called saving memory of the military. This memory justified the military's involvement in the country's political life by claiming the existence of plans for a communist-led foreign invasion. After losing credibility in previous years due to these groups' weakness, it now gained renewed currency and was more aggressively promoted through propaganda and repression.[18] All of this contributed to erode the MIR's efforts to move closer to anti-dictatorial sectors and lay bare certain problems in the MIR's military strategy that had been debated since Operation Return.

These problems had to do with the ways in which the dictatorship should be combated. What role did armed struggle play? Did it contribute to the growth of the social movement or could it ultimately result in that movement's isolation? How could the risks of the voluntaristic, *foquista*, and militaristic deviations into which many organizations had fallen in the 1960s and 1970s be avoided? In short, how could the tension between political and military aspects be resolved at a time in which the military power of dictatorships had given ample proof of their effective ability to control any form of resistance.

In the case of Operation Return, these discussions had been present at the central committee meeting that defined Plan 78. The decision to adopt the plan had in fact won by only one vote.[19] Those who opposed it expressed doubts, arguing that the dictatorship was too stable and that social struggles were still too weak to ensure the return of militants. As with other cases mentioned in this book – for example, the Tupamaros' discussion over the possibility of returning to Uruguay from Buenos Aires in 1974 – some accounts reveal the weight that emotions and loyalties had in the decisions made at that moment. The guilt many felt over not being in the country, and the urgency to do something, carried an emotional charge that was much stronger than any cold-headed analysis of Chile's situation that these exiles could make, an analysis that was moreover based on the fragmented information that was available to them.[20]

For some, the discrepancies in this process were so intense that they led them to leave the MIR. Víctor Toro Ramírez, a prestigious leader of the urban settlement movement who was in Cuba, stepped down from the leadership of the MIR and left for Mexico. There he published a document whose heated tone reveals the harshness of the internal discussions in the MIR at that time. In it he denounced "the group of comrades who have monopolized certain positions in the steering committee [which] has been increasingly operating as a true faction within the Chilean MIR, purging and expelling hundreds of comrades who criticized the lack of internal democracy in our party, the voluntarism, the petit-bourgeois revolutionarism, their bureaucratic and authoritarian styles."[21]

The tone it was written in was brutal, expressing the high levels of confrontation within the organization, the bulk of which was in exile. The disagreements had to do both with the possibility of implementing internal democracy mechanisms under such circumstances and with the military strategy issue. Those who were against the military strategy did not deny the need for armed struggle in the context of the transition, but they disagreed over the modes it should adopt. Most were in favor of insurrectional strategies linked to the social protests and were against guerrilla actions such as the failed operation in Neltume. This was the debate on the surface, but there was another, deeper underlying discussion that divided the MIR along with the other Southern Cone organizations and that had to do with the weight of political and military aspects in this new context.

Despite the persecutions and losses suffered in the years 1984 and 1985, the MIR tried to regain some initiative by furthering certain forms of violent resistance among the mobilized working-class neighborhoods: by participating in the human rights movement through the Corporación de Promoción y Defensa de los Derechos del Pueblo (Corporation for the Promotion and Defense of the People's Rights, or CODEPU), and at the political level in the Movimiento Democrático Popular (Popular Democratic Movement), the left-wing coalition that refused to negotiate with Pinochet for an end to the dictatorship.[22] The context within the Left had changed. As noted above, the emergence of the Frente Patriótico Manuel Rodríguez, an armed group connected with the Communist Party, transformed the traditional relationship between MIR militants and communists. This opened doors, but also introduced a new competitor that challenged the MIR's leadership among certain sectors of the social movement. Despite these political efforts by the MIR to remain standing, the military apparatus continued to sustain losses and by 1986 the organization no longer had the capacity to conduct military actions.[23]

During this period, the 1978 debates regarding the tension between militarist and political options, and which should prevail, began to reemerge in the face of the MIR's repeated defeats and the impossibility of reorganizing. Although the MIR had gained a significant presence in some of the organizations active in the mass movement against dictatorship, the other part of the strategy of Operation Return, which had to do with the MIR's military actions, turned out to be impossible to carry out. This tension was evident at a meeting of the steering committee, in which leaders who prioritized social work and believed that military action should come later as a result of social mobilization were pitted against those who saw this position as subordinating military goals to social aims. In the months that followed, the two groups split into two factions: MIR Renovation (also known as the Political MIR), headed by Nelson Gutiérrez, who for the most part represented militants connected with social movements; and the Historical MIR, which was led by Andrés Pascal Allende and gathered most of the members of the party apparatus. In 1988, following its congress, the first group declared:

For the vast majority of militants this event was a new experience, which strengthened democratic ideas about the party. We will not see a repetition of the situations that enabled a voluntaristic tendency to take hold of the top leadership, through antidemocratic procedures, despite the obvious mistakes made from 1981 to 1984.[24]

This was contrasted by the vindication of the Neltume actions by a group within the Historical MIR faction, which declared that the Chilean Left's greatest problem was still:

the lack of a people's armed and military power [which is] what has prevented us from moving firmly forward in the struggle to seize power. As revolutionaries we must acknowledge that despite our efforts we have failed to build such a power, because we have been mistaken in our force-building strategy, which has been unable to overcome and defeat repression, and which has spread us too thinly in multiple tasks, preventing us from focusing on armed and military struggle, which is the core and the engine of all forms of struggle that are part of the revolutionary process.[25]

Once again, the problem of the Left's renovation was linked to the military–political dichotomy, and to the fact that, in theory, the two categories were not antagonistic but in the context of democratization appeared to be. This rift occurred in a particular context in which the transition was starting to change course. The FPMR's failed assassination attempt against Pinochet unleashed a fierce wave of repression that affected the entire Left. This created divisions between those who continued to wager on a revolutionary end to the dictatorship and the majority sectors of the Left that began to lean toward a negotiated solution in alliance with Christian Democratic sectors. The latter would emerge as the sectors with the greatest capacity for leadership and the ones that were to effectively guide the transition toward a negotiated end to the dictatorship, which would finally come in 1990 with the Patricio Aylwin government.

The last years of the democratic transition were very difficult for the fragmented MIR, with the historical sector suffering another fracture in 1987 led by Hernán Aguiló, head of the military commission, followed by two further breakaways, and in 1990 two new rifts. Although the members of MIR Renovation were still significantly divided over what approach to take, the faction remained relatively stable behind its project of participating in the parliamentary elections along with the Partido Amplio de Izquierda Socialista (Broad Socialist Left Party). However, as of the year 1990, it split into four factions that in practice resulted in its virtual disappearance. Some left to join the Socialist Party, others tried to form a new group with breakaway sectors of the Izquierda Cristiana (Christian Left, or IC) and the Communist Party, and others sought to take up again the legacy of the MIR. By 1990 there were eight groups claiming the identity of the old MIR, spanning a wide range of positions with respect to the situation in the country. At one end of the spectrum were those who argued against a negotiated democracy, and for the need to continue with armed struggle; at the other were those who joined the Socialist Party amidst that party's process of reunification, and would ultimately be appointed to government positions among the members of the governing Concertación de Partidos por la Democracia (Coalition of Parties for Democracy, or Concertación).[26]

This political fragmentation and uncertainty with which the MIR met the new democracy was compounded by the legal situation in which several of its jailed militants found themselves. Although initially the new democratic government expressed its will to implement a broad amnesty policy for the 400 political prisoners who were still in jail, pressure from the opposition and the armed forces was too strong, particularly with respect to those imprisoned in the 1980s for violent crimes. The fact that various groups, which supported the MIR or the FPMR, maintained or renewed their armed actions in the context of the nascent democracy further complicated the situation. The attempt on air force general and post-coup junta member Gustavo Leigh's life, by FPMR-A militants just ten days after the inauguration of the democratic government, generated a difficult situation for President Patricio Aylwin, with the media raising the specter of left-wing "terrorism" again and the Concertación government resorting to harsh measures so as not to yield any spaces to the Right. All of this delayed the liberation of the prisoners of the dictatorship, a process that involved long negotiations. By late 1992, after various proceedings that entailed case-by-case reviews, 300 prisoners had been freed. The most problematic cases – those connected with the FPMR attempt on Pinochet's life – were settled in the final days of the Aylwin administration, by commuting the forty-year jail sentences of the militants involved for their exile in Belgium.[27]

The new government also developed a counterinsurgency strategy aimed at dismantling the armed leftist groups that were still active. That strategy was not entrusted to military officers trained under the national security doctrine but to old comrades of the same ideological families who now took on the counterinsurgency tasks. To that end, in 1991 a Public Security Coordinating Council was formed to coordinate the intelligence tasks involved in the surveillance of these armed groups and to organize related police action. In addition to being headed by socialist militant Marcelo Schilling, the council was assisted by other militants who had insurgency and counterinsurgency experience, had been trained in Eastern Europe, and were now engaged as advisors. One of the legal instruments that played a key role in structuring the persecution of these militants was the Repentance Act. In addition, the sentences established under prior laws (the Interior Security of the State Act, the Weapons and Explosives Control Act, and the Anti-Terrorist Act) were toughened and a high security prison (Cárcel de Alta Seguridad, or CAS) was created, which would later be called into question because of the isolation and punishment mechanisms used against militants.[28]

This was the difficult context in which the MIR faced democracy. Even for those who had chosen to renounce armed struggle it was very difficult to shed the stigma created under the dictatorship and which was now reshaped by the first democratic government with much greater legitimacy. All of this led to a complete fragmentation from which the MIR has yet to recover and which appears irreversible.

The last two decades, however, have shown a particular presence of the Chilean Left in different areas of the country's social and cultural life.

The testimonial work produced in various formats, ranging from film documentaries to written memoirs, has found numerous militants from that experience contributing to a collective reflection that has to do with their own organizations but also with the country as a whole.[29] In academic circles a group of prominent historians with different historiographic approaches reference their MIR experience as a major part of their intellectual development.[30] In the field of human rights, particularly with respect to memory policies, various groups have set out to tell the experiences suffered by MIR militants under state terrorism.[31]

The reflection generated by these multiple experiences of social and cultural activism is an open one. While in general terms it is marked by the denunciation of the state violence perpetrated by the dictatorship and the moral defense of the political actions of these militants, it has also created spaces for self-critical reflection on multiple aspects of the political culture of that experience. The documentaries, in particular, reveal the gender conflicts that stemmed from the prevailing sexist culture but which had remained hidden in the 1970s under a guise of equality. For their part, the voices of the sons and daughters of these militants have raised the issue of the conflict between family and revolutionary projects. Some studies by Gabriel Salazar also contain an explicit criticism of the authoritarian dimension of the vanguardism of the 1970s. This process of reflection has had a certain influence on youth movements that have adopted a critical view of the experience of the Concertación in these past decades.

To some extent these forms of activism have played a more important role in memory struggles than they have in elections and political battles, where MIR militants as an organized group have been unable to form a common front since the 1990s. Marco Enríquez Ominami's experience in recent years, however, shows in a somewhat ambiguous and opaque way how those political struggles for memory have affected electoral politics.

Marco Enríquez Ominami is the son of MIR historical leader Miguel Enríquez and journalist Manuela Gumucio. After his father was killed by the dictatorship, his mother, who was already separated from Miguel Enríquez, decided to leave the country. In 1975 Gumucio became involved with socialist politician Carlos Ominami. Upon returning to Chile, her son Marco decided to add Ominami to his last name, in recognition of his adoptive father.

During the first years of democracy, Enríquez Ominami alternated his political activism with his work as a communicator and documentary filmmaker. In 2006, as a Socialist Party candidate he was elected to the lower chamber of parliament. In 2009, he left the party to form a political group outside the Concertación and run for president. He received a range of supports, spanning different sectors and ideas. These included sectors with an MIR background. One group that supported his bid for presidency was La SurDa, an organization made up of former MIR and communist militants from the 1980s, as well as MIR members from the 1970s, who established an MIR culture committee, with the participation of Andrés Pascal Allende. In the 2009 presidential election Enríquez Ominami obtained twenty percent of the vote, in what was an unprecedented result in a system strongly marked by a two-party institutional tradition.

In 2014, at a presentation of a biography of Miguel Enríquez, his son Marco said that he "would have been an MIR militant" in the 1960s, as he considered it "a brilliant intellectual movement." Marco Enríquez Ominami's bid for presidency generated endless debates among former MIR militants, with many identifying with his platform. But what is most interesting in his relatively successful political career is how the cultural value of that tradition appears to have some political currency in today's Chile.

Argentina: A Strange Return

The PRT-ERP experience was less visible in Argentina's transition. While, during exile, this group also thought about organizing a return, its internal situation and the political dynamics in Argentina made it difficult to feasibly implement such a process. The vicissitudes faced by this organization outside Argentina were marked by a deep rift between two sectors. On the one hand, members exiled primarily in Europe were drawn to the international communist movement, leaving behind the old definitions of the Latin American New Left of the late 1960s. This sector, led by general secretary Luis Mattini (the name taken by Arnold Kremer in the late 1960s), raised increasing objections to the idea of resuming armed actions in Argentina. On the other hand, a minority sector settled in Cuba, under the direction of Enrique Gorriarán Merlo, and in 1978 it participated in Nicaragua in the offensive actions of the FSLN's southern front. As of that moment, this sector's militants assumed a strong commitment with the Nicaraguan Revolution. Some human rights organizations working abroad, made up primarily of PRT-ERP members or former members, acted as a bridge of sorts between the two opposing sectors within the organization.[32]

It was through Gorriarán Merlo's group that, following the victory of the Sandinistas, some one hundred Argentine militants went to Nicaragua to participate in different government activities. This group's support to the revolution was not limited to assistance within Nicaraguan borders, as in 1980 a commando unit led by Gorriarán Merlo gunned down former dictator Anastasio Somoza Debayle in Paraguay. According to Gorriarán Merlo, this assassination was not merely an act of revenge, as the aim was to stop the counterrevolutionary actions that Somoza forces were carrying out with the collaboration of the governments of Paraguay and Argentina.[33]

According to accounts, between 1980 and 1981 both factions were considering a plan to return to Argentina. But a range of reasons are given for the failure to launch such an operation. Julio Santucho recalls that the sector that was in Europe moved to Mexico in 1980 with the idea of preparing the return. However, the kidnapping of the daughter of a mining industrialist linked to Mexico's Partido Acción Nacional (National Action Party, or PAN), perpetrated by Gorriarán's group for financing purposes, alerted the intelligence services. This led to the arrest of fifty militants of the other PRT-ERP faction who were operating legally and publicly in Mexico, and in turn put an end to any return preparations on Mexican soil.[34]

After participating in Somoza's assassination, the group led by Gorriarán went on to take a nine-month course in rural guerrilla tactics. These militants returned to Argentina via the province of Salta, resuming the guerrilla tradition of setting up camp in rural areas of northern Argentina with the aim of developing a rural *foco*, as Masetti and the ERP itself had done in the 1970s. This attempt, however, did not progress past initial exploratory incursions.[35] The Malvinas/Falklands War, the defeat of the Argentine armed forces in that war, and the dictatorship's subsequent crisis led these militants to conclude that conditions were not ripe for this kind of initiatives, and they returned to Nicaragua.

According to Gorriarán Merlo, after realizing that the military regime was in its last days, the group of PRT-ERP militants in Nicaragua who had ruled out the possibility of forming a *foco* in northern Argentina embarked on a different political path that clearly acknowledged the new political state of affairs in Argentina and certain renovating processes in the Latin American Left. Although initially this group of militants represented the minority faction of the ERP, as their prestige grew among fellow militants due to their participation in the FSLN's southern front, followed by their involvement in the revolutionary government, and finally their role in Somoza's assassination, they acquired a halo of respect and admiration in the coming years. The group became the core of the organization, channeling proposals aimed at reorganizing political projects that had points of contact with the PRT-ERP experience.[36]

Gorriarán Merlo's group began launching press projects as early as 1982, anticipating the political spirit that these militants would embrace in the coming years. The magazine *Frente* (published in 1982 and 1983) and the second publishing project called *Entre Todos* (a magazine published as of 1984) expressed the pluralist will of that new moment in the armed leftist experience of the 1960s. The magazine *Entre Todos* – whose title was completed with the subtitle *Los que queremos la liberación (peronistas, radicales, intransigentes, cristianos, socialistas, comunistas, independientes)*, so that it read something like "All together, Those of us who want liberation (Peronists, Radical Party followers,

Intransigent Party followers, Christians, socialists, communists, independent activists)" – expressed the aim of building a broad and plural political movement that would gather together the different progressive sectors of Argentine society in the context of redemocratization.[37] The reasons behind this aim had to do with the realization that, in Argentina, there was a powerful social movement with a variety of leftist political positions with which it was possible to build a new form of political movement. They also had to do with the Central American experience, where the construction of political fronts that brought together Christian, Marxist, and social democrat sectors had been the key to the success of the FSLN in Nicaragua and appeared to be yielding good results in El Salvador.

Entre Todos clearly expressed that form of politics. Its pages showed a pluralist political approach that sought to bring together all those who had an anti-imperialist discourse and an affinity with those sectors, regardless of their political affiliation. Moreover, the publication replaced the highly ideologically-charged language of the PRT newsletters with a more popular language closer to the imaginary of Latin American nationalism. Local social movements, culture, and human rights featured prominently in its articles. Also underlying these articles was the idea that the leading conflict was between authoritarianism and democracy. The publication was written by a staff of journalists and intellectuals who in some cases were connected with the ERP experience, but others came from other generations or political sectors within the Left. Renowned figures such as the Nobel Peace Prize laureate and SERPAJ leader Adolfo Pérez Esquivel, the journalists Horacio Verbitsky and Manuel Gaggero, the theologian Rubén Dri and the friar Puigjane, connected with liberation theology, and the poet and cultural journalist Jorge Boccanera contributed to this magazine from the start.

During this period, Gorriarán Merlo's group was particularly interested in promoting cultural projects that could expand the voice of center-left sectors. The human rights lawyer Eduardo Luis Duhalde founded the influential publishing house Editorial Contrapunto with the support of the group, and several accounts reveal that the group's financing was instrumental in the founding of the newspaper *Página 12*.[38]

The group had significant economic resources. The origins of such resources are not entirely clear, but some investigations by journalists connect them with the close relationship that Gorriarán Merlo forged with Cuba's Americas Department. Also, as was seen in the case of Mexico, there had been networks of illegal activities abroad (robberies and kidnappings) through which funds had been obtained to carry out this kind of cultural ventures.[39]

Although this political strategy began to yield some returns, it had a limit determined by the extent of Gorriarán Merlo's circle and the position in which the transitional context and the human rights policy of the new democratically-elected president Raúl Alfonsín had put ERP militants.

The transition process in Argentina was marked by a fast and somewhat chaotic retreat by the military. As they withdrew they tried to impose a self-amnesty two weeks before the elections. That attempt was thwarted by Alfonsín's victory at the polls, as in his campaign Alfonsín had shown his support for the cause of human rights. Upon taking office in December 1983, the new president called for the repeal of the self-amnesty law, ordered the arrest and prosecution of the members of the first three military juntas, reformed the military code, and convened a commission to investigate the crimes committed by the dictatorship in connection with forced disappearances.[40]

However, the guerrilla groups would have to play a role within the strategy of the new democratic government in order to justify the prosecution of the military commands. The same day the president issued Decree 158, ordering the arrest of the military junta members on charges of human rights violations committed under the dictatorship; he also issued another decree ordering the arrest of the surviving members of the "terrorist leadership" of the Montoneros and the ERP. In the case of the ERP, he specifically ordered Gorriarán Merlo's arrest, as he was the sole surviving member of the group's historical leadership.[41] In this sense, the discursive and political strategy on the issue of human rights that has been labeled by some as the "theory of the two demons" had two clear targets: the armed Left of the 1970s; and the military, which were placed in a past that the new democracy wished to leave behind.[42]

Another specific consequence of this policy was delayed liberation of political prisoners, as Alfonsín did not grant a general amnesty at the start of the democratic government. The reasons for not granting it were explained in the grounds of Decree 157, which ordered the capture of the guerrilla leaders. According to the decree, the amnesty granted in 1973 at the beginning of the democratic government of Héctor Cámpora had furthered the regrouping of the existing guerrilla organizations that had been controlled under the previous dictatorship. However, the circumstances in 1984 were different from those in 1973, as by then no guerrilla groups remained active, and many had apparently expressed their will to join the social struggles of the time. The other argument was that an amnesty would have a destabilizing effect on the military. In this sense, this policy also entailed a concession to military sectors that retained a certain degree of power and could view a unilateral punishment as a form of revenge.

Faced with increasing protests from human rights organizations and from the prisoners themselves through a series of hunger strikes, the government proposed a law for the commutation of sentences that gradually released most political prisoners. In 1987, there were still thirteen political prisoners of the 114 who were still in jail at the end of the dictatorship.[43] This policy also affected several exiled militants, who decided to remain abroad upon seeing the situation the prisoners faced, afraid that if they returned they would be put on trial.[44]

This explains why in 1986 the Movimiento Todos por la Patria (Everyone for the Homeland Movement, or MTP), a group linked to the news venture *Entre Todos*, was formed in Managua. The magazine was dominated by the figure of Gorriarán Merlo, who met with different leaders in Managua and Brazil, and in some cases in Argentina where he would enter secretly as he was wanted by the Argentine authorities. These leaders would later form the MTP. The founding group included a number of hard core militants of the PRT-ERP, whose direction they recognized, and with whom they had been involved through several of its previous plans. Gorriarán Merlo's situation was a complicated one. He was the brains behind the project, but he remained in the shadows, as it was not wise to have someone wanted by the law as the leader of a legal organization. The activities carried out by the *Entre Todos* project gathered together a range of activists: old ERP militants who had survived persecution; left-wing Peronists; young people who identified with the experience of the 1970s, several of whom had joined the Intransigent Party during the democratic transition; Catholic sectors that sympathized with liberation theology; and human rights movement activists and lawyers, many of whom traveled to Managua to participate in the founding of the MTP. Also present in Managua for the founding of the movement was Tupamaro leader Raúl Sendic, who had been recently released from prison and was visiting Nicaragua.[45]

The first positions adopted by the MTP were featured in the May 1986 *Entre Todos* issue.[46] The article that introduced the movement is surprising if we consider that the head of the movement was one of the leaders of the 1970s PRT-ERP who insisted on hard-line ideological definitions. This text had little of the old Marxist orthodoxy and much more of a populist Latin Americanism that seemed more in line with traditions that dated back to the late 1950s.

After referring to a number of national and popular traditions, ranging from San Martín to Yrigoyen and Perón, the introduction called for the construction of a new national historical movement. The main objectives of the movement's program focused on the ideas of participatory democracy (which did not go against the principles of liberal democracy), economic independence, human rights, a Latin Americanist foreign policy that would further the region's integration, and a reform of the armed forces. This declaration of principles was signed, among others, by many of the people who had been involved in the *Entre Todos* experience.

Although the MTP appeared to have a somewhat positive impact within the Argentine Left and initially the movement saw relative growth, a series of internal and external events led to a radical shift in this organization between 1986 and 1989.

The fact that Gorriarán Merlo – who was among the "demons" of the transition – was leading from the shadows, made it difficult to build the movement's identity. And it placed him and the MTP in a complicated position, as the most progressive aspect of Alfonsín's policy – his approach to the issue of human rights – rested on the stigmatization of the experience of the 1960s. In 1988, speaking from an undisclosed site, Gorriarán Merlo himself declared that he would refuse an amnesty if that amnesty would be granted in exchange for an amnesty for the military junta members.[47]

In addition, a number of events further complicated the actions of the MTP. First, the bid to participate in provincial elections in 1987 was apparently not very successful. Alliances with other leftist groups were formed in several provinces, but they failed to secure any legislative seats or government positions. Second, the military reaction against the Alfonsín government in the form of the Carapintada movement had a major influence in the reading this group made of the country's political process.[48]

During the Alfonsín government there were three uprisings by military forces that opposed the human rights policy implemented in the initial years of the return to democracy. The first uprising took place in 1987, in the week prior to Easter. Although it was crushed and its leaders were arrested and prosecuted, the passing of the Due Obedience and Full Stop Acts in the following months showed the impact that these military actions were having on the government's human rights policy. While there was a large pro-democracy sector of society that took to the streets to support Alfonsín during those days, after the Due Obedience Act it became increasingly clear that the political establishment was divided in its position with respect to these uprisings. There were those who were not willing to negotiate with the military rebels and those who admitted the need to reach some agreements with them. The second and third uprisings aggravated the conflict with certain political and social sectors that demanded a firmer stand from the Alfonsín government in response to the blackmailing situation generated by the military. The third uprising sparked skirmishes with social and political activists from left-wing parties who surrounded the barracks seized by the military rebels.

Several sectors of the Left, and even of the Radical Party, began to fear the possibility of a military coup as a feasible scenario. They believed they needed to be prepared to resist such a threat. In their book *La Tablada*, researchers Pablo Waisberg and Felipe Celesia provide several accounts of young communists, left-wing Peronists, and Intransigent, and even Radical, Party sympathizers who began to seriously consider that possibility and began gathering weapons, practicing shooting, and engaging in other similar activities.[49]

This idea had a greater effect on the MTP militants who had been linked to the official structure of the PRT-ERP. The aim of building a great inclusive political movement was dropped very quickly; the old issues and discourses of the 1970s were taken up again. The key question was once again how to go about consolidating the revolutionary vanguard. In a practical sense, this had to do with the development of a military-political apparatus that would coexist in secret and in parallel with the organization. Celesia and Waisberg note that what first pushed Gorriarán Merlo toward a skeptical reading of the possibilities offered by the nascent democracy was the 1986 Full Stop Act, which amounted to an amnesty for several military officers implicated in human rights abuses. As of that moment, an "analysis group" was formed under Gorriarán Merlo's supervision with the aim of monitoring the military's advance. This interpretation gained ground in 1987 and 1988 following the two military uprisings. In a document on the second uprising, the MTP alarmingly noted: "The military are advancing. What do we do?" And it declared: "The people must take the defense of democracy into their own hands."[50]

Internally, this debate over expanding the political movement or developing a military apparatus to prepare for an adverse situation, such as a military coup, exacerbated the conflicts that were emerging between Gorriarán Merlo and other political leaders of the MTP.[51] Gorriarán Merlo – who remained in Nicaragua and was still very much defined by his revolutionary past – and a group of Argentines, who were more connected with political and social action, and who realized how far removed Argentine society was from the imaginaries of revolutionary heroism of the 1970s, envisioned vastly different paths for facing a possible military reaction. This led to a series of internal fractures in the MTP that meant that by 1988 the group had been reduced to Gorriarán Merlo's inner circle.[52]

This group began planning a military operation that was put into action in January 1989. The operation involved spreading the rumor that a coup was imminent, thus justifying an attack on military barracks. There were actually no solid grounds for fearing a coup threat. Although the possibility was not entirely unfounded, in the summer of 1989 there was nothing specific that could lead to the belief that it was imminent. Subsequent events would prove that it was all part of a sham to prepare for the attack on the Cuartel de La Tablada military barracks.

With the Cuartel de la Tablada assault, this group intended to gain entry into the barracks by pretending to belong to a coup faction, throwing flyers in the air and chanting the names of the Carapintada leaders, to then seize the barracks and the tanks. Once the barracks had been seized, the people would be called on to defend democracy. A number of militants were prepared to surround the barracks and convene social organizations. Afterwards, they would head to Plaza de Mayo and call on the people to rise up in an insurrection to demand that a popular and revolutionary army be formed.

The action was one of the most resounding failures in the history of Argentina's guerrilla organizations. Of the forty-six individuals who participated in the action, thirty-three died, some of them executed after they were taken into custody, four were seized by the military and disappeared, and in the days that followed several militants were captured and thrown in jail. Gorriarán Merlo escaped and remained on the run until 1995 when he was arrested in Mexico. The action failed to generate any of the effects sought. In the armed forces, it strengthened the officers' esprit de corps in the repression of social protests and by raising again the threat of subversion it legitimized their memories and their past and present actions.[53] Social and left-wing organizations tried to distance themselves from the action, which they saw as absurd, and they warned that it would have harsh consequences for the political development of the Argentine Left, and that it would bring back the discourse of national security that was re-emerging among the military and conservative civilian sectors.[54] There were some exceptions, such as Hebe de Bonafini, a member of the Mothers of Plaza de Mayo, who on the anniversary of the coup, on March 24, 1989, in a rally convened under the slogan "To resist is to combat," warned of the characteristics of the military officers who had crushed the action in La Tablada.[55] This disastrous action seemed to mark the end of a historical cycle. This is how various academics and journalists who have studied the events at La Tablada explain it, as is evidenced by the titles chosen for their works.[56]

After a significant silence that followed the Tablada action, in the second half of the 1990s a number of developments in the human rights movement showed that the memory of the guerrilla organizations of the 1970s was still alive in Argentine society. Federico Lorenz has examined how in 1996, in the context of the commemoration of the March 24, 1976 coup, a new generation of activists of the human rights movement, who formed an organization under the acronym H.I.J.O.S (which stands for Children for Identity and Justice and against Forgetting and Silence, but also means "children"), proposed a shift in the memory policies within the movement. Whereas, until then, the strategy of the human rights movement had been to omit any references to the revolutionary activism of the 1970s, the members of this new generation posed the need to recover the memories of their parents not only as victims of state terrorism but also as key political actors of the previous decades.[57]

This social movement was in tune with a publishing boom that included numerous testimonial and journalistic accounts of the revolutionary militant experience, written in an open and pluralist tone, in which from a position of familiarity certain positive values were recognized while taking distance from the militarist practices of that generation and from certain issues connected with gender and family relations.[58] While the latter were criticized in such works, the political violence perpetrated by these organizations was largely ignored. In 2004, however, a discussion regarding a 1964 event in which the EGP had sentenced some of its members to death triggered a long controversy that lasted a year and a half, and engaged many intellectuals linked to the experiences of the 1960s and 1970s.[59] This production of books and magazines had a major impact among readers, with bookstores across Buenos Aires featuring sections devoted to these issues for years to come. The publishing of these accounts was also accompanied by the development of a film documentary subgenre, as well as plays, produced primarily by sons and daughters of disappeared militants.[60]

This movement's influence increased after the events connected with the 2001 crisis, when a wave of social protests erupted in a context of acute economic recession. Street clashes resulted in some forty protesters being killed by police and security forces, forcing President Fernando de la Rúa, of the Radical Civic Union party, to resign. These events opened up a new political chapter in the history of Argentine democracy. The following year saw two interim presidencies and in 2003 Carlos Saúl Menem – who had been president before de la Rúa and was a major exponent of the neoliberal policies of the 1990s – came in first in the initial round of the presidential elections, with twenty-four percent of the votes. The governor of Santa Cruz, Nestor Kirchner, also of the Justicialista Party, came in second with twenty-two percent of the votes. In the run-off election, however, Menem withdrew his candidacy, as he feared lowing what promised to be a very difficult race.

Nestor Kirchner's victory as a democratically-elected president following the 2001 political crisis marked the beginning of a new historical era shaped by the development of a novel political movement that engaged in a very fluid dialog with the memory discourses that had been circulating at a cultural and social level since the mid-1990s. It was at this time that Nestor Kirchner appropriated these discourses. In March 2004, in the prolog to a poetry book by a fellow militant who had been disappeared, President Néstor Kirchner wrote:

Once upon a time in this Country there was a generation marked by the desire to wipe out inequality and injustice from its soil. Daughter of proscriptions and intolerance, nurtured in its youth by the French May, it moved forward in Argentina without heeding the limits of the times or leaving any room for speculation. I am part of that generation.[61]

This was one of the first times that the new president identified with that legacy and linked it to his human rights policies. That entailed certain changes with respect to the view of the past built during the Alfonsín government.

An example of this new policy was the rewriting of the prolog to the *Never Again* report, which now stated that "any attempt to justify state terrorism by explaining it as a reaction to rival forms of violence is unacceptable, because when a nation and state deviate from functions that are inherent to them and cannot be renounced, there is no justification to be found in any symmetry of individual actions," obviously alluding to Alfonsín's so-called theory of the two demons, of which the earlier prolog was a clear expression.[62]

It was in this post-2001 crisis context that Gorriarán Merlo was pardoned in 2003, after staging a hunger strike that lasted 162 days. Upon his release, he resumed his political activity, forming the Partido para el Trabajo y el Desarrollo (Work and Development Party), with a discourse that was in line with the progressive tone of the times. His death in 2006, however, put an end to this new venture before it could really take off.

Uruguay: The Rocky and Successful Road to Legal Activity

In Uruguay, the events of La Tablada also had a certain impact. By 1989, the Tupamaros had been participating legally in the country's political life for four years and had explicitly declared their will to do so. However, solidarity, previous ties, and the close relationship forged between Raúl Sendic and Gorriarán Merlo during the former's visits to Nicaragua following his release from prison all led the Tupamaros to issue a public statement that triggered a small political quake within the Uruguayan Left. While most leftist groups on both sides of the Plata River tried to distance themselves from the action, in their statement the Tupamaros said:

The MLN cannot give an opinion neither in general nor in abstract. We are and want to be an organization committed with the struggle of our people and the struggle of the peoples of our sister nations. We have and want to have comrades and we respect them as such, especially when their voices are silenced and they give their lives on the battlefield. Comradeship and solidarity cannot be separated from criticism when in conscience we understand that that criticism is just. But we must be very careful with it when it refers to those who can no longer defend themselves or argue back because they have given their lives to defend their ideas. It may also turn out that we are the ones who are wrong and life – what a paradox! – will prove that the dead were right.

But today, with the elements we have, and we admit that we do not have all the elements, we are convinced that our comrades were wrong and the error that pains us most is that they denied us the possibility of having their great heroism and selflessness for the future.... The MLN reaffirms its decision and its will to live together peacefully, waging a clear and defined political struggle to achieve a full and participatory democracy, to struggle tirelessly against any form of control that does not come from the sovereignty of the people; to combat fascism. It rules out any possibility of combat that does not involve the great popular majorities, the only ones that can carry out, with their own hands, the task that the future has in store for all of us.[63]

This statement earned them public criticism from the other leftist groups, which questioned its position and demanded that the Tupamaros adopt a firmer stance in condemning what was interpreted by the other organizations as an action disconnected from reality that revived the imaginary of armed struggle and went against the democratic struggles built by social movements in the transition.[64] In response to this, Sendic himself categorically replied that they could not renounce armed struggle and he explained that the conditions in Argentina differed from what was happening in Uruguay.[65]

Solidarity also led many of the militants that fled Argentina to seek refuge in Uruguay through the Tupamaros.[66] These solidarity ties were not just a whim from the past, but had also been forged through contacts developed in Nicaragua. Sendic and Gorriarán Merlo had met several times there. And while the two groups had practically the same views of the transitional processes, the difference in their national contexts led them to diverge as they developed their interpretations.

A key milestone in the reconstruction of the Tupamaros occurred in 1985. Ten days after Uruguay's return to democracy, a law granted an amnesty to prisoners of conscience and commuted the sentences of those political prisoners who were implicated in violent crimes, in consideration of the inhumane conditions they had suffered during their incarceration. As a result, all political prisoners were set free and a favorable climate was ensured for the return of exiles, as they would not be prosecuted on charges connected with the past.[67] The Tupamaros' attempt at reorganizing began that very same day, which was celebrated as a day of rejoicing. Immediately after they were set free, the members of the old MLN-T leadership – who since 1972 had been held under hostage conditions, marked by constant abuses and complete isolation – gave a press conference in which they acknowledged the new stage the country was embarking on.

As spokesman, Eleuterio Fernández Huidobro recognized that they were witnessing a unique moment in the history of the country:

We believe that a stage of burgeoning democracy has opened up in our country. Democracy is a fact that is not to be found in votes. Nor is it to be found in the results of the elections. It is in the streets. Democracy in Uruguay, the democracy we have today, was forged by the Uruguayan people. And we understand that you would have to be blind not to see that reality, we would have to be blind not to see it; it has to be respected because it is an order of the people. So we are going to abide that order of the people.... It is not a decrepit democracy like that of 1972 and 1971, in which the forces of reaction were trampling the people. A democracy with militarized workers and imprisoned comrades. This democracy is different, it is a democracy in which, as you can see, prisons disappear.[68]

They also issued a public document declaring that they would respect the law and would enter a process of internal discussions among the members released from prison, those returning from exile, those who had survived in the country, and the young people who had joined the movement. Raúl Sendic, the organization's historical leader, did not participate in the press conference as he had difficulty talking due to a bullet wound on his face that had remained untreated since he was shot in 1972. He sent a letter apologizing for not being present and backing the concepts raised at the conference. In that letter he also anticipated a program that basically defended democracy and proposed a constitutional reform based on non-payment of the foreign debt contracted during the dictatorship, an agrarian reform for establishments larger than 2,500 hectares, and nationalization of the banks.[69]

After the initial idyllic moment in which hundreds of Tupamaro militants reunited, problems began to arise in the movement's reorganization. The distances between those who had been exiled in different places, those who had been in prison, and those who had remained in the country began to be felt. For almost a decade, numerous groups throughout the world, even inside various prisons and in the country, had developed different political interpretations of the defeat of the MLN-T, as well as of the events leading up to the process of democratization.

Astrid Arraras, a political scientist who studied this process of reorganization, identifies at least four groups in1985: the Tendencia Proletaria (Proletarian Tendency) group formed in Argentina in 1974 during the exchanges with the ERP; the Movimiento 26 de Marzo (March 26 Movement) group in Uruguay, connected with militants who regrouped during the transition; the historical leaders, who had remained in prison and were marked by abuse and severe isolation; and various groupings of exiles. The meeting of these groups sparked highly intense debates. Several of these debates had to do with the issue of self-criticism and referred back to old disagreements dating from the 1970s, disagreements which had not been openly expressed due to the persecution under the dictatorship. The diverse experiences of the exiled militants also affected how the old issues of the revolutionary aims and the new issues of democracy were analyzed.[70]

However, despite disagreements, the organization gradually regrouped and the Tupamaros began to carry out social actions that had an impact at the popular level. In the first years, in certain districts of Montevideo the organization's influence grew as it focused on social work and engaged in a direct dialog with the people through open meetings known as *mateadas* (named for the popular Uruguayan infusion, *mate*, shared at these sessions), in which MLN-T leaders gathered in neighborhood plazas to talk with anyone wishing to meet the historical leaders who had been imprisoned for years. The Tupamaros were also particularly concerned with communications, launching their weekly publication *Mate Amargo*, where in a renewed style they engaged in a political journalism that sought to appeal to popular sectors, a radio station that achieved a significant audience, and a publishing house, Tupac Amaru Ediciones, where Fernández Huidobro published a series of testimonial and historical books that became bestsellers in the 1980s.[71]

Moreover, although initially the Tupamaros defined themselves as social activists, they would gradually move closer to the Frente Amplio, the left-wing coalition toward which they had shown their sympathy since its creation in 1971 but which they had never officially joined. In the new state of affairs imposed by legal political life, joining the Frente Amplio and aligning themselves with certain groups in the coalition seemed inevitable.

Another issue, in which the Tupamaros began to have an active role, had to do with the mobilization in defense of human rights. In December 1986, amidst rumors of a military coup, sectors of the governing Colorado Party and of the National Party voted in parliament to pass Law 15,848 on the Expiry of the Punitive Claims of the State (or Expiry Act). The aim of this law was to stop any possible court actions against military personnel implicated in crimes against humanity committed during the dictatorship. The Tupamaros were the first to pose the need to call for a referendum to repeal the law.[72]

In January 1989, at the time of the events at La Tablada, Uruguay was preparing to hold the referendum to repeal the Expiry Act, after the social movement organized to call the referendum succeeded in gathering signatures representing twenty-five percent of eligible voters, as required by the constitution. In that context the MLN-T issued a statement underlining the importance that the cause of human rights had for the organization:

Here we are waging the historical battle of the referendum. The eyes of the world will be on us, to see what our people decide on April 16. For the first time ever in the Southern Cone and perhaps in the entire continent, the issue of human rights violations and the punishing of such crimes, how the military problem can be dealt with under a controlled democracy, and the definition regarding what kind of democracy we want will be determined by popular decision. This decision was made possible because the people themselves have secured it against all odds and not obtained it as a generous gift from anyone.[73]

Human rights had achieved a certain centrality and were re-conceptualized in terms of a battle against the remnants of power that the military still retained from its hold during the dictatorship. The issue was linked to the defense of the nascent democracy which, from the perspective of the MLN-T, had been achieved as a result of popular struggle. This did not entail a complete break from the tradition of armed struggle and the conspiratorial practices of the 1970s. In their discussion of the events of La Tablada, Tupamaro leaders stressed that they too could take up arms again if the threat of a dictatorship arose. Thus, in the context of the coming referendum and with the risk of a military reaction, the organization devised contingent military plans and security operations.

According to a testimonial biography of one of the historical leaders, Jorge Zabalza, who showed a greater inclination to maintaining the organization's conspiratorial practices and resisted the political adaptation process that would unfold in the 1990s, a group was formed within the MLN-T, known as the Seventeen, which gathered most of the historical leaders outside the organization's official governing bodies with the aim of determining its international relations with the revolutionary movement, seeking forms of financing for the organization's new communication projects, and discussing security measures to adopt in the event of military threats. Zabalza reveals that the efforts to find forms of financing included contacts with Gorriarán Merlo and the Argentine MTP, ETA, and Peru's MRTA. In that book he also mentions certain robberies committed in Uruguay by Tupamaro militants with the purpose of obtaining funds for the organization.[74]

All of this shows how the tension between political and military aims still existed within the MLN-T. Although initially the more political side of the organization had prevailed, the conflict was still latent. This tension was aggravated in the 1990s. The year 1989 was marked by a series of events that had a negative impact on the Uruguayan Left. The end of the Cold War, with the ensuing crisis of communism, affected even those who, like the Tupamaros, did not see themselves as part of that world but who did recognize the difficulties of the globalized new world order of the post Cold War era. Also, the defeat of the FSLN at the polls had negative repercussions for the Tupamaros, who had become involved in the Nicaraguan experience during the revolution, maintained close ties with that organization, and saw it as a model to follow.[75] Lastly, in April of that year two local events shook the MLN-T. The outcome of the referendum, which upheld the Expiry Act with fifty-seven percent of the votes, was a huge blow, and marked the end of a cycle of the social movement that had gradually been built during the process of democratization, and that as a result retreated after this defeat. The death of Raúl Sendic, the top Tupamaro leader, only twelve days after that defeat exacerbated the feelings of loss and despondency. These events, together with the neoliberal reforms of the new democratic government of the National Party, with the election of Luis Alberto Lacalle in 1990, ushered in a different period, that seemed to close the cycle of the popular anti-dictatorship movement built during the transition.

In that context, of contraction of social mobilization and the emergence of a neoliberal agenda, the Fifth Convention of the MLN-T, held in 1991, leaned toward the views within the organization that were closer to the imaginary of armed struggle. Discussions at the convention confronted those who posed the need to build a political and military organization (Organización Político Militar, or OPM), which would operate legally but would be prepared for future scenarios of armed violence, against those who stressed the need to focus on election-based politics and social mobilization. The defenders of the OPM made a negative assessment of the economy, which in their view would lead to an increased social response and state repression, with predictable authoritarian reactions from the state. On the other side were those who while sharing certain elements of that diagnosis insisted on the need to further the work on the political front and who, in particular, wanted to move away from the conspiratorial and militarist practices of the past. The overwhelming triumph of the former youth-led sectors and some leaders connected with the media projects to distance themselves from the organization. However, internal discussions continued. Although the call to build an OPM was the majority position, it had different meanings for the various groups of militants that supported it. For some it entailed a path for generating the conditions to take up arms again, while for others it was a sort of safeguard against possible authoritarian returns.[76]

The year 1989 also brought positive developments for the Left. For the first time ever, the Frente Amplio won the municipal elections of Montevideo, the country's capital. The growth of the coalition showed that with each new election it was closer to the possibility of successfully disputing the national government. That year the MLN-T had formally become part of the Frente Amplio and joined other radical sectors of the Left in a sub-coalition known as Movimiento de Participación Popular (Popular Participation Movement, or MPP). The Tupamaro leaders refused to participate in the lists of candidates for parliament but enthusiastically supported the initiative.[77]

After the Fifth Convention in 1992 the debate on what the organization's approach to the electoral process should be continued and it became more heated as a result of an incident that, according to political scientist Adolfo Garcé, divided once and for all those who tried to keep an insurrection imaginary alive from those who were more in favor of participating in elections. Two months before national elections were to be held in 1995, a series of clashes between demonstrators and police forces in the vicinity of the Filtro Hospital caused a stir within the MLN-T. The clashes occurred when the police tried to remove three Spanish nationals who were accused of being members of ETA and were holding a hunger strike to protest their extradition to Spain. Several social and political organizations had convened a demonstration outside the hospital to call for asylum for the Spanish nationals and to oppose their removal from the hospital. When the police arrived to take them to the airport, a number of demonstrators tried to stop the police from leaving the hospital. From its radio station, the MLN-T urged demonstrators to prevent the removal of the Basque prisoners. Some demonstrators were particularly defiant, engaging in a number of actions that were uncommon for the marches staged during the transition, which had mostly been peaceful. For their part, the police responded with clearly excessive force, firing their weapons directly at the demonstrators. The repression left two dead and approximately eighty wounded. The MLN-T's radio station was shut down, accused of inciting the clashes.

The Filtro episode, or "massacre" as it would be known, was an issue of debate in the election campaign and within the Left. The National and Colorado Parties used it to brandish again the old stigmas of the violent nature of the Left, in line with the national security discourses of past decades. In the Left, many organizations within the Frente Amplio questioned the role of the Tupamaros in that incident and the failure to reflect on how that event would be used against the Left in the election campaign. The Frente Amplio candidate Tabaré Vázquez lost by only 1.8 percent of the votes. Several sectors of the Left were convinced that they lost the elections because of the Filtro episode.[78]

Within the MLN-T, the Filtro episode and the elections that year exacerbated the conflict between those who presaged scenarios of greater repression, and demanded the consolidation of a political and military organization that would contribute to an insurrectional strategy, on the one hand; and, those who focused on elections and had their hopes pinned on the electoral growth of the Frente Amplio, on the other. For both, 1994 had confirmed their intuitions. In the case of the former, the Filtro massacre was a rehearsal of what was to come, of the way in which the dominant sectors would act in reaction to rising social mobilization. For the latter, what that year revealed was that a victory of the Left at the polls was a real possibility in the medium term.

Moreover, for this second group there was a development that would have major consequences in the coming years. Although the Tupamaros participated in the MPP and backed its candidates, they had consistently refused to present the historical leaders of the MLN-T as candidates for legislative seats. In 1994, for the first time José Mujica ran for a seat in the lower chamber of parliament as an MPP candidate. His participation in parliament would have major implications for both his future and the future of his organization. During his term in parliament he made a significant public impact. Various aspects of his work as legislator were highly valued and he stood out for his unique style. He went to work on a Vespa motorcycle and dressed informally, in what was not a demagogic gimmick, but an attempt to retain certain authenticity that politics, both to the right and left, seemed to distort. He also spoke in a clear, simple manner, with a discourse that was not overly ideological but was based on certain leftist principles and backed by much preparation that enabled him to give an opinion on the range of topics touched on by legislative activity. Lastly, his non-confrontational and conciliatory tone in legislative debates earned him the sympathy of some politicians from the traditional parties.[79]

Although some aspects of this success had to do with his charismatic personality, it was also linked to the historical experience he represented. Certain ideas and values of the 1960s were translated in his work as legislator. Aspects of the militant life – self-sacrifice, giving oneself entirely to the cause, militant ethics – were reinterpreted in the context of the 1990s in this national representative, who donated a large part of his salary, had no material interests dictating his actions, and engaged with common people in a direct way. With respect to his guerrilla past, Mujica expressed no regrets, although he did appear self-critical regarding various actions or ways of thinking of that decade.

This discursive strategy enabled him to open up to more moderate political agendas without sacrificing the political capital inherited from his armed struggle experience. Moreover, his fighting life as a guerrilla and his twelve years as victim of state abuses and isolation while he was held hostage by the dictatorship afforded him a symbolic power of sorts that he was able to capitalize on in the elections. He emerged as a figure that, after such an experience, would not yield to any form of pressure. In that halo of respect that formed around him it was evident that revolutionary action still had a significant appeal but was translated in other ways. All of that political capital paved the way for his leadership within the Left, which culminated with him becoming president of Uruguay in 2010.

Conclusion

In all the groups there was a tension between the past of the 1970s and the present of the 1980s. For some this entailed abandoning armed struggle for the time being, while for others it meant rethinking the ways in which armed struggle would be developed in a new context.

After the Malvinas/Falklands War, the surviving Argentine ERP members did not believe that conditions were ripe for resuming armed struggle and, therefore, focused on building a political movement, that was later embodied in the MTP and which represented the new historical moment. As the Tablada episode showed, for some the decision to abandon armed struggle was only temporary. In Uruguay's case, the defeated MLN-T, which began reorganizing in 1985, also understood that conditions were not ripe for taking up arms again. However, as seen earlier in this chapter, there were some militants who were particularly concerned with resuming that strategy.

The Chilean case was somewhat different. The decade began with the MIR's Operation Return. While the MIR was not without internal conflicts, such divisions had not led to the levels of fragmentation that affected the organizations in Argentina or Uruguay. The MIR was also the only organization that received the support from Cuba to carry out its project. Lastly, the scenario of Chile's transition, marked by Pinochet's victory in the 1980 plebiscite, left the country's political forces with much less margin for political negotiation and encouraged a radicalization among other sectors of the Left, including the influential Chilean Communist Party, which also backed the idea of developing an armed strategy through the FPMR. All of this led to the emergence of a strong social movement between 1983 and 1986, where the insurrectionist ideas developed by the MIR and by the FPMR were somewhat appealing. The MIR renewed the military strategy it implemented in the 1970s, with the aim of incorporating the social mobilization. After the movement began to wane in 1986 due to the increasing political repression and the decision of certain sectors of the Left to negotiate, the MIR had to dramatically face the choice of taking a political path or resuming a military path, as was expressed by the factions that emerged at that moment.

In short, for all of these groups the tension between revolutionary political culture inherited from the past and social struggle linked to the social and political movements of the transition was the central element of this period. The experience of the Nicaraguan Revolution, as explained by the MIR's open letter, helped build a bridge between the old and the new. It was a revolution forged by militants who had come together during the armed struggle of the 1970s, to whom several Southern Cone militants were close as a result of their involvement in that process, and who in the early 1980s had an agenda with renovation-related issues, such as democratic pluralism, forms of mixed economy, and the relationship with social movements.

Abandoning conspiratorial practices and armed struggle was in no case a decision brought on by a radical ideological transformation; rather, it was the result of an assessment of the historical conditions that these actors were facing. For some it was the realization that the development of the armed apparatuses of the terrorist states left guerrilla strategies little room to maneuver. For others it had to do with the awareness that social movements were being more effective in carrying out their protest repertoires. Several practices were nonetheless maintained. This chapter shows various accounts of activities connected with regional solidarity and financing networks that illegally raised funds for some projects carried out by militants who belonged to these organizations but were working outside of them.[80]

The way in which the tension between revolutionary political culture and political strategies of the 1980s was resolved depended on the feasibility and continuity of these political projects. The key to success lay in achieving some sort of balance in which certain aspects connected with that political culture, such as the militant ethics of the 1970s associated with self-sacrifice, giving oneself to the cause, and egalitarian notions, coexisted with a pragmatic and critical acceptance of the rules of democracy and the market. The most successful experience appears to be that of the MLN-T, with one of its leaders, José Mujica Cordano, securing the highest elected office in the country in 2010 and becoming one of the most popular presidents in the history of Uruguay.

Generally speaking, successfully overcoming that tension was not only due to the ability of the actors involved, but also to the structure of political opportunities that enabled the political process of each transition. In her insightful study, Vania Markarian showed how certain Uruguayan leftist militants gradually incorporated the human rights discourse developed internationally, as that language allowed them to effectively combat the dictatorship. Building on Nancy Bermeo's notion of "political learning," Astrid Arraras proposes something similar when she analyzes the Tupamaros' incorporation into Uruguay's political system. According to both approaches, it was not a liberalist ideological illumination that led them to embrace certain political principles, but rather the realization that those strategies would allow them to move closer to attaining certain political objectives. What are the key aspects that made this possible in Uruguay?

The answer goes beyond the scope of this chapter, but, allowing for differences in more general aspects such as national political cultures and the degree of stability of each political system, there is a very specific aspect that can be observed in comparative terms. The amnesty and exile return policies can provide clues for understanding which strategies were most successful. In the cases of Chile and Argentina there were policies that hindered the integration of the sectors that had engaged in armed struggle in the 1970s. Chile's case was particularly complex because these groups continued to be active in the 1980s. In Argentina and Uruguay, all armed groups had been disarmed by the time these countries returned to democracy.

Argentina had a very active role with respect to disappeared militants, but the situation was somewhat more complicated when it came to the living. Political prisoners were not freed en masse, and the orders for the arrest of the Montonero and ERP leaders impacted the exile community. To a certain extent this made reorganizing efforts difficult. For example, the MTP, whose main leader acted from the shadows due to an order for his arrest from Argentina's courts, reveals how the possibilities for integration in the new democratic climate were not just determined by the ideological mindsets that these militants brought from the 1970s, but also had to do with the political opportunities offered by each transition.

In contrast to what happened in Argentina, in Uruguay all political prisoners were freed, which made those who had taken up arms in the past more inclined to believe in the feasibility of operating under the new state of affairs. While there were also sectors that favored a more militarist approach, they failed to take their proposals further, unlike what occurred in Argentina. Although the case of Brazil is not discussed in this chapter, it should be mentioned here as it also appears to support the hypothesis that political amnesties enabled a greater integration of armed leftist groups into the new democracies. The 1979 amnesty law that opened the process of democratization in Brazil, the liberation of political prisoners, and the return of exiles to the country helped dissipate the doubts of those who were still considering the possibility of taking up arms again. Moreover, many of the actors involved in armed struggle joined the Partido dos Trabalhadores (Workers' Party, or PT), successfully competing in elections, which led to former armed militant Dilma Rousseff being elected president in 2010 and reelected for a second term in 2014.

In any case, regardless of the successes and failures of each of these groups, the fact is that in the first years of the twenty-first century their legacy proved effective and appears to have played a major role in the wave of progressive governments that emerged in the Southern Cone. In the second decade of the century, significant sectors of the governing parties of Argentina, Bolivia, Brazil, and Uruguay admit to having some kind of connection to this armed struggle experience.

The denunciations by the human rights movements helped break down the stigmatization of these left-wing organizations that had prevailed during the authoritarian regimes. As Gilda Zwerman and Patricia Steinhoff have argued in their studies on New Left activists in the United States and Japan, state actions have long-term effects, and what might initially be seen as a victory may be inverted in the long run if the state lacks sufficient legitimacy to sustain its actions.[81] The struggles for truth and justice, and against the legacies of authoritarian states, gave rise to questions that had been relatively silenced during the transitions to democracy. In the framework of these struggles, different left-wing political experiences of the 1970s, both armed and legal, were vindicated. In the case of armed groups, this entailed a resignification that minimized aspects connected

Figure 5.a. "No vai ter golpe:" stencil denouncing the coup d'etat against Dilma Rouseff. The image is based on a picture taken by the Brazilian dictatorship when Rouseff was captured, accused of being part of a guerrilla organization.

with violent practices and highlighted the supposed ethical integrity of the armed organizations and the final goals that guided their projects. In the current circumstances, then, the notions of defeat and victory discussed throughout this study tend to be relativized. The involvement of some militants from that period in politics today, as well as the sympathy of some sectors of the voting public prompt a reassessment of these political experiences.

Notes

1 MIR, "Carta Pública del MIR. Unidos avancemos en la guerra popular a la dictadura," *Correo de la Resistencia. Special edition. no. 9*, February 1981, p.18.
2 See Pascale Bonnefoy, Claudio Perez, and Angel Spotorro, *Internacionalistas: chilenos en la Revolución Popular Sandinista* (Santiago de Chile: Brigada 30 Aniversario de la Revolucion Popular Sandinista, 2008); Enrique Haroldo Gorriarán, *Memorias de*

Enrique Gorriarán Merlo: de los setenta a La Tablada (Buenos Aires: Planeta, 2003); Víctor Estradet, *Memorias del Negro Pedro: Tupamaros en la revolución sandinista* (Montevideo, Uruguay: Editorial Fin de Siglo, 2013).

3 For the impact of the emergence of the discourse of human rights in the global order, see Samuel Moyn, *The Last Utopia, Human Rights in History* (Cambridge: Harvard University Press, 2010), and Barbara J. Keys, *Reclaiming American Virtue, the Human Rights Revolution of the 1970s* (Cambridge: Harvard University Press, 2014). To understand the impact of human rights discourse in Latin America, see Vania Markarian, *Left in Transformation* (New York: Routledge, 2005), James Green, *We Cannot Remain Silent: Opposition to the Brazilian Military Dictatorship in the United States* (Durham, NC: Duke University Press, 2010), and Kathryin Sikkink, *The Justice Cascade: How Human Rights Prosecutions Are Changing World Politics* (New York: W.W. Norton & Co., 2011).

4 Two texts that show Gramsci's influence in the 1980s are: José Aricó, *La cola del diablo. Itinerario de Gramsci en América Latina* (Buenos Aires, PuntoSur Editores: 1988), and Ernesto Laclau and Chantal Mouffe, *Hegemonía y estrategia socialista. Hacia una radicalización de la democracia* (Madrid, Siglo XXI, 1987).

5 On the Chilean case, see: Katherine Hite, *When the Romance Ended: Leaders of the Chilean Left* (New York: Columbia University Press, 2000), and Cristina Moyano Barahona, *El MAPU durante la dictadura: saberes y prácticas políticas para una microhistoria de la renovación socialista en Chile, 1973–1989* (Chile: Ediciones Universidad Alberto Hurtado, 2010). On Argentina, see Cecilia Lesgart, *Usos de la transición a la democracia: ensayo, ciencia y política en la década del '80* (Rosario, Argentina: Homo Sapiens Ediciones, 2003).

6 See Fernando Calderón G and Elizabeth Jelin, *Clases y movimientos sociales en América Latina: perspectivas y realidades* (Buenos Aires: Centro de Estudios de Estado y Sociedad, 1987).

7 On Operation Return, see Julio Pinto and Sebastian Leiva "Capítulo II. Punto de quiebre: El MIR en los ochenta," in Verónica Valdivia et al., *Su revolución contra nuestra revolución. La pugna marxista-gremialista en los ochenta. Vol. II* (Santiago, Chile: LOM Ediciones, 2008), and Igor Goicovic, *Movimiento de Izquierda Revolucionaria* (Concepción, Chile: Equipo Editorial, 2012). For accounts from this period, see Patricio Rivas, *Un largo setiembre* (Santiago, Chile: LOM Ediciones, 2007), and Comité Memoria Neltume, *Guerrilla en Neltume. Una historia de lucha y resistencia en el sur chileno* (Santiago, Chile: LOM Ediciones, 2003).

8 For information on Plan 78, see endnote 2 and interview by the author with Muñoz, Torres, and Zarriscueta. See MIR press *El correo de la resistencia* and *El Rebelde en la clandestinidad*.

9 See Rolando Alvarez, "'Aún tenemos patria, ciudadados'. El partido comunista de Chile y la salida no pactada de la dictadura (1980–1988)," in Valdivia et al., *Su revolución contra nuestra revolución. Vol. II*, 22–42.

10 Rivas, *Chile, un largo septiembre*, 189–90.

11 Rivas, pp. 164–166. Hernan Vidal, *El Movimiento de la Izquierda Revolucionaria (MIR) de Chile en la justicia transicional* (Hernan Vidal, 2013) http://ideologiesandliterature.org/VIDAL-%20Justicia%20Transicional%20III.pdf. 80–137; interviews with Muñoz, Zarricueta, and Pascal Allende conducted by the author. On the Chilean Communist Party, see: Rolando Alvarez, "'Aún tenemos patria, ciudadados'," in Valdivia et al., *Su revolución contra nuestra revolución. Vol. II*, 22–42; and Claudio Pérez Silva, "De la guerra contra Somoza a la guerra contra Pinochet. La experiencia internacionalista revolucionaria en Nicaragua y la construcción de la Fuerza Militar Propia del Partido Comunista de Chile," in Pablo Pozzi and Claudio Pérez (ed.), *Historia oral e historia política. Izquierda y lucha armada en América Latina, 1960–1990* (Santiago: Lom Ediciones, 2012).

12 In *Correo de la Resistencia*. October 1979, no. 8, p. 13.

13 Interview with Zarricueta. On Chilean participation in the FSLN's Southern Front, see Pascale Bonnefoy Miralles, Claudio Perez, and Angel Spotorno. *Internacionalistas. Chilenos en la Revolución Popular Sandinista. Second Expanded Edition* (Santiago, Chile: Editorial Latinoamericana, 2009), 10–16.

14 Pinto and Leiva, 91.

15 Ascanio Cavallo, Manuel Salazar, and Oscar Sepúlveda. *La historia oculta del regimen militar* (Santiago: Grijalbo, 1997), 257–64, 295–303.

16 For an official version on Neltume from the MIR, see "Una experiencia guerrillera," in *El rebelde*, no. 180, November 1981. See also Comité, *Guerrilla en Neltume.*

17 Leiva and Pintos, 106–7.

18 Steve J. Stern, *Battling for Hearts and Minds: Memory Struggles in Pinochet's Chile, 1973–1988* (Durham: Duke University Press, 2006), 222.

19 Rivas, 183.

20 See Rivas, 145–98. Interview with Torres.

21 *Boletín Miguel Enríquez*, No. 3, February 1980, 20.

22 On CODEPU's activities, see Patricio Orellana; Elizabeth Q Hutchison. *El movimiento de derechos humanos en Chile, 1973–1990* (Santiago de Chile: Centro de Estudios Políticos Latinoamericanos Simón Bolívar, 1991), 34–6.

23 See Hernan Aguiló. "Inicio de un balance autocrítico de mi militancia revolucionaria," 2005 in Archivochile.com

24 "Contra la dictadura y por la liberación popular," *Comunicado del IV Congreso del MIR (Politico)*, 1988 in Archivochile.com.

25 "Única vía a la democracia," *El Combatiente. Periódico oficial de la Comisión Militar*, no. 1 March 1988, 2.

26 For descriptions of the political fragmentation, see Pinto, Leiva, 125–36, and Goicovic, 87–98.

27 Steve J. Stern, *Reckoning with Pinochet: the memory question in democratic Chile, 1989–2006* (Durham, NC: Duke University Press, 2010), 36–7; Brian Loveman and Elizabeth Lira, *Las ardientes cenizas del olvido: vía chilena de reconciliación política 1932–1994* (Santiago: LOM Ediciones: DIBAM, 2000), 490–539.

28 See CODEPU, Informe de Derechos Humanos, 1990–2000 (Santiago: LOM, 2001), chap. II; Igor Goicovic, "Transición y violencia política en Chile (1988–1994)," in *Ayer. Revista de Historia Contemporánea* (Madrid, 2010) 79; Pedro Rosas, *Rebeldía, subversión y prisión política* (Santiago: LOM, 2004), Chapter IV.

29 See, for example, Carmen Castillo, *Calle Santa Fé* (2007), and Macarena Aguiló, *El edificio de los chilenos* (2010). For written testimonial accounts, see: Carmen Castillo, *Un día de octubre en Santiago* (Mexico: Ediciones Era, 1982); Guillermo Rodríguez, *Hacia el final de la partida* (Santiago: LOM Ediciones, 2007); Rivas, *Chile, un largo septiembre.*

30 For example, Mario Garcé, Julio Pinto, Gabriel Salazar, and Igor Gocovich.

31 There are MIR groups with influence in the memorial sites established in various former detention and torture centers, including Villa Grimaldi, Londres 38, and the José Domingo Cañas Memorial. See Ministerio del Interior, "Programa de Derechos Humanos," *Geografia de la Memoria* (Santiago, Chile: Ministerio del Interior, 2010).

32 For a reflection on the paths taken by the various groups from the perspectives of the participants, see: Julio Santucho, *Los últimos guevaristas: la guerilla marxista en la Argentina* (Buenos Aires: Vergara, Grupo Zeta: Ediciones B Argentina, 2004), chapter 3; Daniel de Santis, *La Historia del PRT-ERP por sus protagonistas* (Temperley: Estación Finlandia, 2010), chapter 28. See interviews with Daniel de Santis (Archivo oral, Memoria Abierta), and interview with Enrique Gorriarán Merlo and Luis Mattini (Archivo de Historia Oral, Instituto Gino Germani, UBA). For a historical approach, see: Vera Carnovale,

"De *Entre Todos* a La Tablada. Redefiniciones y permanencias del ideario setentista," in *PolHis*, year 6, no. 12, second semester, 2013; Claudia Hilb, "La tablada: el último acto de la guerrilla setentista, in Claudia Hilb, *Usos del Pasado. Qué hacemos hoy con los setenta* (Argentina: Siglo XXI, 2013).

33 See Samuel Blixen, *Conversaciones con Gorriarán Merlo* (Buenos Aires: Editorial Contrapunto, 1988), 266; Claribel Alegría and D. J. Flakoll, *Death of Somoza* (Willimantic, CT: Curbstone Press, 1996). With respect to the coordination between Central American militaries and the Argentine army, see Ariel Armory, *Argentina, the United States, and the anti-communist crusade in Central America, 1977–1984* (Athens: Ohio University Center for International Studies, 1997).

34 See Julio Santucho, *Los últimos guevaristas*, 256–9, and Enrique Gorriarán Merlo, Enrique Gorriarán Merlo, *Memorias de Enrique Gorriarán Merlo: de los sesenta a La Tablada*.(Argentina: Planeta, 2003).

35 De Santis, *La historia del PRT-ERP*, 674.

36 Interview with Enrique Gorriarán Merlo (IGG, UBA), session 3, and Enrique Gorriarán Merlo, *Memorias de Enrique Gorriarán Merlo*.

37 See the *Entre Todos* collection. The subtitle was maintained from the first issue of November 1984 to the 25th issue, printed in February 1987. After that the reference to the various groups was removed and only the phrase "Those of Us Who Want Liberation" was left.

38 Felipe Celesia and Pablo Waisberg, *La Tablada. A vencer o morir. La última batalla de la guerrilla argentina* (Buenos Aires: Aguilar, 2013) 103–5, 145–56.

39 Ibid.

40 To understand the strategy of the government and its context, see: Claudia Feld and Marina Franco, *Democracia: hora cero. Actores, políticas y debates en los inicios de la posdictadura* (Buenos Aires: Fondo de Cultura Económico, 2015); Marcos Novaro and Vicente Palermo, *La dictadura militar, 1976–1983: del golpe de estado a la restauración democrática* (Buenos Aires: Paidós, 2003).

41 See Decree 157/1983.

42 See: Emilio Crenzel, *La historia política del Nunca más: la memoria de las desapariciones en la Argentina* (Buenos Aires, Argentina: Siglo Veintiuno Editores, 2008) 57–63; and Marina Franco, "La 'teoría de los dos demonios' en la primera etapa de la posdictadura," in Feld and Franco, *Democracia hora cero*.

43 Santiago Garaño and Werner Pertot, *Detenidos-aparecidos: presas y presos políticos desde Trelew a la dictadura* (Buenos Aires: Editorial Biblos, 2007), 293.

44 Soledad Lastra, *Los retornos del exilio en Argentina y Uruguay. Una historia comparada de las políticas y tensiones en la recepción y asistencia en las posdictaduras (1983–1989)*. PhD dissertation in History, Facultad de Humanidades y Ciencias de la Educación (UNLP), La Plata, March 2014.

45 Celesia and Waisberg, *La Tablada*, 119; Samuel Blixen, *Sendic* (Montevideo, Trilce, 2000), 328.

46 "Una nueva propuesta política. Todos por la Patria," *Entre Todos*, no. 17, May 1986, 20–1.

47 Samuel Blixen, *Conversaciones con Gorriarán Merlo: treinta años de lucha popular* (Buenos Aires: Editorial Contrapunto, 1988), 355.

48 See "La democracia amenazada," *Entre Todos*, no. 28, 1st fortnight, June 1987, 10–11.

49 Celesia and Waisberg, *La Tablada*, 212–14.

50 MTP, "Los militares avanzan. Que hacemos?"

51 See Gorriarán Merlo, *Memorias*, and oral interview with Gorriarán Merlo, AHO IGG, UBA. Session 4.

52 See Ibid.

53 "Anunció Alfonsín medidas para la lucha contra la subversión. Afirmó que retorna la guerrilla de ultraizquierda," *Clarín*, January 25, 1989, 2–13; "Integran las Fuerzas Armadas el Consejo de la Nación," *Clarín*, January 26, 1989, 4.

54 By way of example, see the coverage in the magazine *El Porteño*, February 1989, in paticular, the article by Eduardo Blaustein, "Un alfiler menos," page 13, or by Eduardo Aliverti, "Un comando de maniaticos," page 17.

55 Federico Lorenz, "¿De quién es el 24 de marzo? Las luchas por la memoria del golpe de 1976," in Elizabeth Jelin (coord.), *Las Conmemoraciones: las disputas en las fechas "infelices"* (Buenos Aires: Siglo XXI de España Editores, 2002), 79–80.

56 See Hilb, "La Tablada: el último acto de la guerrilla setentista," Celesia and Waisberg, *La Tablada*.

57 Lorenz, "¿De quién es el 24 de marzo?," 87–90.

58 See, for example: Eduardo Anguita and Martín Caparrós, *La voluntad: una historia de la militancia revolucionaria en la Argentina* 3 tomos (Barcelona; Buenos Aires: Grupo Editorial Norma, 1998); and Marta Diana, *Mujeres guerrilleras: la militancia de los setenta en el testimonio de sus protagonistas femeninas* (Buenos Aires: Planeta, 1996).

59 Pablo René Belzagui, Héctor Jouvé, and Oscar del Barco, *No matar: sobre la responsabilidad* (Córdoba, Argentina: Ediciones del Cíclope: Universidad Nacional de Córdoba, 2007).

60 See: Nicolas Prividera, *M* (2007); Albertina Carri, *Los rubios* (2003); and María Inés Roque, *Papa Iván* (2004). For an analysis of some of these testimonial and documentary productions, see Alejandra Oberti and Roberto Pittaluga, *Memorias en montaje. Escrituras de la militancia y pensamientos sobre la historia* (Buenos Aires: El cielo por asalto, 2006).

61 See: Néstor Carlos Kirchner, *Prólogo*, http://anamariaponce.blogspot.com.ar/; and Federico Lorenz and Peter Winn, "Las memorias de la violencia política y la dictadura militar en la Argentina: un recorrido en el año del Bicentenario," in Peter Winn et al., *No hay mañana sin ayer. Batallas por la memoria histórica en el cono sur* (Santiago de Chile: LOM, 2014), pp. 42–3.

62 Secretaría de Derechos Humanos, Comisión Nacional sobre la Desparación de Personas (CONADEP), *Nunca más: Informe de la Comisión Nacional sobre la Desaparación de Personas.* (Buenos Aires: Ed. Eudeba, 2006), 8.

63 MLN-T, "El documento del MLNT," *Brecha*, February 3, 1989.

64 "Los ecos de la Tablada: Polémica en la izquierda local," *Búsqueda*, February 9, 1989, 4.

65 "Raul Sendic: en Argentina puede haber nuevas acciones armadas para resistir una sublevación castrense," *Búsqueda*, February 2, 1989, 5.

66 Federico Leicht, *Cero a la izquierda: una biografía de Jorge Zabalza* (Montevideo, Uruguay: Letraeñe Ediciones, 2007), 168–9.

67 María Eugenia Allier, *Batallas por la memoria* (Montevideo: Trilce, 2010), 31–46.

68 "Conferencia del MLN," *Las Bases*, March 11, 1985.

69 Ibid.

70 Astrid Arraras, *Armed Struggle, Political Learning and Participation in Democracy: the Case of the Tupamaros* (PhD dissertation, Princeton University, January, 1999).

71 See: Eleuterio Fernandez Huidobro, *Historia de los tupamaros*, three volumes (Montevideo: TAE, Tupac Amaru Editores, 1986–1988); and Mauricio Rosencof and Eleuterio Fernández Huidobro, *Memorias del calabozo* (Montevideo: Tae, 1988).

72 Centro Uruguay Independiente (1987), *Documentos, documento político n. 2: Referéndum* (Montevideo: CUI, 1987), 65.

73 "Editorial. El momento exige grandeza," *Mate Amargo*, February 2, 1989.

74 Leicht, *Cero a la izquierda*, 163, 173–95.

75 See Victor Estradel, *Memorias del Negro Pedro. Tupamaros en la revolución sandinista* (Montevideo: Ediciones Fin de Siglo, 2013).

76 For an overview of that process, see MLN-T, *Resoluciones de la V Convención Nacional. Junio-Julio 1990.* For an analysis of the conflict, see Adolfo Garcé, *Donde hubo fuego: el proceso de adaptación del MLN-Tupamaros a la legalidad y a la competencia electoral (1985–2004)* (Montevideo: Editorial Fin de Siglo, 2006), Chapter V.

77 Mario Mazzeo, *MPP: orígenes, ideas y protagonistas* (Montevideo, Uruguay: Ediciones Trilce, 2005).

78 Garcé, *Donde hubo fuego,* 130–1.

79 See, "El 'fenómeno Mujica'. La seducción de un intruso," *Brecha,* October 8, 1999.

80 In 1989, several people were arrested in Brazil for the kidnapping of businessman Abilio Diniz, including five Chileans, two Argentines, and one Brazilian. The militants later admitted that the operation was prepared in Managua and that it was meant to obtain funds for the MIR and other Latin American organizations. See "Reportaje exclusivo a los huelguistas de hambre de Brasil. 'Estamos dispuestos a llegar al fin'," *Página 12,* December 5, 1998, 19.

81 Gilda Zwerman and Patricia Steinhoff, "When Activists Ask for Trouble: State-Dissident Interactions and the New Left Cycle of Resistance in the United States and Japan," in Christian Davenport, Hank Johnston, and Carol Mueller (editors), *Repression and Mobilization* (Minneapolis: University of Minnesota Press, 2005).

Conclusion: Revolutionaries without Revolution

In early 2015, Brazilian president Dilma Rousseff and Uruguayan president José Mujica met in the Uruguayan department of Colonia for the inauguration of a small-scale symbol of what we must do, multiplying the presence of partner states in America, not with the aim of taking ownership of everything but in order to exercise sovereignty." While acknowledging that there was still much to be done in terms of Latin America integration, President Mujica recognized that it was a historic moment: "We are far from achieving integration, but for the first time ever the governments of Latin America are consulting each other, looking to each other, discussing, dialoguing, and agreeing. Never before has Latin America seen this political reality." Rousseff took up the ideas put forward by Mujica and went one step further. After recognizing Mujica's political values in his "struggle for democracy and human rights," President Rousseff looked back at the colonial and neocolonial past that had divided the two nations, and welcomed the new historic moment, as "today the technological barriers imposed by historical colonialism on our integration in the field of energy are being torn down." Rousseff closed her speech with a series of optimistic phrases regarding the dreams that were being realized in the new era that was dawning in Latin America.[1]

Mujica's statement was not strictly true. Integration efforts in Latin America dated back many years and had been linked to various currents of Latin American thought. From the developmentalism of the late 1950s to the military governments with their obsession for national security to the Southern Cone presidents of the neoliberal climate of the 1990s, they had all developed different forms of integration (whether economic, commercial, or security-related integration). What was new, in this period, was the fact that integration was being furthered by a political generation that had been removed from the state for many decades. Rousseff and Mujica are major representatives of that generation and of the legacy of their political actions and the effects that that legacy has had, and still has, in contemporary Latin American politics. They both participated in guerrilla organizations, championed a Latin American model of socialism, and were jailed and subjected to inhumane treatment. Under the democratic transition that followed the region's dictatorships, both Rousseff and Mujica joined political projects, furthered by leftist groups, that operated legally and which combined social mobilization with participation in elections, while maintaining a radical ideology agenda. In the last two decades they tempered their discourse, taking up again developmentalist traditions that posed the possibility of linking national capitalist development to the aim of improving the welfare of popular sectors. Throughout this period, both have retained a certain Latin Americanist profile that can be traced back to the Guevarista idea of a continental strategy for the revolution and can be found in the integration ideals that have been promoted in the last decade.[2]

Not every story of survivors of armed struggle was as successful as Rousseff's and Mujica's. The path taken by Enrique Gorriarán Merlo in the 1980s reveals other tragedies and a certain impossibility or slowness to adapt to the new political context of liberal democracy that began to set in during that decade in the region.

After the assault on La Tablada discussed in Chapter V, Gorriarán Merlo moved from country to country, relying on past contacts, until he was arrested in Mexico in 1995 and extradited to Argentina. In 2003, President Duhalde pardoned him. In 2006, Gorriarán Merlo launched a new legal party, which showed a certain capacity to adapt to the new political times, with the aim of bringing together all the forces that opposed neoliberalism and were in favor of Latin American integration. At that time he praised the human rights and foreign policies of the Kirchner administration but pointed out its economic and social limitations imposed by corporate pressures. As noted in the previous chapter, Gorriarán Merlo's last project was cut short when he died of a heart attack that same year.[3]

What has remained of that experience of the 1960s and 1970s in today's progressive politics is a heatedly debated issue that has sparked harsh arguments among the survivors of those decades. It is not the aim of this conclusion to settle that debate, but merely to note that the permanence of a common language and the sense of being part of a shared tradition would appear to reveal the persistence of several of the issues addressed in this book and which as a whole have been referred to as political culture. This presence of that political culture of the 1960s and 1970s is an example of what has been discussed in this study.

That legacy had its foundational moment in the 1960s. The three leaders mentioned above became politically active during that decade. Aged thirty-three in 1968, Mujica was among the older members of his organization (one of the viejos), whereas Gorriarán was twenty-seven and Rousseff only twenty-one. In that vertiginous decade, a difference of five years was significant. While Mujica and Gorriarán had been connected with populist and reformist traditions in the 1950s and in the early 1960s they were

already participating in the New Left, Rousseff first joined one of the political organization of the New Left, Politica Operaria (Polop), in 1964 when
she was just seventeen, the same year as the coup that toppled Goulart.

In this sense, the emergence of these militants in their countries' political life cannot be disconnected from the global sixties. In this region of the
world, however, the 1960s were more linked to the idea of the global anti-
imperialist revolution as put forward by Wallerstein than to the superficial language of dissent of the baby boomers suggested by Jeremi Suri.[4]
The Latin American 1960s were influenced, more by the language of anti-
colonialism and national liberation, than by the language of "imagination
to power" of the French May '68. In this region, the global sixties were
translated into events such as the Tricontinental Conference and the OLAS,
promoted by Cuba but called for by several sectors of Latin America's Left.
As Jeff Goodwin said, "many more radical, or "social," revolutions occurred
during the Cold War era than had occurred in all previous history prior
to the Second World War."[5] Odd Arne Westad, in his book The Global
Cold War, explains that the ideologies of the Cold War put certain areas
of the Third World in a semi-permanent state of war. This situation was
often associated with the local elites' conviction that violence was necessary to eradicate colonial legacies and morally justifiable to attain the
various visions of progress that the Cold War bipolar scheme proposed.[6] In
this sense, it may be argued that the revolutionary aspirations of Southern
Cone activists were the norm rather than the exception, at a moment in
time that was shaped by a permanent war that was waged primarily in
the Third World. It would have been surprising if the Southern Cone had
remained untouched by a war that was fought in three continents and that
spawned the greatest number of revolutions in the history of humanity.
This explains why some of these groups had to draw on early nineteenth-
century emancipators, such as José de San Martín or José Gervasio Artigas,
in order to establish historical connections with their countries' traditions
and take up again issues connected with independence and national sovereignty, which in South America, at least with respect to political independence, had been resolved in the previous century.

Nonetheless, in Latin America there were also aspects similar to the
countercultural practices of the central countries. In the 1950s and 1960s
the countries of the Southern Cone saw a significant growth in secondary school and university enrolment. These places of learning were one
of the main spaces of political socialization for this generation. A large
part of these students represented processes of upward social mobility that
were beginning to show their limitations in the context of the crisis of the
industrialist models. A feeling of discontent associated with the divorce
between the expectations and the realities of these middle classes, similar
to what was happening in the First World, influenced the commitments

and criticisms that arose among youth sectors.[7] Moreover, in this region of the world these middle-class sectors adopted methods of radical struggle in dialog with various experiences of social mobilization connected with popular sectors. The crisis of the import-substitution models prompted two forms of conflict within labor sectors. On the one hand, were urban working-class sectors that had improved their standard of living, and were now affected by inflationary processes that threatened their recently attained welfare, thus leading them to protest actively. On the other, rural workers who had come late to the process of modernization and were now standing up for their social rights, as they had been left out of the benefits afforded to their urban peers in previous decades. As these urban and rural labor sectors began to converge with each other, and with the youth movement, they became more and more radicalized. Many young people in the region were closely following the development of countercultural proposals that questioned the way of life and the values of the middle classes in consumer societies, but most of that critical potential was channeled through radical political action and efforts to organize lower-class sectors that had been ignored by the traditional Left.

The social and demographic characteristics of the countries of the Southern Cone affected the way in which anti-colonial discourses were interpreted and recreated – and to a certain extent the way they were linked to counter-cultural discourses in the region. As seen in Chapter I, through trial and error, these militants gradually became aware of what they had in common with, but also what set them apart from, other experiences of anti-colonial struggle in the Third World. Adapting the repertoires of protest to more urbanized countries with larger middle classes, urban workers with a long-standing labor tradition, and small rural populations posed a challenge that Southern Cone militants had to address. They did so with a creativity and intelligence that led them to occupy a specific place in the circulation of ideas and the networks of the global sixties. In particular, the way they adapted the repertoire of Third World struggles to countries with greater urban development and significant middle sectors was what enabled these movements to have a major influence in national political spheres and later made it possible for European and U.S. armed and radical groups to look for inspiration in the repertoires they developed. It was in this way that organizations such as the Weather Underground in the United States, the Red Army Faction, the Revolutionary Cells, and other minor groups, including Tupamaros-West Berlin, in Germany, and the Red Brigades in Italy hailed the Tupamaros as an example to be followed. This also explains the enormous solidarity with which Chilean MIR militants were received by Italy's Lotta Continua, PdUP, and Avanguardia Operaia, or Germany's Kommunistischer Bund, France's Politique Hebdo and Ligue communiste, when they were exiled in Europe after the coup.

These gestures of solidarity were what led Edgardo Enríquez to comment on a revolutionary movement that transcended borders and united the struggle of his comrades back in Chile with that of the revolutionaries in Italy, and to conclude that in that process the revolutionary Left was overcoming its weaknesses and gaining increasing consistency.[8] For this reason, we can say that the 1960s were not merely an outside influence, rather they were a cycle of global protests in which these Southern Cone groups positioned themselves, actively reinterpreting the influences they received and in turn influencing subsequent processes.

This active re-creation of the global sixties was developed in dialog with local processes. Starting in the mid-1950s, and with increasing visibility in the second half of the 1960s, a number of social and political actors in the Southern Cone began a process of radicalization. That radicalization was connected with the failure of other transformation projects that in general terms can be described as reformists.[9] The term radicalization is used here to express the political behavior of actors who during the crisis of traditional forms of political participation proposed forms of collective action that entailed a break with past practices. However, initially radicalization did not necessarily entail embracing practices of organized revolutionary violence and was instead connected with rising unrest in the streets, sparked by clashes between security forces (police and military) and increasing numbers of mobilized workers and students who engaged in a diversity of actions, ranging from forms of nonviolent protest to disruptive social mobilization.

Radicalization also expanded as a result of the growing authoritarianism with which democratic states met social demands, and was fueled later by the authoritarian responses deployed by the 1964 and 1966 military coups in Brazil and Argentina, which showed what would happen to any government who yielded to social mobilizations. Journalists, academics, and militants linked to these groups of the nascent New Left had an interpretation of the regional political process that was built simultaneously with the development of armed organizations. They posited that a conservative and authoritarian reaction supported by the United States was inevitable. This argument was not just the result of ideologized approaches to the characteristics of the bourgeois state, linked to a certain Marxist reductionism, it was also based on the new role that the military, formed in the doctrine of national security and sponsored by the United States, assumed first in the Brazilian dictatorship and later in the Argentine dictatorship, and on the social polarization that was connected with the crisis of the previous development models. In this sense, the experience of the pre-dictatorship democracies of the Southern Cone evidenced the more structural limitations of the Cold War democracies in progressively adapting to the processes of social change that increasingly larger sectors of the population were demanding since the 1950s.

This interpretation regarding the inevitability of authoritarianism and the role of the United States in that process once again linked the local to the global and put into question the ways in which geographies were considered by the actors of Latin America's Cold War. The period seemed to change how borders were conceived, altering the way in which the national and the foreign were viewed. Thus, speaking at West Point in 1965, General Onganía announced a transformation in the role of Argentina's armed forces that involved going from the defense of natural borders to the defense of ideological borders. Guevara in his message to the Tricontinental Conference called for a global war against imperialism, where nations were locations of a war that transcended them. This does not mean that the concept of nation was replaced by forms of internationalism or that nationalism as an ideology was abandoned. On the contrary, the 1960s saw a boost in nationalist ideas associated with projects both to the left and right of the political spectrum. During this period, under the framework of national liberation ideas and the dependency theory, the notion of national sovereignty gained special relevance in the Left, much more than in the first half of the century, when internationalism prevailed. What was different about this period were the ways in which these ideas of nation were linked to other geographical and political identities that transcended it, such as Latin Americanism and Third Worldism.

Social radicalization, increasing authoritarianism, and the global dimension of the 1960s, contributed to the development of this cycle of armed left-wing organizations that had characteristics that were different from those of other regions of Latin America. The regional dynamics of the political process gradually forged a shared experience among armed left-wing organizations that emerged into public life in the mid-1960s and became key actors in the processes that preceded the consolidation of authoritarianism in the Southern Cone. It was a laboratory in which militants assessed each local event and drew conclusions that would influence the coming struggles. These regional dynamics also helped postpone national defeats. Exile within the region was not seen by these militants as traditional exile but as a continuation of their national struggles. As long as there were countries in the region that provided a safe place to retreat into, there could still be hope for a revolution. This situation changed radically after the 1976 coup in Argentina, as authoritarian regimes had spread across the region and the possibilities for organizing strategic rearguard forces were greatly limited.

These dynamics fostered a transnational political culture among militants, which resulted from the coming together of the various ways in which militants experienced local political processes and linked them to their interpretations of global processes. As noted in the introduction, the term "political culture" is used to describe a number of different aspects. These aspects were examined from four key dimensions: actions, ideas and interpretations of the political process, a common political subjectivity, and definitions of a transnational community.

These groups were formed in opposition to the traditional Left. Initial criticism focused on the gradualist strategies proposed by the old Left, and, in some cases, its dogmatic positions. At first they proposed a heterodox, open, plural view of Marxism centered on the development of new political practices connected with the repertoires of contention mentioned in Chapter I. They countered them with a view that was Latin Americanist and entailed a break from the past. This view drew theoretically on several of the arguments that the dependency theory was beginning to formulate in the late 1960s and a political interpretation of the Latin American Cold War that warned of the inevitability of an authoritarian response to the growing social movement, which would have its ultimate expression in Chile. As a result, however, of the impact of certain intellectual currents (Althusserianism), transformations in the discourse of the Cuban Revolution, and the dynamics of the political process of the Southern Cone, they started veering toward more orthodox positions which, in the late 1970s, led some groups to align themselves with the Soviet orthodoxy of the communist world.

These political ideas were accompanied by the subjective construction of the figure of the militant, forged through a common sentimental interpretation of certain events in the region (Guevara's Bolivia campaign, the reaction to state authoritarian practices), as well as a criticism of certain middle-class values. In this process, an idealized figure of the revolutionary soldier and the proletarian emerged, which militants were called to emulate.

With respect to transnational ties, these groups had a common Southern Cone vision that was underpinned by practical reasons, that had to do with the need to continue their political struggle through regional exile, and was made possible thanks to a shared social and cultural background (as they were mostly middle-class or educated working-class in origin) that facilitated relations among the region's militants. That movement across borders was also based on certain Latin Americanist and, at times, internationalist conceptions that were incorporated by these groups as the Southern Cone experience became connected with other international actors and processes, such as the Cuban Revolution and Europe's non-parliamentary Left.

This political culture was not merely the result of a number of preformed ideas. Rather, it resulted from the interaction of previously held ideas and the political process that these militants had to face. It was in that process that they gradually developed a unique political culture, which was built in the course of the regional exchanges that were born of the uncertain historical contingency of local processes that often led them to places that were inconceivable in the mid-1960s.

Since the return to democracy, much has been written about the relationship of this militant political culture with democratic values. The 1980s saw the emergence of a literature that emphasized how, under the influence of Marxism, there was a tendency to promote a criticism of liberal democratic values. In the 1990s, other less political and more cultural perspectives also found authoritarian elements in the internal culture of these organizations and the ways in which gender and ethnic conflicts were resolved within them. However, it should be noted that these approaches were motivated by political and academic concerns that emerged gradually in the post-dictatorship era, a time that differed considerably from the 1960s. A present time, in which the distinction between "space of experience" and "horizon of expectation" proposed by Reinhart Koselleck as a characteristic element of modernity, seemed suspended; or in other words, a time in which the idea of revolution, which accepted the sacrifice of a certain present for a future horizon, no longer had the persuasive force that fueled ideologically-diverse projects across the continent, over a significant part of the nineteenth and twentieth centuries.[10] As noted by Friederich Engels in "On Authority," a "revolution is certainly the most authoritarian thing there is; it is the act whereby one part of the population imposes its will upon the other part by means of rifles, bayonets, and cannons – authoritarian means, if such there be at all."[11] The revolutionaries of the 1960s were certainly closer to what the nineteenth-century philosopher thought, than to our conceptions on politics and violence and the social order. It is from that particular regime of historicity – namely, modernity – that historians must draw their questions and understand the problems faced by those political actors.

This situation leads us inevitably to an epistemological problem typically faced in historical operations: namely, the issue of anachronism. How can a revolution be assessed looking back from non-revolutionary times? Against the grain of historiographic orthodoxy, François Dosse has argued in favor of "the legitimacy of a controlled anachronism" in considering historical phenomena.[12] Many interpretations made in the last decades can be considered under this approach. These have certainly been more productive than both the sugarcoated or condemnatory readings by diehard defenders or critics of that experience.

Even several survivors of that experience reassessed the past under a lens influenced by that democratic perspective. In the last chapter I showed how changing political conditions, both nationally and internationally, allowed some militants to adjust to the new political opportunities that arose. For some, the weight of the past was too much and it prevented them from adapting to the new era. For others, this readjustment did not entail abandoning the legacy of the revolutionary culture built in the 1960s and 1970s, but they were able to adapt to the new conditions and build bridges between past and present experiences with a great deal of success.

This, however, should not detract from the idea that there are certain aspects of historical events that need to be understood in their own terms, in light of how the social change in question was conceived in that period. In this sense, political conflict was primarily associated with ideas connected with the violent transformation of the economic and political order. Other issues, such as race, gender, or political rights, were secondary to the goal of economic transformation. This is not to say that such issues were "inconceivable" in the 1960s.[13] On the contrary, these movements opened up possibilities for thinking about gender, race, and political rights, among other things. Such issues, however, were subsumed under the totalizing discourse of revolution. That several participants in those experiences were able to see the limits or problems of such approaches is perfectly valid, but that does not mean that a number of questions regarding that era are not still relatively open. The tragic fate of many thousands throughout the Southern Cone revealed the depths of the limits posed by the Cold War world on any attempts to achieve social change in this region of the planet. Such issues are still very much relevant in current discussions, both globally and in the continent, which, despite social transformations in the last decades, is still the most unequal continent in the world.

Notes

1 www.presidencia.gub.uy/comunicacion/comunicacionnoticias/mujica-dilma-artilleros
2 For biographical information see: Ricardo Batista Amaral, Vida quer é coragem: a tra-jetória de Dilma Rousseff, a primeira presidenta do Brasil (Rio de Janeiro: Primeira Pessoa, 2011), and Miguel Ángel Campodónico, Mujica (Montevideo, Uruguay: Editorial Fin de Siglo, 1999).
3 Enrique Gorriarán Merlo. Memorias de Enrique Gorriarán Merlo: de los sesenta a La Tablada (Argentina: Planeta, 2003).
4 See: Jeremi Suri, Power and Protest: Global Revolution and the Rise of Détente (Cambridge: Harvard University Press, 2003), and Immanuel Wallerstein et al., Anti-Systemic Movements (London, New York: Verso 1989), Chapter V.
5 Jeff Goodwin, No Other Way Out: States and Revolutionary Movements, 1945–1991 (Cambridge; New York: Cambridge University Press, 2001), 3.
6 Odd Arne Westad, The Global Cold War: Third World Interventions and the Making of Our Times (Cambridge: Cambridge University Press, 2005), 398.
7 Aldo E Solari, Estudiantes y politica en América Latina (Caracas: Monte Avila Editores, 1968).
8 See quote by Edgardo Enríquez in Chapter IV, p. 251, footnote 112: Edgardo Enríquez, "Discurso del compañero Edgardo Enriquez. Roma 14 de setiembre de 1974," Correo de la Resistencia, nos. 3–4, September–October, 1974.

9 For Chile's case, see Manuel Garretón and Tomás Moulian, "Procesos y bloques políticos en la crisis chilena, 1970–1973," Revista Mexicana de Sociología 41, no. 1, Análisis de Coyuntura (January–March 1979). For Argentina's case, see Juan Carlos Portantiero, "Clases dominantes y crisis política en la Argentina actual," in Pasado y Presente, no. 1, new series (April–June 1973). For Uruguay's case, see Aldo Solari, Estudios sobre la sociedad uruguaya (Montevideo: Arca, 1964).

10 Reinhart Koselleck, Futures Past: On the Semantics of Historical Time (New York: Columbia University Press, 2004).

11 Friedrich Engels, "On authority," in Marx-Engels Reader (New York: W. W. Norton and Co., second edition, 1978), 730–3.

12 François Dosse, "Del uso razonado del anacronismo," in El Giro reflexivo de la historia. Recorridos epistemológicos y atención a las singularidades (Santiago de Chile: Ediciones Universidad Finis Terrae, 2012).

13 In the sense put forward by Michel Trouillot in Silencing the Past: Power and the Production of History (Boston, Mass.: Beacon Press, 1995), chapter 3.

Bibliography

Primary Sources

Archival Documents

Argentina

Archivo del Centro de Documentación e Investigación de la Cultura de Izquierda (CEDINCI).
Archivo de la Dirección de Inteligencia de la Provincia de Buenos Aires (DIPBA).
Archivo de Historia Oral del Instituto de Investigaciones Gino Germani.
Archivo Intermedio del Archivo General de la Nación.
Colecciones del Ministerio del Interior y Justicia.
Archivo Oral, Memoria Abierta.

Chile

Archivo General Histórico, Ministerio de Relaciones Exteriores, Santiago.
Centro de Investigación y Documentación en Historia de Chile Contemporáneo. Archivo Nacional.
Biblioteca Nacional.

United States

National Archives and Records Administration, College Park, Maryland.
Hoover Institution Archives, Stanford University.

Uruguay

Archivo administrativo, Ministerio de Relaciones Exteriores.
Archivo Histórico Diplomático, Ministerio de Relaciones Exteriores.
Archivo de la Dirección de Inteligencia del Ministerio del Interior.
Archivo de la Lucha Armada "David Cámpora" en Archivo del Centro de Estudios Interdisciplinarios Uruguayos, Facultad de Humanidades y Ciencias de la Educación, Universidad de la República.

Online Archives

Archivo Chile Documentación de Historia Político y Social y Movimiento Popular con-
temporáneo de América Latina y el Caribe. www.archivochile.com/
Archivo El topo blindado. Centro de Documentacion de las organizaciones Político
militares argentinas. www.eltopoblindado.com/
Marxists internet archives. www.marxists.org/
Fondo Digital Eugenio Ruiz Tagle, FLACSO, Chile. www.fondo.flacso.cl/

Newspapers and Periodicals

Argentina:

Boletin Interno, PRT (1972–1976)
Che (1960–1961)
Confirmado (1967)
Cristianismo y Revolución (1966–1971)
Cuadernos de Pasado y Presente (1963–1965)
Entre Todos (1984–1988)
Estrategia (1964–1968)
Estrella Roja (1971–1977)
El Combatiente (1968–1976, 1977–1979)
Norte Argentino (1964–1965)
Nuevo Hombre (1971–1976)
Palabra Obrera (1963–1965)
Primera Plana (1962–1968)

Chile

Arauco (1960–1967)
Chile Hoy (1972–1973)
Cuadernos del Centro de Estudios Socioeconómicos (1966–1968) (1970–1971)
Cuadernos de la Realidad Nacional (1969–1973)
Correo de la Resistencia (1974–1979)
Estrategia (1965–1969)
El Mercurio (1967, 1970–1975)
El Rebelde (1962–1965, 1965–1973, 1976)
El Siglo (1967, 1972)
Ercilla (1964, 1970–1973)
Punto Final (1965–1969) (1969–1973)
Revolución (1966)
Qué Pasa (1971–1975)
Teoria y práctica. Problemas de la revolución Brasilera (1972–1973)

Uruguay

Brecha (1985–1996)
Barricada (1964)
Carta (1972–1973)
El Tupamaro (1974–1975)

Época (1963–1967)
Estudios (1964–1973)
Las Bases (1985)
Marcha (1962–1973)

Others

Revista Casa de las Américas (1967–1970)
Revista Che Guevara (1974–1977)

Oral Interviews

Interview with Jorge Selves conducted by Clara Aldrighi and contributed by her.
Interview with Manuel Cabieses conducted by the author – April 6, 2009.
Interviews with Daniel de Santis conducted by Vera Carnovale in Archivo Oral, Memoria Abierta – June 23, 2008; July 7, 2008; July 14, 2008.
Interview with Hilda Amalia Garcés conducted by the author – September 12, 2008.
Interviews with Enrique Gorriarán Merlo conducted by Archivo de Historia Oral, Instituto Gino Germani – August 9, 2005; August 11, 2005; September 15, 2005; October 27, 2005.
Interviews with Efrain Martínez Platero conducted by the author – January 25, 2008; February 1, 2008; March 14, 2008.
Interviews with Luis Mattini (pseudonym) conducted by Archivo de Historia Oral, Instituto Gino Germani – May 5, 2004; June 24, 2005; June 29, 2005.
Interviews with Gaston Muñoz conducted by the author – September 26, 2008.
Interviews with Andres Pascal Allende conducted by the author – October 8, 2008; April 7, 2009.
Interview with Osvaldo Torres conducted by the author – September 25, 2008.
Interview with Carlos Zarricueta conducted by the author – October 4, 2008.

Memoirs, Interviews, and Historical Documents

Agee, Philip. *La CIA por dentro, diario de un espía*. Buenos Aires: Editorial Sudamericana, 1987.
Aldrighi, Clara. *Memorias de insurgencia*. Montevideo: Ediciones de la Banda Oriental, 2009.
Alegría, Claribel , D J Flakoll, *Death of Somoza*. Willimantic, CT: Curbstone Press, 1996.
Allende, Salvador. *Cuba: un camino*. Santiago: Prensa Latinoamericana, 1960.
   "Discurso en la Primera Conferencia Tricontinental, La Habana, 5 de enero de 1966," in *Salvador Allende: pensamiento y acción* edited by Frida Modak. Buenos Aires: CLACSO – FLACSO- Brazil, 2008, 289–90.
Anguita, Eduardo Anguita and Martín Caparrós, *La voluntad. Una historia de la militancia revolucionaria en la Argentina*. Six volumes. Argentina: Booket, 2006.
Artés, Matilde. *Crónica de una desaparición. La lucha de una abuela de Plaza de Mayo*. Madrid: Espasa, 1997.
Assman, Hugo. *Teoponte. Una experiencia guerrillera*. Oruro: CEDI, 1971.
Benedetti, Mario. *Cuaderno cubano*. Montevideo: Ed. Arca, 1967.
Bengochea, Angel and J.J. López Silveira. *Guerra de guerrillas*. Montevideo: Editorial Uruguay, 1970.
Bernhard, Guillermo and Alberto Etchepare. *Reportaje a Cuba*. Montevideo: Ediciones América Nueva, 1961.

Bustos, Ciro. *El Che quiere verte: la historia jamás contada del Che en Bolivia.* Buenos Aires: Javier Vergara Editor, 2007.

Castillo, Carmen. *Un día de octubre en Santiago.* Mexico: ERA, 1982.

Castro, Fidel. "Discurso pronunciado en el acto clausura de la Primera Conferencia de Solidaridad de los Pueblos de Asia, África y América Latina (Tricontinental), en el Teatro Chaplín, La Habana, el 15 de enero de 1966," www.cuba.cu/gobierno/discursos/

"Discurso pronunciado en el acto clausura de la Primera Conferencia de la Organización Latinoamericana de Solidaridad (OLAS), celebrada en el Teatro Chaplín, La Habana, 10 de agosto de 1967," www.cuba.cu/gobierno/discursos/

Primer Congreso del PCC

Chelén, Alejandro. *La Revolución Cubana y sus proyecciones en América Latina.* Santiago: Ed. Prensa Latinoamericana, 1960.

CODEPU, *Informe de Derechos Humanos, 1990–2000.* Santiago: LOM, 2001.

Collazo, Ariel. *Historia de una pasión política.* Montevideo: s.n., 2004.

Comité Memoria Neltume. *Guerrilla en Neltume. Una historia de lucha y resistencia en el sur chileno.* Santiago: LOM Ediciones, 2003.

Conteris, Hiber. *Cono sur.* Montevideo: Ediciones de Marcha,1963.

Contorno: Edición Facsimilar. Buenos Aires: Biblioteca Nacional, 2007.

Cultelli, Andrés. *La revolución necesaria.* Montevideo: Colihue, 2006.

Debray, Regis. "El castrismo: la gran marcha de América Latina." Pasado y Presente, year 2, no. 7–8 (October 1964–March 1965).

"¿Revolución en la revolución?," *Cuadernos de la Revista Casa de las Américas* 1.Havana: Casa, 1967.

Los Tupamaros en acción. Mexico: Editorial Diógenes, 1972.

La crítica de las armas. Mexico: Siglo XXI, 1975.

Alabados sean nuestros señores. Una educación política. Barcelona: Editorial Sudamericana, 1999.

Dos Santos, Theotônio. *Socialismo o fascismo, el dilema latinoamericano.* Santiago: Prensa Latinoamericana, 1969.

Socialismo o Fascismo, el nuevo carácter de la dependencia y el dilema latinoamericano. Argentina: Ed. Periferia, 1972.

"André Gunder Frank – recordatorio", in e-l@tina, vol. 3, no. 11 (April–June 2005);

El Kadri, Envar and Jorge Rulli. *Diálogos en el exilio.* Argentina: Forosur, 1984.

Eloy Martinez, Tomás. *La pasión según Trelew.* Buenos Aires: Granica Editor, 1973.

Enríquez, Miguel. *Con vista a la esperanza.* Santiago, Chile: Escaparate Ediciones, 1998.

Miguel Enríquez y el proyecto revolucionario en Chile: discursos y documentos del Movimiento de Izquierda Revolucionaria. Santiago: LOM Ediciones: Centro de Estudios Miguel Enríquez, 2004.

Estradel,Victor. *Memorias del Negro Pedro. Tupamaros en la revolución sandinista.* Montevideo: Ediciones Fin de Siglo, 2013.

Frondizi, Silvio. *La Revolución cubana: su significación histórica.* Montevideo: Editorial Ciencias Políticas, 1960.

Gallardo Lozada, Jorge. *De Torres a Banzer: diez meses de emergencia en Bolivia.* Buenos Aires: Ediciones Periferia, 1972.

INDAL. *Movimiento de Liberación Nacional (Tupamaros): documentación propia.* Belgium: Heverlee-Louvain: Information documentaire d'Amérique latine, 1973.

Domecq, Sergio, Carlos Ramírez, and Juan Candela (pseudonyms). *El único camino para la toma del poder y el socialismo.* Ediciones Combate, 1969.

De Santis, Daniel. *A vencer o morir: PRT-ERP, Documentos.* 2 Vols. Buenos Aires: Eudeba, 1998–2000.

Entre tupas y perros. Buenos Aires: Ed. R y R, 2005.

La historia del PRT-ERP por sus protagonistas. Buenos Aires: Estación Finlandia, 2010.

Duhalde, Eduardo and Eduardo Pérez. *De Taco Ralo a la alternativa independiente. Historia documental de las Fuerzas Armadas Peronistas y del Peronismo de base*. La Plata: De la campana, 2003.

FAMUS. *Operación independencia*. Buenos Aires: FAMUS, 1988.

Frank, Andre Gunder. *Capitalismo y subdesarrollo en América Latina*. La Habana: Instituto del Libro, Editorial de Ciencias Sociales, 1970.

Quién es el enemigo inmediato?: América Latina, subdesarrollo capitalista o revolución socialista. 1. ed. Buenos Aires: Editorial Centro de Estudios Políticos, 1974.

Gaggero, Manuel J. "El encuentro con el Che: aquellos años." In *Che, el argentino* edited by Fernando Martínez Heredia. Buenos Aires: Ediciones de Mano en Mano, 1997.

Guevara, Ernesto. "Discurso en la reunión del CIES," 1961, Punta del Este, Uruguay, in www.archivochile.com

"Discurso en la Universidad de la República," August 17, 1961, www .archivochile.com.

"Mensaje a los argentinos," in Claudia Korol, *El Che y los argentinos*. Buenos Aires: Ediciones Dialéctica, 1988.

Pasajes de la guerra revolucionaria. Cuba: Unión, 1963.

El diario del Che en Bolivia," Punto Final, no. 59, 1st fortnight of July 1968.

La guerra de guerrillas. Lima: Fondo de Cultura Popular, 1973.

Guillén, Abraham. *Teoría de la violencia; guerra y lucha de clases*. Buenos Aires: Editorial Jamcana, 1965.

Estrategia de la guerrilla urbana. Montevideo: Manuales del pueblo, 1966.

Desafío al Pentágono; la guerilla latinoamericana. Montevideo: Editorial Andes, 1969.

"Entrevista con Abraham Guillén." Bicicleta, Revista de comunicaciones libertarias, October 1978, España.

Gorriarán Merlo, Enrique. *Memorias de Enrique Gorriarán Merlo: de los sesenta a La Tablada*. Argentina: Planeta, 2003.

Harnecker, Marta. *Los conceptos elementales del materialismo histórico (versión corregida y ampliada*. Mexico, Spain, Argentina: Siglo XXI Editores, 1985.

Hernández Vázquez, Martín. *El pensamiento revolucionario de Bautista Van Schouwen (1943–1973)*. Concepción: Ediciones Escaparate, 2004.

Huidobro, Eleuterio Fernández. *Historia de los Tupamaros*, 3 vol. Montevideo: Tupac Amaru, 1986.

Jorge, Graciela and Eleuterio Fernández Huidobro. *Chile roto*. Santiago: LOM Ediciones, 2003.

Junta de Comandantes en Jefe, *Las Fuerzas Armadas al pueblo oriental. La subversion*, vol. 1 Montevideo: Junta de Comandantes en Jefe, 1978.

Madres y Familiares de Detenidos Desaparecidos (Uruguay). *A todos ellos: informe de Madres y Familiares de Uruguayos Detenidos Desaparecidos*. Montevideo: Madres y Familiares de Uruguayos Detenidos Desaparecidos, 2004.

Marambio, Max. *Las armas de ayer*. Santiago: La Tercera, Debate, 2007.

Marini, Ruy Mauro. *Subdesarrollo y Revolución*. Mexico: Siglo Veintiuno Editores, 1969.

Memoria, Ruy Mauro Marini, in Ruy Mauro Marini Escritos page, at www.marini-escritos.unam.mx/002_memoria_es.htm

Martínez Estrada, Ezequiel. *En Cuba y al servicio de la revolución. Mi experiencia cubana* Montevideo: Siglo Ilustrado, 1965.

Martínez Moreno, Carlos. *El paredón*. Barcelona: Seix Barral, 1962.

Masetti, Jorge Ricardo. *Los que luchan y los que lloran*. Buenos Aires: Editorial Jorge Álvarez, 1969.

Mattini, Luis. Hombres y mujeres del PRT-ERP: La pasión militante. La Plata: Ed. de la Campana, 2003.

Los perros. Memorias de un combatiente revolucionario. Buenos Aires: Continente, 2006.

Los perros 2: memorias de la rebeldía femenina en los '70. Buenos Aires: Continente, 2007.

Mechoso, Juan Carlos Mechoso. *Historia de FAU*, 3 vol. Montevideo: Ediciones Recortes, 2005–2011.

Mendoza y Caamaño, Hector. *Chile surgimiento y ocaso de una utopía, 1970–1973. Testimonio de un diplomático mexicano.* Mexico: Secretaría de Relaciones Exteriores, Acervo Histórico Diplomático, 2004.

Methol Ferre, Alberto. *Regis Debray y la ideología de la revolución en América Latina*, Cuadernos Latinoamericanos. Montevideo: Instituto de Estudios Americanos, 1968.

MIR, MIR, dos años en la lucha de la resistencia popular del pueblo chileno, 1973–1975. Madrid, Ed. Zero, 1976.

Ministerio del Interior, *7 meses de lucha antisubversiva; acción del Estado frente a la sedición desde El 1° de Marzo al 30 de setiembre de 1972.* Montevideo: Ministerio del Interior, 1972.

  Programa de Derechos Humanos, *Geografía de la Memoria.* Santiago: Ministerio del Interior, 2010.

MLN-T. *Simposio de Viña del Mar.* Montevideo: MLNT, undated.

  Actas tupamaras. Buenos Aires: Schapire, 1971.

  Actas tupamaras. Bogotá: Editorial Ibérica, 1971.

National Intelligence Estimate, NIE 80/90–68 Washington, March 28, 1968. "The potential for revolution in Latin America," in *Foreign Relations of the United States, 1964–1968: Volume XXXI, South and Central America; Mexico* edited by David C. Geyer, David H. Herschler. Washington: United States Government Printing Office, 2004. 170–2.

OAS. Council of the Organization of American States, *Special Consultative Committee on Security. Statutes*, April 23, 1963.

OLAS. *Primera conferencia de la Organización Latinoamericana de Solidaridad.* Montevideo: Nativa Libros, 1967.

  El imperialismo: deformador de nuestra tradición histórica. Havana, 1967.

  Actuación de la OEA: Guatemala (1954), República Dominicana (1965), Cuba (1959–1967), Intervencionismo y Fuerza Interamericana de Paz. Havana: Primera Conferencia de Solidaridad de los Pueblos de América Latina, 1967.

Ortolani, Luis. "Moral y proletarización," *Políticas de la memoria*, no. 4, Summer 2004–2005, 96.

Pascal Allende, Andrés, *El MIR Chileno, una experiencia revolucionaria.* Argentina: Ediciones Cucaña, 2003.

Peredo, Osvaldo "Chato." *Volvimos a las montañas. Santa Cruz, Bolivia*: Osvaldo Peredo Leigue Edición, 2003.

Piñeiro, Manuel. *Che Guevara y la revolución latinoamericana.* Colombia: Ocean Sur, 2006.

Poder Ejecutivo Nacional. *El terrorismo en la Argentina: evolución de la delincuencia terrorista en la Argentina.* Buenos Aires: Poder Ejecutivo Nacional, 1979.

PRT. *El Peronismo ayer y hoy.* Mexico: Editorial Diógenes, 1974.

Presidencia de la República. *Movimiento de Liberación Nacional-Tupamaros (MLNT-T), Índice cronológico de documentos, Actualización histórica sobre detenidos desaparecidos.* Uruguay: Presidencia de la República, 2011. www.presidencia.gub.uy/wps/wcm/connect/presidencia/portalpresidencia/comunicacion/informes/investigacion-historica-sobre-detenidos-desaparecidos

Quiroga Zamora, Patricio. *Compañeros: el GAP: la escolta de Allende.* Santiago de Chile: Aguilar, 2001.

Rey, Amalio Juan. *Sobre el mensaje del Che Guevara a los argentinos el 25 de mayo de 1962.* Córdoba: Narvaja Editor, 1999.

Rivas, Patricio. *Chile, un largo septiembre.* Santiago: LOM Ediciones, 2007.

Rodriguez, Guillermo. *Hacia el final de la partida*. Santiago de Chile: LOM Ediciones, 2007.

Rovira, Carlos and Filomena Grieco. *Veinte años después del 14 de abril de 1972*. Montevideo: Ediciones de la Plaza, 1993.

Sandoval Ambiado, Carlos. *Movimiento de Izquierda Revolucionaria, 1970–1973*. Concepción: Ediciones Escaparate, 2004.

Santucho, Mario Roberto. "Argentinos! A las armas!," *El Combatiente*, no. 210, March 31, 1976, 2, 15.

Seman, Elías. *Cuba Miliciana*. Buenos Aires: Ediciones Ubicación, 1961.

Tavares, Flavio. *Memórias do esquecimento*. Sao Paulo: Globo, 1999.

Torres, Simón and Julio Aronde, "Debray and the Cuban Experience," *Monthly Review* 20, no. 3 (July–August 1968).

Acdel Vilas, Tucumán, enero a diciembre de 1975, www.nuncamas.org/investig/vilas/acdel_00.htm

Peter Weiss, "Testimonio: Che Guevara," *Punto Final*, no. 45, January 2, 1968, 22–3.

Secondary sources

Published

Aarao Reis Filho, Daniel. *Ditadura militar, esquerdas e sociedade*. Rio de Janeiro: Zahar, 2000.

Aldrighi, Clara. *La izquierda armada: ideología, ética e identidad en el MLN-Tupamaros*. Montevideo, Uruguay: Ediciones Trilce, 2001.
  La intervención de Estados Unidos en Uruguay (1965–1973): El caso Mitrione. Montevideo: Trilce Ediciones, 2007.

Aldrighi, Clara and Guillermo Waksman. "Chile, la gran ilusión," in *El Uruguay del exilio, gente, circunstancias, escenarios*, Silvia Dutrenit Bielous (ed.) Montevideo, Uruguay: Trilce Ediciones, 2006.

Allier, Maria Eugenia. *Batallas por la memoria*. Montevideo: Trilce, 2010.

Alonso, Rosa and Carlos Demasi. *Uruguay, 1958–1968: crisis y estancamiento*. Montevideo: Ediciones de la Banda Oriental, 1986.

Alonso, Jimena. "Tupamaros en Chile. Una experiencia bajo el gobierno de Salvador Allende," in Encuentros Uruguayos, Revista Digital, 3rd year, number 3 (2nd part) September 2010.

Altamirano, Carlos. *Bajo el signo de las masas (1943–1973)*. Buenos Aires: Ariel, 2001.

Andersen, Martin Edwin. *Dossier Secreto. Argentina's Desaparecidos and the Myth of the Dirty War*. Boulder, Colorado: Westview Press, 1993.

Anderson, John Lee. *Che Guevara: A revolutionary life*. New York: Grove Press, 1997.

Angell, Allan. *Chile de Alessandri a Pinochet: en busca de la utopía*. Santiago: Andrés Bello, 1993.

Arrate, Jorge and Eduardo Rojas. *Memoria de la izquierda chilena, tomo I*. Santiago: Ediciones B, 2003.

Arrighi, Giovanni, Terence K. Hopkins and Immanuel Wallerstein. *Movimientos antisistémicos*. Madrid: AKAL, 1999.

Armony. Ariel C. *La Argentina, los Estados Unidos y la cruzada anticomunista en América Central, 1977–1984*. Bernal, Argentina: Universidad Nacional de Quilmes, 1999.

Arquidiocese de São Paulo. *Brasil Nunca Mais*. Petrópolis: Ed. Vozes, 1985.

Aseff, Marlon. *Retratos do Exilio, Solidariedade e Resistencia na Fronteira*. Santa Cruz do Sul: EDUNISC, 2009.

Avendaño, Daniel and Mauricio Palma. *El rebelde de la burguesía: la historia de Miguel Enríquez*. Santiago, Chile: Ediciones CESOC, 2001.

Aznarez, Carlos A. and Jaime E. Cañas. *Tupamaros? Fracaso del Che?* Buenos Aires: Ediciones Orbe, 1969.

Becerra Ramírez, Manuel. "Marco Kaplan, un científico social," biographical sketch in www.bibliojuridica.org/libros/4/1785/4.pdf

Bender, Thomas. "Introduction. Historians, the Nation, and the Plenitude of Narratives," in *Rethinking American History in a Global Age* edited by Thomas Bender. Berkeley: University of California Press, 2002.

Beigel, Fernanda. "La Flacso chilena y la regionalización de las ciencias sociales en América Latina (1957–1973)," *Revista Mexicana de Sociología* (Mexico) 71, no. 2 (April–June 2009), 319–49.

Berger, John. "Che Guevara: The Moral Factor," *The Urban Review* vol. 8, no. 3 (September 1975).

Blanco, Cecilia. "El socialismo argentino de la euforia a la crisis de identidad, 1955–1958. Un análisis de la ideología política del PS desde el periódico La Vanguardia." Lecture, II Jornadas de Historia de las Izquierdas, CEDINCI, Buenos Aires, December 11, 12, and 13, 2002.

Blixen, Samuel. *Conversaciones con Gorriaran Merlo.* Buenos Aires: Editorial Contrapunto, 1988.

El vientre del Cóndor: del archivo del terror al caso Berríos. Montevideo, Uruguay: Ediciones de Brecha, 1995.

Sendic. Montevideo: Ediciones Trilce, 2000.

Boonefoy Miralles, Pascale and Claudio Perez y Angel Spotorno. *Internacionalistas. Chilenos en la Revolución Popular Sandinista. Segunda Edición Ampliada.* Santiago: Editorial Latinoamericana, 2009.

Boccia Paz, Alfredo, Myriam Angélica González, and Rosa Palau Aguilar. *Es mi informe. Los archivos secretos de la policía de Stroessner.* Asunción: CDE, 1994.

Brands, Hal. *Latin America's Cold War.* Cambridge: Harvard University Press, 2010.

Bruno, Mauricio. *La caza del fantasma. Benito Nardone y el anticomunismo en Uruguay (1960–1962).* Montevideo: FHCE, Colección Estudiantes, no. 28, 2007.

Burgos, Raul. *Los Gramscianos argentinos: cultura y política en la experiencia de "Pasado y Presente."* Buenos Aires: Siglo Veintiuno de Argentina Editores, 2004.

Calveiro, Pilar. *Política y/o violencia: una aproximación a la guerrilla de los años 70.* Buenos Aires: Norma, 2005.

Cancino, Hugo. *Chile. La problemática del poder popular en el proceso de la vía chilena al socialismo 1970–1973.* Aarhus: Aarhus University Press, 1988.

Cardozo, Marina. "'El cordero nunca se salvó balando': reflexiones acerca de los relatos de un militantes de la izquierda armada," in several authors, *Recordar para pensar. Memoria para la democracia. La elaboración del pasado reciente en el cono sur de América Latina.* Santiago de Chile: Ediciones Böll Cono Sur, 2010.

Carnovale, Vera. *Los combatientes: historia del PRT-ERP.* Buenos Aires: Siglo Veintiuno Editores, 2011.

"De Entre Todos a La Tablada. Redefiniciones y permanencias del ideario setentista" en PolHis. Año 6. n. 12. Segundo semestre. 2013.

Castañeda, Jorge G. *Utopia Unarmed: the Latin American Left after the Cold War.* New York: Knopf 1993.

Compañero: the Life and Death of Che Guevara. New York: Knopf, 1997.

Cavallo, Ascanio, Manuel Salazar and Oscar Sepúlveda. *La historia oculta del regimen militar.* Santiago: Grijalbo, 1997.

Caviasca, Guillermo. *Dos caminos. ERP-Montoneros en los setenta.* Buenos Aires: Centro Cultural de la Cooperación Floreal Gorini, 2006.

Ceballos, Carlos. *Los estudiantes universitarios y la política (1955–1970)*. Buenos Aires: Centro Editor de América Latina, 1985.

Celesia, Felipe and Pablo Waisberg. *La Tablada. A vencer o morir. La última batalla de la guerrilla argentina*. Buenos Aires: Aguilar, 2013.

Céspedes, Roberto and Roberto Paredes. "La resistencia armada al stronismo: panorama general," in *Revista Nova Polis* 8, August, 2004.

Chagas, Jorge and Gustavo Trullen. *Pacheco, la trama oculta del poder*. Montevideo: Rumbo, 2005.

Childs, Matt D. "An Historical Critique of the Emergence and Evolution of Ernesto Che Guevara's Foco Theory," *Journal of Latin American Studies* 27, no. 3 (October 1995), 593–624.

Cibelli, Juan Carlos. "Orígenes de la FAL," Lucha Armada en la Argentina, no. 1.

CLAEH, *Indicadores básicos, Cultura, sociedad y política*. Montevideo: CLAEH, 1991.

Collier, David, Fernando Henrique Cardoso, and Joint Committee on Latin American Studies. *The New authoritarianism in Latin America*. Princeton, N.J.: Princeton University Press, 1979.

Comisión Nacional de Verdad y Reconciliación. *Informe Rettig*. Santiago: Ed. del Ornitorrinco, 1991.

Corradi, Juan E., Patricia Weiss Fagen and Manuel A. Garretón Merino. *Fear at the Edge: State Terror and Resistance in Latin America*. Berkeley: University of California Press, 1992.

Costa, Omar (ed.). *Los Tupamaros*. Mexico: Ediciones Era, 1971.

Crenzel, Emilio *La historia política del Nunca más: la memoria de las desapariciones en la Argentina*. Buenos Aires, Argentina: Siglo Veintiuno Editores, 2008.

Crozier, Michael, Samuel P. Hunttington and Joji Watanuki. *The Crisis of Democracy. Report on the Governability of Democracies to the Trilateral Commision*. New York: New York University Press, 1975.

Cultelli, Andrés. *La revolución necesaria, contribución a la autocrítica del MLN-Tupamaros*. Buenos Aires: Colihue, 2006.

D'Elía, German. *El Uruguay neobatllista (1946–1958)*. Montevideo: Ediciones de la Banda Oriental, 1982.

Dandan, Alejandra and Silvina Heguy. *Joe Baxter, del nazismo a la extrema izquierda La historia secreta de un guerrillero*. Argentina: Editorial Norma, 2006.

Davenport, Christian, Hank Johnston, and Carol Mueller. *Repression and Mobilization*. Minneapolis: University of Minnesota Press, 2005.

De Almeida Silva, Catia Cristina. "Resistencia no exterior: os exilados brasileiros no Chile (1969–1973)," paper presented in the conference Usos de Pasado: XII Encuentro Regional de Historia, ANPUH-RJ, 2006.

De Barcelos, Thatiana Amaral, and Ana Paula Goulart Ribeiro. "Militantes e jornalistas: A imprensa editada por exilados políticos brasileiros durante a ditadura," paper presented at Intercom – Sociedade Brasileira de Estudos Interdisciplinares da Comunicação: XIV Congresso de Ciências da Comunicação na Região Sudeste – Rio de Janeiro – May 7–9, 2009.

Della Porta, Donatella. *Social Movements, Political Violence, and the State: A Comparative Analysis of Italy and Germany*. Cambridge; New York: Cambridge University Press, 1995.

Dinges, John. *The Condor Years: How Pinochet and his Allies Brought Terrorism to Three Continents*. New York: The New Press, 2004.

Dominguez, Jorge I. *To Make a World Safe for Revolution. Cuba's Foreign Policy*. Cambridge: Harvard University Press, 1989.

Dosal, Paul. *Comandante Che. Guerrilla Soldier, Commander, and Strategist, 1956–1967*. Pennsylvania: Pennsylvania State University Press, 2003.

Drake, Paul W. *Socialism and populism in Chile, 1932–1952*. Urbana: University of Illinois Press, 1978.

Dunkerley, James. *Rebellion in the Veins, Political Struggle in Bolivia, 1952–1982*. Verso: London, 1984.

Duré, Victor R. and Agripino Silva. "Frente Unido de Liberación Nacional (1959–1965), guerra de guerrillas como guerra del pueblo," *Revista Nova Polis* 8, August, 2004.

Echeverría, Mónica. *Antihistoria de un luchador: (Clotario Blest 1823–1990)*. Santiago, Chile: LOM Ediciones, 1993.

Faúndez, Julio. *Izquierdas y democracia en Chile, 1932–1973*. Santiago: Ediciones BAT, 1992.

Feld, Claudia and Marina Franco. *Democracia: hora cero*. Actores, políticas y debates en los inicios de la posdictadura. Buenos Aires: Fondo de Cultura Económico, 2015.

Fermandois, Joaquín. *Chile y el mundo, 1970–1973, La política exterior del gobierno de la Unidad Popular y el sistema internacional*. Santiago: Ediciones Universidad Católica de Chile, 1985.

Foran, John. "Theories of Revolution Revisited: Toward a Fourth Generation?" *Sociological Theory*, Vol. 11, no. 1 (March 1993), 1–20.

Fraga, Rosendo. *Ejército: del escarnio al poder (1973–1976)*. Buenos Aires: Planeta, 1988.

Garcé, Adolfo. *Donde hubo fuego: el proceso de adaptación del MLN-Tupamaros a la legalidad y a la competencia electoral (1985–2004)* Montevideo: Editorial Fin de Siglo, 2006.

Galasso, Norberto. *La izquierda nacional y el FIP*. Buenos Aires: Centro Editor de América Latina, 1983.

Galván, Valeria and Florencia Osuna (comp). *Política y cultura durante el "Onganiato". Nuevas perspectivas para la investigación de la presidencia de Juan Carlos Onganía (1966–1970)*. Rosario, Prohistoria, 2014.

Garaño, Santiago and Werner Pertot. *Detenidos-aparecidos: presas y presos políticos desde Trelew a la dictadura*. Buenos Aires: Editorial Biblos, 2007.

Garcés, Mario and Sebastián Leiva, *El golpe en La Legua. Los caminos de la historia y la memoria*. Santiago: LOM Ediciones, 2005.

García Naranjo, Francisco. *Historias derrotadas: opción y obstinación de la guerrilla chilena (1965–1988)*. Morelia, Mexico: Universidad Michoacana de San Nicolás de Hidalgo, Instituto de Investigaciones Históricas, Departamento de Historia Latinoamericana, 1997.

Garretón, Manuel A. and Javier Martínez (dir.). *La reforma en la Universidad de Chile*. 3 vols. Santiago: Ediciones Sur, 1986.

Garretón, Manuel A. and Javier Martínez and Tomás Moulian. "Procesos y bloques políticos en la crisis chilena 1970–1973," *Revista Mexicana de Sociología* 41, no. 1, *Análisis de Coyuntura*. (January–March 1979), 159–204.

Garretón, Manuel A. and Javier Martínez and Tomás Moulian and Carmen Garretón Merino. *Por la fuerza sin la razón. Análisis y textos de los bandos de la dictadura militar*. Santiago: LOM Ediciones, 1998.

Gasparri, Elio. *A ditadura escancarada*. Sao Paulo: Editora Schwarcz, 2005.

As ilusões armadas. A ditadura envergonhada. Sao Paulo: Companhia das Letras, 2002.

Gatto, Hebert. *El cielo por asalto: el Movimiento de Liberación Nacional (Tupamaros) y la izquierda uruguaya (1963–1972)*. Montevideo, Uruguay: Taurus, 2004.

Gaudichaud, Frank. *Poder popular y cordones industriales: Testimonios sobre el movimiento popular urbano 1970–1973*. Santiago: LOM Ediciones, 2004.

Gilio, Maria Esther. *La guerrilla tupamara*. La Habana: Casa de las Américas, 1970.

Gill, Lesley. *The School of Americas. Military Training and Political Violence in the America*. Durham: Duke University Press, 2004.

Gillespie, Richard. *Soldiers of Perón, Argentina's Montoneros*. Oxford, New York: Clarendon Press; Oxford University Press, 1982.

Gilman, Claudia. *Entre la pluma y el fusil: debates y dilemas del escritor revolucionario en América Latina*. Buenos Aires: Siglo Veintiuno Editores Argentina, 2003.

Gleijeses, Piero. *Conflicting Missions, Havana, Washington, and Africa, 1959–1976*. Berkeley: The University of North Carolina Press, 2002.

Goicovich, Igor "Transición y violencia política en Chile (1988–1994)" en *Ayer. Revista de Historia Contemporánea*. Madrid, 2010.

Movimiento de Izquierda Revolucionaria. Concepción: Chile, Escaparate, 2012.

Goldstone, Jack A. "Theories of Revolution: The Third Generation," *World Politics*, Vol. 32, no. 3 (April 1980), 425–53.

Gómez, Luis. "Entrevista con el profesor Sergio Bagú, El periplo intelectual de un científico social latinoamericano," in *La Insignia*, Mexico, February 2006.

González, Ernesto (ed.). El trotskismo obrero e internacionalista en la Argentina, vol. 3, *Palabra Obrera, el PRT y la Revolución Cubana*. Buenos Aires: Ed. Antídoto, 1999.

González Canosa, Mora. "Modelo para armar: itinerarios y ámbitos disidentes del Partido Comunista Argentino en la gestación de uno de los grupos fundadores de las Fuerzas Armadas Revolucionarias (1960–1967)," Izquierdas, 4/12/2012, www.izquierdas.cl

González Sierra, Yamandú. *Los olvidados de la tierra. Vida, organizacion y lucha de los sindicatos rurales*. Montevideo: Montevideo: FEDESUR-CIEDUR-Nordan Comunidad, 1994.

Gorender, Jacob. *Combate nas trevas: a esquerda brasileira: das ilusões perdidas à luta armada*. Sao Paulo: Editora Atica, 1987.

Goodwin, Jeff. *No other way out: States and Revolutionary Movements, 1945–1991*. Cambridge; New York: Cambridge University Press, 2001.

Goodwin, Jeff, James M. Jasper and Francesca Polletta (ed.) *Passionate Politics. Emotions and Social Movements*. Chicago: University of Chicago Press, 2001.

Gott, Richard. *Guerrilla Movements in Latin America*. Calcutta, London, New York: Seagull Books, 1970.

Gould, Jeffrey L. "Solidarity Under Siege," *American Historical Review*. April, 2009.

Grandin, Greg. *The Last Colonial Massacre: Latin America in the Cold War*. Chicago: University of Chicago Press, 2004.

"H-Diplo Roundtables, Grandin on Jeremi Suri" www.h-net.org/~diplo/roundtables/PDF/Grandin-Suri.pdf

"Living in Revolutionary Time: Coming to Terms with the Violence of Latin America's Long Cold War," in Greg Grandin and Gilbert M. Joseph (eds.), *A century of Revolution: Insurgent and Counterinsurgent Violence during Latin America's Long Cold War*, Durham [NC]: Duke University Press, 2010.

Greg Grandin and Gilbert M. Joseph. *A Century of Revolution: Insurgent and Counterinsurgent Violence during Latin America's long Cold War*. Durham [N.C.]: Duke University Press, 2010.

Green, James. *We cannot remain silent: opposition to the Brazilian military dictatorship in the United States*. Durham, NC: Duke University Press, 2010.

Halperín Donghi, Tulio. "Dependency Theory and Latin American Historiography," *Latin American Research Review* 17, 1982, 1.

Harari, José. *Contribución a la historia del MLN (Tupamaros)*. Montevideo: Editorial Plural, 1987.

Harmer, Tanya. *Allende's Chile and the Inter-American Cold War*. Chapel Hill: University of North Carolina Press, 2011.

"The view from Havana: Chilean exiles in Cuba and early resistance to Chile's dictatorship, 1973–1977," *Hispanic American Historical Review* 96, 2016, 1.

"Two, three, many revolutions: Cuba and the prospects for revolutionary change in Latin America, 1967–1975," *Journal of Latin American Studies* 45, 1, 2013, 61–89.

Healey, Mark Alan. "El interior en disputa: proyectos de desarrollo y movimientos de protesta en las regiones extrapampeanas," in Daniel James (ed.), *Violencia, proscripción y autoritarismo (1955–1976). Nueva historia argentina. Tomo IX*. Buenos Aires: Sudamericana, 2003.

Hilb, Claudia. "La tablada: el último acto de la guerrilla setentista," in www.historia politica.com

Hilb, Claudia and Daniel Lutzky. *La nueva izquierda argentina*. Buenos Aires: Centro Editor de América Latina, 1984.

Hite, Katherine. *When the romance ended: leaders of the chilean left*. New York: Columbia University Press, 2000.

Huggins, Martha K. *Political Policing. The United States and Latin America*. Durham: Duke University Press, 1998.

Hunt, Lynn. *Politics, Culture and Class in the French Revolution*. Berkeley: University of California Press, 1984.

Instituto de Economía. *El proceso económico del Uruguay*. Montevideo: Universidad de la República, 1969.

Iriye, Akira. "Internationalizing International History," in Thomas Bender (ed.) *Rethinking American History in a Global Age*. Berkeley: University of California Press, 2002.

Izaguirre, Inés and others. *Lucha de clases, guerra civil y genocidio en la Argentina. Antecedentes, desarrollos y complicidades*. Buenos Aires: Eudeba, 2009.

James, Daniel. *Resistance and integration, Peronism and the Argentine Working Class 1946–1976*. Cambridge: Cambridge University Press, 1988.

Elizabeth Jelin (coord.) *Las Conmemoraciones: las disputas en las fechas "in-felices"*. Buenos Aires: Siglo XXI de España Editores, 2002.

Johnson, John J. *Political Change in Latin America, The emergence of middle sectors*. Stanford, California, Stanford University Press, 1958.

Jocelyn-Holt Letelier, Alfredo. *El peso de la noche. Nuestra frágil fortaleza histórica*. Chile: Planeta/Ariel, 1999.

Joseph, Gilbert, Catherine LeGrand and Ricardo Donato Salvatore (ed.). *Close encounters of empire: writing the cultural history of U.S.-Latin American relations*. Durham, N.C.: Duke University Press, 1998.

Reclaiming the Political in Latin American History. Essays from the North. Durham: Duke University Press, 2001.

Joseph, Gilbert, Catherine LeGrand and Ricardo Donato Salvatore and Daniela Spenser (ed.). *In from the cold: Latin America's new encounter with the Cold War*. Durham: Duke University Press, 2008.

Keck Margaret E. and Kathryn Sikkink. *Activists Beyond Borders*. Ithaca, NY: Cornell University Press, 1998.

Keys, Barbara. J. *Reclaiming American Virtue, the Human Rights Revolution of the 1970s* Cambridge: Harvard University Press, 2014.

Klimke, Martin. *The Other Alliance: Student Protest in West Germany and the United States in the Global Sixties*. Princeton, N.J.: Princeton University Press, 2010.

Kohan, Nestor. *La rosa blindada, una pasión de los '60*. Buenos Aires: La Rosa Blindada, 1999.

Kornbluh, Peter. *The Pinochet file: a declassified Dossier on Atrocity and Accountability*. New York: New Press, 2004.

Kunzle, David. *Che Guevara. Icon, Myth, and Message*. Hong Kong: Regents of the University of California, 1997.

Lastra, Soledad, *Los retornos del exilio en Argentina y Uruguay. Una historia comparada de las políticas y tensiones en la recepción y asistencia en las posdictaduras (1983–1989)*. Tesis para optar por el grado de Doctora en Historia. Facultad de Humanidades y Ciencias de la Educación (UNLP) La Plata, Marzo de 2014.

Labrousse, Alain. *Una historia de los Tupamaros: De Sendic a Mujica.* Montevideo: Editorial Fin de Siglo, 2009.

Langland, Victoria. *Speaking of Flowers. Student Movements and the Making and Remembering of 1968 in Military Brazil.* Durham and London: Duke University Press, 2013.

Lanusse, Lucas. *Montoneros: el mito de sus 12 fundadores.* Buenos Aires: Vergara, 2005.

Leacock, Ruth. *Requiem for Revolution.* Ohio: Kent University Press, 1990.

Leibner, Gerardo. *Camaradas y compañeros. Una historia política y social de los comunistas del Uruguay.* Montevideo: Trilce, 2011.

Leicht, Federico. *Cero a la izquierda. Una biografía de Jorge Zabalza.* Montevideo: Letraeñe Ediciones, 2007.

Leiva, Sebastian and Mario Garcé. Perspectivas de análisis de la Unidad Popular, opciones y omisiones, Informe de Avance, octubre 2004, Universidad ARCIS, Historia y Ciencias Sociales, in www.archivochile.com/Ideas_Autores/leivas/leivas0006.pdf

Lesgart, Cecilia. *Usos de la transición a la democracia: ensayo, ciencia y política en la década del '80.* Rosario, Argentina: Homo Sapiens Ediciones, 2003.

Lessa, Alfonso. *La revolución imposible: los tupamaros y el fracaso de la vía armada en el Uruguay del siglo XX.* Montevideo, Uruguay: Editorial Fin de Siglo, 2002.

Linz, Juan. *The Breakdown of Democratic Regimes.* Baltimore, London: Johns Hopkins University Press, 1978.

Lucas da Cruz, Fabio. "Frente Brasileño de Informaciones e Campanha: os jornais dos brasileiros exilados no Chile e na França (1968–1979)," paper presented at the Encontro de Pós-Graduandos da FFLCH-USP. Sao Paulo: November 2009.

Longoni, Ana. *Traiciones: la figura del traidor en los relatos acerca de los sobrevivientes de la represión.* Buenos Aires: Grupo Editorial Norma, 2007.

López Chirico, Selva. *Estado y las fuerzas armadas en el Uruguay del siglo XX.* Montevideo: Ediciones de la Banda Oriental, 1985.

Loveman, Brian and Elizabeth Lira. *Las ardientes cenizas del olvido: vía chilena de reconciliación política 1932–1994.* Santiago: LOM Ediciones: DIBAM, 2000.

Mallon, Florencia E., *Courage tastes of blood. The Mapuche Community of Nicolás Ailío and the Chilean State, 1906–2001.* Durham: Duke University Press, 2005.

Marchesi, Aldo. "Imaginación política del antiimperialismo: intelectuales y política en el Cono Sur a fines de los sesenta," *E.I.A.L.* no. 17, 1, 2006–2007.

"El pasado como parábola política: Democracia y derechos en los informes Nunca Más del cono sur," *Stockholm Review of Latin American Studies*, no. 7, December 2011.

"Geografías de la protesta armada, guerra fría, nueva izquierda y activismo transnacional en el cono sur, el ejemplo de la Junta de Coordinación Revolucionaria (1972–1977)," Sociohistórica, Cuadernos del Cish 25, second semester 2009, Universidad Nacional de la Plata, Argentina.

Marchesi, Aldo and Jaime Yaffé "La violencia bajo la lupa: una revisión de la literatura sobre violencia y política en los sesenta" Revista Uruguaya de Ciencia Política Vol. 19, no. 1.

Marín, Juan Carlos. *Los hechos armados.* Buenos Aires: La Rosa blindada: P.I.CA.SO., cop. 1996.

El ocaso de una ilusión. Buenos Aires: Colectivo ediciones, 2007.

Markarian, Vania. *Left in transformation: Uruguayan exiles and the Latin American human rights networks, 1967–1984.* New York: Routledge, 2005.

et al. *1958 el gobierno autonómico.* Montevideo: Universidad de la República, 2008.

El 68 Uruguayo. El movimiento estudiantil entre molotovs y música beat. Bernal: Universidad Nacional de Quilmes Editorial, 2012.

Martínez Heredia, Fernando (comp.). *Che, el argentino.* Buenos Aires: Ediciones De Mano en Mano, 1997.

Martins, Carlos Eduardo. "Theotônio dos Santos: introducción a la vida y obra de un intelectual planetario," in Francisco López Segrera (ed.). *Los retos de la globalización. Ensayo en homenaje a Theotônio dos Santos.* Caracas: UNESCO, 1998.

Mayer, Arno J. *The furies: violence and terror in the French and Russian Revolutions.* Princeton, N.J.: Princeton University Press, 2000.

Mazzeo, Mario *MPP: orígenes, ideas y protagonistas.* Montevideo, Uruguay: Ediciones Trilce, 2005.

McAdam, Douglas, Sidney G. Tarrow and Charles Tilly. *Dynamics of Contention.* Cambridge; New York: Cambridge University Press, 2001.

McSherry, Patrice. *Los estados depredadores: la operación Cóndor y la guerra encubierta en América Latina.* Uruguay: Ediciones de la Banda Oriental, 2009.

Merenson, Silvina. "(Des)marcaciones (trans)nacionales. El proceso de movilización y radicalización política de la Unión de Trabajadores Azucareros de Artigas, 1961–1972," *Revista Contemporánea* 1, 2010.

Milos, Pedro. *Historia y memoria: 2 de abril de 1957.* Santiago: LOM: Ediciones, 2007.

Moraña, Mabel and Horacío Machín (comp.) *Marcha y América Latina.* Pittsburgh: Biblioteca de América, 2003.

Moyano Barahona, Cristina. *El MAPU durante la dictadura: saberes y prácticas políticas para una microhistoria de la renovación socialista en Chile, 1973–1989.* Chile: Ediciones Universidad Alberto Hurtado, 2010.

Moyano, Maria José. *Argentina's Lost Patrol: Armed Struggle, 1969–1979.* New Haven: Yale University Press, 1995.

Moyn, Samuel. *The Last Utopia, Human Rights in History.* Cambridge: Harvard University Press, 2010.

Naranjo, Pedro et al. *Miguel Enríquez y el proyecto revolucionario en Chile.* Santiago: Lom, 2004.

Nicanoff, Sergio and Alex Castellano. *Las primeras experiencias guerrilleras en la Argentina: la historia del "Vasco" Bengochea y las Fuerzas Armadas de la Revolución Nacional.* Buenos Aires: Centro Cultural de la Cooperación Floreal Gorini, 2006.

Nun, José. "A Latin American Phenomenon: The Middle-Class Military Coup," James Petras and Maurice Zeitlin (eds.), in *Latin America, reform or revolution? A reader.* Greenwich, Conn.: Fawcett Publications, 1968.

Ñáñez, Guillermo Daniel. "Abraham Guillén: Los remotos orígenes de la guerrilla peronista 1955–1960," in Historia, Publicación del Instituto Superior de Formación Docente (Berazategui), 50, año 4, no. 3.

O'Donnell, Guillermo et al. *Transitions from Authoritarian Rule. Latin America.* 3 vols. Baltimore: Johns Hopkins University Press, 1986.

O'Donnell, Guillermo *Contrapuntos. Ensayos escogidos sobre autoritarismo y democratización.* Buenos Aires: Paidós, 1997.

Orellana, Patr icio and Elizabeth, Q Hutchison. *El movimiento de derechos humanos en Chile, 1973–1990.* Santiago de Chile: Centro de Estudios Políticos Latinoamericanos Simón Bolívar, 1991.

Ortiz, Oscar. *Crónica anarquista de la subversión olvidada.* Santiago: Ediciones espíritu libertario, 2002.

Palieraki, Eugenia. *¡La revolución ya viene!: el MIR chileno en los años sesenta.* Santiago: LOM Ediciones, 2014.

Panizza, Francisco. *Uruguay: Batllismo y después. Pacheco, militares y tupamaros en la crisis del Uruguay Batllista.* Montevideo: Banda Oriental, 1990.

París de Oddone, Blanca. *La Universidad de la República. Desde la Crisis a la Intervención 1958–1973.* Montevideo: Universidad de la República, 2010.

Peirano Basso, Luisa. *Marcha de Montevideo.* Barcelona; Buenos Aires: J. Vergara Editor, 2001.

Pérez, Cristián. "El Ejército del Che y los Chilenos que continuaron su lucha," *Estudios Públicos* 89. Summer, 2003.

Pinto Vallejos, Julio. "Hacer la revolución en Chile" in *Cuando hicimos historia, la experiencia de la Unidad Popular* edited by Julio Pinto Vallejos. Santiago: LOM Ediciones, 2005.

Plis-Sterenberg, Gustavo. *Monte Chingolo. La mayor batalla de la guerrilla argentina.* Buenos Aires: Booket, 2006.

Portantiero, Juan Carlos. "Clases dominantes y crisis política en la Argentina actual," in Pasado y Presente, 1, new series, April–June 1973.

Potash, Robert. *El ejército y la política en la Argentina, 1962–1973: de la caída de Frondizi a la restauración peronista.* Buenos Aires: Editorial Sudamericana, 1994.

Pozzi, Pablo A. *Por Las Sendas Argentinas: El PRT-ERP, La Guerrilla Marxista.* Buenos Aires: Eudeba, 2001.

Pozzi, Pablo A. and Claudio Pérez (ed.), *Historia oral e historia política. Izquierda y lucha armada en América Latina, 1960–1990.* Santiago: Lom Ediciones, 2012.

Puciarelli, Alfr edo (ed.). *La primacía de la política. Lanusse, Perón y la Nueva Izquierda.* Buenos Aires: EUDEBA, 1999.

Rama, Germán W. *La democracia en Uruguay.* Buenos Aires, Argentina: Grupo Editor Latinoamericano, 1987.

Reca, Inés Cristina. "El movimiento estudiantil y el proceso de reforma de la Universidad de Chile," *Revista Mexicana de Sociología* 32, no. 4 (July–August 1970), 893–947.

Rey Tristan, Eduardo. *A la vuelta de la esquina, la izquierda revolucionaria uruguaya, 1955–1973.* Montevideo: Editorial Fin de Siglo, 2006.

Reyes, Hernán. "Abraham Guillén: teórico de la lucha armada," *Lucha Armada* no. 4, September–November 2005.

Rico, Álvaro (coord.). Investigación Histórica sobre la dictadura y el terrorismo de estado en el Uruguay (1973–1985), 4 vols. Montevideo, UDELAR-CSIC.

Ridenti, Marcelo. *O fantasma da revolução brasileira.* Sao Paulo: UNESP, 1993.

"Esquerdas armadas urbanas: 1964–1974," in Marcelo Ridenti and Daniel Arao Reis (comp.), *Historia do Marxismo no Brasil.* Campinas: Unicamp, 2007.

Rodriguez Ostria, Gustavo. *Sin tiempo para las palabras, Teoponte, La otra guerrilla guevarista en Bolivia.* Cochabamba: Grupo Editorial Kipus, 2006.

Rollemberg, Denise. *Exílio: entre raízes e radares.* Rio de Janeiro: Editora Record, 1999.

O apoio de Cuba a luta armada no Brasil: O treinamento guerrilheiro. Rio de Janeiro: Mauad, 2001.

"Debate no exilio: Em busca da Renovação," in *Historia do Marxismo no Brasil.* Marcelo Ridenti and Daniel Arao Reis (eds.), Campinas: Unicamp, 2007.

Romero, Luis Alberto. "La violencia política en la historia argentina reciente: un estado de la cuestión," in Anne Pérotin-Dumon (ed.), Historizar el pasado vivo en América Latina. www.historizarelpasadovivo.cl/

Rosas, Pedro. *Rebeldía, subversión y prisión política.* Santiago: LOM, 2004.

Rot, Gabriel. *Los orígenes perdidos de la guerrilla en la Argentina: la historia de Jorge Ricardo Masetti y el Ejército Guerrillero del Pueblo.* Buenos Aires: Ediciones El Cielo por Asalto, 2000.

"Notas para una historia de la lucha armada en la argentina. Las Fuerzas Argentinas de Liberación," *Politics de la Memoria,* no. 4, Summer 2003–2004.

Ruiz, María Olga. "Historias y memorias de traición. Reflexiones en torno a la Conferencia de Prensa de los cuatro miristas de 1975" in *Recordar para pensar. Memoria para la democracia. La elaboración del pasado reciente en el Cono Sur de América Latina.* Santiago de Chile: Ediciones Boll Cono Sur, 2010.

Sandoval, Carlos. *M.I.R. (una historia).* Santiago: Sociedad Editorial Trabajadores, 1990.

Movimiento de Izquierda Revolucionaria, 1970–1973. Concepción, Chile: Escaparate Ediciones, 2004.

Movimiento de Izquierda Revolucionaria. Coyunturas y vivencias (1973–1980). Concepción, Chile: Escaparate Ediciones, 2011.

Santucho, Blanca Rina. *Nosotros, los Santucho*. Santiago del Estero, 1997.

Seoane, María. *Todo o nada, la historia secreta y pública de Mario Roberto Santucho, el jefe guerillero de los años setenta*. Buenos Aires: Sudamericana, 2003.

Serpaj. *Uruguay, Nunca Más*. Montevideo: Serpaj, 1989.

Seveso, Cesar. "Escuelas de militancia: La experiencia de los presos políticos en Argentina, 1955–1972," *A contracorriente*. Vol. 6, no. 3, Spring 2009, 137–65.

Sewell Jr., William H. "Historical Events as Transformations of Structures: Inventing Revolution at the Bastille," *Theory and Society*, Vol. 25, no. 6, December, 1996, 841–81.

Sigal, Silvia. *Intelectuales y poder en Argentina en la década del sesenta*. Argentina: Siglo XXI, 2002.

Sikkink, Kathryn. *International Human Rights and Sovereignty in Latin America*. New York: Columbia University-New York University Consortium, 1991.

The justice cascade: how human rights prosecutions are changing world politics. New York: W.W. Norton & Co., 2011.

Sivak, Martin. *El asesinato de Juan José Torres: Banzer y el Mercosur de la muerte*. Buenos Aires: Ediciones del Pensamiento Nacional, 1998.

Slobodian, Quinn. *Foreign Front: Third World Politics in Sixties West Germany*. Duke University Press, 2012.

Solari, Aldo. *Estudios sobre la sociedad uruguaya* (Montevideo: Arca, 1964).

(ed.). *Estudiantes y política en América Latina*. Caracas: Monte Avila Editores, 1968.

Spenser, Daniela (ed.). *Espejos de la guerra fría: México, América Central y el Caribe*. Mexico DF: CIEAS-Miguel Ángel Porrúa Editor, 2004.

Stern, Steve J., *Battling for hearts and minds: memory struggles in Pinochet's Chile, 1973–1988* Durham: Duke University Press, 2006.

Reckoning with Pinochet: the memory question in democratic Chile, 1989–2006. Durham, NC: Duke University Press, 2010.

Suri, Jeremi. *Power and Protest: Global Revolution and the Rise of Detente*. Cambridge, MA: Harvard University Press, 2003.

Svampa, Maristella. "El populismo imposible y sus actores. 1973–1976," in *Violencia, proscripción y autoritarismo (1955–1976) Nueva Historia Argentina*, vol. 9, Daniel James (ed.) Buenos Aires: Editorial Sudamericana, 2003.

Sznajder, Mario and Luis Roniger. *The Politics of Exile in Latin America*. Cambridge University Press, 2009.

Sweig, Julia. *Inside the Cuban Revolution: Fidel Castro and the Cuban Underground*. Cambridge, Mass.: Harvard University Press, 2002.

Tapia, Luis. *La producción del conocimiento local. Historia y política en la obra de René Zavaleta*. La Paz: Muela del Diablo, 2002.

Tarcus, Horacio. *El Marxismo olvidado en la Argentina: Silvio Frondizi y Milcíades Peña*. Buenos Aires: Ediciones El Cielo por Asalto, 1996.

Tarrow, Sidney. *Power in Movement. Social Movements and Contentious Politics*. 2nd ed. New York: Cambridge Press, 1999.

The New Transnational Activism. New York: Cambridge University Press, 2005.

Tavares, Flavio. *Memorias do Esquecimento*. Sao Paulo: Globo, 1999.

Tcach, Cesar. "Golpes, proscripciones y partidos políticos," in *Violencia, proscripción y autoritarismo (1955–1976) Nueva Historia Argentina*, vol. 9, Daniel James (ed.) Buenos Aires: Editorial Sudamericana, 2003.

Terán, Oscar. *Nuestros años sesentas: la formación de la nueva izquierda intelectual en la Argentina, 1956–1966*. Buenos Aires, Argentina: Puntosur Editores, 1991.

Torre, Juan Carlos (dir.) *Los años peronistas, 1943–1955*. Buenos Aires: Editorial Sudamericana, 2002.

Tortti, María Cristina. *El "viejo" partido socialista y los orígenes de la "nueva" izquierda: 1955–1965*. Buenos Aires: Prometeo Libros, 2009.

Uchoa Cavalcanti, Pedro C. and Jovelino Ramos (comp.), *Memórias do exílio, Brasil 1964/ 19?? De muitos caminos*, vol. 1. Sao Paulo: Livramento, 1978.

Valdivia, Verónica. *El golpe despues de Chile. Leigh vs. Pinochet, 1960–1980*. Santiago: LOM Ediciones, 2003.

Valdivia, Verónica, Rolando Álvarez y Julio Pinto. *Su revolución contra nuestra revolución. Izquierdas y derechas en el Chile de Pinochet (1973–1981)* Vols. 1, 2, Santiago: LOM, 2006, 2008.

Valenzuela, Arturo. *The Breakdown of Democratic Regimes: Chile*. Baltimore: Johns Hopkins University Press, 1978.

Varela Petito, Gonzalo. *El movimiento estudiantil de 1968: el IAVA, una recapitulación personal*. Montevideo: Trilce, 2002.

Varon, Jeremy. *Bringing the War Home: The Weather Underground, the Red Army Faction, and Revolutionary Violence in the Sixties and Seventies*. Berkeley: University of California Press, 2004.

Vidal, Hernan. El movimiento de la izquierda revolucionaria (mir) de Chile en la justicia transicional. Hernan Vidal: 2013. ideologiesandliterature.org/VIDAL-%20Justicia%20 Transicional%20III.pdf

Vitale, Luis. *Contribución a la historia del MIR*. Santiago: Ed. Instituto de investigación de Movimientos Sociales "Pedro Vuskovic," 1999.

Vezzetti, Hugo. *Pasado y presente: guerra, dictadura y sociedad en la Argentina*. Buenos Aires: Siglo XXI, 2002.

Sobre la violencia revolucionaria: memorias y olvidos. Buenos Aires: Siglo Veintiuno, 2009.

Weisz, Eduardo. *El PRT-ERP: Nueva izquierda e izquierda tradicional*. Buenos Aires: Centro Cultural de la Cooperación, Depto. de Historia, 2004.

El PRT-ERP: claves para una interpretacion de su singularidad, Marxismo, Internacionalismo y Clasismo. Buenos Aires: Centro Cultural de la Cooperación Floreal Gorini, 2006.

Westad, Odd Arne. *The Global Cold War: Third World Interventions and the Making of Our Times*. Cambridge, New York: Cambridge University Press, 2005.

Wickham-Crowley, Timothy P. *Guerrillas and Revolution in Latin America: a Comparative Study of Insurgents and Regimes since 1956*. Princeton, N.J.: Princeton University Press, 1991.

Williams, Raymond. *Marxism and Literature*. Oxford: Oxford University Press, 1977.

Winn, Peter. *Weavers of Revolution: The Yarur Workers and Chile's Road to Socialism*. New York, Oxford: Oxford University Press, 1986.

"The Furies of the Andes: Violence and Terror in the Chilean Revolution and Counterrevolution," in *A Century of Revolution: Insurgent and Counterinsurgent Violence during Latin America's Long Cold War* Greg Grandin and Gilbert Joseph (eds.), Durham, London: Duke University Press, 2010.

et al. *No hay mañana sin ayer. Batallas por la memoria histórica en el cono sur*. Santiago de Chile: LOM, 2014.

Wood, Elizabeth Jean. *Insurgent Collective Action and Civil War in El Salvador*. New York: Cambridge University Press, 2003.

Zavaleta Mercado, René. *Documentos de trabajo n. 8: El poder dual (contribución a un debate latinoamericano)*. Santiago: Universidad Católica de Chile, 1973.

Zolov, Eric. "Expanding our Conceptual Horizons: The Shift from an Old to a New Left in Latin America," *Contracorriente* 5, no. 2, Winter 2008.

Unpublished

Alfonso Valdés Navarro, Pedro. "Elementos teóricos en la formación y desarrollo del MIR durante el período 1966–1970." Undergraduate dissertation. Universidad de Valparaíso, 2006. Archivochile.com.

Arrarás, Astrid. "Armed Struggle, Political Learning and Participation in Democracy: The Case of the Tupamaros." PhD Dissertation, Princeton University, 1998.

Barrientos, Claudio. "Emblems and Narratives of the Past: the Cultural Construction of Memories and Violence in Peasant Communities of Southern Chile, 1970–2000." PhD Dissertation, University of Wisconsin-Madison, 2003.

Cassol, Gissele. "Prisão e tortura em terra estrangeira: a colaboração repressiva entre Brasil e Uruguai (1964–1985)," MA thesis, Universidade Federal de Santa Maria 2008.

Cortina, Eudald. "Historia del Movimiento Revolucionario Oriental y de las Fuerzas Armadas Revolucionarias 'Orientales'." Masters thesis in Contemporary History. Universidad de Valencia. Valencia, 2010.

Diez, María A. "El dependentismo en Argentina, una historia de los claroscuros del campo académico entre 1966 y 1976." PhD dissertation, Universidad Nacional del Cuyo, 2009.

Harmer, Tanya. "The Rules of the Game: Allende's Chile, the United States and Cuba, 1970–1973." PhD dissertation, London School of Economics and Political Science, 2008.

Pezzonia, Rodrigo. "Revolução em DEBATE: O grupo DEBATE, o exílio e a luta armada no Brasil (1970–1974)" Masters thesis in History, Universidad Estadual de Campinas, 2011.

Lozoya, Ivette. Pensar la revolución: Intelectuales y Pensamiento Latinoamericano en el Mir chileno (1965–1973), Tesis para optar al grado de Doctora en Estudios Americanos IDEA-Universidad de Santiago de Chile.

Schlotterbeck, Marian E., Everyday Revolutions: Grassroots Movements, the Revolutionary Left (MIR), and the Making of Socialism in Concepción, Chile, 1964–1973, PhD dissertation, Yale University, 2013.

Simões Fernandes, Ananda. "Quando o inimigo ultrapassa a fronteira: as conexões repressivas entre a ditadura civil-militar brasileira eo Uruguai (1964–1973)." Porto Alegre, MA thesis, Historia Universidade Federal do Rio Grande do Sul, 2009.

Documentaries

Aguiló, Macarena. *El edificio de los chilenos* (Chile: Producciones Aplaplac / Les Films d'Ici / Instituto Cubano del Arte e Industrias Cinematográficos (ICAIC), 2012).

Arruti, Mariana. *Trelew* (Argentina: Fundación Alumbrar, 2004).

Albertina Carri, *Los rubios* (Argentina: 2003).

Carmen Castillo, *Calle Santa Fé* (Chile, France: Les Films d'Ici / Les Films de la Passerelle / L'INA / Parox et Love Stream productions, 2007).

Getino, Aldo et alters, *Gaviotas Blindadas. 3 vols* (Argentina: Córdoba: Mascaró Cine Americano, 2006–2007).

Guzmán, Patricio. *La Batalla de Chile. 3 vols I*: (Equipo Tercer Año, 1975, 1977, 1979).

Nicolas Prividera, *M* (Argentina: Trivial, 2007).

María Inés Roque, *Papa Iván* (México: Centro de Capacitación Cinematográfica, CCC/ Fondo Nacional para la Cultura y las Artes México / Zafra Difusión S.A., 2004).

Katz, Leandro. *El día que me quieras* (United States, 1997).

Index

CPSIA information can be obtained
at www.ICGtesting.com
Printed in the USA
LVHW020538011221
704952LV00002B/188